CW00536316

Best W

Gordon Fraser

SPORTING GENES

100 Years of
Sporting Achievements

The author can be contacted at:

gordon@sportinggenes.com

www.sportinggenes.com

First published 2015 by DB Publishing, an imprint of JMD Media Ltd, Nottingham, United Kingdom.

ISBN 9781780914558

Copyright © Gordon Fraser 2015.

All Rights Reserved. No part of this publication may be reproduced, stored in a retrieval system, or transmitted in any form, or by any means, electronic, mechanical, photocopying, recording or otherwise without the prior permission in writing of the copyright holders, nor be otherwise circulated in any form or binding or cover other than in which it is published and without a similar condition being imposed on the subsequent publisher.

SPORTING GENES

100 Years of
Sporting Achievements

Gordon Fraser

CONTENTS

	ACKNOWLEDGMENTS	9
	PREFACE	10
1.	BRUCE RANKIN AT EVERTON (1901-06)	14
2.	BRUCE ON THE MOVE (1906-09)	54
3.	BILLY RANKIN AT MARINE FC (1931-34)	97
4.	BILLY AND BASEBALL (1932-60s)	122
5.	GEORGE RANKIN AT EVERTON (1946-56)	142
6.	GEORGE AT SOUTHPORT FC (1956-60)	184
7.	ANDY RANKIN AT EVERTON (1961-71)	237
8.	ANDY AT WATFORD (1971-76) – THE SLIDE FROM DIVISION TWO TO DIVISION FOUR	299
9.	ANDY AT WATFORD (1976-79) – THE CLIMB BACK TO DIVISION TWO	327
10.	ANDY AT HUDDERSFIELD (1979-82)	357
11.	GAVIN FRASER (1979-00)	378
	BIBLIOGRAPHY	418

For our son, Gavin
Thank you for the many happy and proud moments.

Acknowledgments

Sporting Genes started out as a simple family history project about eight years ago. I am indebted to my cousin, David Angus, and Tony Higginson of Formby Books for encouraging me to turn that project into a book and to have it published.

I am extremely grateful to the following people who provided information and/or photographs about the clubs or organisations in brackets: David Barber (The FA); Alan Cozzi (Watford FC); Gary James (Manchester City); Michael Philpott (West Bromwich Albion FC); David Threlfall-Sykes (Huddersfield Town FC); Gilbert Upton (Tranmere FC); Roger Wash (Luton Town FC); Colin Williams (English Baseball Association); and David Wotherspoon (Marine FC).

I am obliged to the individuals who agreed to be interviewed for the book. In particular, I must mention Howard Kendall, Terry Rankin (brother of Andy), Billy Rankin (brother of George), who was on holiday in Merseyside with his wife Wyn from his home in New Zealand when I met him and Sue Rankin (George's daughter-in-law), who also allowed me access to George's memorabilia. I am also grateful to George Allen and Alan Deutsch, who both provided me with information about George Rankin's life after football.

My thanks must also go to Mary and Ian Cover for proof reading my original manuscript.

Finally, I must thank my long-suffering wife, Maureen, for tolerating my many visits to libraries, both in Merseyside and other parts of the country, and the many hours I spent writing up my research and then turning it into this book.

I do hope that I have not forgotten anyone who deserves a mention. If I have, please accept my sincere apologies.

PREFACE

This book is about the sporting achievements of four generations of the one family.

It all began with Bruce Rankin, who played for Everton from 1901 to 1906 and later a number of other clubs. His son, Billy Rankin, turned out for Marine FC in the 1931/32 FA Amateur Cup Final, represented England at baseball and later became a baseball referee. Billy's elder son, George, and grandson of Bruce, played for Everton in the early to mid-1950s and then joined Southport FC. Another of Bruce's grandsons, Andy Rankin, was one of Everton's goalkeepers in the 1960s and early 1970s, before playing more than 300 games for Watford and then finishing his career at Huddersfield. Finally, Gavin Fraser, Bruce's great grandson, played rugby union for Waterloo, London Scottish and other clubs, as well as representing Scotland at different levels.

Throughout my research for this book, I have failed, to find a family in which four consecutive generations have achieved significant sporting success. That is not to say it has not happened, more that I cannot find anyone who has written about it.

Why am I writing this book? In May 1964, I married Maureen Don, one of Bruce Rankin's granddaughters and Gavin Fraser, one of the subjects of the book, is our son.

When I married Maureen, I knew that her grandfather had played for Everton and that her cousin, Andy Rankin, was a goalkeeper on Everton's books. In fact, I had crossed paths with Andy a few years earlier. I had joined the Liverpool City Police Cadets in 1960 and was their goalkeeper, playing in the Liverpool Boys Association League. Neil Ablett, the father of Gary Ablett of Liverpool and Everton, who died in 2012, was a clever winger in the team and went on to represent the British Police. In late 1961, Andy Rankin also joined the Police Cadets and, needless to say, I immediately lost my place in goal to him.

Predictably, Maureen's family were all Evertonians. So was I, fortunately. I was a Dundee FC supporter before coming from Scotland to Liverpool and, some months before I arrived in the city in September 1960, Jimmy Gabriel had joined Everton from Dundee for a fee of £27,000. So, it had to be Everton for me.

Once I had finally retired in 2003, I began to research my family tree. About that time, I read an article about how to write up a family history. One of the suggestions was to tackle it by themes. So, having learned that other members of Maureen's family had achieved sporting success, I decided that I would pick up the sports theme and write about her family's achievements.

The first port of call for my research was, of course, my wife's immediate family. Surprisingly, they were only able to provide the most basic information. My next source was the various books that listed the records of individual football players, including the clubs they had played for, the number of appearances made and goals scored. Next, it was a case of visiting local libraries in Liverpool, Southport, Crosby and Birkenhead to read the various match reports and relevant articles in the local newspapers. I then had to travel further afield to carry out research in libraries in Birmingham, Huddersfield, Luton, Watford and Wrexham.

I was amazed that more than a hundred years after Maureen's grandfather had played for Everton that I was able to read all the match reports in the local papers. In the early 1900s, the only real coverage of football, certainly in the local papers, was the match reports. There was no daily speculation about the team or revelations about the players' private lives. The language used was different, for example, the ball was the leather, and match reports were sent by telegraph and sometimes by pigeon post, a far cry from the technology of today.

I can still recollect the thrill of finding the report of Bruce's first game for Everton in the Liverpool Echo, albeit that it was for the Reserves or Combination team as it was called then. I can also recall the disappointment and annoyance that I felt when I found that Bruce was almost always dropped once Jack Sharp, an Everton legend, was available for selection, despite the fact that Bruce had played well the previous week. No doubt Bruce experienced similar emotions.

As part of my research, I also wrote to the various football clubs and the Football Association (FA). They were really helpful, providing relevant information and photographs where possible. In the case of Manchester City, however, their records had been destroyed in 1920 when their main stand at Hyde Road burned down. The English Baseball Association also provided information that I would otherwise never have obtained.

An unexpected and most valuable source of information was the Everton Collection, which contains a vast assortment of Everton memorabilia dating back to the 1880s, including match programmes, the minutes of Directors' meetings, financial data, correspondence and photographs of the various teams and individual players. The Collection was amassed over a period of 25 years by David France and was bought by The Everton Collection Charitable Trust in 2007 with the help of a grant from the Heritage Lottery Fund, and with the blessing of David France himself, for a fraction of the money spent by him in assembling the historical material.

Whilst the Collection is physically housed in the Liverpool Record Office, much of it was made available on-line in 2009. It allowed me to uncover information that would not have been available to me through any of my other research sources.

As I mentioned earlier, I had spoken to a number of members of the Rankin family. However, it was a great disappointment when Andy Rankin, one of only two surviving subjects of the book, did not wish to be interviewed.

What is also disappointing is that there were a number of missed opportunities for me. Billy Rankin died in 1980 and his son, George, passed away nine years later, 25 years after I had married Maureen, but I never met them. Maureen's mother was one of 12 children and whilst she maintained contact with her sisters, she was not in touch with her brothers or their families.

Another missed opportunity was meeting Tommy Clinton, a former Everton full-back who had played with George. When I was a young probationary constable, my beat included the area around Goodison Park. Tommy Clinton lived in Goodison Avenue, a cul-de-sac next to the ground, in what may have been an Everton club-house. I reported Tommy for some minor traffic offence; I cannot remember the details now. Although our initial contact was less than amicable, we eventually became quite friendly and I would pop into his house on occasions for a cup of tea when I was on my beat. I missed the chance to hear some really interesting stories from him about George and his Everton team-mates, but I did not realise the significance of the meeting some fifty years before I started writing this book.

In the hundred years or so since Bruce joined Everton, there have been many changes in the sport of football, for example, the introduction and use of substitutes, goal average vs goal difference, the number of points for a win and so on. Where appropriate, these are discussed at the pertinent point in the book.

Is there likely to be a fifth generation of sporting success? It is too early to say as several of that generation are not yet of school age. Two of Bruce's great-great granddaughters, however, have got close.

Charlotte Buckingham, who is 22 years of age, was Athlete of the Year at Greenbank High School in Southport for four years in succession and represented the school at seven different sports. She was Merseyside County Schools Champion at triple jump and represented Merseyside Schools in the pentathlon event. She has won a number of badminton trophies and has represented the Southport Badminton League and Lancashire. Her 20-year-old sister, Hannah, has represented Lancashire at badminton since she was 12 years of age. She too has won numerous badminton trophies. Their senior school, Greenbank High School, represented England Schools in the World Schools Badminton championships in Spain in 2008 and both sisters played in the team against Belgium, China Taipae (Taiwan), Italy, Luxembourg, Spain and Turkey.

Gordon Fraser
January 2015

1

Bruce Rankin at Everton (1901-06)

Introduction

Bruce Rankin's birth certificate shows that he was born in Liverpool on 5th July 1879, although various other records (1) misleadingly suggest that his birthplace was Glasgow in 1880. Indeed, even two of his daughters, Elsie and Alice (known as Teeny) believed that he had been born in Scotland. His father, also Bruce Rankin, was born in Liverpool too, but his mother, Sarah Hind, was a native of Dumfries in Scotland. Perhaps it was his mother's Scottish ancestry that made him claim that he had been born there.

Bruce was the second of six children, with an elder brother William, younger brothers George and Andrew, and two sisters Mary and Isabella. His father was a ship's steward and later a ship's cook and the family lived in the Walton area of Liverpool.

Nothing is known about Bruce's schooldays, other than that he attended Walton Lane Council and St Bernard's Schools. He is unlikely to have played football at school as playing organised games such as football did not become part of the school curriculum until after 1900. However, as a youngster, he appears to have been a budding athlete. When he was ten years old, he won a 100 yards handicap race at the Beaver Line Sports Day in Chester and also a half-mile race at a local gathering. (2)

Bruce's father was a merchant seaman, certainly from 1873 to 1906, so he may well have sailed with the Beaver Line, which ran a weekly passenger service from Liverpool to Canada and the United States. That could well be the reason that Bruce was able to participate in the Beaver Line Sports Day at Chester.

As a youngster, Bruce lived in Neston Street, which runs right to the front of Goodison Park, the home of Everton FC since 1892. Bruce would have been 12 or 13 years old when Everton moved from Anfield to Goodison Park. (3) So, the crowds making their way to watch Everton on a Saturday afternoon would have been a common sight for him. It may have been the excitement of seeing those crowds bustling past his home, or the thrill of hearing the cheers of the crowd from the ground itself, or maybe even seeing Everton play having sneaked into Goodison that encouraged his interest in football.

Of course, the crowds in the 1890s and early 1900s were not the 39,000 or so that turn up to watch Everton today. Attendances averaged about 13,000 in those days.

Spectators at that time were mainly drawn from the semi-skilled and skilled working class and lower-middle class and were predominantly male. The minimum admission price of 6d probably deterred the less well off. However, some women and boys did attend games and were usually charged half price. At one stage, some clubs admitted women free of charge until directors realised that, on occasions, they were losing significant revenue.

Many football teams were formed by or associated with churches as sport in general was seen by the clergy as character forming and offering an alternative to drink, gambling and crime for young men. A number of League clubs, including Everton, Aston Villa and Bolton, can trace their origins to a particular church. Others, such as Arsenal, West Ham, Stoke and Crewe, developed from teams set up at workplaces, often with the support of the employers.

Like many young men of his era, Bruce was drawn into football through a local church, starting out as inside-right with St Luke's Bible Class team as a teenager. St Luke's is the famous Anglican Church that stands at the corner of Goodison Park, between the Gwladys Street End and Goodison Road stands, and it was just a stone's throw from Bruce's home in Neston Street.

After several years, he moved to City Villa again playing at inside-right, which he apparently always considered to be his best position. Two or three years later, when he was 19 or 20 years old he joined White Star Wanderers, a member of The Combination League, which included teams such as Bangor, Birkenhead,

Middlewich, Nantwich, Newton-le-Willows, Rhyl, Tranmere Rovers, Winsford United, Witton Albion and Wrexham.

Following half a season with White Star, he gave up football and went to sea. His father was a merchant seaman at this time, so he may have been encouraged by his father's tales of trips to other countries to follow in his footsteps. However, it would seem that seafaring did not suit Bruce, for he left after a few months.

On coming ashore, he worked as a telephone jointer, taking up football again, this time with Kirkdale FC, one of the top teams in the 1 Zingari League. Whilst at Kirkdale, he represented Lancashire against Cheshire at inside-right.

1901-02 Season

Bruce joined Everton in 1901. The club was one of the twelve founding members of the Football League in 1888 - the others were Accrington Stanley; Aston Villa; Blackburn Rovers; Bolton Wanderers; Burnley; Derby County; Notts County; Preston North End; Stoke City; West Bromwich Albion; and Wolverhampton Wanderers. When the League was formed, Bootle was actually the top team on Merseyside. But it was not the playing success of a team that proved to be the key factor in deciding which Merseyside team joined the League. It was the fact that Everton had a purpose-built ground – Anfield, now the home of Liverpool FC – which was enclosed, accessible, and capable of holding the large crowds that would help to pay the wages of the professional players.

By 1901, when Bruce joined Everton, there were two Divisions, each comprising 18 teams; the Second Division had been formed in 1892. Only eight of the founding members were still in the First Division in 1901: Accrington Stanley, Burnley, Preston North End and West Bromwich Albion had been demoted. The eight remaining original members had been joined in the First Division by Bury, Grimsby, Liverpool, Manchester City, Newcastle United, Nottingham Forest, Sheffield United, Sheffield Wednesday, Small Heath (later re-named Birmingham) and Sunderland.

It was in the 1901/02 season that Everton began to wear their now famous royal blue jerseys and white shorts. When they first moved to Goodison Park in

1892, they played in salmon shirts and blue shorts, later adopting ruby shirts with a blue trim and dark blue shorts.

Whilst at Kirkdale, Bruce had played in several trial matches for Everton, including a friendly against Liverpool Reserves. However, it was not as a footballer that he joined the club, for he was invited to join Everton as the Assistant Trainer. The Minutes of the Meeting of the Board of Directors on 2nd May resolved that he "*be engaged (as Assistant Trainer) at 25/- per week and he to make himself generally useful*". The term "*generally useful*" was not defined but he would obviously have worked under the direction of the Trainer, a Mr. Elliott, whose re-engagement was also confirmed at the same Board meeting, "*at £2.10.0 per week and (he) be offered bonuses on results of matches as the Board may hereafter decide*".

Why Bruce was appointed as Assistant Trainer is not clear. He may have had some appropriate qualifications or he may have shown an interest in that side of the sport. In any case, that is how he started his career at Everton.

What is rather strange, however, is that Bruce then played four games at outside-right for Tranmere in The Combination league in the September and October, some four months after becoming Everton's Assistant Trainer. There is nothing in the match reports to suggest that he "set the place on fire" at Tranmere, and his final game on Saturday 5th October, away to Witton Albion, whose home ground was in Northwich, was an experience he would not want to repeat.

The team and officials left Lime Street Station by train sometime after mid-day. They alighted at Runcorn for the train to Northwich, the railway company having notified Tranmere's secretary in writing that they should change there for Northwich. At Runcorn, they learned that the train service had been altered that very day and that the trains were going directly to Northwich. The next train would not get them to the ground until well after kick-off. So a "wagonette", a horse-drawn open carriage with benches along the two sides with the passengers sitting facing each other, was hired at the cost of £2 to take the team on the 13 mile journey to Northwich. The journey was anything but pleasant as the weather was "*very showery and boisterous. After the drive the whole team were stiff and cramped with cold*" and they arrived an hour late. (4) This obviously affected the players' performance, as they suffered their first defeat of the season by a goal to nil, having already defeated Witton Albion 3-0 in their second game of the season.

Bruce made his Everton debut for the Combination (Reserve) team on Monday, 16th September. He was selected at right-half for the fixture against Glossop Reserves at Glossop in the Lancashire Combination League, which Everton won 1-0. That game fell between his first two appearances for Tranmere – against Witton Albion and Newton-le-Willows on 14th and 21st September respectively.

As mentioned earlier, Bruce played his last game for Tranmere on Saturday, 5th October, returning then to Everton. Why did he play four matches for Tranmere? Was it because Tranmere asked to have him for a trial period with a view to signing him permanently, but then sent him back to Everton because they did not think he was suitable? Or, was it because Everton released him to Tranmere for experience and then recalled him because they wanted him for their Combination team? There is nothing in the newspaper reports or in the minutes of the Meetings of the Everton Directors of that time to provide an answer.

Bruce appeared for the Everton Combination team against Bury Reserves on Saturday, 20th October and he turned out for them the following week against Blackburn Rovers Reserves. Three days later, on 30th October, the Board of Directors *"resolved that the Secretary obtain an Assistant Trainer and that Rankin be instructed to train as a player".* His salary was increased by 5/- to 30/- a week.

The Football Association had imposed a maximum wage of £4 a week for the 1901/02 season and, at the same time, had banned the payment of bonuses based on the results of matches and limited the signing on fee to no more than £10. There had been no maximum wage previously, so some players found that their weekly pay was reduced. Some clubs ignored the restrictions, for a number of them, including Sunderland, Manchester City, Middlesbrough and Glossop, were fined in the first few years for illegal payments and a number of players who received them were banned from playing.

In the early 1900s, the wages of the First and Second Division players easily exceeded the salary of skilled and semi-skilled workers and even foremen. For example, in 1906, when Bruce was being paid £4 a week by Everton, the average weekly earnings for a foreman were £2.2s.4d (£2 .13p), whilst the weekly wage of a labourer about that time was only £1.2s.7d (£1.15p). (5)

The players, however, had to accept certain rules set by their clubs. For example, in October 1901, Everton's Directors resolved that any injured or sick player should not leave his home without a written recommendation from the club doctor and the consent of the Chairman or Vice-Chairman and that, in addition to their normal attendance for treatment, they should also report to the doctor on Tuesday of each week.

Bruce continued to play regularly for the Combination team and their biggest game of the season was against Liverpool Reserves, at Goodison Park, on 18th January 1902. The game was played before a crowd of 15,000 in *"beautifully fine and crisp"* weather (6). Bruce appeared at right-half. During the match, two penalties were awarded, one to each side, and both had to be retaken, with differing results. Liverpool were awarded a penalty in the first half *"for a trip"*. Wilson scored from the spot, but the kick was ordered to be retaken *"owing to some informality"*. On the second occasion, he shot past the post.

In the second half, Everton were awarded a penalty for a hand-ball by Wilson. Boyle failed to score with his first kick, but the referee ordered the penalty to be retaken; the match report offering no explanation. This time, Boyle *"netted the leather and made Everton 2 up"*. Everton won 2-0.

The crowd of 15,000 for that Reserve game was as good as, if not better than, attendances at many First Division matches. Indeed, the Everton first team only averaged just over 16,000 that season.

In the first season of the Football League in 1888, an average of 2,250 watched each game; by 1905/06, the average match attendance was 13,200; and in 1913/14, the average crowd for a game was 23,100. The larger cities such as Liverpool, Manchester, Birmingham and Sheffield attracted the bigger crowds. Watching football on a Saturday afternoon, particularly in the North and Midlands, was becoming increasingly popular. Most workers had Saturday afternoon off, so "the match" was something to do and it allowed them to escape the hardship and toils of working class life for a few hours.

Bruce eventually made his debut for Everton's first team on 1st February 1902 against Sheffield United, replacing Jack Taylor at inside-right. Taylor was essentially a centre-half, but played in seven different positions during his 14-year career at Goodison Park. The previous Saturday, Everton had drawn 2-2 in the first round of the FA Cup against Liverpool at Anfield, and had then been unexpectedly beaten 2-0 in the replay at Goodison the following Thursday. Liverpool were in the Second Division at the time.

After the Cup-tie, *"the Everton eleven were at once taken away to Castleton, where it was hoped the invigorating air might bring them back to something like reasonable form. They stayed at the Derbyshire health resort whence they came into Sheffield this morning. The weather in the cutlery capital was bright and fine, though bitterly cold, and the journey from Liverpool, made by a handful of enthusiasts was through a country hidden beneath a mantle of snow. The Sheffielders had had no special preparation for the meeting, but a hard fought game was nevertheless anticipated, and there was an excellent crowd of spectators present when the rival teams turned out. There were several changes in the Everton ranks from Thursday, no less than three new men being brought in. These were Singleton and Proudfoot, who replaced Bell and Bowman, and Rankin, who took the place of Taylor. Neither Singleton nor Rankin had hitherto appeared in First League football, and their debut was, therefore, watched with considerable interest."* (7)

The game was drawn 0-0 and it would appear that Bruce had a fairly quiet debut. He received two mentions in the match report, one of which states that *"some fine work by Rankin gave Young a fine opening but the Everton player dallied too long with the result that he was neatly robbed when about to shoot"*.

The game against Sheffield was Bruce's only first team appearance of the season. He continued to play in the Combination team, primarily on the right wing and, on at least one occasion, at right-half. Everton's Combination team played in the Lancashire Combination, which included the Reserve teams of the Lancashire clubs from the two Football Leagues, as well as teams from local towns, such as Darwen, Rossendale and Oswaldthistle.

Young (fourth from the left on the middle row in the photograph on Page 22) who is also mentioned in the report of the game against Sheffield United, is considered to be an Everton "all-time great", having appeared in 314 League and

FA Cup games and scoring 125 goals in his 10 years with the Club. After leaving Everton in 1911, he played for Tottenham Hotspur, Manchester City and South Liverpool, and then, in 1914, emigrated to Australia. The following year, Young was charged with the murder of his brother, but was found guilty of manslaughter on the basis of evidence from football officials from England that, during his playing career, he had been subject to fits of temporary insanity. He was sentenced to three years imprisonment, but he was not released immediately on completion of his sentence; he was detained for a further period of time on the grounds of 'mental weakness'. He eventually did return home to Scotland and died on 17th September 1959 in an Edinburgh asylum.

In the middle of April, Bruce re-signed for the forthcoming season for 50/- a week, an increase of £1 on the weekly wage he had been receiving since signing for the club as a player some six months earlier (8).

The end of the season was marred by a disaster at Glasgow's Ibrox ground on Saturday, 5th April. Scotland were playing England and Everton's Settle was in the England team. Ten minutes into the game, part of the western terrace supporting a new stand behind England's goal collapsed, throwing hundreds of spectators some 40 feet below, striking metal girders and wooden joists on their way down. Several thousand people flooded on to the touchline. Clearly something was wrong. The referee stopped the game and as the players were leaving the field "*a crowd of people swarmed round them and although there was some hooting there was no attempt to molest them*". (9) Whilst the players were off the pitch, the Scottish FA met. They were aware that a number of people had been killed but decided that the game should continue, probably because they feared a riot if the match was abandoned. After a delay of 20 minutes, play resumed with the vast majority of the 80,000 or so in the ground unaware of the tragedy – there was no public address system in those days. The final result was 1-1, with Settle scoring England's goal. Twenty six people died and more than 500 were injured.

The result was subsequently declared void by the Scottish and English FAs. The match was replayed at Villa Park in Birmingham on 3rd May and ended 2-2. All the proceeds being donated to the Ibrox disaster fund.

Sadly this was not to be the last major disaster at a football ground, or indeed at Ibrox.

Nothing is new in football. In June that year, Everton's Secretary, Mr. Cuff, and the Trainer, Mr. Elliott, were suspended without pay by the FA from the 9th June to 1st October 1902 for having illegally approached a player, Robertson of Crewe Alexandra. Later, the FA agreed that Elliott could receive half of his salary.

1902-03 Season

The week before the football season started, the Football Echo included a short biographical sketch of the players of each Club in the League. The entry for Everton described the football strip as *"Colours – Blue Shirts, White Knickers"* and included 22 biographical sketches. Bruce's entry was: *"Rankin (forward) – A useful Combination winger, occasionally drafted into League service." (10)*

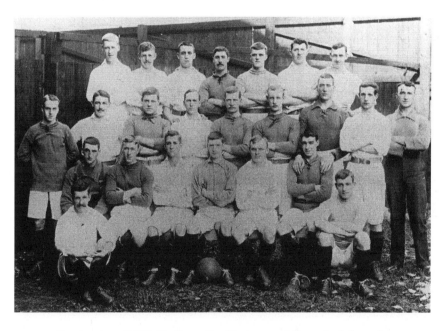

Everton team 1902-03. Bruce Rankin is second from the left on the
seated row. Courtesy of The Everton Collection Charitable Trust,
Reference 796EFC/26/1/32

Today's players would not be too pleased to be described as wearing knickers although, surprisingly, the word still appeared in match programmes until the 1960s when "*shorts*" took over. (11)

It will have been noted that the words "*the leather*" were used in the match report of the Everton Combination-Liverpool Reserve game earlier. In the early 1900s, the terminology used in the match programmes and newspaper reports reflected the language of the day – players gave "*a capital display*", had "*champion games*", committed "*dastardly conduct*" and made "*dashing runs*".

Surprisingly, perhaps, having only joined Everton as a player some six months earlier, Bruce was appointed captain of the Combination team, while goalkeeper Whitley was chosen as "*sub-captain*". The first team's captain and sub-captain were named as Tom Booth and William Balmer respectively. (12)

Bruce did not have to wait too long for an opportunity in the first team that season, as the match report for the Everton-Wolves game on 20th September indicates:

"*So far this season, although three games have been played, the Everton team up to this morning had not earned a single point. The team left Liverpool in the charge of the chairman of the club at noon today, Wolverhampton being reached about half past two, the weather was beautifully fine, and there was a large crowd present before the start. There were three changes in the Everton eleven from last week. Sharp and Settle are both on the sick list, the former suffering from an injury. The third absentee was Balmer, who has been seized with influenza. The forward line was reinforced by Sheridan who took Settle's place and Rankin, who appeared in the position normally occupied by Sharp; while Balmer's place was taken by Crelly.*" (13)

The game ended in a 1-1 draw, giving Everton their first point of the season after four games. Bruce scored Everton's only goal and his first for the Club's senior team.

He must have been somewhat disappointed to learn that he was not selected for the next first team game, against Liverpool at Goodison Park, particularly as it would appear that he had played well against Wolves. The Everton-Liverpool match report begins by giving the team changes:

> *"As regards the teams, Liverpool put forward their full strength; but on the home side the front rank was of a somewhat experimental nature, Rankin, who played such a hard game last Saturday, at Wolverhampton, stood down in favour of Sharp."* (14)

Bruce did not play in the first team again until 15th November, an away game against Sunderland. He replaced Sharp, who was suffering from a strained tendon, on the right wing. Sharp is one of the few players to have represented England at both football and cricket. In his eleven years with Everton, he made a total of 342 appearances and scored 80 goals and was capped twice by England. Probably his greatest cricketing achievement was scoring 105 runs for England against Australia at the Oval in 1909. Later, he served as an Everton director for many years.

Sharp was not the only Everton player of that era to represent England at both sports. Harry Makepeace, a half-back, played 336 games for Everton between 1902 and 1915, winning four caps for England and making five appearances for the Football League; he also made almost 500 appearances in first class matches for the Lancashire County Cricket Club, representing England in four test matches.

Everton lost 2-1 to Sunderland on 15th November before a crowd of 10,000. Bruce received one mention in the match report:

> *"Everton gradually forced their way along the right and Watson had to concede a corner. The place kick was splendidly taken by Rankin. The ball struck the upright and Young getting the return. This success came after eight minutes play and naturally infused great spirit into the visitors who ran down again on the right and Rankin sent a long oblique shot which caused Doig to run out in order to effect a clearance."* (15)

Sharp must have still been injured the following week because Bruce continued on the right wing against Stoke City at Goodison Park. Everton lost for the second successive week, this time to a 1-0 scoreline.

Bruce then had a run of five games in the first team over the Christmas and New Year period, but at outside-left rather than on the right wing. This sequence started with the game on 13th December against West Bromwich Albion at Goodison Park. Everton won 3-1 before 15,000 spectators. It would seem that Bruce had a reasonable game, as he was mentioned a number of times in the match report, and his pace and strength were already catching the eye:

> "Lee restarted, and after a few exchanges the Evertonians went to the front, Rankin making a strong run, and having a great struggle with Kifford."

> "Rankin gave a taste of his speed, and wound up with a perfect centre, which Nurse cleared before Taylor could get to it."

> "Rankin had been responsible for some work, which resulted in a fine opening. After he had beaten Kifford, he stumbled inside the penalty line, and it looked as though he had been hipped. A penalty claim was disregarded, however." (16)

He then played four games in 13 days: against Notts County (away) on 20th December, losing 2-0; against Grimsby Town (away) on Christmas Day, which resulted in a goalless draw; against Bolton Wanderers at home on 27th December, winning 3-1; and finally, against Bury (away) on New Year's Day, a 4-2 defeat.

Bruce's next game in the first team was on 31st January 1903 against Sheffield United at Goodison Park. He was again selected on the left wing and, before a crowd of 16,000, he scored the only goal of the game in the second half:

> "Rankin fastened on it (the ball) about fifteen yards from goal and let fly without any hesitation. Lewis had little chance as the ball was travelling very fast indeed and found the net after twenty minutes play. There was

nothing fluky about the goal, which was entirely due to Rankin's splendid work." (17)

Three days later, an interesting letter to the Editor appeared in the Liverpool Echo:

"Sir, There was a general feeling abroad amongst the crowd at Everton on Saturday that if Jack Sharp was to take his proper place as centre-forward, and let Rankin take Sharp's present position, the arrangement would work well. Hoping the Committee will take it into consideration. Yours &c Evertonian." (18)

The Committee took no heed. Having scored the winner against Sheffield United, Bruce would have again been frustrated to discover that he was not in the team for the FA Cup-tie against Portsmouth at Goodison Park the following Saturday. Being named as reserve for wingers Sharp and Bell and being among the sixteen players, who spent three days at Blackpool in preparation for the Portsmouth tie, would not have been much consolation. However, the special training paid dividends as Everton progressed to the next round by beating Portsmouth five goals to nil.

Interestingly, at their meeting on 6th February, the Board of Directors requested the Secretary to convey their appreciation of the manner in which the players conducted themselves whilst at Blackpool.

Bruce was back in the first team a week later, on 14th February, as two of Everton's forwards, Sharp and Settle, were absent on international duty for England against Ireland. Everton lost 1-0 to Aston Villa at Goodison Park before a crowd of 20,000 spectators. From the match report, it would seem that Bruce played well against Villa and reports about him were beginning to glow:

"The homesters broke away, and from a pass by Bowman, Rankin skimmed the cross bar."

"Suddenly, Rankin attained possession and raced away, closely attended by the two opposing backs. The Everton man eventually rounded Leake very

prettily and centred, but between them Bowman and Abbott made a hash
of the proceedings."

"The Everton forwards never looked like really meaning business, not one of
them being dangerous, excepting Rankin, who made some smart dashes but
was well attended by Leake." (19)

Bruce also won a penalty, from which Everton might have gained a point:

"Following a run by Rankin, Leake handled the ball in the penalty area and
a penalty was awarded. Abbott was entrusted with the kick but he sent the
ball on to the goalkeeper and consequently failed to score."

Bruce made his FA Cup debut the following week against Manchester United at
Goodison Park. Whether this was because of his performance against Villa the
week before or because Sharp was injured is not clear (there was no international
match), but neither Sharp nor Settle were included in the team. Manchester
United were in the Second Division at this time, but the game had added interest
as United had knocked Liverpool out of the Cup in the previous round. They were
unable to repeat the feat against Everton, who won 3-1 watched by a crowd of
15,000 spectators. Regrettably, Everton were themselves knocked out in the next
round of the Cup by Millwall from the Southern League.

Bruce played for the first team on three more occasions before the end of the
season: against Stoke City (away) on 21st March, a game which Everton lost 2-0;
against Newcastle United (away) on 1st April, Everton losing 3-0; and on 4th April,
against Sheffield Wednesday at Goodison Park in a 1-1 draw.

One of the games Bruce missed was the 3-0 home defeat at the hands of
Blackburn Rovers on Easter Monday, 13th April. The Press later claimed that the
Everton players had allowed Blackburn to win. *"After a most exhaustive examina-*
tion of every member of the team and upon a review of the evidence adduced," the
Board *"unanimously resolved that there was no evidence to support the allegation"*
and informed the media accordingly. (20)

Having finished runners-up in 1901/02, so much was expected of Everton the following season, but they finished a disappointing 12th of the 18 clubs.

Bruce was a regular during the season for Everton in the Lancashire Cup. He played in their 2-1 victory over Glossop at Goodison in the First Round on Monday afternoon, 29th September 1902.

He was selected for a Second Round replay against Manchester City, from Division Two, on the afternoon of Monday, 10th November. The match was *"favoured by autumn weather…(but) failed to attract more than a few hundred spectators. Everton played a mixed team, while the Manchester eleven was nearly at League strength"*. (21) At full-time, the score was 2-2 but Everton managed to win in extra time.

An episode in this cup-tie was described some years later in Bee's Sports Notices in the 3rd October 1917 issue of the Liverpool Echo as the *"funniest incident that ever happened at Goodison"*. In the second-half, an Everton defender's clearance struck the referee, a Mr Howcroft, and knocked him out. Frost, the Manchester City right-half, *"ran and picked up the referee but the ball had bounded down the field and the Everton winger, Bruce Rankin, had fastened on to the same and with several players on both sides, who seemed unaware of the incident, was in full career for the City goal. Poor Frost was now torn by conflicting emotions, whether to help the afflicted referee, or to drop the unconscious man and fly to the defence of his goal. Suddenly, he had a positively brilliant idea. Seizing the fallen man's whistle he blew a shrill blast, brought the play to a standstill and solved both questions at one and the same time. As an example of quick wit on the football field I think this will take a lot of beating."*

In the next round, the semi-final, on 19th January 1903, a crowd of about 4000 spectators saw Everton beat Blackburn Rovers three goals to nil at Blackburn. Bruce was on the right wing.

In the final, Everton faced Bury, who, days earlier, had won the FA Cup at Crystal Palace when they beat Derby County by six goals to nil, still the biggest win in an FA Cup Final. They went on to add another trophy to their collection as they were 1-0 victors over Everton. Everton's team was:

Whitley; W. Balmer, R. Balmer; Wolstenholme, Booth, Abbott; Rankin, Taylor, Dilly, Settle, McEwan.

The highlight of Bruce's season, however, was his selection for the North v South on 26th January 1903 in a game that was *"of chief importance as an international trial"*. (22) The game was played at Tottenham Hotspur's ground and attracted 11,000 spectators. The teams lined up as follows:

North: Linacre (Notts Forest); Iremonger (Notts Forest) and Spencer (Aston Villa) (captain); Jackson (Sunderland), Wilkinson (Sheffield United) and Warren (Derby County); Rankin (Everton), Garraty (Aston Villa), Raybould (Liverpool), Sagar (Bury) and Goddard (Liverpool). When the team was originally selected, Goddard and Rankin were on opposite wings.

South: Clawley (Tottenham Hotspur); Stokes (Reading) and H Smith (Oxford City); Morris (Tottenham Hotspur); Walls (Reading) and Houlker (Portsmouth); Craggs (Reading), Cunliffe (Portsmouth), V J Woodward (Chelmsford and Tottenham Hotspur), R E Foster (Old Malvernians) and Barlow (Southampton).

The North won 2-1, a result that made *"the record of wins equal, each having been successful seven times, while the drawn games in the series number three"*. Bruce did not get a mention in the match report.

Immediately after the game, the selectors chose the England team to play Ireland on 14th February. Of the original selections for the North and South teams, four players were chosen for the international side – Spencer and Garraty, both of Aston Villa; Woodward of Tottenham Hotspur; and Molyneux of Southampton, who was originally selected at left-back for the South, but missed the game itself following an attack of quinsy. Smith of Oxford City replaced him.

This had been an extremely successful season for Bruce. He had played 14 games for Everton's first team and had been selected to play for the North against the South in an international trial. He clearly had a promising future.

Bruce was re-signed by Everton in April. His weekly wage was increased by

£1 to £3.10s. This rise would have been very welcome indeed as, at 23 years of age, he had married Mary Jane Jackson on 20th October 1902, and the first of their twelve children, Nellie Evelyn Rankin, was born just six months later, on 26th April 1903. Perhaps the increase came as a surprise, for the Directors had turned down a request by Bruce for a rise in his wages in October, the month of his marriage.

1903-04 Season

During the close season, Bell, who had played regularly on the left wing for the first team, moved to Preston North End and Brearley, who had sometimes played at inside forward for the senior side, and Clarke, a Combination team player, moved to Southern clubs. In the meantime, Everton had acquired a number of new recruits, including McDermott, an inside forward from Celtic, and Hardman, an amateur winger from Blackpool, to replace the outgoing players.

In all, Everton had 30 players on their books and, according to the Football Echo on 22nd August 1903, *"excellent things are expected of Dilly and Rankin"*. Bruce and Whitley were again appointed as captain and sub-captain of the Combination team, whilst Booth and William Balmer were named as captain and sub-captain respectively of the first team.

The paper also carried a report of Everton's first practice match, which had been played that afternoon at Goodison Park before *"a large and eager crowd"*. The teams lined up as follows:

Blues (League defence and Combination forwards): Kitchen; Balmer and Crelly; Wolstenhome, Booth and Abbott; Rankin, McDermott, Dilly, Sheridan, Corrin.

Stripes (*Combination defence and League forwards*): Whitley; Gordon and Murray; Chadwick, Russell and Makepeace; Sharp, Taylor, Young, Settle, Hardman.

The Blues ran out 4-1 winners.

Unfortunately, despite the promise shown during the previous season, Bruce did not play for the first team until the final third of the season. He was kept out of the first team by the English international Jack Sharp and, somewhat surprisingly, Hardman, the new signing, took the left wing berth from the first game of the season. Hardman did go on to play 156 first team games for Everton as an amateur, scoring 29 goals. He won ten amateur caps and four full caps for England and also earned a gold medal with the Great Britain team in the 1908 Olympics Games.

In September, Bruce had been admonished by the Board of Directors for his poor displays in the Reserves. He appeared before the Board again on 16th February 1904 and was once more admonished by the Directors but, on this occasion, the minutes of the Board meeting did not record the reason.

A week later, one of the Directors, Mr Bainbridge, reported to the Board on his trip to watch the Bury v Sheffield United match that he had seen *"Whitley, Rankin and McMullen in Exchange Station under circumstances which aroused his suspicion as to their intentions for next season".* (23) There was no further mention of the incident. However, at the beginning of the following season, Whitley was transferred to Stoke for £325, whilst Bruce remained with Everton for a further two years. McMullen was not a first team or Reserve team player and it is not known what happened to him.

Despite this, days later Bruce made his first appearance of the season at inside-left in the away game against Nottingham Forest on 27th February. Although Everton won 4-0, the Liverpool Daily Post reporter was far from satisfied with the game. He wrote, *"... the game cannot by any stretch of the imagination be called a good one. The pace was slow throughout, and at times was positively dull,"* and then he went on to say, *"the wretched weather no doubt had something to do with the lack of enthusiasm, but the general opinion of those present was that the exhibition was not calculated to inspire it."* (24)

Bruce was not spared in the reporter's comments, although he had scored one of the goals: *"...Rankin was by no means a success though once or twice he partnered Hardman to some advantage."*

His next game was away against Derby County on 16th April and, this time, he was playing in his usual position at outside-right, as Sharp was rested. The Everton team was:

Whitley; Balmer, Creely; Wolstenholme, Booth, Abbott; Rankin, Taylor, Young, Settle, Hardman.

Everton won 1-0 and Bruce's play obviously created a more positive impression this time: *"On one occasion, Rankin, who was playing a capital game, dashed down the right wing and centred with fine judgment, but Settle just missed putting the finishing touch on the effort, and the Derby goal escaped."* (25)

Bruce played again for Everton two days later at Goodison Park against West Bromwich Albion. Everton won 4-0 and Bruce, who was on the right wing, scored one of the goals.

Having managed only three first team games that season, Bruce must have been extremely disappointed, particularly as he would have been full of hope following his success of the previous campaign.

He did play regularly for the Combination team, which topped the League by six points from Accrington Stanley, losing only two of its 34 games. At the Board of Directors meeting on 14th June, it was resolved that 15 players should be awarded Combination medals. The players were: Whitley, R. Balmer, Wildman, Gordon, Murray, Clayton, T. Chadwick, Russell, O'Hagan, Roberts, Dent, Rankin, Sheridan, Dilly, and Makepeace. The Club Secretary was instructed to apply to the Combination for permission to obtain 15 medals rather than the usual 11 and to have the players' names inscribed on them. Poor consolation for Bruce!

The first team finished third in the League, four points behind the leaders Sheffield Wednesday, but they had been knocked out of the FA Cup in one of the early rounds.

Just before the season ended, Everton received a letter from Bolton Wanderers asking the price for Wolstenholme and Rankin. (26) There is no record of Everton's reply but, within days, Wolstenholme was transferred to Blackburn Rovers for £600, whilst Bruce remained with the Club for almost another two years. Wolstenholme had made 170 appearances for Everton in seven years, had been capped by the English League against the Scottish League in 1902 and had made his full England debut earlier in the year against Scotland.

An interesting little episode was reported in the Board's minutes during the close season. In June, the trainer, Mr. Elliott, had been sent to Scotland to sign Hutchinson, a midfielder from Blantyre Victoria, for a weekly wage of 50/-, with a £5 bonus. For some reason, the Club had to send a £10 money order to Elliott, but it was lost in transit. Enquiries by the Post Office quickly revealed that the money order had been paid into the North and South Wales Bank. At the Board of Directors meeting on 16th August, the Secretary reported that his office boy, Thomas Moorcroft, had been arrested for stealing the money order, had pleaded guilty at the Court, and was being sentenced the following day. The Board instructed the Secretary to attend the Court hearing and ask for leniency; he was also directed to write the loss off and to exercise greater supervision in the future in the dispatch of money orders.

The compassion shown by the Directors in this instance was again revealed in an entry in the minutes of a Board meeting on 16th February the following year when the Secretary was instructed to write a letter to the widow of the ticket holder who had collapsed and died during the match on the previous Saturday.

1904-05 Season

In an effort to cut costs that season, Everton and Liverpool decided to issue a joint match programme, an arrangement that continued for the next 30 years. The programme had 16 pages and contained theatre and film news, as well as football gossip and advertisements. The club whose first team was at home would get the most coverage. It meant that the identical programme was on sale at both football grounds at the same time.

Bruce got an early opportunity to show his worth, replacing the injured Sharp in the fourth game of the season against Newcastle at St James Park on 17th September. Sharp was not the only absentee; Booth and Abbott were also missing from the half-back line. The Everton team *"journeyed north on Friday afternoon, breaking the tedium of travelling at Harrogate, where the night was quietly spent"*. (27)

Everton had never beaten Newcastle at St James Park, but 25,000 spectators saw them come close to breaking that unwanted record. They were down 2-1 at half-time, then Settle equalised with four minutes to go but Newcastle restored their lead two minutes later.

The match programme for the following week's game gave Bruce a glowing report: *"...and Rankin gave one of his best exhibitions. He ran and centred with as much accuracy as his comrade (Sharp), whose place he was temporarily occupying, could have accomplished, and on this form is worthy of a position in any team."* (28)

He continued in the first team for the next two games. The first was on 24th September at Goodison Park against Preston North End, who were unbeaten after four games, with three wins and a draw. Everton ended Preston's good run with a 1-0 victory before a crowd of 20,000.

The second game was against Middlesbrough away from home the following Saturday. The match report began:

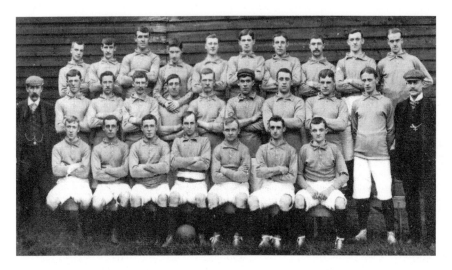

Everton 1904-05: Bruce Rankin is extreme left on the front row. Courtesy of The Everton Collection Charitable Trust, Reference 796EFC/26/1/37

"Following their usual custom, the players and directors left Liverpool yesterday afternoon and the tedium of the long journey was agreeably broken at Harrogate. The fashionable Yorkshire spa was left shortly after ten o'clock this morning and Middlesbrough was reached at noon. The weather was beautifully fine and great interest was manifested in the encounter. Although the home eleven have not been performing as well as their supporters could wish their prospects were considered bright in remembrance of the fact that last season they defeated the Goodison Park contingent by three clear goals. It had been hoped that both Sharp and Booth would be able to

turn out for Everton but this was found impossible and the team had to undergo some slight rearrangement. Rankin once more deputised for Sharp and the half back line was arranged by putting Taylor in the centre position and playing Ashworth the ex-Manchester amateur at right-half back. The home team was at full strength and in brilliant sunshine and before about 12,000 spectators." (29)

Everton lost 1-0, but Bruce's performance drew some positive comments in the local press:

"A brilliant breakaway by Rankin forced Blankett (the Middlesbrough left-back) to concede a corner…";

"Everton returned to the attack immediately, and Rankin sent in a glorious shot, which the home custodian was lucky to intercept and throw clear."

"… and a shot from Rankin was luckily diverted by Blankett."

Sharp returned to the first team on 8th October, but was unable to play the following week against Bury away, and was replaced by Bruce. On a sunny afternoon, before a crowd of 10,000 spectators, Everton won 2-1. The match report began:

"The Everton team were due at Bury this afternoon, and in view of the wretched form which the Giggs Lane contingent have so far exhibited this season, the prospects of the visitors were considered very bright. At the same time, it was remembered that the Bury men have invariable played well against Everton when on home territory and it will be remembered that last year's encounter ended in a goalless draw. The weather today was delightfully bright and fine, and a large number of the Club's supporters accompanied the Everton brigade from Exchange Station. In the cotton town itself, the game was anticipated with great interest, and there appeared to be a feeling of confidence that the home eleven for once in a way render a good

account of themselves. There were two changes in the composition of the Everton side, Ashworth, who is playing in the Inter-League match with Ireland was an absentee, and his place was taken by Makepeace, who crossed over from the other side and made room for Abbott, who reappeared after his knee trouble. In the front line, Sharp was unable to play and Rankin took his place." (30)

Most fans could only afford to watch their team at home games, so it is rather surprising to note from the Bury match report on the 15th October that *"a large number"* of Everton fans travelled to Bury. Whilst it could hardly be described as a "derby" game, Bury was one of several Lancashire sides in the League, whose grounds were fairly easily accessible for Everton fans by train.

Bruce kept his place the following week against Aston Villa at Goodison Park. It had been anticipated that *"Sharp would have sufficiently recovered to have been able to turn out but at the last moment it was found that it was not so, and the directors and the player himself exercised their wisdom in not running further risks"* (31). Before a crowd of 25,000 spectators, Aston Villa were leading 2-1 in the second half, but Everton managed to score twice to win 3-2.

Bruce continued in the first team against Blackburn Rovers on 29th October. According to the match report:

"After their handsome victory over Aston Villa at Goodison last Saturday, the Everton eleven travelled to Blackburn today, full of the brightest anticipation. The famous Rovers have in the past shared in many strenuous struggles with the Evertonians, but the latter as a rule have cut a very formidable figure when performing at Ewood Park. Last season, the Goodison Park brigade secured a two goal to nothing victory, and it was generally expected that they would make a bold bid for achieving similar honours this afternoon. The team, accompanied by several directors, and quite a large number of club supporters left Exchange Station at noon, Blackburn being reached in good time. The weather was delightfully mild and fine, and as a consequence, there was a large turnout of local enthu-

siasts. There was only one change in the composition of the visitor's team from last week. Walter Abbott strained his injured leg last Monday and was perforce an absentee, his place being filled by the extremely useful player, Makepeace." (32)

Blackburn scored the only goal of the game after 50 minutes, so Everton were unable to maintain their good run.

Sharp was fit again for the game against Nottingham Forest on 5th November. Bruce returned to the Combination side and he turned in some excellent performances, including in the Reserve derby at Goodison Park on 12th November and the matches against the two Manchester clubs over the festive period.

Bruce was *"the chief factor in the downfall"* of Liverpool Reserves in their unexpected 6-2 defeat, *"and three of the later goals were absolutely due to his fine centres after dashing runs."* (33) In the 1-1 draw with Manchester City on Christmas Eve and the 2-0 victory over Manchester United at Goodison Park on Boxing Day, *"the most prominent figure in each game was Rankin, who also had the good fortune to score the three goals gained by his side in the these matches."* (34)

Bruce returned to the first team against Derby County at Derby on 27th December, for his third game in four days. Everton's travel arrangements and team changes are described in the match report:

"After the handsome victory over Wolverhampton at Molyneux Ground on Monday, the Everton players were taken to witness the Villa match, and then took the train for Derby, where the evening was quietly spent. Several hundred ardent enthusiasts braved the journey from Liverpool to Derby yesterday morning and they made the sleepy town ring with their "war cries". The weather, though fine, was misty, and at one period of the morning it looked as though the fog might interfere with the game. The keenest interest was evinced in the meeting, and the local supporters of the Rams turned out in great numbers. The Everton directors decided to make four changes in the team from Monday. Thus Scott appeared in place of Roose, Makepeace took Ashworth's position, Rankin superseded Sharp,

and McLoughlin figured in the centre position instead of Young, who was
rather badly injured." (35)

Before a capacity crowd, Everton secured a 2-1 victory when Hardman scored
with 20 seconds to go.

Everton supporters were reported to have walked through the streets of
Derby, on their way to the ground, chanting their *"war cries"*. In the early 1900s,
supporters certainly sang when walking in groups and at the games, and cheered
and waved rattles. They would not be dressed in replica shirts, a modern creation,
although they did wear rosettes in the colours of their favourite team. For the big
matches, such as FA cup-ties, they might also wear hats and carry fancy umbrel-
las. Typically, football crowds were well-behaved throughout Bruce's years as a
professional footballer, although there were instances of disorder but mostly at
non-league matches.

Following Bruce's appearance in the victory over Derby County, he was not
selected for the next League game, but returned to the first team on 7th January
1905 against Sheffield United away. Everton lost 1-0, which meant that Sheffield
United went to the top of the First Division, with Everton in third place. Bruce,
*"who was filling the outside-right position owing to Sharp being incapacitated with
a twisted knee, gave a capital display, and on the occasions when he has turned
out with the league eleven this season has shown great improvement upon his performances of previous years. He finishes his work more accurately now and should
prove an acquisition to the first team."* (36)

Bruce retained his place the following week against Newcastle at Goodison
Park. Before a crowd of 25,000, Everton went behind early in the second half, but
"Rankin equalised with a glorious oblique shot, swift as an arrow". (37) Settle then
scored a second goal to secure a 2-1 victory for Everton.

Bruce continued in the first team against Preston North End at Deepdale
on 21st January, not on the right wing this time, but partnering Sharp, who had
returned after injury. It was centre-forward Young, who was unfit on this occasion. McDermott moved from inside-right to centre-forward, whilst Bruce took
his place. Everton could only manage a 1-1 draw, despite leading at half-time.

Sharp was missing from the first team for the next game, against Middles-brough at Goodison Park, on 28th January and Bruce replaced him at outside-right. A crowd of 15,000 saw Makepeace gain a 1-0 victory for Everton with a second half penalty. Everton were now top of the First Division, equal on points with Sheffield United, but having played a game less.

The following Saturday, 4th February, Everton faced Liverpool at Anfield in the First Round proper of the FA Cup. Once again, Bruce lost his place to Jack Sharp and played on the right wing for the Reserves against Liverpool Reserves at Goodison Park, before a 10,000 crowd, in what is now called the "mini-derby". The half-time score was 1-1, Bruce scoring Everton's goal from the penalty spot. However, Liverpool went on to find the net three times after the interval, without any Everton reply.

In the meantime, the FA Cup derby ended 1-1, with Everton winning the midweek replay at Goodison Park. Bruce was not selected for the replay, but he was back in the first team for the home League game against Bury on 11th Febru-ary. Everton were leading 1-0 at half-time and Settle scored a couple of minutes from the end to clinch a 2-0 victory.

Bruce returned to the Reserve team for the next few weeks, although he did not appear in the friendly against the amateur side Northern Nomads at Goodison Park on Saturday, 18th February. Everton used the opportunity to give a trial to a number of local players, including Bruce's younger brother George (38), who would have been 20 years old at that time. The team was:

Kitchen, Kerr and Rothwell; Stott, Chadwick and Evans; J L Jones,
G Rankin, Thorburn, Dilly and Phillips.

Although George scored in the 2-2 draw, he obviously failed to impress as the Minutes of the Directors Meeting of 20th February reported, "*the left-back Rothwell deserved further trial. The wing-halfbacks (Stott and Evans) were moderate as were the right wing (Jones and Rankin) and outside-left Phillips.*"

Despite these comments in the Minutes of the Directors meeting, George certainly played at least two further Reserve games for Everton in the early weeks of the following season. The first was against Northern Nomads on Thursday, 14th September 1905. He also appeared nine days later against Ripley Athletic at Goodison on Saturday, 23rd September. Everton won 2-0, George netting the first goal from a free-kick.

George had actually played in Tranmere Rovers' public trial on Saturday, 26th August at Prenton Park and then lined up at centre-forward against Broughton United in the opening Combination league fixture the following Saturday. The Combination, at that time, included teams such as Birkenhead, Chester, Crewe Alexandra, Glossop Reserves, Rhyl Athletic, Oswestry United and Wrexham.

According to the Birkenhead News on 5th September: "*On the Tranmere side there was only one change (against Broughton United) in the composition of the team as compared with last season's set, this being Rankin who, brother of the Everton forward, came in vice Archie Hughes who has joined Earlestown.*" George made an immediate impact on his debut, scoring two goals to put Tranmere 2-1 ahead at half-time. In an exciting second-half, Tranmere fell behind 3-2, scored two more goals to move 4-3 ahead and then saw goalkeeper Robertson save a penalty to deny Broughton a point.

In all, George appeared 13 times for Tranmere's senior side during the 1905-06 season, scoring four goals; he also played for the Reserves on a number of occasions. His final first team game was against Harrowby on Saturday, 24th October 1906 in a Liverpool Shield semi-final replay, which ended 1-1. Tranmere lost the second replay, although George was not selected for that match. Based on the various newspaper reports, George could be summed up as a talented forward, who tended to be somewhat nervous in front of goal and therefore did not score as many goals as his play deserved and, on occasions, had a habit of trying to beat too many players.

On 31st August that year, the Manchester Courier and Lancashire General Advertiser reported that Rossendale "*have secured Rankin, a brother of Bruce, who formerly played for Everton, but who is now a member of the West Bromwich Albion team*".

Following his run in the Reserves, Bruce was restored to the first team against Sheffield Wednesday at Goodison Park on Saturday, 11th March 1905, when he took Hardman's place at outside-left. Everton won 5-2, having been awarded three penalties.

However, the next few games saw him back in the Reserves. He received a number of mentions in the first half report of the game against Nelson in the Lancashire League game at Goodison Park on 1st April:

> *"Booth passed cleverly to Rankin, and the latter, after safely beating Morton gave to McLoughlin, who mulled a splendid opening."*

> *"Rankin was again prominent with an accurate centre, and McLoughlin tipped the leather to Caldwell, who failed miserably to open the score when the merest touch must easily have defeated the Nelson keeper."*

> *"Rankin's centres had been the most prominent feature of the game, but his colleagues had failed to profit from them through bad judgment."* (39)

Sharp had been injured whilst on international duty on Saturday, 1st April and Bruce took his place for the next three League games. The first of those was at Goodison Park on Wednesday, 5th April against Woolwich Arsenal. The report of the fixture began:

> *"The visit of the Arsenal to Liverpool this afternoon was the result of the postponement of the March 25 fixture, when Everton, instead of entertaining the Gunners, journeyed to Stoke for the English Cup game with the Villa. The Blues paid the Londoners a visit on November 26, on which occasion the demon fog robbed them of apparently certain victory, as they were 3 goals to 1 when the referee summarily terminated the proceedings. On this form, today's game seemed more than likely to provide the Blues with a couple more points, and thereby consolidate their championship prospects which have brightened considerably since Saturday with Newcastle biting the dust and Manchester scoring a single. The Evertonians had to turn out minus Sharp, who was rendered hors de combat in Saturday's*

international. His place was filled this evening by his capable understudy, Rankin." (40)

The match kicked off at 5.15pm with only 5000 spectators in attendance. Everton scraped a 1-0 win, which put them at the top of the League, two points ahead of Newcastle and one ahead of Manchester City.

Bruce's next game was against Stoke City at Stoke three days later. According to the Liverpool Echo report:

> *"Everton's engagement at Stoke this afternoon was fraught with exceptional interest. In the first place, the Goodison Park brigade had serious designs in winning the League Championship honours and they therefore desired a couple of points; in the second place, the Stoke Club, as usual, were struggling to keep out of the Second Division, and whose incentive to win was, therefore, equally as great as that of their opponents, and there was the additional influence at work in the remembrance that it was Everton that knocked the Potters out of the English Cup competition. Under these circumstances, the meeting was anticipated with the liveliest interest in the Staffordshire town, and favoured by a beautiful springlike weather, the encounter attracted a great crowd to the Victoria Ground. The Everton team left Liverpool at twelve o'clock and reached Stoke shortly after two. It was hoped that Roose would be able to appear for Everton, but the injury to his leg which he received on Wednesday when playing against Arsenal precluded this, and his place was taken by Scott. Crelly was also an absentee and his place was filled by Robert Balmer. These changes were made at the last moment and they rather altered the complexion of the chances of the visitors. The Stoke team were at full strength and there were 6000 people present."* (41)

After listing the two teams, the report adds, *"It will be noticed that Sharp was still an absentee owing to his injured shoulder, and the reason for Crelley's absence was that he injured his knee in getting out of the train."*

Stoke managed to gain a 2-2 draw with what was, according to the Liverpool Daily Post, a dubious equaliser:

"Until about ten minutes from the finish of the game, there was every likeli-hood that the league leaders would gain an easy victory. (The draw) is only just to the Stoke players notwithstanding the fact that no little doubt exists as to the legitimacy of the first goal which the referee awarded. It is always a moot point whether the referee or the linesman, who are up the field, can decide as to whether a custodian steps back over the line. The goal which Mr Kirkham awarded was one of this description, which is always more or less unsatisfactory. However, the referee, after consulting one of the linesmen, granted Stoke's claim." (42)

It would appear that Bruce had a poor game. The Daily Post continues:

"The Everton forwards were not at their best, and the wing men were not sufficiently plied with work from the centre. Sharp's absence was distinctly missed, for Rankin when in possession, showed little assurance, and several fine openings were allowed to go a begging by faulty returns to the centre."

Despite his apparent poor performance against Stoke City, Bruce was again selected on the right wing in the next League game, at home against Small Heath. Somewhat surprisingly, Everton were down 1-0 at half-time, but in the second half, Young equalised and Makepeace scored from a penalty to secure a 2-1 win for Everton. Again, it would seem that Bruce did not have a good game. According to the report in the Football Echo of 15th April, *"Unfortunately, Rankin and Taylor could not make successful partners…"*; Taylor had been moved from the defence into the forward line for this game.

Everton then had three away games in four days at the end of April – Manchester City on 21st; Woolwich Arsenal the following day; and Nottingham Forest on 24th. Bruce did not play in any of those games, although he did travel as reserve for the Woolwich Arsenal game.

Everton lost 2-0 to Manchester City, but would be League champions if they won their remaining two games. The Everton - Woolwich Arsenal match on 22nd April was a replayed game; the original fixture in November had been abandoned because of fog, when Everton were leading 3-1. Sadly, Woolwich Arsenal won 2-1 on the 21st April to deprive Everton of the League championship, for Everton won the Nottingham Forest game two days later. Newcastle United were champions with 48 points from 34 games, Everton were runners-up with 47 points and Manchester City were in third place, a point behind Everton.

Everton were desperately unlucky not to win the League. The abandonment of the game against Woolwich Arsenal when Everton were leading 3-1 and the subsequent loss in the replayed game some five months later was cruel. Two points from the original game would have been sufficient to ensure that Everton were champions. The incident involving the disputed goal which gave Stoke a 2-2 draw against Everton was also unfortunate although, to be fair, an additional point from that game would not have won Everton the League as Newcastle had a superior goal average to the Blues. It was a disappointing end to the season, however.

In the close season, Everton embarked on their very first international tour. A party of 20 players and officials left Exchange Station for Budapest at 2.10pm on Thursday, 27th April. The journey took two full days, with overnight travel on the boat from Harwich to Hook of Holland and then on the train from Dresden to Vienna, finally arriving on the Saturday afternoon in Budapest, where they stayed at the Grand Hotel Royale. The players who travelled were:

Roose and Scott, goal; R. Balmer and Crelly, backs; Taylor, Booth and Abbott, halves; Rankin, McDermott, Young, McLoughlin, Settle and Hardman, forwards. Accompanying them were club officials Dr. Baxter, Dr. Whitford, and Messrs Baimbridge, Wade, Kelly and Cuff, as well as the trainer Mr. Elliott.

Their first game was in Budapest on Sunday, 30th April against local club Magyar Athletikai. The long journey had little or no effect on the Everton players for they trounced their opponents by 11 goals to 2.

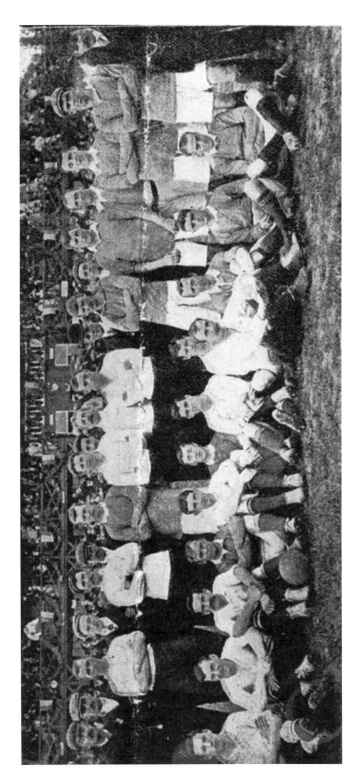

The Everton and Spurs teams that faced each other in Prague when Everton won 1-0. Bruce Rankin is sixth from the left on the front row.

Courtesy of The Everton Collection Charitable Trust, Reference 796EFC/19/3/1/0001

The following afternoon, the party travelled by train to Vienna, where they stayed at the Hotel Royale. They played three matches in Vienna. The first two, on 2nd and 5th May, were against First Vienna FC and an Austrian XI, both of which Everton won. Everton's first real test was on Sunday, 7th May, when they faced Tottenham Hotspur, who were then in the Southern League and were also on tour. Some 7,000 spectators turned up to watch Everton beat Spurs 2-0 and see them presented with a trophy in the shape of a tankard to commemorate their victory.

Following the win over Spurs, the party had a day at leisure in Vienna before setting off for Prague, where their headquarters was the Hotel Schwarzes Roff. There, Everton defeated two local sides, Athletikklub Sparta and Sportklub Slavia, and recorded a second win over Spurs, this time by the only goal of the game, which was scored by Roose, the goalkeeper, who was playing on the right wing. Roose only appeared in goal for one game on the tour, as he injured a thumb in training.

The party left Prague on the evening of 16th May, travelling by train overnight to Berlin, arriving at 7.30am the following morning. In Berlin, they stayed at the Hotel Central for one night, catching the train for Rotterdam the next morning, the 18th May, at 11.40am. Sailing overnight on the ferry from Hook of Holland to Harwich, they eventually arrived at Liverpool Exchange Station on Friday afternoon , 19th May, where they were welcomed by a group of directors, players and ladies. "*All the men looked exceedingly well when they stepped on to the platform*". (43)

The Austro-Hungarian tour was a considerable success. Everton won all their games, including two victories over Spurs, the weather was excellent and the club's reception at each ground was enthusiastic. The only complaint from the players was that the grounds were so hard that their studs hurt the soles of their feet.

One of the club officials told the reporters that "*the game (in the countries visited) is getting a good hold on the people and it will be the most popular sport in time*". On the subject of the referees there, however, he said, "*Oh, over here we may have a little grumble, but draw the veil over foreign referees*."

Bruce would have been fairly pleased with himself that season, having played 16 games for the team that was runners-up in the League. He had given a number of good displays during the season, although it would seem from newspaper reports that his performance had fallen away in his final two games. He will have suffered from continued disappointment, however, knowing that whenever Jack Sharp was fit, he would always be the first choice for the right wing position.

His inclusion on the Austro-Hungarian tour must have been a great thrill. Travelling abroad at that time was fairly unusual, certainly for someone of Bruce's background, and to have visited four great capital cities of Europe must have been a unique experience, not to mention playing against teams from three of the countries visited.

Bruce re-signed for the following season on the maximum weekly wage of £4.

1905-06 Season

Although *"all the men who did so well last year have been retained"*, Everton made a number of signings during the close season. These included W. Kelly, a goal-keeper, who was a nephew of one of the directors; Harry Cooke, an inside forward, who was persuaded by Bruce to join the Club (44), and who later became the club trainer; Hannon and Black from Celtic, a full-back and half-back respectively; Hill, another full-back, from Southampton; and Oliver, a forward, from Brentford.

Goodison Park in 1905 with St Luke's Church on the far right – Bruce played for the Church's Bible Class team as a youngster. Courtesy of The Everton Collection Charitable Trust, Reference 796EFC/26/4/1

Bruce played in the first match of the season against Middlesbrough at Goodison Park. The Football Echo of 1st September reports, *"On the right wing, Sharp was an absentee as a result of his cricket exertions, but Everton are fortunate in having a brilliant substitute in Rankin, who seems to improve at every appearance and has a host of admirers"*. Everton won the game 4-1, Bruce scoring the third goal in the second half.

Bruce was replaced by Sharp in the next game, but returned to the first team on 23rd September against Aston Villa at Villa Park in the place of McDermott, who was dropped. Everton lost the game before a crowd of 25,000. From the match report, it would seem that Bruce did not have a particularly good game, although he did hit the crossbar in the first half. He was dropped from the first team again, sometimes playing in the Reserves and, on occasions, travelling as 12th man for the first team.

In October, McDermott, who had been signed from Celtic in the summer of 1903, was transferred to Chelsea for £350, having first refused a move to Bury. He had had a poor disciplinary record with Everton. He had failed to turn up for training and had admitted to drunkenness on a number of occasions and, as a result, had been fined and suspended at different times. Despite these transgressions, he continued to play regularly in the first team. However, the Board of Directors eventually lost patience with him when he failed to appear for training on 19th September, and the Secretary was instructed to inform clubs that they were willing to accept offers of not less than £250 for his transfer. In almost two years at Everton, McDermott had made 71 appearances, scoring 19 goals. At Chelsea, he played in 31 league games, but his form was inconsistent, and he returned to Scotland to secure regular first team football, signing for Dundee, one of his former clubs. Within a year, he was back in England, joining Bradford City but he moved on quickly to a number of other clubs before returning to amateur football.

Bruce re-appeared in the first team against Blackburn Rovers at Ewood Park on 11th November. He replaced Sharp, who had been injured in the match with Woolwich Arsenal the previous week. It was a surprise to the match reporter *"to find the Evertonians in striped costumes instead of the time honoured blue"*. (45) Everton were losing 1-0 at half-time. However, early in the second half *"the*

wretched form of the Evertonians was brightened by a fine run by Rankin, who car-
ried the ball along perfectly at his toe, then passed to little Settle, who was waiting,
and seemed to steady himself a moment, and the equalising was achieved." Everton
took the lead 15 minutes from the end and then, with four minutes to go, Bruce
scored direct from a corner. Despite conceding a goal in the dying seconds of the
game, Everton won 3-2.

The following week, Bruce played against Sunderland at Roker Park in what
proved to be his last first team game for the Club. The match report describes the
team's journey to Sunderland and the team changes:

> *"The players left Liverpool under the care of Mr Horace Wright, one of the*
> *directors, and Mr Cuff, the Secretary, yesterday afternoon, arriving at the*
> *Durham town early in the evening. After a couple of hours at the theatre,*
> *the players went early to bed and did not turn out until late in the forenoon,*
> *preferring rest to recreation. In this they were not unwise, for the weather*
> *was almost arctic in character. There had been a keen frost overnight and*
> *this morning the atmospheric outlook was the reverse of promising, for, in*
> *addition to the low temperature there was a threatening of fog, and at one*
> *o'clock it was quite doubtful whether the game would be played to a finish.*
> *There were several interesting changes to the composition of the Everton*
> *eleven. For the first time this season, Harold Hardman had to stand down*
> *owing to an injury to his leg and his place was filled by Rankin. Oliver reap-*
> *peared in the centre and Young partnered Sharp on the right, while in the*
> *back division, the elder brother supplanted his brother. The fog was hanging*
> *heavily over the enclosure when in the presence of 10,000 spectators, the*
> *players lined up."* (46)

The half-time score was 1-1 but, because of the worsening weather, play restarted
without the players leaving the pitch. Everton lost 2-1, the match reporter con-
cluding that *"in the present case the composition and disposition of the forward line*
was not a success. Rankin, with every desire to do well, was quite out of the picture
at outside-left, and Oliver failed to reach the standard suggested by his sensational

debut against Notts County." (Oliver had scored a hat-trick in his first game on 14th October)

Following the Sunderland game, Bruce returned to the Reserve team and he scored several goals, including two against Southport Central on 30th December, one of which was a penalty. On New Year's Day, however, he missed a penalty against Manchester City Reserves at Goodison Park, sending *"the ball into the hands of Youde, who easily saved"* (47). The game ended in a 0-0 draw before a crowd of 2000 spectators.

Bruce continued to play in the Reserve team during January 1906 and his last game in the Everton colours was on the right wing against Southport Central on the 27th. A few days later West Bromwich Albion, who were then in the Second Division, submitted an offer of £100 for Bruce's transfer. Everton's Directors wanted more money for him and, subsequently, West Bromwich increased their offer to £250. The Everton Directors were satisfied with the new offer and, on 6th February, agreed to allow Bruce to go. (48)

Just twelve months earlier, in February 1905, the country had seen the first four-figure transfer when Alf Common was transferred from Sunderland to Middlesbrough for £1000. Sunderland had bought him from Sheffield United just a year previously for £350, when transfers were normally around £400. So, Bruce's transfer fee was not particularly high for that time.

Bruce's transfer was reported in the Liverpool Daily Post on 9th February:

"West Bromwich Albion have signed Bruce Rankin, the Everton player. Born in Everton twenty-three years ago, he helped such clubs as City Villa, St Luke's Bible Class, White Star Wanderers and Kirkdale in youthful days. In 1902-03, he played with the first team and, in all, fourteen times appeared among the seniors. Last season, he scored against Newcastle with a goal that will long be remembered. He has represented Lancashire, has numerous medals, and assisted the North versus the South at Tottenham in 1902-03."

Bruce had not been a regular first team player in his time at Everton. Jack Sharp, an England international, was the first choice at outside-right, Bruce's main position, although he did appear at outside-left and inside forward on several occasions. He had a number of excellent games, but the more recent match reports had been somewhat critical of his performances. Indeed in October, along with Chadwick and Dilly, he appeared before the Board of Directors to be *"spoken to about their indifferent displays"*. (49) It was not at all unusual for players to be admonished for poor performances by the Board of Directors in those days. Even the great Jack Sharp had been called before the Board to be rebuked about his poor play, and one of the directors, Mr. Kirkwood, had been instructed by the Board to give Alex Young *"some tuition in the centre-forward game."* (50)

Bruce had been with Everton for four and a half seasons and, in that time, had played 38 League and FA Cup games, scoring seven goals, as well as appearing in a number of friendlies. Ten of his team-mates were included in "Gwladys Street's Hall of Fame" (51) a disproportionate number when one considers that the Hall of Fame covered 100 years of football and included only 75 players.

He was probably somewhat disillusioned at being in and out of the first team and, perhaps, he was glad of the prospect of proving himself at another club, albeit one in the Second Division, where he was likely to have more opportunities in the first team.

In Tony Matthews' "Who's Who of Everton", Bruce was described as *"an easy-moving, graceful-looking wing forward, clever on the ball and a player who could let fly with a useful telling shot."*

Eight days after Bruce's move, Everton secured the transfer of Donnachie from Newcastle United. Donnachie was reported *"to be equally good at outside-right or left"* (52) and went straight into the first team against Notts County that Saturday. He played 58 games for Everton in the 2½ years he was at Goodison, before being transferred to Blackpool in August 1908.

References

1.   For example records held by Everton FC and "Who's Who of Everton" by Tony Matthews (2004)

2.   Everton v Middlesbrough programme 28th January 1905

3.   See Across the Park by Peter Lupson for the story behind the change of grounds

4.   Birkenhead News, 9th and 12th October 1901

5.   Association Football and English Society 1863-1915 by Tony Mason; The Harvester Press Ltd; 1980

6.   Liverpool Football Echo, 18th January 1902

7.   Liverpool Football Echo, 1st February 1902

8.   Minutes of Meeting of Board of Directors, 15th April 1902

9.   Liverpool Daily Post, 7th April 1902

10.   Liverpool Football Echo, 30th August 1902

11.   Boots, Balls and Haircuts: An illustrated history from then to now by Hunter Davies; Cassell Illustrated; 2003

12.   Minutes of Meeting of Board of Directors, 6th August 1902 Liverpool Football Echo, 20th September 1902

13.   Liverpool Football Echo, 20th September 1902

14.   Liverpool Football Echo, 27th September 1902

15.   Liverpool Football Echo, 15th November 1902

16.   Liverpool Daily Post, 15th December 1902

17.   Liverpool Football Echo, 31st January 1903

18.   Liverpool Echo, 3rd February 1903

19.   Liverpool Football Echo, 14th February 1903

20.   Minutes of Meeting of Board of Directors, 20th April 1903

21.   Liverpool Echo, 10th November 1902

22.   Liverpool Daily Post, 27th January 1903

23.   Minutes of Meeting of Board of Directors, 23rd February 1904

24.   Liverpool Daily Post, 29th February 1904

25.   Liverpool Football Echo, 16th April 1904

26.   Minutes of Meeting of Board of Directors, 25th April 1904

27.   Liverpool Football Echo, 17th September 1904

28.   Everton v Preston North End match programme, 24th September 1904

29.　Liverpool Football Echo, 1st October 1904

30.　Liverpool Football Echo, 15th October 1904

31.　Liverpool Football Echo, 22nd October, 1904

32.　Liverpool Football Echo, 29th October 1904

33.　Everton v Sunderland match programme, 19th November 1904

34.　Everton v Liverpool match programme, 2nd January 1905

35.　Liverpool Daily Post, 28th December 1904

36.　Everton v Newcastle United match programme, 14th January 1905

37.　Liverpool Football Echo, 14th January 1905

38.　Liverpool Daily Post, 18th February 1905

39.　Liverpool Football Echo, 1st April 1905

40.　Liverpool Echo, 5th April, 1905

41.　Liverpool Football Echo, 8th April 1905

42.　Liverpool Daily Post, 10th April 1905

43.　Liverpool Daily Post, 20th May 1905

44.　Liverpool Echo, 9th December 1950

45.　Liverpool Football Echo, 11th November 1905

46.　Liverpool Football Echo, 18th November 1905

47.　Liverpool Daily Post, 2nd January 1906

48.　Minutes of Meeting of Board of Directors, 6th February 1906

49.　Minutes of Meeting of Board of Directors, 17th October 1905

50.　Minutes of Meeting of Board of Directors, 3rd December 1901

51.　Gwladys Street's Hall of Fame by D H France (1998)

52.　Liverpool Daily Post, 17th February 1906

2

BRUCE ON THE MOVE (1906-09)

West Bromwich Albion

1905-06 Season

Like Everton, West Bromwich Albion were founder members of the Football League. They had been relegated for the second time in 1904 and were still in the Second Division when Bruce joined them. Their ground, The Hawthorns, was and still is the highest ground above sea-level in the United Kingdom at 551 feet. The West Bromwich Weekly News welcomed Bruce's arrival:

"The Albion directors on Wednesday signed Bruce Rankin, a forward who has rendered good service to Everton. Rankin, who is 23 years of age (he was actually 26), scales 11st 4lbs and stands 5'8", is one of the best outside-rights in England. He played brilliantly for the North against the South in 1903 – in fact, he was considered unlucky not to receive an international cap. The Albion directors are to be commended for their enterprise for the difficulty of obtaining first class men at this period of the campaign cannot be realised by the ordinary follower of the game. Everton do not want money, and, more-over, they did not want to part with Rankin. But, Rankin this season has been acting as "understudy" to Jack Sharp, and has not relished his part. The Goodison Park officials admit that Rankin is almost, if not quite, the equal of Sharp, but as the ex-Villa man is showing such fine form, they could not drop him in favour of the Albion's latest capture. This is the sole reason why Rankin has left his native town. The amount of the transfer fee has not been divulged, but we are at liberty to state that it is a very substantial one."(1)

Bruce went straight into the first team at outside-right for the home game against Bristol City, the league leaders, on Saturday, 10th February. A large crowd was expected for his debut, but bad weather restricted the attendance to 6400. Before kick-off, some 50 men had removed snow from the ground, which was in a heavy and slippery condition, and the heavy rain during the match did not help matters. It was not to be a winning debut. Albion were two down within the first ten minutes. In the second half, Albion completely outplayed Bristol and should have been on level terms within ten minutes of the re-start, but the referee disallowed what appeared to be two good goals. Later, Pheasant, the Albion centre-half, made it 2-1 from the penalty spot and, although Bristol got a third goal, Albion did most of the pressing.

According to the match reporter for The Chronicle for West Bromwich, Oldbury and District, Albion were unlucky to lose. *"In fact, it was only by some most remarkable refereeing and one might say unfair offside decisions that the Albion were robbed of victory they so richly deserved. To justify this statement I might point out that throughout the game the Albion netted the ball on no fewer than six occasions. Four goals were disallowed on the ground of offside, one in particular was rushed through from a corner, and which could not possibly be offside but which the referee for some reason or other refused to allow all the same."* (2)

In his Football Notes for the West Bromwich Weekly News, Felix Mundi wrote that *"there was much curiosity to see how the new man from Everton shaped and it was a disappointment that he did so little. Still, it must be borne in mind that in strange company and on a new ground he was hardly likely to shine, especially under the conditions that existed. Rankin is a well-built, likely looking player and when he and Simmons get a good understanding, I should think that they will make a good wing."*

Albion's next game, away to Manchester United, ended in a scoreless draw and was watched by 8000 spectators. United were at a disadvantage in the second half, as their centre-forward Beddow was unable to resume because of injury. Despite this, they pressed almost continuously and a magnificent display by the Albion keeper Stringer undoubtedly saved his side. However, the previous week's bad luck still seemed to be with the Albion, as they had a goal disallowed for offside. The view in The Chronicle was that Bruce had certainly performed better than on his debut.

On Saturday, 24th February, Bruce scored his first goal for Albion in a 6-0 win over Glossop at the Hawthorns, watched by a crowd of 7200. Albion were far and away the superior side and right from the start completely outclassed their opponents. *"Rankin, on this occasion was just as brilliant as he was disappointing when he made his debut against Bristol. In fact, the ex-Evertonian was easily the best forward on the field, and his runs and centres were a treat to witness."* (3) In the Weekly News, Felix Mundi wrote, *"On Saturday, he (Rankin) showed himself to be a first-class player and one of the cleverest and neatest performers in the out-side-right position we have seen at the Hawthorns. His display was marked by speed and dash in his runs and remarkably well-judged centring. The goal with which he initiated the scoring was a beauty. He went through quite on his own, and his shot was directed to the likeliest spot for beating the custodian, high in the corner of the stumps. It was principally due to his efforts that from that time to the finish the Albion were all over their opponents."* (4)

West Bromwich Albion had beaten Stockport County 3-1 at the Hawthorns earlier in the season and, towards the end of the return game on Saturday, 3rd March, it looked as if Stockport would gain their revenge; they were leading 2-0. However, in the closing stages, Albion scored twice and were unlucky not to win as centre-forward Simmons hit the post. Bruce's reputation had preceded him for he was well policed by two defenders, although he still managed to put across a few good centres and one of his runs was *"ranked as the finest effort that the match produced".*

Albion were fourth in the league, but this was their seventh draw of the season, which meant that they fell further behind the three leaders, who all won that Saturday.

The following game, at home against Blackpool, was played in cold, drenching rain and saw Albion's fourth victory of the season by five or more goals. Bruce made another good impression - *"...while the more one sees of Rankin the greater becomes the conviction that in him the Albion have secured a bargain. He put in some admirable work and his little touches were a treat to witness. In the last half, he did not get the ball so often as his previous work had warranted."* (5)

A 1-0 win at Bradford on Saturday, 17th March meant that Albion had gone five games without being beaten. Though only one goal separated the teams, Albion produced one of their best displays that season away from home and their superiority was really more marked than the score line suggests. Bruce played a part in Albion's goal - *"Rankin took the measure of Millar and Roberts, and simply made rings round them, while his centres were marked by his usual accuracy. One of them was played back to Heywood, who was standing unmarked, and with the greatest coolness he lifted the ball into the net out of the reach of Daw."* (6)

Albion's next game was against Grimsby Town at the Hawthorns the following Saturday. It was played in a bitterly cold wind, with occasional heavy snow showers, which made things decidedly uncomfortable for both players and supporters. A 2-0 victory kept Albion's unbeaten run going and Bruce scored his second goal since arriving at the Hawthorns. In the 31st March issue of the Weekly News, Felix Mundi wrote, *"Rankin gave another finished exhibition, sprinting and dodging with the cleverness which is characteristic of him."*

During the week following the Grimsby Town match, West Bromwich Albion signed one of Bruce's former Everton teammates - Tom Dilly – for £100. He was selected immediately at outside-right, replacing Perkins for the game at the Hawthorns against Leicester Fosse. Albion won 3-0, watched by more than 10,000 spectators in summer-like weather. The victory made no impression on the promotion race, it simply reinforced Albion's fourth position. Dilly created a good impression on his debut, and was more conspicuous than Bruce, who did not get his usual service from Haycock, who was a replacement for the injured Simmons.

After an undefeated run of seven games - five victories and two draws - West Bromwich Albion were firmly brought down to earth with their heaviest league defeat of the season, 4-0 away to Hull. Albion had more than their share of bad luck, hitting the woodwork twice and captain Pheasant missing a penalty. Bruce and Heywood were the best of the Albion forwards.

Albion's three match Easter programme began on Good Friday, 13th April, with a 3-0 defeat at Barnsley. On the same day, Chelsea played out a draw with Manchester United at Stamford Bridge before a crowd of more than 50,000 spectators.

The trains from Barnsley were operating on a Sunday timetable on Good Friday, so the players had to stay there overnight, returning to the Hawthorns just an hour or so before the kick-off for the Saturday game against Lincoln. No doubt affected by their long journey, the team then gave one of its poorest displays of the season in a 1-1 draw. Many considered them lucky to get a point, although they did the bulk of the attacking and went close to scoring several times.

On Easter Monday, Albion secured an easy away victory against Clapham Orient by two goals to nil. Dilly scored early in the first half and, about 20 minutes later, they went further ahead when Heywood got his head *"to one of Rankin's nice centres and cleverly turning the ball into the net."* (7) The star performers were Bruce and captain Pheasant.

Edward Pheasant had played 168 games for Wolverhampton Wanderers before joining West Bromwich Albion in November 1904. In his five and a half years at the Hawthorns, he made 152 appearances and scored 22 goals, playing primarily at centre-half, but also turning out at centre-forward on occasions. Whilst at Wolves, he was selected to play for the Football League, but refused, preferring to play for Wolves instead. He died of peritonitis within a few weeks of leaving Albion for Leicester Fosse in 1910, at the age of 33.

In their fourth game in six days, Albion were unlucky to be defeated 2-1 away to Gainsborough on Wednesday, 18th April. However, they went on to win their final two games of the season – beating Chesterfield 3-0 away and Burslem Port Vale 4-1 at the Hawthorns. The only disappointment in the final home game of the season was that a mere 4800 people turned up to watch. Bruce signed off the season with a positive performance - he *"delighted the spectators with his exhibition of trickiness and speed."* (8) He was on the retained list for the following season.

1906-07 Season

Four public practice matches were held in preparation for the new season. In the first two, the probable first team forwards were opposed by the probable first team defence, both sides being made up with reserve team players. Bruce played at out-side-right in both games. In the third match, on Monday, 27th August, the full first team opposed the probable reserve side. The players selected for the first team were:

From left to right, back row: Mr. W. Bassett (Director), A. Randle, C. Simmons, W. Bashes (Trainer), J. Stringer, J. Pennington, Mr. C. Couse (Director), Mr F. Everins (Secretary). Middle row: A. Haywood, F. Shinton, F. Busk, E. Pheasant (captain), J. Manners, T. Dilly. Front row: R. Bettelley, B. Rankin. Courtesy of West Bromwich Albion FC

Stringer; Bettelley, Pennington; Randle, Pheasant, Manners; Rankin, Buck, Shinton, Heywood, Dilly.

The last in the series of practice matches took place on Wednesday evening, 29th August, when two full teams of players eligible for the reserves were pitted against each other. The gate receipts for the four games amounted to £56 17s and a cheque for that amount was paid over to the West Bromwich Charity Sports Fund to be distributed between the District Hospital, the Nurses' Home and the Cinderella Club.

For the third successive season, Albion opened their League programme with Burnley as opponents. The game, on Saturday, 1st September, kicked off at Turf Moor at 5.15pm because there was a cricket match between Burnley and Rawtenstall to decide the champions of the Lancashire League; Burnley were the winners. Felix Mundi of the Weekly News commented that the Lancashire locals were much more enthusiastic about their cricket than their counterparts in the Midlands.

The football match was played in glorious weather. Despite a tiring, five-hour rail journey for the Albion players, Buck scored the only goal of the game to give Albion a well-deserved win and an excellent start to the new season. Bruce was at outside-right. The players did not arrive back from Burnley until 3.15am on Sunday morning.

Summer weather again prevailed for the second game of the season, in which Albion routed Leeds City 5-0 at the Hawthorns the following Saturday before 15,500 spectators. Dilly and Bruce were on the wings, the latter being carefully watched by Kennedy, the Leeds half-back. Kennedy's height told when the ball was in the air, but on the occasions when Bruce had possession, his tricks and speed were generally too good for the defender. Perhaps, Kennedy marked Bruce too closely or maybe he did not like the way Bruce beat him on the ground, because in the 14th September issue of the Chronicle it was reported that *"a regrettable incident happened when Rankin and Kennedy began sparring at each other, but this came to nothing and the two players afterwards got on good terms, and many only regarded the affair as a joke."*

The Chronicle considered that Albion's performance against Leeds had raised hopes that they would not be far off the championship by the end of the season. However, the following Saturday, the club and spectators were brought firmly down to earth when they were unexpectedly defeated 2-1 by Burslam Port Vale at Corbridge. Burslam took the lead after five minutes when a shot was diverted past goalkeeper Stringer by an Albion defender. The second goal should not have been allowed. One of the Port Vale players, Beats, brought the ball down with his hand on the halfway line. Although they were in a good position to see the offence, the referee and linesmen missed it. Beats passed the ball to one of his colleagues, who was in an offside position, and ran on to receive a return pass. Stringer pushed out his shot, but a Port Vale forward was on hand to knock the ball into the net. This all took place in the first 15 minutes. Albion managed to pull a goal back, but were unable to rescue the match. Bruce did not have a very good game. Felix Mundi of the Weekly News complained that the Corbridge playing surface was in a dreadful state and placed ball-playing teams at a disadvantage. *"The turf is all tassocks, and there were deep holes in it,"* he wrote, and he went on to suggest that the League should take up the question of the fitness of grounds.

Albion's next match was at Barnsley where they had lost 3-0 the previous season. There was no score at the interval, although Albion were somewhat fortunate to be on level terms as Barnsley missed a penalty. Until ten minutes from the end, it looked as if the game would end in a draw, but a free-kick by Randle was headed into the Barnsley net by Shinton to earn the points for Albion. Although Bruce did some clever things, it was reported that he had *"not yet found his best form"*. Perkins had replaced Dilly on the left wing because he was considered lazy, according to The Chronicle. Albion now had six points from four games, a point behind the leaders, Leicester Fosse.

The top match on Saturday, 22nd September, was West Bromwich Albion against Chelsea at the Hawthorns. It was watched by 25,562 spectators, while the First Division game between Albion's rivals Birmingham and Liverpool only drew a crowd of 9000. Chelsea, who were better in almost every department, won 2-1. However, at no time did the visitors look like winning easily and, in the second half, there were periods when Albion promised to snatch something from the game. Twenty minutes from the end, with Chelsea 2-0 ahead, captain Pheasant missed a penalty.

Bruce had a poor game against Chelsea and was dropped from the first team the following week, a derby game against Wolverhampton Wanderers at Molyneux, which Albion won 3-0. He turned out for the Reserves against Walsall in the Birmingham and District League, scoring the third and final goal in a 3-1 victory. According to the Weekly News report, "*Rankin played with as much indifference – with one or two brief exceptions – as he has shown in the first team and a revival of form will be welcome.*" (9)

Following Bruce's demotion to the Reserves, Albion won six and drew one of their next eight league games without him and were top of the league. One of his games for the Reserves was a 3-0 home win against Coventry City on Saturday, 13th October. During the match there was a remarkable incident, which would not be allowed to happen today. "*Twenty minutes into the second half … the Albion left wing were going for goal, and just as the ball was slipping over the touchline Legge and Haynes both charged at Edwards, the Coventry back, grassing him. The referee obviously thought it was an Albion man down for he awarded a penalty against City. This was altogether wrong but the referee refused to see the mistake and alter the decision and the Coventry players became so disgusted that they prevented the penalty being taken for some time. Every time the ball was placed on the penalty spot, a player would kick it into goal, by the corner flag, or among the spectators, doing this after the referee himself had placed the ball ready for the kick. Such utter defiance should have merited drastic punishment by dismissal from the field, the referee showing lamentable weakness in this respect. After several minutes Haynes was allowed to take the penalty kick. The goalkeeper stopped the shot, and Haynes then headed over.*" (10) Was it a genuine miss by Haynes or did he simply not have the heart to score when the penalty awarded to Albion was not justified? The referee's poor handling of the game allowed the ill-feeling to continue and Heywood, an Albion player, was later sent off – an unwarranted decision, according to the Weekly News reporter. Bruce showed some of his trickery during the game.

On 27th October, Albion won 1-0 at Hull. But, the Second Division games that day were marred by the death of the Leeds City centre-forward - Wilson, aged

23 years - in the game against Burnley. About an hour into the match, Wilson left the field complaining of pains in his chest. Shortly afterwards, on learning that his team were virtually reduced to eight men because of injuries, he insisted on returning to the fray, despite the advice and protests of club doctors and officials. Five minutes later, he was back in the dressing room, where he died soon afterwards of a heart attack.

That same Saturday, the Weekly News also reported that Jack Sharp, the Everton outside-right and former colleague of Bruce, had decided to retire from football at the end of the season as he did not want to risk being injured in view of the fact that his cricket benefit was shortly due. On learning this news, perhaps it crossed Bruce's mind that he might have been better off remaining at Goodison.

Bruce was recalled to Albion's first team for the home game against Chesterfield on 24th November, replacing Broad. Chesterfield scored first but *a brilliant piece of work on the part of Rankin* put Albion on level terms, his shot *being a fair dazzler.* (11) The score remained 1-1 at the interval. Things changed quickly in the second half, however, as Dilly scored three goals in rapid succession and, after Chesterfield had scored again, Shinton headed a fifth to secure a substantial victory. This was the fourth time that Albion had scored five times during the season and Chesterfield scored as many goals against them as any other club had managed. Bruce was clearly a crowd favourite for Felix Mundi wrote in the Weekly News on 1st December, *"If there is one player whom the Albion supporters enjoy to see in form more than another it is Rankin. He has his off days, but when playing at his best his football is delightful. His re-appearance in the first eleven on Saturday was marked by a capital display and he also signalled it by scoring a fine goal."* Albion were still at the top of the league, along with Nottingham Forest, with 21 points from 14 games; Chelsea were third, two points behind, but with a game in hand.

Albion's run of success came to an abrupt end at Leicester the following Saturday with a 3-0 defeat in front of a crowd of almost 20,000. They had been at the top of the table for six weeks but were now in second place, two points behind Nottingham Forest; Leicester were fourth, with Chelsea third on the same number of points as Leicester, but with a game in hand. It was the first time a team had scored three goals against Albion that season; it was also the first time that Albion had failed to score. Perhaps the defeat was not unexpected, as Leicester had won every home game.

There was a chance to regain some of the lost ground the next Saturday when Albion faced Nottingham Forest at the Hawthorns in a top of the table clash. A crowd of 17,000 was thrilled by a 3-1 victory, which regained the top spot for Albion. The first half was keenly contested and, with the score 0-0 at the interval, there was little to choose between the two sides. However, the second half opened in sensational fashion when, within a minute of the restart, "*Rankin, with a beautiful long shot, sent the ball into the corner of the net and the crowd yelled with delight*".(12) According to the Weekly News, Bruce's goal had a great influence on the final result - Albion went about their work with greater confidence and renewed energy, while it took the heart out of the visitors.

Tityrus of Athletic News was at the game and was of the opinion that "*one rarely sees a finer game in the First Division,*" noting that the whistle was blown for offside on only three occasions. He went on: "*Rankin got a very small share of the ball in the first half. Perhaps he took up bad positions, perhaps he was neglected and perhaps he was well-guarded. Among the three we shall find the truth. In the second portion he sallied forth in the most sparkling manner, and was the cause of each goal being notched. With his speed he has fine control of the ball, and he can centre. He is a general, and, above all, a silent man. I have never seen Rankin's lips move when he is on the field. Such men play the game, and contribute to happiness. Rankin ought yet to realise the promise that caused him to be selected for the North against the South – but that was at outside-left.*"

Albion were brought down to earth again the following Saturday. Lincoln deservedly beat them 2-1 on a ground that was as hard as a rock, with a covering of an inch of snow; Lincoln had made no attempt to clear the snow away. Albion's persistence with their short-passing game in these terrible conditions showed a lack of initiative and judgment, as the snow continually held the ball up. Lincoln, on the other hand, adopted the long ball and more direct approach, which was more suited to the situation. The game was won and lost in the first half, for Albion were two down by the interval. Bruce had few opportunities to show his skills.

On Saturday, 22nd December, the Weekly News reproduced a piece, which had appeared in the Sporting Mail the previous week, demonstrating someone's skill in employing the names of some Albion players in the use of the pun:

> *"Two friends at the Forest v Albion match were commenting on individual*
> *players. The first asked: "And what do you think of Shinton?"*
> *"Without a doubt the finest centre-forward in the League."*
> *"Oh, how do you make that out?"*
> *"Well, he has no old **Buck**, is possessed of good **Manners**, has two good*
> ***Legges**, never **Dillys** with the ball and is likely to be **Rankin** amongst the*
> *best when goals are reckoned up at the end of the season."*
> *His friend said no more."*

After the Lincoln match, the Albion players spent the following week at Droitwich in special training for the four Christmas holiday games, which were all at home. Burton Albion, who were bottom of the league, were the first of the visitors on Saturday, 22nd December, a rather cold day. Within 15 minutes, Albion were two up and had failed to convert a penalty. Bruce had a hand in the first goal when he made one of his dazzling runs on the wing and then crossed the ball for Legge to smack the ball past Starbrick, the Burton goalkeeper. Simmons scored from a corner soon afterwards. Burton pulled a goal back before the interval and, for the first twenty minutes after the interval, they held their own. However, two more goals from Shinton and another by Simmons ensured a final score of 5-1 in Albion's favour.

More than 19,000 people were thoroughly entertained at the Hawthorns on Christmas morning when Albion recorded another resounding victory, this time beating Grimsby Town by six goals to one. For the second time that season, Shinton scored four in a game and went on to become the first Albion player to score four hat-tricks in a single campaign.

On Boxing Day, Albion recorded their third victory, defeating Burslem Port Vale 3-0. Their opponents were half-an-hour late in arriving at the Hawthorns, excusing their delay on the grounds that they had had to travel by tram from

Birmingham because of the snow. In order to finish the game before darkness fell, the teams agreed to dispense with the interval. The ground was covered in snow and was hard and slippery but, in spite of this, the game was fast and exciting. Shinton missed an early penalty before Bruce scored the only goal of the first half with a brilliant, long shot beating the Port Vale keeper all ends up. Goals by Dilly and Shinton after the interval secured a well-deserved victory to put Albion back at the top of the table.

After the match, the Albion players were taken to the Prince of Wales Theatre in Birmingham. They then returned to Droitwich to continue their special training until Saturday when the Christmas holiday matches were to be brought to a close with a home game against Burnley. Despite the bitterly cold weather, there was a reasonable crowd of 12,000 people to see the game. Albion made it four victories out of four during the holiday period, although this proved to be their most difficult match. Snow had been removed from around the goals, but the frost made the ground very slippery. Burnley took an early lead when the Albion reserve goalkeeper, Jones, let the ball slip through his hands. Dilly scored from the spot, and a goal by Shinton gave Albion a 2-1 advantage at the interval. In the second half, honours were even, with each side scoring once, but Burnley pressure towards the end of the game caused considerable anxiety among the spectators, who thought Albion were going to be deprived of the victory which had previously seemed certain.

Following those matches, Bruce was dropped from the first team *"for some cause or other"*. (13) In the first of the games that he missed, Albion were beaten 3-2 by Leeds City away on Saturday, 5th January 1907. The next match was an FA Cup tie at home against Stoke City, the bottom club in the First Division, which ended in a 1-1 draw.

Bruce was recalled at outside-left for the replay at Stoke on Thursday, 17th January. The game, which ended in a 2-2 draw after extra-time, was full of excitement from start to finish. Albion opened the scoring after 12 minutes, when Bruce beat the Stoke keeper Roose, a former Everton colleague, with a tremendous shot but, straight from the re-start, Stoke went down the field and equalised. Stoke scored again before half-time but, five minutes after the interval, Albion were back on level terms with a goal from Randle, whose long-range shot should have been saved by Roose. There were no goals in extra time. *"Rankin did splendidly in his new role of outside-left, and centred as accurately with his right foot."* (14)

Albion's home game with Barnsley on 19th January was abandoned ten minutes before the end, with the score at 0-0, because it was too dark for the match officials to see what was going on. The visitors were three-quarters of an hour late arriving at the Hawthorns, which meant that the spectators had a long, cold wait for the kick-off. Albion had all the play, but could not score. Buck did have the ball in the net once, but the referee ruled that the ball was out of play before it was centred; he also hit the crossbar on another occasion. *"Rankin and Dilly played a fine game and the former at outside-left showed the crowd what he could do."* (15)

Albion and Stoke met again on Monday, 21st January to try to decide their FA Cup tie, this time at a neutral venue – Villa Park. A crowd of more than 32,000 watched Albion dominate the game, apart from the first 15 minutes, and go through to the next round with a 2-0 win. Bruce was at outside-left. In total, 79,500 spectators watched the three cup-ties, bringing in receipts of £2373.

Albion seemed to have benefited from the special training at Droitwich during the Christmas period. As a result, after the victory over Stoke on Monday, the directors decided to send the players to Brighton, which avoided a long train journey on the morning of Saturday's game at Chelsea. It was all to no avail. Chelsea defeated Albion 2-0 before a crowd of more than 41,000 and might have scored eight or ten goals but for some poor finishing and some splendid saves by Stringer.

The following Saturday, Albion were to play Norwich City in the second round of the FA Cup, and the players were taken to Rhyl to prepare for the game. The trip had dire consequences for Bruce. Under the headline, *"Rankin Suspended"*, Felix Mundi filed the following report in the 2nd February issue of the Weekly News:

"It is a matter of genuine regret that the directors have found it necessary this week to suspend Bruce Rankin sine die. He was one of the players taken to Rhyl on Monday to prepare for the cup-tie today. On Tuesday, owing to his insubordination, Mr Fred Everiss (secretary) felt compelled to order his return to West Bromwich. On Wednesday, a special meeting of the directors

was held, at which the secretary was present, and after hearing the details of the matter Rankin was suspended. The supporters of the club may take it for granted that this drastic punishment would not have been inflicted had not the player fully merited it. They were very reluctant to take the step, but in the interests of the club and for the maintenance of proper discipline no other course was left to them.

Rankin is as clever a footballer as there is, not alone in the Albion ranks, but throughout the country, and the followers of the Albion have a high opinion of what he can do when he likes. The course of conduct, however, which he has pursued during this present season has not been in his own best interests or those of the club, and while previous breaches of training regulations have not been so severely dealt with as they might have been, the latest offence was too serious to admit of the directors taking any other course than the one they have. We believe that in their determination to maintain the state of affairs which should exist in a well-regulated and properly-conducted organisation the directorate have the full support and confidence of the supporters of the club."

It would appear that the incident did not affect the other Albion players, as the team beat Norwich to progress to the next round of the Cup, although they were later beaten by Everton in the semi-final. Bruce missed the opportunity to face his former club.

Two of Bruce's daughters voiced the opinion that the *"insubordination"* incident was fuelled by drunkenness. Yet, whilst at Everton there was nothing in the Minutes of the Meetings of the Board of Directors to suggest that Bruce was *"a drinker"*. There were occasions when other players, notably McDermott and Corrin, were admonished by the Board for drunkenness. Whilst at Everton, Bruce would have been living at home but, after signing for Albion, he was probably living in lodgings in the Birmingham area. The temptations of drink were no doubt more difficult to resist.

Bruce made a great start to his stay at Albion, playing some dazzling and effective football. However, he failed to stamp his personality on the games at the beginning of the following season and he was dropped from the team for a sequence of eight games. On his recall in November, he was back to his best, particularly in the match against Nottingham Forest when he was influential in the 3-1 win in the top-of-the-table clash. After that match, Tityrus wrote in the Athletic News that Bruce *was "a general, and above all, a silent man"* and that he had never seen his *"lips move when on the field."* And yet, a few weeks after Tityrus had penned these thoughts, Bruce's behaviour was so outrageous during the special training trip to Rhyl that the Albion Directors felt that they were left with no option other than to ban him sine-die and to transfer him as soon as possible. He was clearly a great favourite with the Albion supporters; he could have had a very successful career at Albion, but he spoiled it all by his own foolish behaviour.

Manchester City (1906-07)

1906-07 Season

Surprisingly, within days, Bruce signed for Manchester City, for a reported fee of £500. (16) The transfer fee is more likely to have been in the region of £250, the amount Albion paid Everton for him. Indeed, Bruce's transfer from Everton to Albion is reported as £500 in the *"Who's Who of Everton"*, but was actually recorded as £250 in the Minutes of Meeting of Everton's Board of Directors.

Manchester City had joined the Football League as founder members of the Second Division in 1892 and were in the First Division when Bruce joined them. So, he was presented with an unexpected opportunity to resurrect his career with a club in the top division of the League.

Bruce made his first team debut on the right wing against Preston North End at Deepdale on Saturday, 9th February. The City team was:

Smith; Hill, Norgrove; Dorsett, Eadie, M'Oustra; Rankin, Grieve, Thornley, Jones, Conlin.

In its match preview that day, the Sporting Chronicle stated, *"...but if Rankin does his abilities justice, the right wing will be much stronger for George Stewart gives one the impression that he is just in England for his own innocent amusement and is not inclined to take football too seriously. If he likes he is a fine player; and exactly the same can be said of Rankin. Consistency is a most desirable attribute and to be perfectly frank Manchester City would be in a better position than at present if they possessed eleven men who always put all their heart and soul into their operations."*

City defeated Preston 3-1, and Bruce, *"who was making his first appearance, did fairly well, and taken on the whole, the line played better than I have seen for a long time."* (17)

Bruce was replaced by Stewart for the next game, but appeared for City on the left wing in their 4-1 defeat at the hands of Aston Villa at Villa Park on Saturday, 23rd February. Two of City's regular forwards were missing – outside-left Conlin was ill, while his partner, Jones, was on international duty in Belfast – and the two full-backs, Hill and Norgrove, were both injured. The team was:

Smith; Kelso, Christie; Dorsett, Eadie, M'Oustra; Stewart, Grieve, Thornley, Ross, Rankin.

Bruce did not play again in City's first team, but he did appear for the Reserves in a dozen or so games, scoring two goals. At the end of the season, he was transferred to Luton Town.

According to Gary James, Manchester City's Museum Manager, the club's records were destroyed in 1920 by a fire in the main stand at their Hyde Road ground, so it was impossible to tell why Bruce was transferred. However, James suggested that, as George Stewart and Jimmy Conlin *"became major (City) stars"* and vied for the same position as Bruce, his departure may simply have been due to the competition for places. But, why would a major Club pay a substantial fee for a player, play him twice and then move him on within a few months. It could have been that Bruce did not play to his potential, but it may well have been that his behaviour and commitment to training left a lot to be desired, leaving the City

Directors, like their Albion counterparts, with little choice but to transfer him out of the Club. However, that is only conjecture and may be widely inaccurate speculation.

Luton Town (1907-08)

1907-08 Season

Luton Town was formed in 1885, three years before the formation of the Football League and, four years later, became the first southern team to go professional. In those early days, fixtures were arranged on a friendly basis with other southern clubs, although Luton did enter the FA Cup, without any success. The Club was nicknamed the Hatters as the town's economy at that time relied heavily on the millinery trade.

In 1894-95, Luton became a founder member of the Southern League, along with clubs such as Millwall, Hotspur, St Albans, Southampton and Ilford. Three years later, they were elected as members of the Second Division of the Football League, but were soon back in the Southern League, after being relegated at the end of the 1899-1900 season. The Southern League now included clubs such as Southampton, Fulham, West Ham and Plymouth Argyle.

In 1906-07, the season before Bruce joined them, Luton had finished fourth in the Southern League. So, their pre-season hopes for the following year were high – *"the sterling defence and majestic halves were to be given the precision scoring forward line they clearly deserved"*. (18) The new forwards were Farrant signed from Workington, Hall of Bradford City, and Pearson from Hull City, all of whom were inside forwards; Rigate, an outside-right came from Hastings; Walders, another winger, was signed from Oldham Athletic; and, of course, Bruce, who had moved from Manchester City.

There is no record of Luton having paid a transfer fee for Bruce and, according to Roger Wash, the club's historian, Luton were not in the habit of paying fees at that time. However, Bruce did receive a £10 signing on fee and was to be paid £4 a week during the playing season and £3 a week in the close season.

All of the new players featured in the three public trial games in August 1907.

After the second match, the reporter from The Luton News and Bedfordshire Chronicle wrote, "*the left wingers, Rankin and Pearson, confirmed the good impressions on Wednesday.*" (19)

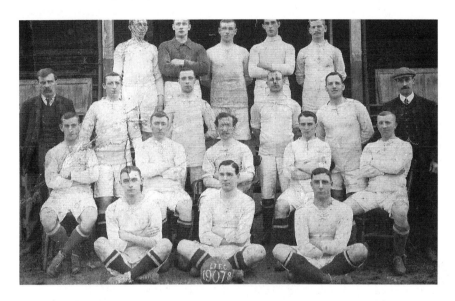

Luton Town team 1907-08: Bruce is 2ⁿᵈ from left in row seated on chairs.
Courtesy of Luton Town FC

The first game of the season was away to Southampton on Monday, 2ⁿᵈ September. Luton included four of the new forward signings in the team, which was:

Platt; Hogg, McCurdy; F. Hawkes, White, Jones; Walders, Hall, Brown, Pearson, Rankin.

In heavy rain, Southampton scored within a minute of kick-off, which meant that Luton faced an uphill battle right from the start. However, they nearly equalised soon after the Southampton goal when the Saints goalkeeper allowed the ball to go through his legs, only for it to stop dead just before the goal-line, enabling him to turn round and recover it. Towards the end of the first half, the rain was so heavy that many thought that the referee would stop the game, but it cleared during the interval.

Photo   **BRUCE RANKIN**   *Albert Wilkes.*

Is a native of Liverpool and 23 years of age. After being con-
nected with Everton for four-and-a-half seasons he went to West
Bromwich Albion and was subsequently transferred to Manchester City. Rankin has played in all forward positions except
centre, but his favourite place is outside right, though four
seasons ago he performed at outside left for North *v.* South.
Height 5ft. 7in., weight 11st. 6lbs.

25

Biography of Bruce from the Luton Town Handbook 1907/8.

Courtesy of Luton Town FC

Bruce was prominent early in the second half; a shot from 30 yards was just over the crossbar, and then, shortly afterwards, he hit the upright. Luton equalised midway through the second half from the penalty spot following a handball. But, ten minutes before the final whistle, Southampton got the winner. Bruce was the most effective of the Luton forwards.

Luton made one change for their next game at Northampton on Saturday, 7th September, Bob Hawkes replacing Jones at left-half. The game was a drab 0-0 draw, with a disappointing display from the forwards.

The following Saturday, Luton faced Southampton again for their first home game. Walders and Pearson were dropped, Bruce moved to the right wing to partner Hall and close-season signing Farrant and Latheron were paired on the left. Southampton scored in the 25th minute and were unfortunate not to score their second goal until eight minutes from the finish, dashing any hopes Luton may have had of rescuing a point. According to the match reporter, *"this was the most disheartening show given on Luton's ground for a long time"*. (20)

Luton's next league game was at Plymouth. The team left Luton on Friday afternoon and travelled to Teignmouth, where they stayed overnight. There were two changes to the team that had faced Southampton – Bob Hawkes moved from left-half to inside-left, replacing Farrant, whilst Jones came in at left-half. Thus, the team read:

Platt; Hogg, McCurdy; F. Hawkes, White, Jones; Rankin, Hall, Pearson, R. Hawkes, Latheron.

Luton had the greater share of the play for the first twenty minutes but, then, both Jones and McCurdy stood appealing for offside, allowing one of the Plymouth forwards to run through and score. The referee ignored the appeals. Within ten minutes, Luton equalised, when Hall headed home from a Pearson cross – it was the first goal scored against Plymouth that season. Two minutes later, Pearson hit the upright from 20 yards but the ball bounced back to the Plymouth keeper. Luton were far the better team up to the interval. With twenty minutes to go to the final whistle, Plymouth went ahead against the run of play and, encouraged by this unexpected success, the home team now played better than at any stage; Luton never looked like getting a second goal. Although they lost the match, this was a much better display. Bruce played well, but received some criticism in the match report for bringing the ball back towards his own goal on several occasions, allowing the home defence to fall back. Luton were now firmly rooted at the bottom of the table along with Portsmouth, both teams having only one point from four games.

In midweek, Luton had beaten West Ham 1-0 at home in the first Western League game of the season, despite having to play only three men up front, after they had lost two players through injury. So, the 7,000 crowd on Saturday was full of optimism when Luton again faced West Ham at home in the Southern League. The team was:

Platt; Jones, McCurdy; F. Hawkes, White, R. Hawkes; Rankin, Hall, Brown, Moody, Latheron.

Luton were a goal down by the interval. *"Rankin was really the originator of the disaster, for he dallied about with the ball near the centre of the field until Taylor rushed in and robbed him of it, and the consequence was that the visitors were immediately placed on the offensive. Somehow, the Luton defence got in a mix up, allowing Grasson (inside-right) to beat Platt."* (21) People were still optimistic enough to believe that Luton might save the game in the second half, but their hopes were dashed within a minute of the restart, when White completely missed the ball to allow the West Ham centre-forward to score. Later, West Ham scored again and, quarter-of-an-hour before the end, many of the spectators were leaving the ground.

Bruce, along with others, was dropped for the next three League games, in which Luton were beaten away by Queens Park Rangers (1-3) and Swindon (0-4), but were winners against Tottenham Hotspur (3-1) at home.

Whilst out of the first team, Bruce played at outside-right in the Reserves in the South-East League, but he was recalled to the first team at centre-forward for the home game against Crystal Palace on Saturday, 26th October. The team was

Platt; McCurdy, Dimmock; R. Hawkes, White, Jones; Rigate, F. Hawkes, Rankin, Moody, Walders.

The experiment of playing Bruce in the middle certainly paid off and Crystal Palace were completely outclassed by Luton, who were worthy 4-0 winners, although, with a little luck, they might have had six or eight. The win was *largely due to the wonderfully good play by Rankin in his new position,"* and *"the way in which he made openings for the other forwards frequently eliciting the admiration of the spectators with such judicious passes it would have been odd indeed had Luton not scored."* (22) Bruce nearly scored in the first half, he then hit the bar with a great shot after the interval and, later, eventually managed to snatch a goal. This victory lifted Luton off the bottom of the table – Tottenham had three points from nine games, Luton had five points from the same number of games, and Brighton and Hove had six points from eight games.

Following their excellent victory the previous week, Luton fielded the same team for the next home game against New Brompton. However, they were unable to provide their supporters with a repeat performance, losing 2-1, despite scoring first. Brompton equalised before the interval and took the lead early in the second half. Later, the home side was awarded a penalty for hands. Jones hit the post with his spot kick and the ball was cleared for a corner. Luton continued to press strongly for an equaliser and, five minutes before the end, practically everybody thought Moody had scored. Martin, the visitor's goalkeeper, caught the ball near the post but dropped it. The ball seemed to be well behind the goal line before he recovered and turned it round the post for a corner.

Although defeated, Luton played well; they forced 13 corners to New Brompton's four. But, the forwards were not as effective as the previous week, principally due to the fact that Bruce was not as prominent. Defeat left them second from bottom of the table.

Luton had high hopes for their next game, away to Brighton and Hove Albion, who had not won since the opening day of the season. But there was disappointment again when the team lost 1-0. Luton's team was:

Platt; Hogg, McCurdy; Jones, White, R. Hawkes; Rigate, F. Hawkes, Rankin, Moody, Walders.

Brighton missed a penalty in the first half and, ten minutes later, Bruce wasted a relatively straightforward opportunity when, with only the goalkeeper to beat, he shot over the bar. Soon afterwards, he missed the upright by a few inches. Brighton went ahead just before the interval and, in the second-half, Luton pressed strongly for an equaliser but, towards the end of the game, it was Platt, who was the busier keeper.

Saturday, 16th November, saw a battle between the two bottom teams in the league, with Luton overcoming Portsmouth at home by two goals to nil. Luton had to make an enforced change. Left-back McCurdy was injured, missing his first game of the season, and was replaced by Dimmock. Bruce had several shots saved in the first half, whilst Platt did not have to make a single save. After the interval, Bruce was off the field injured when Luton took the lead following a header by Moody. Two or three minutes after he resumed, Bruce got possession of the ball some way from goal. His shot rebounded from the crossbar to Fred Hawkes, who had no difficulty scoring. Luton were still second from bottom – three points ahead of Portsmouth and two behind Brentford.

Bruce's injury prevented him from playing in the next game against Bradford Park Avenue, which Luton lost 1-0. He was not selected for the home game against Millwall the following Saturday, a 3-1 victory for Luton. However, he was given a run out at centre-forward in the Reserve game at Maidstone, scoring Luton's first goal in a 2-1 victory.

Bruce was back in the first team to face Brentford in the away match on Saturday, 7th December; Brentford were unbeaten at home. Luton's Bob Hawkes was unavailable, as he had been selected for the England amateur team, whilst Bruce was preferred to Walders at outside-left. The team was:

Platt; Hogg, McCurdy; H. Parsons, White, Jones; Rigate, F. Hawkes, Pearson, Moody, Rankin.

Soon after the kick-off, Bruce *"put in a brilliant run and, beating off all the opposition sent the ball all along the ground direct to Moody, who was standing unmarked, with no one but Montgomery to beat… but Moody lifted the ball over the bar with a wild shot."* (23) It was a bad miss, for some minutes later Luton found themselves a goal behind. Just before the interval, Pearson had a great opportunity to equalise. He could have walked the ball into the net, but chose to shoot, allowing a defender to knock the ball away. In the second half, Luton went two down and then pulled one back with 12 minutes of the game remaining. There seemed a chance for Luton to save a point but, within a couple of minutes, a mix up between Platt and two of his defenders presented the Brentford centre-forward with an open goal to score a third.

Bruce retained the outside-left berth for the 2-0 home defeat by Bristol Rovers the following Saturday in what was described as *"one of the worst exhibitions given by a Luton team for many a long day".* (24) However, he lost his place to Walders for the next two games – a 5-0 away defeat by Clapton Orient on Saturday, 21ˢᵗ December and a 1-1 draw in the home game with Watford on Christmas Day.

He was recalled for the goalless draw at home with Norwich on Boxing Day and the 3-1 home win over Reading on Saturday, 28ᵗʰ December. Reading opened the scoring in the 20ᵗʰ minute and Moody equalised just before the interval. *"Five minutes after the resumption some smart passing in the Luton left wing took the ball up the field in fine style and Rankin headed through from Walders' centre. It was the most cleverly worked goal seen in the Luton ground for some time."* (25) Walders scored Luton's third.

Luton's next match was an FA Cup-tie at home against Fulham from the Second Division of the Football League on Saturday, 11ᵗʰ January 1908. The team was:

Platt; Watkins, McCurdy; Jones, White, R. Hawkes; Rigate,
F. Hawkes, Rankin, Moody, Walders.

The snow-covered and frost-bound ground was so slippery, that it took the players sometime to get used to the tricky conditions. The 5,500 spectators were treated to eleven goals, the highest total scored in any first team match on the ground. Three goals were scored in the first eleven minutes and no fewer than seven before half-time.

Luton went ahead after three minutes with a goal by Rigate. Four minutes later Fulham equalised, only for Luton to go ahead again, when Bruce scored after the Fulham goalkeeper could only push out a stinging shot from Walders. Fulham pulled level for a second time, and minutes later, Bruce's shot hit the post and went behind for a goal kick. That was a crucial point in the game for Fulham scored three times before the interval to go in leading 5-2 at the break. Luton worked hard for the first quarter of an hour in the second half and pulled a goal back with a headed goal from Moody. However, Fulham scored next from the penalty spot and, after this, Luton were a beaten team. Fulham's seventh goal was scored ten minutes before the finish, followed by another five minutes later. Despite the heavy defeat, Luton were far from disgraced, taking the lead twice and giving the crowd a game which they would remember for a long time.

The next match was a scoreless draw away to Plymouth, one of the best teams in the Southern League. Bruce was at centre-forward and an early shot by him went yards wide. In the last minute of the first half, Bruce was fouled in the box as he attempted to convert a centre by Rigate, but the referee dismissed the claims for a penalty. Towards the end of the game, Luton had another penalty appeal rejected when one of the Plymouth players handled the ball. Bruce then had the best shot of the match, but the goalkeeper instinctively stuck out his arm to divert the ball for a corner. Luton were unlucky not to score as they did almost all of the attacking. Luton were still second from bottom with 14 points from 21 games, two points behind Brentford, who had played a game more.

Luton were extremely unlucky to lose their next game at West Ham on Saturday, 20th January by a goal to nil. Bruce was at inside-right. The only goal of the game came midway through the second half when Platt saved at the feet of one of the West Ham forwards, only to see the ball rebound to another opponent, who scored easily.

In their next League match on Saturday, 8th February, Luton recorded their first away win of the season when they defeated Tottenham Hotspur 2-1, despite going a goal down in the first half. Bruce was at inside-right. Both Luton's goals were scored by outside-left Porter.

The following week, Luton had their first home game for a month when they faced Swindon. The match was spoiled by the weather - it rained the whole time and, early in the second half, the downpour was so heavy that the referee stopped the game for a minute or two. The result was more to Luton's liking than the weather, however, a 1-0 victory. Bruce scored the only goal 15 minutes from the end. He eluded the Swindon centre-half, Bannister, and shot low and hard into the bottom corner of the net. Luton had earlier been awarded a penalty for handball, but Walders hit his spot-kick straight at the Swindon goalkeeper, who saved easily.

There was no League game for Luton the next weekend, as it was FA Cup Saturday. Then, on Saturday, 29th February, the team recorded its second consecutive away win with a 1-0 victory over New Brompton, with a Moody goal scored 20 minutes after the start. Bruce was at inside-right.

Following a midweek 4-2 away defeat at the hands of Crystal Palace, Luton defeated Brighton 1-0 at home on Saturday, 7th March. Moody scored the decisive goal, to make it four goals in the last three games for him.

Luton faced Portsmouth at Fratton Park the following Saturday. Having never managed to win a point at Portsmouth, it was hardly surprising that they lost, albeit by the smallest of margins. Luton had the greater share of the first half and began in the same vein after the interval. However, Pompey scored with half-an-hour to go, and dominated the next 20 minutes. Luton's desperate attempts to get an equaliser, included a fine run and an excellent shot by Bruce, which was saved by the Portsmouth goalkeeper.

The best game seen in Luton for a long time was played on Saturday, 21st March and resulted in a 1-0 victory over Bradford Park Avenue. Luton might easily have won by four or five goals, such was their superiority. The only goal of the game was scored by Bruce in the 20th minute.

Following that victory, Luton were 16th in the league of 20 teams. They had 25 points from 30 games; Watford had the same number of points and games; Brighton & Hove Albion had 24 points from 28 games; New Brompton had 23 points from 30 games; whilst Clapton Orient had 20 from 31 games.

After a 0-0 draw at Millwall, who were third in the League, Luton fielded the same team for the fourth match in succession for the home game against Brentford on Saturday, 4th April. The team was:

Platt; Dimmock, McCurdy; F. Hawkes, Jones, R. Hawkes; Rigate, Rankin, Pearson, Moody, Latheron.

Moody scored the only goal of the game. However, Luton should have been awarded two penalties. In the first half, the Brentford centre-half handled a corner in the box, but the incident was missed by the referee. After the interval, the same player fisted away a shot from Bruce. The referee stopped play and, although the infringement was committed inside the penalty area, the referee placed the ball on the 18-yard line, much to the annoyance of the Luton supporters.

Luton's next fixture was away to Bristol Rovers on Saturday, 11th April. The only change was Albone at left-half for Bob Hawkes, who was unavailable because of business commitments. It was another victory by the narrowest of margins. Bruce was the best forward on the field and it was he who scored the decisive goal ten minutes after the interval. *"A clearance was headed to Rankin, who had plenty of time to make up his mind, and this time, instead of shooting with terrific force, he coolly glided the ball low and slow towards the right of Cartlidge (the Bristol goalkeeper) and it took the post low down and rebounded into the net."* (26)

Having won three and drawn one of their last four games, the players and supporters were anticipating a successful Easter programme. It was not to be. A 2-1 away defeat at Watford on Good Friday, followed by 3-0 and 1-0 home defeats by Clapton Orient and Northampton respectively on Easter Saturday and Easter Monday meant that it was a *"pointless"* weekend for Luton. Bruce was inside-right for the three games.

There were over 8000 spectators at the Watford game. Special trains had been laid on from Luton and hundreds of cyclists also made the journey. Bruce gave Luton the lead 15 minutes into the first half with a headed goal. Their lead was short-lived, however, as a minute later Platt was beaten by a free kick from 20 yards out. Watford scored the decisive goal five minutes after the interval when they converted a penalty kick after Albone tripped one of the Watford forwards. Luton deserved at least a share of the points – they were the better team in the first half and dominated after Watford's second goal. Again, Bruce had an excellent game and was as good as any of the forwards.

Platt had injured himself trying to save Watford's penalty on Good Friday and was unable to play on the Saturday at home to Clapton Orient. His place was taken by Jarvis. Left-back McCurdy had also been injured in the same game and was replaced by White. Twenty minutes after the start, White had the misfortune to head into his own goal. That was the first goal conceded by Luton at home in 1908. Clapton increased their lead a few minutes after the interval and 15 minutes later scored again.

The match against Northampton on Easter Monday, 20th April, was Luton's last home game of the season. There were more than 7000 spectators there, but a snowstorm half-an-hour before kick-off probably kept many away. It was any-one's game until a defensive error halfway through the second half lost Luton the points. A centre from the Northampton outside-left dropped in front of goal and, although Jarvis was ready to deal with it, Nicholson, who had replaced White at left-back, allowed the ball to roll over the line.

In the penultimate game of the season, Luton were thrashed 6-1 by Norwich. Bruce played in that game and was included in the team for the final match away to Reading on Saturday, 25th April. However, when the team turned up at Reading's ground, they found that there were no spectators and no referee. Once the referee did arrive, he decided that the conditions were too bad for the match to be played. The Luton players then had to make their way back into town using the trams; the service was disrupted as they had found when trying to reach the ground. Accord-ing to the Luton News and Bedfordshire Chronicle on 30th April, the ground was in such a state that it was surprising that the officials of the Reading Club did not try to stop the Luton players at Paddington or even send a message to Reading station. However, the directors had gone up to London for the Cup Final, which was won by Wolves with a 3-1 victory over Newcastle United at Crystal Palace.

The Reading game was played the following Wednesday but, for some reason, Bruce was not included in the team. It ended with another defeat for Luton, which meant that they finished the season 18th of the 20 teams in the league, three points ahead of Leyton and five ahead of New Brompton.

Having been fourth the previous season, the directors and spectators had harboured ambitions to do even better, particularly as the Club had engaged a number of new players, to strengthen the forward line in particular. The critics and supporters pointed the blame at the new "stars". Bruce's performances had been mixed, ranging from outstanding in the victory over Crystal Palace and the defeat at the hands of Watford to poor in the home defeats by West Ham and Bristol Rovers. Following those defeats, he was omitted from the first team. In all, he played 31 games for the first team, scoring seven goals, at least three of which won the points for Luton, so he was far from the worst of the newcomers.

When the list of players who had re-signed was published in The Luton News and Bedfordshire Chronicle, Bruce was not included, but neither was he reported as having left the club. However, he did move on for some reason, whether it was his choice or at the club's insistence is unclear.

Wrexham FC (1908-09)

1908-09 Season

After leaving Luton at the end of 1907-08 season, Bruce played for Egremont Social and Wirral (27), before signing for Wrexham sometime after the start of the 1908-09 season.

Wrexham were formed in 1872 and, at the time Bruce joined them, they were playing in the Birmingham and District League. Other League members included the reserve sides of Midland League clubs such as Aston Villa, Birmingham and Stoke and teams from towns such as Dudley, Kidderminster, Stourbridge and Walsall. Wrexham played at The Racecourse, which hosted internationals until 1991.

Bruce's first game for Wrexham was on Saturday, 19th December 1908, away to Wellington Town who were bottom of the table, so Wrexham anticipated winning both points. It was not to be, as the home team emerged worthy winners by three goals to one. The Wrexham team was:

Percival; Chappell, Davies; Huffadine, Williams, Price; Berry, Wynne, Mason, Smith, Rankin.

The only mention of Bruce in the match report was that *"Rankin, an old Everton and West Brom player, was tried at outside-left"*. (28)

Wrexham made three changes for the home game on Boxing Day against Stafford. Blew came in at left-back, which enabled Davies to move forward to left-half, while Price vacated the left-half berth to take the place of Mason at centre-forward. Despite the cold east wind, the crowd of about 3,000 was delighted when Wrexham were two up at half-time. They were less than happy, however, when Stafford scored twice after the interval to gain a point. Bruce hardly had a single chance to distinguish himself in the first half and fared no better when he changed places with Hayden Price during the second half.

Bruce retained his place for the next fixture, a 4-2 defeat away to Stoke Reserves on Monday, 28th December. This defeat left Wrexham in 11th place in the league of 18 teams, with 14 points from 13 games.

Wrexham crushed Dudley 4-1 at The Racecourse on Saturday, 2nd January 1909, for Bruce's first winning appearance. The team was:

Husbands; Chappell, Blew; Huffadine, Williams, Davies; Berry, Wynne, Rankin, Mason, Price.

Wrexham kicked off into a slight wind, but were ahead within ten minutes when Bruce converted a cross from outside-right Berry. Haydn Price scored the second a minute or so before the interval, but Husbands, who was making his debut for Wrexham in the Birmingham League, had been called upon earlier to make several excellent saves for which he was loudly applauded. Wrexham kept up the pressure in the second half, scoring two more goals. On both occasions, the Dudley keeper had saved shots from Bruce only to see Mason and then Wynne follow up to push the ball into the net. Just before the final whistle, Husbands was beaten for a consolation goal for Dudley. The following Saturday, Wrexham beat Oak Alyn Rovers 4-0 away from home in the Third

Round of the Welsh Senior Cup. Bruce was ineligible, having signed too late for Wrexham.

On Saturday, 16th January, Wrexham faced Exeter City from Division One of the Southern League in the FA Cup at The Racecourse before a crowd of some 5,000, despite the miserable conditions. The team was:

Husbands; Chappell, Blew; Huffadine, Williams, Davies; Berry, Wynne, Rankin, Smith, Price.

Exeter won the toss and elected to play with the advantage of the strong breeze behind them. Almost from the kick-off, Bruce broke away and struck the ball hard, only to be thwarted by a full-length save by the Exeter keeper. But, Wrexham were not to be denied, taking the lead shortly afterwards when a shot from Smith struck the inside of the post and went into the net. The Wrexham players and fans then thought that they had a second goal. Berry crossed the ball and Hayden Price's header appeared to have crossed the line when Robinson, the Exeter goal-keeper, caught it. The referee dismissed Wrexham's protests without even consulting his linesmen. Exeter equalised 15 minutes before half-time. The heavy ground seemed to have taken its toll, for both teams seem to tire in the second half. The game finished 1-1, although both sides had opportunities to win.

The replay was at Exeter the following Wednesday. The players and officials left Wrexham on the Tuesday, breaking their journey overnight at Bristol, and arriving in Exeter about noon. Wrexham fielded the same eleven, but Exeter were forced to make one change, as their left-back's elder child had died only three days earlier after a short illness. Wrexham took the lead in the first half through Bruce, but Exeter equalised late in the second half from the penalty spot, following a handball by one of the Wrexham defenders. Full-time arrived at 2.25pm and, as visibility was beginning to fail, the players re-started without leaving the pitch. Exeter got the winner in extra-time. Afterwards, it was generally agreed that the Welsh club played by far the better game and that Bruce had had an excellent match, orchestrating the forward line. Rover of The Devonshire Press wrote: "*I have never witnessed a more exciting tie and Exeter's case certainly looked hopeless up to 10 minutes from the finish, for it was just about that time that the penalty came along. Wrexham are a fine cup-fighting team, and really one must confess that, from the point of view of cup methods, so to speak, they deserved their half-time lead."*

The next league game was at home to Birmingham Reserves, one of the highlights of the season for the Wrexham supporters. Bruce was moved to outside-right in place of Berry, whilst Mason came in at centre-forward. Wrexham were a goal up at the interval and were the better team in the second half, but a miskick by right-back, Chappell, allowed Birmingham to equalise with ten minutes to go. Encouraged by their supporters, Wrexham pressed for the winner and were rewarded when Hayden Price shot into the net three minutes from time.

Wrexham lost their next two league matches, both away from home – Halesowen scored the only goal of the game 15 minutes from the end on 30th January, whilst Walsall were easy 5-0 victors on 6th February. Bruce was at centre-forward in both games.

Bruce was eligible to face the Druids away in the Fourth round Welsh Senior Cup-tie on Saturday, 13th February. The team was:

Husbands; Chappell, Blew; Huffadine, Evans, Davies; Rankin, Wynne, Mason, Smith, Price.

There was a sensational start to the game when the Druids scored in the first minute as a result of a misunderstanding in the Wrexham defence. Five minutes later, Wrexham were on level terms and began to have the better of the play. Soon afterwards, however, Evans, the Druids' right-back, injured his knee and was unable to continue, leaving his team down to ten men. Wrexham scored two further goals and just before half-time, *"Rankin directed a hot drive towards his opponents' goal and, in its transit, Owens, the Druids' left-half, handled the ball within the prescribed area and a penalty kick was awarded. This was entrusted to Hayden Price who made no mistake by scoring Wrexham's fourth goal."* (29)

On the Monday after the Druids game, Blew and Hayden Price were both selected for Wales against Scotland at The Racecourse. Wynne was called up later and all three played in the match. Blew, Wrexham born and bred, was the club's captain and spent most of his career there, winning 22 caps for Wales. He played only two matches in the Football League, both in 1906 - one was for Manchester United, the other for Manchester City. The United game was against Chelsea at the end of the 1905-06 season. Blew helped United win the point they needed for promotion to the First Division and, after the match, he was presented with a special gold medal by United in recognition of this.

For some reason, Bruce missed the league game the following Saturday, 20th February, a 3-0 defeat away to Stourbridge and was also absent for the 2-2 draw in the semi-final of the Welsh Senior Cup at Chester against Connah's Quay.

However, he was back in the team for the replay at Chester on Wednesday, 3rd March. Wrexham's team showed two changes - Bruce for Mason at centre-forward, while the absence of Smith led to the inclusion of Yuill, the captain of Northern Nomads, at outside-right. The team read:

Husbands; Chappell, Blew; Huffadine, Williams, Davies; Yuill, Berry, Rankin, Wynne, Price.

Deep snow had been cleared from the ground prior to kick-off. Wrexham were straight into the attack, forcing three early saves from the Connah's Quay goalkeeper, one of which was from Bruce. After ten minutes, Bruce gave Wrexham the lead. From about 25 yards out, he shot into the top corner of the net, giving the keeper no chance. Connah's Quay seemed to settle down after the goal and pressed for an equaliser. However, Wrexham began to have the better of the play again and went two up through Berry. Bruce scored a third shortly before the interval. In the second half, Wrexham seemed content to rest on their laurels but Bruce completed his hat-trick before the end, ensuring that Wrexham went through to the final by 4-0.

The away game with Wolves Reserves on Saturday, 6th March, was postponed because of a blizzard. On the following Monday, Wrexham were beaten 1-0 at home by Kidderminster, although they were the better team throughout. Left-back Chappell left the field with an injury just before the interval, returning after treatment to outside-left. Bruce was at centre-forward and *"set the forwards going in fine style*" (30), but they lacked a marksman. This defeat left Wrexham fourth from bottom of the League with 18 points from 19 games, although the teams around them had played five or six games more.

Wrexham lost again on Saturday, 13th March, a 3-0 defeat away to Burton United. Two days later, however, they secured two points with a home victory over Shrewsbury Town by two goals to one. Wrexham's team was:

Husbands; Davies, Morris; Huffadine, Williams, Hughes; Cook, Mason, Rankin, Pike, Evans.

Shrewsbury were leading 1-0 at half-time, but Bruce equalised within three minutes of the restart. Wrexham pressed for the winner, with Cook and Bruce prominent. Despite a heavy snowstorm midway through the second half, it was still all Wrexham, and Pike gave them the lead, which they held on to for both points.

The following week, Wrexham suffered their heaviest defeat that season when Aston Villa recorded a 7-0 victory in Birmingham in front of 3000 spectators. They were far from full strength with Blew, Berry, Price and Wynne missing. A respectable score of 1-0 at the interval gave no clues as to what was to happen later.

Two home victories followed: 2-1 over Stoke Reserves and 9-0 against Burton United. In the first half against Stoke, Bruce was prominent at centre with three excellent shots, but it was Price from the penalty spot who gave them the lead. Smith then put Wrexham two up, before Stoke reduced the arrears just before half-time. Wrexham should have increased their lead after the interval, hitting the post twice, and Price missed a penalty.

Bruce scored the first goal for Wrexham against Burton with a fierce shot, which gave the goalkeeper no chance. He notched their third before half-time when he "*and Wynne made an excellent run, and Wynne centred to Rankin, who breasted the ball into the net.*" (31) Sandwiched between those two goals was a Burton own goal. With a 3-0 lead at half-time, Wrexham then ran away with the game in the second half with four goals from Wynne and two from Mason. The forwards shot at every opportunity and could do no wrong. Bruce had another good game, leading the forward line very effectively. Wrexham were now in 11th position in the League with 24 points from 26 games.

Wrexham failed to make it three wins in a row when they lost 3-1 at Crewe on Saturday, 3rd April, but returned to winning ways on the Monday beating Walsall 2-0 at The Racecourse. The team against Walsall was:

Husbands; Chappell, Blew; Huffadine, Williams, Hughes; Cook, Wynne, Rankin, Mason, Pike.

A strong wind made conditions difficult for the players to control the ball, but Bruce held on to a pass from Cook and struck the ball fiercely into the net to give Wrexham the lead at the break. The visitors got the upper-hand early in the second half and hit the crossbar with Husbands well beaten. With half-an-hour left, Walsall's keeper injured his arm and was unable to continue. Wrexham found it difficult to make their numerical advantage count but, then, Bruce increased their lead when he received the ball directly from a Walsall goal kick and immediately struck the ball into the net from 20 yards out.

On Good Friday, Wrexham earned a point in a hard-fought 1-1 draw with Birmingham Reserves at Birmingham; Bruce was at centre-forward. For the fixture the following day, with the Welsh Senior Cup Final coming up on Easter Monday, Wrexham rested seven players – Husbands, Blew, Davies, Williams, Price, Wynne and Cook – for the away game with Kidderminster Harriers. Bruce was retained at centre-forward. With so many first-team regulars missing, it was hardly surprising that Wrexham slumped to a 6-1 defeat.

The Welsh Senior Cup Final against Chester was played at The Racecourse on Easter Monday afternoon, 12th April. The teams were:

Wrexham: Husbands; Chappell, Blew; Huffadine, Williams, Davies; Cook, Wynne, Rankin, Smith, Hughes. Hayden Price was missing as he had been injured on Good Friday against Birmingham.
Chester: Keeley; Russell, Davies; Matthews, Grainger, Gordon; Stockton, Roberts, Cotton, Lappin, Jones.

It was a sunny afternoon with a strong wind and the pitch was in excellent condition. Chester, the cup-holders, were the better team in the early stages of the first half with Husbands being called upon to make several saves. As the match progressed, however, it became more evenly balanced. A centre by Hughes was smartly headed away by Russell, Bruce collected the ball and shot just over. Shortly after, another shot by Bruce rebounded away off one of the Chester defenders. Wrexham were the more satisfied of the two teams at the interval, having played against the wind and keeping the score at 0-0. The spectators were entertained with a gymnastic display during the break.

After the resumption, Bruce was prominent in Wrexham attacks forcing Keeley to save on one occasion and shooting over on another. Chester did have the occasional foray into their opponents' half, but thirty minutes after the interval, Huffadine scored his first goal of the season when he headed a corner in just under the bar. Wrexham practically monopolised play after the interval and Bruce had another four attempts at goal. There were no more goals and the Welsh Cup found its way back to Wales. This was the seventh time that Wrexham had won the Welsh Cup, the previous occasion being in 1904-05. Mr John Davies, President of the Welsh Football Association, presented the cup to Wrexham captain, Horace Blew.

Caption for previous page: From left to right, back row – Ted Robinson (secretary), R.L. Ellis (director), E. Sideway (referee), Ernie Chappell, Ted Husbands, Horace Blew, J.A. Mossford (director), Frank Edwards (trainer), W.H. Parry (director). Middle row – Ernie Huffadine, Pryce Williams, Llew Davies. Front row – Fred Cook, Arthur Hughes, Bruce Rankin, Alf Smith, Haydn Price. George Wynn had played in the final but had been transferred to Manchester City before this photograph was taken. Hayden Price missed the final through injury. From Wrexham Football Club 1872-1950 compiled by Gareth M Davies & Peter Jones.

Following the Cup-final, Wrexham completed their League programme with four games in ten days. In the 2-0 win over Stourbridge at The Racecourse on Tuesday, 13th April, Bruce scored the second goal just on full-time from the penalty spot, after the visitor's right-back handled the ball in the area. Wrexham were well-beaten in their next two games, which were both away from home – going down 3-1 to Brierley Hill Athletic on Saturday, 17th April and losing 5-0 to Worcester City the following Thursday. Bruce was at centre-forward in both matches. In their final fixture of the season, at the Racecourse, on Saturday, 24th April, Wrexham easily defeated Wellington Town 5-1, with Bruce scoring the fifth and final goal. The team was:

> Husbands; Chappell, Blew; Huffadine, Williams, Davies; Cook, Hughes, Rankin, Smith, Price.

They finished a disappointing 11th place in the League, following a very respectable sixth place the previous year. Aston Villa Reserves won the title.

Bruce had played in 22 League games and five FA and Welsh Cup-ties, scoring seven and four goals respectively and winning a Welsh Cup-Winners medal. Several of his league goals were crucial and he scored a hat-trick in the 4-0 semi-final victory over Connah's Quay, so he had made a significant contribution to Wrexham's season in the four months that he was there.

"The Who's Who of Everton" by Tony Matthews shows that Bruce retired as a player in May 1912. It is not clear who he was playing for at that time. It would seem that he left Wrexham at the end of the 1908-09 season for he does not feature in the list of players in "Wrexham: A Complete Record 1872-1992" by Peter Jones in any of the following seasons, nor is he included in the list of re-signed players published in the 15th May issue of The Wrexham Advertiser and North Wales News.

The team is unknown. Bruce Rankin is seated second from the right on the front row and he looks some years older than in the Wrexham photograph of 1909. The placard being held by the player to the left of Bruce may read 'MacIvers'. The MacIver family were Liverpool shipping agents and steamship owners. Bruce's death certificate shows that he was a 'Docks Goods Checker (retired)'. So, there may be a connection there.

Life after Football

Once a professional footballer's career was over, few remained in the game in another capacity. However, according to Bruce's youngest daughter, Teeny, her father was offered the job as groundsman at Everton; he turned it down, saying, *"I'm being no groundsman, I used to play on that ground."* The 1911 census shows

Bruce as a railway porter, but he worked later on the Liverpool Docks as a goods checker. In those days, there was no guarantee of regular employment.

Teeny's recollections of her father were that he was "*a quiet man, unassuming, didn't use bad language and was never rude. I never heard him shout, he never laid a finger on anyone of us and although he liked a drink, I never saw him drunk.*" As far as she remembered, her mother and father got on well, although she did add that her mother was too strong a character for her father. Her father, Teeny said, liked going out to work, even when he was unable to get any because, in her view, "*for men at that time, getting out of the house was a way of putting their worries out of their mind*". However, she could also recall him "*lying in bed on many a Sunday until tea-time, when he went out for a pint*".

Perhaps, Bruce spent too much of his wages on drinking, for his wife, despite having seven daughters and five sons, as well as a number of miscarriages, worked until her death at the age of 76. Teeny maintained that if it had not been for her mother there would have been no food on the table.

Only one of Bruce's children was still alive on completion of this book at the beginning of 2015 – Bobby, aged 88, a widower, living in Perth, Australia. According to Bobby, it was "*normally left to my Mum to cover the rent and food. She took in washing and ironing to make ends meet and also went picking spuds.*" He went on to say that when his father "*didn't have the bus fare to get to the docks, he would walk there to get a job*". At that time, the family lived in Walton, some miles from the docks.

Bruce never spoke to Bobby about his football career. He was never encouraged by his father to play football and never went with him to see a match. Indeed, Bobby said that his father was keen for him to take up boxing but he was not interested in pursuing it.

Bruce was clearly a gifted footballer who, perhaps, did not realise his full potential. Selected to play in an England trial early in his career, it was unfortunate that he had to vie with Jack Sharp, an Everton legend, for the outside-right berth. Following his move to West Bromwich Albion, he was undoubtedly a great favourite with the supporters there and may well have gone on to greater things with the club had it not been for the unfortunate incident of insubordination, which led to his transfer to Manchester City. There was no indication of any problems with his behaviour at Goodison.

His stay at The Hawthorns was short-lived and was followed by half-a-season at Manchester City, one season at Luton and then part of another at Wrexham. He would certainly have had to live in lodgings at Luton, while his family remained in Liverpool. Maybe he was unhappy with that particular lifestyle and that may have been the reason he left Luton. From the match reports, it would not appear to be because of too many poor performances.

During his season at Wrexham, he would have resided in Liverpool as the football club would not have expected him to move into Wales, according to Geraint Parry, the Club Secretary. In any case, even at that time, there was a direct train service from Liverpool to Wrexham, and the station was next to the football ground. Unfortunately, it has not been possible to unearth any concrete evidence to explain the nomadic end to Bruce's career.

Bruce may also have been an excellent cricketer. His daughter Teeny recalled seeing a newspaper article describing her father as a wonderful cricketer. Yet, he was not selected for Everton in the annual cricket matches with Bootle in each of the close seasons. However, according to his granddaughter, Marjory Rankin, on joining the Liverpool City Treasurer's Department at 14 years of age, the City Treasurer asked her if she was any relation to Bruce Rankin. When she said she was, he told her, "*Your granddad was a great footballer, but a marvellous cricketer.*"

Bruce died in hospital on 16th February 1954, aged 74, from bronchopneumonia and tuberculosis. His wife, Mary Jane Jackson, survived him by six and a half years. She died in Walton Hospital in December 1960 at 76 years of age, from acute bronchopneumonia following a fracture of the right femur when she was blown over by the wind about seven in the morning on her way to work as an office cleaner.

References

1.   West Bromwich Weekly News, 10th February 1906

2.   The Chronicle for West Bromwich, Oldbury and District, 16th February 1906

3.   The Chronicle, 2nd March 1906

4.   Weekly News, 3rd March 1906

5.   Weekly News, 17th March, 1906

6.   Weekly News, 24th March 1906

7.   Weekly News, 21st April 1907

8.   Weekly News, 5th May 1907

9.   Weekly News, 6th October 1906

10.   Weekly News, 20th October 1906

11.   The Chronicle, 30th November 1906

12.   The Chronicle, 14th December 1906

13.   The Chronicle, 11th January 1907

14.   Weekly News, 19th January 1907

15.   The Chronicle, 25th January 1907

16.   "Who's Who of Everton" by Tony Matthews; 2004

17.   Athletic News, 11th February 1907

18.   The Luton Story – 1885 – 1985 by Timothy Collings; 1985

19.   The Luton News & Bedfordshire Chronicle, 22nd August 1907

20.   The Luton News & Bedfordshire Chronicle, 19th September 1907

21.   The Luton News & Bedfordshire Chronicle, 3rd October 1907

22.   The Luton News & Bedfordshire Chronicle, 31st October 1907

23.   The Luton News & Bedfordshire Chronicle, 12th December 1907

24.   The Luton News & Bedfordshire Chronicle, 19th December 1907

25.   The Luton News & Bedfordshire Chronicle, 2nd January 1908

26.   The Luton News & Bedfordshire Chronicle, 16th April 1908

27. Football League Players' Records 1888-1939 by Michael Joyce; SoccerData 2002

28. The Wrexham Advertiser & North Wales News, 26th December 1908

29. The Wrexham Advertiser & North Wales News, 20th February 1909

30. The Wrexham Advertiser & North Wales News, 13th March 1909

31. The Wrexham Advertiser & North Wales News, 3rd April 1909

3

BILLY RANKIN AT MARINE FC (1931-34)

Introduction

William or Billy Rankin, Bruce's eldest son, was born in Liverpool on 2nd October 1904. At that time, the family lived in Gwladys Street, which runs alongside Goodison Park.

Nothing is known about Billy's childhood and teenage years. One would think that he must have been influenced by his father's success at football but whether or not Bruce actually encouraged Billy to play football is a matter of conjecture.

Billy was on Everton books as an amateur at some stage, probably in the mid to late 1920s, although he never played for the first team. The professional game had changed little since his father had played, although the maximum wage had doubled to £8 a week during the season and £6 in the summer.

Facilities at football grounds were much the same, however, and the crowds were still generally well-behaved, with the occasional incidents of disorder.

1931-32 Season

Billy joined Marine FC in the summer of 1931 at the age of 26 years, after playing for local amateur teams Bootle Celtic and Howsons. Marine were one of the foremost amateur teams in the Liverpool area, playing in the Liverpool County Combination. Their home ground was in Crosby.

His first season at Marine must have exceeded his wildest dreams. The Mariners, as they were known, reached the final of the FA Amateur Cup for the first and only time in their history and then created another record by winning the Lancashire Amateur Cup for the second season in succession.

Some 300 clubs entered the FA Amateur Cup. Marine's journey to the final began on Saturday, 12th December 1931 with a 4-2 home win against Northampton Nomads. The team was:

Drury; Kerr, Rankin; Peet, Kelly, Crilley; Harrison, King, O'Donnell, Garvey, Davies.

Northampton Nomads took the lead in the first half, but Marine equalised almost immediately. Then, an inspired period early in the second half, when they added three goals in almost as many minutes, gave Marine victory, although the Nomads scored a second goal towards the end of the game. Despite the win, the Waterloo and Crosby Herald match reporter thought that Marine had a weakness in the half-back line. He wrote, *"Peet was not as guilty to the same extent as Kelly and Crilley, who repeatedly advanced too far up the field, and leaving a gap in the centre so vulnerable that Kerr and Rankin had the utmost difficulty in covering up. Indeed, it was only sheer hard work on the part of the two full-backs and several mighty saves by Drury that prevented disaster."* (1)

In the second round, Marine faced South Bank on Saturday, 16th January 1932. The team travelled to Middlesbrough on the evening before the game, leaving Lime Street on the 5.45pm train and staying at the Grand Hotel. To strengthen the half-back line, Marine moved Kerr forward to right-half and brought in Jackson, who had been playing with Everton Reserves, to take Kerr's place at right-back; the inside-forwards, Garvey and King, swapped positions. Marine had much the better of the early exchanges, but did not take the lead until the 30th minute when O'Donnell raced through to score. For the remainder of the first half, the home goal had a charmed life, but Marine could not score again before the interval. Ten minutes into the second half, Drury brought down the South Bank centre-forward to concede a penalty. He saved the resulting kick brilliantly, but could not stop one of South Bank's forwards following up the rebound to equalise. Marine responded to the reverse by attacking their opponents' goal and, despite playing up a slope and against the wind, King scored 15 minutes from time to take Marine through to the third round.

In the next round, to be played on 6th February, Marine were lucky enough to get a home draw against Maidenhead United, who played in the Spartan League and were holders of the Berkshire Senior Cup. Maidenhead were never in the hunt. Marine scored in the third minute and were four goals up within the first half an hour. Maidenhead's consolation goal came seven minutes from the end. Marine's team was:

Drury; Jackson, Rankin; Crilley, Kelly, Halsall; Kerr, Garvey, O'Donnell, King, Davies.

Marine's luck held when they were drawn at home again in the quarter-final, this time against Leyton from the Athenian League. Leyton had won the FA Amateur Cup in successive years, in 1926-27 and 27-28, and were beaten finalists in 1928-29. Their secretary George Smith told the Press, "*I may sound bombastic about it, but we feel we have the Cup almost within our grasp*." (2) His feelings were misplaced, however, for Marine beat Leyton 3-0, fielding the same team that had played in the previous round. Just as they had done against Maidenhead United, Marine went ahead in the third minute. They scored a second before half-time and then again after the interval to seal the game. According to the Liverpool Echo, "*Drury had hardly one shot of any strength – perhaps that was due to the safety first play and stern tackling of Jackson and Rankin, who had as much credit for the side's success as any*". (3) The game was watched by some 6,000 spectators, a record for Marine's ground.

The semi-final draw pitted Marine against Yorkshire Amateurs, who were probably favourites for the Cup as they had knocked out the holders, Wycombe Wanderers, in the third round. The game was played at Filbert Street, Leicester City's ground, on Saturday, 5th March. Marine made only one change to the victorious quarter-final team, bringing Wady in to replace left-winger Davies, who had broken his collar-bone. To the delight of the 200 or so supporters who had travelled from Crosby, Marine won 2-1.

Yorkshire almost went ahead midway through the first half. Their left-winger outpaced both Crilley and Jackson to cross the ball dangerously into the penalty area but, at full stretch, Billy just managed to divert the ball away with two opponents rushing in on goal. Marine went ahead five minutes from the interval through O'Donnell and then scored again within five minutes of the restart to make it 2-0. Shortly afterwards, Billy miskicked allowing outside-right Craven a chance to shoot but Drury smothered the ball. However, with 15 minutes to go, Yorkshire pulled a goal back when one of their forwards smashed the ball into the back of the net after Drury could only push a shot out into the goalmouth. The Marine defence then came in for its biggest test, but held out. *"Yorkshire, despite their defeat, were undoubtedly a fine team and as a combination were superior to Marine in the day's display, but they hadn't a Garvey or a Drury, or a pair of backs like Jackson and Rankin…"* (4) The game was watched by only 2839 spectators, whilst 27,340 turned up at Selhurst Park to see Dulwich Hamlet beat Kingstonians by a solitary goal in the other semi-final.

The Final was played at Upton Park on Saturday, 16th April. Marine travelled down to London *"in a reserved saloon attached to the 5.20pm train on Friday for the players, officials and friends".* They stayed at the Regents Palace Hotel in Regent Street and, on the morning of the match, placed a wreath at the Cenotaph and went on to watch the Changing of the Guard – hardly the sort of preparation that would be undertaken today, even by an amateur team. The team showed one change from the semi-final – Bamford in place of Wady on the left wing. The book, "The Mighty Mariners" included the following profiles of each player:

Harry Drury: goalkeeper, had only missed one game since joining in 1928. He had signed amateur forms for Manchester United, but preferred to stay at Marine. He had previously played for Seaforth Albion.

George Jackson: right-back, had also been playing for Everton Reserves that season and by the time of the AGM the following June had turned professional with them.

Billy Rankin: left-back, was the son of former Everton player Bruce Rankin and weighed 12stone 9lb. He had previously played for Bootle Celtic and Howsons and was also a baseball international. (5)

LONDON COMBINATION.

	P	W	D	L	For	Ag.	Pts.
Arsenal	38	27	7	4	106	35	61
Brentford	36	25	5	6	93	45	53
Crystal Palace ...	36	20	8	8	81	52	48
West Ham United ...	39	19	6	14	91	63	44
Fulham	37	17	10	10	88	70	44
Tottenham Hotspur	35	19	5	11	83	73	43
Chelsea	35	16	8	11	72	63	40
Portsmouth... ...	37	16	8	13	77	74	40
Q.P. Rangers ...	36	16	7	13	72	79	39
Luton	35	16	3	16	75	74	35
Charlton Athletic ...	35	13	7	15	66	70	33
Clapton Orient ...	37	14	5	18	57	74	33
Southend United ...	35	14	4	17	52	79	32
Leicester City ...	34	12	8	14	80	79	32
Reading	35	11	8	16	71	78	30
Millwall	35	11	7	17	58	77	29
Swansea Town ...	37	10	8	19	48	80	28
Watford	35	10	8	17	53	69	28
Coventry City ...	36	10	8	18	54	80	28
Southampton ...	37	8	11	18	71	87	27
Brighton & H. Alb.	35	10	4	21	45	86	24
Cardiff City... ...	35	6	5	24	51	94	17

MUSICAL PROGRAMME

Arranged by AUDIBLE ADVERTISING, LTD.

83A Valetta Road, Acton, W.3. Tel.: Shep. Bush 1044

SELECTIONS FROM THE FOLLOWING

RECORDS

WILL BE PLAYED OVER

THE RADIO-RECORDION EQUIPMENT

1 March—" Song of the Guards "
{Feldman —Black Diamonds Band   Zono.   6024

2 " Begone couldn't help it " (Campbell
Connelly)—The Million-Airs   Decca F2210

3 " The Rose-Beetle goes a-Wooing "
—Ferdy Kaufman's Orch.   HMV B3507

4 " Quand Madelon "—International
Novelty Orch.   B3600

5 " My Bluebird's back again " (Lawrence Wright)—The Rythmic Eight   Zono.   5003

6 " Amazon's Ride "—Mandoline
Concert Society   HMV B3334

7 " For You " (Feldman)—J' Hylton's
Orch.   Decca F2085

DULWICH HAMLET
Colours—Pink and Blue

RIGHT   LEFT

1
R. Miles

2   **3**
A. J. Hugo   **B. Osmond**

4   **5**   **6**
C. Murray   **A. H. Hamer**   **A. T. Aitken**

7   **8**   **9**   **10**   **11**
L. Morrish **E. Kail** **W. G. Goodliffe** **H. Moseley** **H. Robbins**

Referee: Mr. A. H. ADAMS (Nottingham)

Linesmen—Sergt. S. WATERS (Red Stripe Flag)   Mr. W. PARSONS (Blue Stripe Flag)
(Oxfordshire)   (Hertfordshire)

12   **13**   **14**   **15**   **16**
A. Bamford **L. King** **G. F. O'Donnell** **J. Garvey** **N. Kerr**

17   **18**   **19**
W. L. Halsall   **A. S. Kelly**   **J. P. Crilley**

20   **21**
W. Rankin   **G. Jackson**

22
H. J. Drury

LEFT   RIGHT

LIVERPOOL MARINE
Colours: White

GOAL SCORERS

FOOTBALL LEAGUE		LONDON COMBINATION		OTHER MATCHES
Watson 22	Yews 1	Wood 8	Barrett 1	Deacon 1
Norris 4	Chalkley 1	Gamble 18	Young 1	Fenton 2
Weldon 2	Morton 1	Earle 3	Pollard 7	Watson 2
Ruffell 16		James 11	Weldon 3	Weldon 1
Wood 2		Deacon 6	Yews 1	
Gibbins 5		Musgrave 2	Morton 3	
Phillips 3		Phillips 5	Norris 1	
Barrett 2		Watson 3	Fenton 8	
Cadwell 1		Harris 2		

The page of the Cup Final programme naming the two teams.

Courtesy of David Wotherspoon..

Jack Crilley: right-half, was a former Bootle schoolboy who had become captain. He was described as a clever dribbler despite being 13 stone and had won many representative honours. He had joined in 1928-29 from Linacre Gas Works, having played for the County.

Stan Kelly: centre-half, had been promoted from the Reserves after Almond, the previous captain, was injured. He had previously played for Liverpool Reserves and Northern Nomads and used his 6 feet height effectively.

Wally Halsall: left-half, the youngest member of the side had already signed amateur forms for Bolton Wanderers. He had come through the Reserve side.

Norman Kerr: outside-right, had played full-back up until the Leyton game when he moved to the right wing and made a quick impression with his speed and hard shot. He had joined in 1928-29 from Everton, having played for Liverpool County.

Joe Garvey: inside-right, had been with the club for seven years and had gained FA honours. He was an exceptionally clever and tricky player.

George O'Donnell: centre-forward, was in his sixth season and had won several 100 yards championships and assisted a number of League clubs. He was the leading goalscorer.

Lol King: inside-left, formerly with Old Xaverians and was in his first season, having represented Liverpool County and Zingari League sides. He was a clever dribbler and tireless.

Arthur Bamford: outside-left, a clever and speedy player, who has had wide experience with Lytham, Burscough Rangers and Skelmersdale.

Bamford's career at Marine was short but memorable. He played over Easter and in the Final, but did not feature in any further games.

Marine were never in the game itself. Although they were only down 1-0 at half-time, they conceded a further six goals in the second half and managed to score a consolation goal themselves, all in the space of 20 minutes. According to the Waterloo and Crosby Herald published the Saturday following the final, "*For twenty five minutes, Drury, Jackson and Rankin held the fort, often they were aided by Dulwich's bad finishing, but for sheer grit they were the outstanding men in the match.*" The reporter added, "*One does not desire to lay the blame of defeat at the door of any particular department, but it was undoubtedly contributed to by the weakness in Marine's half backs.*" However, The Daily Telegraph thought that there was another reason for Marine's defeat, "*At home I am told Marine play on a grassy ground superlatively well drained, and the layer of slime which passes for Turf at West Ham beat them from the start.*" And, in his Local Sports and News column in the Waterloo and Crosby Herald on 23rd April, Cantab "*was surprised and delighted to see that a fairly lengthy film of the match was being presented at the various local cinemas for it will give the local public a convincing idea of the playing pitch, which probably no words of mine could adequately express or impress.*" Of course, Dulwich Hamlet had played under the same conditions and managed to score seven times.

Not everyone laid the blame for Marine's defeat on the muddy pitch. The match reporter for the Liverpool Post and Mercury wrote, "*the reason for Marine's defeat is easy to explain. First, the lethargy of the half-backs when Dulwich were throwing in the ball with a quickness uncommon in Northern football; two, the failure of the half-backs to cope with the men who acted better on the heavy going; three, the lack of confidence as the team became further and further away from winning chances; and four, the failure of passes to reach the extreme wingers.*" No mention of the pitch there. He added, "*Devastating as the score was, no disgrace attaches to the beaten side. They did their best, but their best was not good enough.*" (6)

Marine 1931-32: Back row (left to right): Tommy Halton, Stan Berney, Harry Gilmour, Walter Halsall, Harry Drury, Stan Kelly, Billy Rankin, Tom Stephens (referee), Freddie Lake. Front row: Sam Harrison, Joe Garvey, Jack Crilley, George O'Donnell, Lol King and Arthur Bamford. George Jackson and Norman Kerr played in the FA Amateur Cup Final instead of Gilmour and Harrison. Courtesy of David Wotherspoon.

After the match, the Marine players and officials attended the 9pm performance at the Holborn Empire and, after another night spent at the Regents Park Hotel, returned to Liverpool by train on Sunday afternoon.

Marine gained some consolation for their loss in the FA Amateur Cup Final four days later when they won the Lancashire Amateur Cup for the second year running. They defeated The Casuals from the Liverpool Zingari League by four goals to two at Goodison Park. The Marine team was:

Drury; Jackson, Rankin; Crilley, Kelly, Wady; Kerr, Jones, O'Donnell, King, Kinder.

Billy (on the goal line) in action in the FA Amateur Cup Final for Marine against Dulwich Hamlet. Courtesy of David Wotherspoon.

Early in the second half, Marine had established a three goal lead with Billy netting the second from the penalty spot. With five minutes to go, the Casuals pulled the score back to 3-2, and pressed fiercely for the equaliser but, *"only steady and deliberate work by Jackson and Rankin frustrated the fierce rushes."* (7) Centre-forward O'Donnell scored in the last minute to seal the game for Marine. The Lord Mayor of Liverpool, Alderman J Cross, presented the Cup and medals to the players.

Billy had played in all of the Lancashire Amateur Cup matches. After beating Old Blackburnians 7-0 at home and then Manchester YMCA 3-2 away, on a ground that resembled a miniature lake, Marine were held to a 2-2 draw by Old Boltonians, coming from behind twice despite having 75 percent of the play. However, they made amends in the replay on 9th January 1932, scoring four goals before half-time and finishing 5-1 winners. At the end of the month, they beat Collegiate Old Boys 2-0 in the semi-final played at Formby.

Holders Marine also reached the final of the George Mahon Cup, losing 3-2 to Liverpool Cables on 5th May. Billy was at left-back in that game and also appeared in the earlier rounds, the highlight of which was probably the 4-1 first round defeat of Liverpool A on 10th October 1931.

Marine were also invited to play in the Lythgoe Memorial Cup along with

Peasley Cross Athletic and the Liverpool and Everton Central League sides. They were drawn against Peasley in the semi-final, which was played at College Road on Monday 25th April 1932. The game ended in a 2-2 draw after extra time. It was only their poor shooting that prevented Marine from sealing the game for they were clearly the better team. Marine scored early in the first half, only for Peasley to equalise in the last minute of the game. Peasley then went ahead in the first half of extra time, but Marine equalised in the second period. According to the Waterloo and Crosby Herald of 30th April, Jackson and Rankin were outstanding in defence. Marine had played six games in nine days and still had a semi-final replay in the George Mahon Cup and two League games to complete before the end of the season. As a result, they withdrew from the Lythgoe Memorial Cup competition, allowing Peasley to progress to the final by default.

Marine, the holders, were knocked out of the Liverpool Amateur Cup by The Casuals in a first round replay in January 1932. In the first game, a week earlier, Marine had been leading 4-3 in extra time when the referee unexpectedly abandoned the game seven minutes from the end on the grounds that he could not follow the flight of the ball. The fixture had started 15 minutes late because a number of The Casuals' players were late in arriving for the game. Marine had gone two goals up early in the first half, but The Casuals had equalised by half-time. Ten minutes into the second half, Harrison, the Marine outside-right, was injured and had to be taken off. Marine battled on and scored through an own goal. However, a few minutes from time, a foul was given against Drury, the Marine goalkeeper. The free kick was to be taken practically on the goal line and Marine packed their line. The ball was blocked, but not cleared properly, allowing Casuals to lob the ball into the net for the equaliser. At the start of extra-time, Harrison resumed for Marine but, almost immediately, Peet, their right-half, had to leave the field with an injury. Despite the handicap of playing with only ten men, Marine scored again to take the lead and it was a great surprise when the referee abandoned the game seven minutes from time. The Marine team was:

Drury; Kerr, Rankin; Peet, Kelly, Crilley; Harrison, Garvey, O'Donnell, King, Davies.

Peet was not fit for the replay at College Road, and his replacement, Halsall, was the only change to the side that had been leading 4-3 three weeks earlier. Unfortunately, Marine lost 2-1, *"because of over-confidence to a certain extent"*. (8)

The other major Cup competition contested by Marine was the English FA Cup. They were 3-2 victors over Whiston at College Road on Saturday, 26th September 1931 in a preliminary qualifying round. It was a hard-earned victory as far as Marine were concerned. With the score at 1-1 before the interval, Marine's centre-half Almond fell in a tackle and broke his arm. Soon after the re-start, Marine surprisingly took the lead. Then, they went down to nine men when Peel, struck by the ball full in the face, had to leave the field for treatment, resuming shortly afterwards. *"Marine battled on. Rankin saved the position times without number with mighty first time clearances. Again and again, the half back line was over-run, but Kerr and Rankin were there, clearing from the feet of the keen Whiston forwards with desperate tackling when all seemed lost."* (9) Drury, the Marine goalkeeper let the ball slip through his hands and into the net for Whiston to equalise, *"with Rankin making a desperate bid to kick it out again."* Then, Marine scored the winner when Campbell, their outside-left, and the Whiston goalkeeper collided in going for the ball. With the goalkeeper on the ground, Jackson, who was following up, banged the ball into the empty net. Whiston appealed madly, surrounding the referee, only giving up their protests after their centre-half was booked.

Marine's passage into the second qualifying round of the FA Cup was a far easier affair, with a 5-0 home victory over the Cheshire side, Timperley, on 3rd October.

However, their interest in this particular trophy ended two weeks later when they lost 3-1 to Prescot away from home before 5,000 spectators. In the 24th October issue of the Waterloo and Crosby Herald, Cantab's view was, *"Marine will not be sorry to quit this particular competition where, of course, they have not the slightest chance of progressing far against even the minor professional sides, who have fitness and training on their side with which to a great extent amateur sides cannot cope."*

Marine had been Liverpool County Combination champions for the 1930-31 season but, by Boxing Day 1931, it was fairly clear that they were not going to retain the league title when they lost 3-1 at home to their bogey team, Everton A. Their attempt to retain the championship had got off to a disastrous start on Saturday, 5th September when they were unexpectedly beaten 4-0 at home by Peasley Cross Athletic from St Helens, who were only in their second season in the league. The Marine team was:

Drury; Kerr, Rankin; Green, Almond, Hunter; Harrison, Jackson, O'Donnell, Wotherspoon, Campbell.

In their next league game, Marine had a good win, beating Liverpool A away by three goals to two. Marine took a two-goal lead, only to be pulled back by one goal just before half-time. After the interval, Liverpool caused the Marine defence considerable trouble, culminating in Billy putting through his own goal. After that setback, Marine were the better team and deservedly scored the winning goal late in the match.

Marine won two of their next three league games before shattering Peasley Cross Athletic's unbeaten league record with a remarkable 5-2 victory to avenge their own defeat in the first game of the season. Billy played in all of those games.

On 12th March 1932, Marine had to field two teams in an endeavour to reduce the extraordinary fixture congestion as a result of their continuing interest in several cup competitions, not least of which was the FA Amateur Cup. The first team lost by one goal at Whiston, dashing any lingering hopes they had of retaining the championship title. Indeed, by the end of the month, they were bottom of the league although they had played fewer games than their closest rivals, Blundell-sands and Bootle.

By the end of the season, Marine had managed to climb to fifth position in the league. Their final game was a thrilling affair. Whiston needed only one point at College Road on Saturday 7th May to become the Liverpool County Combination champions. However, Marine beat their visitors 1-0 to rob them of the title and hand the season's league honours to Everton A. Marine's team for that game was:

Drury; Jones, Rankin; Winn, Crilley, Halsall; Rogers, Constantine, O'Donnell, Shennan, Kinder.

1932-33 Season

Marine began their league campaign with a 5-2 victory at home on Saturday, 3rd September 1932 over league newcomers Liverpool Trams. Despite a strong wind in their faces, Marine held their opponents to 2-2 at the interval. However, with the wind behind them in the second half, Marine scored a further three times without conceding any further goals. The Marine team for the opening game was:

Drury; Kerr, Rankin; Crilley, Worsley, Harrison; O'Donnell, Constantine, Roberts, Jones, Davies.

The following Saturday, Marine overcame Peasley Cross Athletic away from home by three goals to one, only to drop a point in their next game when they drew 3-3 with Liverpool Cables. Marine full-backs, Kerr and Billy defended steadily but in the 25th minute "*Rankin slipped down and deflected the ball into the net for Cables equaliser. Drury appeared to have the ball covered when the ball struck the upright and rolled over the line*". (10) Outside-left Davies restored Marine's lead before the interval, but ten minutes after the restart Cables equalised again. Later in the game, after Marine had taken the lead for the third time, Cables managed to draw level yet again.

On Saturday, 24th September, Marine slipped to their first defeat when they lost 2-1 away to Liverpool A. Billy was a doubtful starter, but was selected at left-back. Although they had lost their unbeaten record, Marine still remained top of the league.

Billy then missed a number of games through injury, returning at left-back for the home game against Skelmersdale on Saturday, 12th November. In a match played at a cracking pace throughout, Skelmersdale scored after two minutes and went on to win 3-1. This was Marine's fifth defeat in the league, leaving them in fifth place.

The following Saturday saw Marine gain their first away win of the season when they defeated league leaders Liverpool Cables 2-1. Cables went ahead in the 12th minute against the run of play but, undeterred, Marine scored two goals before the interval. Marine's sound defence prevented any further goals, with *"Kerr and Rankin meeting all raids with solid tackling and clever clearing."* (11)

Everton A were Marine's opponents for their Boxing Day game at College Road and they completed the double over the Mariners with a 5-2 victory. Everton scored all their goals before the interval virtually killing any further interest for the large crowd. Everton were clearly the superior team; the Marine defence was unsteady and *"Rankin was at fault with weak kicking that presented Everton with opportunities they should never have had."* (12)

Whiston could be forgiven for believing that Marine was their bogey team. In the last game of the 1931-32 season, Marine robbed Whiston of the league title when they defeated them 1-0. Whiston had only needed one point to become champions but their defeat handed the title to Everton A. On Saturday, 4th March 1933, Whiston travelled to College Road as joint league leaders but were well and truly beaten 4-1 by Marine, who scored three goals in the second half. That defeat meant that Whiston slipped two points behind Everton A, albeit with two games in hand. The Marine team was:

Drury; Kerr, Rankin; Worsley, Kelly, Duffy; O'Donnell, Garvey, George Davies, Jones, Glynn Davies.

Marine then had back-to-back games against New Brighton Reserves, the first match at College Road on 11th March ending in a 2-2 draw. Marine had established a well-deserved 2-0 lead at the interval but, in the second–half, the Marine half-backs were unsettled and full-backs, Kerr and Billy, had to get through a tremendous amount of work to keep New Brighton's rally down to two goals. *"In defence, Rankin earned the chief honours in covering a weak half-back in Reynolds with great tackling and clean kicking."*(13)

In the away game the following weekend, New Brighton won 2-1 and, in his weekly 'Local Sports and News' column in the Waterloo and Crosby Herald,

Cantab wrote, "*A feature of the game was the form of Rankin at left-back, his tackling and kicking throughout was accuracy itself...*"

For the final home league game on Saturday, 22nd April, Marine faced Liverpool A. Marine's team was:

Drury; Kerr, Rankin; Worsley, Kelly, King; Constantine, Garvey, George Davies, Talon Jones, Glynn Davies.

However, they had to start with ten men as Billy was a late arrival. The match was no end of the season affair; it was a hard-fought game with bright spells and thrilling moments. The first half was goalless, but up to the interval, Liverpool were "*the more workmanlike side, but repeatedly stumbled over the sound rearguard of Kerr and Rankin.*" (14) Two minutes after the resumption, Marine found themselves a goal down following a blunder by Drury when he allowed the ball to bounce over him into the net. Marine equalised when George Davies hooked the ball on to the upright and Jones ran the rebound into the net. Davies scored a brilliant goal with a few minutes to go to seal victory.

The top two positions in the League were reversed that year with Whiston as champions and Everton A as runners up. Marine finished fourth, eight points behind Whiston.

As losing finalists in the previous year's FA Amateur Cup, Marine avoided the qualifying rounds for the FA Cup and went straight into the draw for the first round proper. They drew Hartlepool United at home. Hartlepool were next to bottom in the Northern Section of the Third Division, so Marine's hopes of progressing in the competition were high.

The game was played on Saturday, 26th November 1932 in blustery conditions. The crowd was a disappointing 2000. Marine's team was:

Drury; Kerr, Rankin; Worsley, Kelly, King; O'Donnell, Garvey (capt), Constantine, Talon Jones, Davies.

Despite being completely outplayed in the first half, Marine were only two goals down at the interval. In the second half, even with a strong wind in their backs, they went further behind, but a goal from Constantine raised their supporters' hopes. Two further goals from Hartlepool emphasised their superiority and ended Marine's hopes of progressing in the FA Cup.

The Mariners anticipated a good run in the FA Amateur Cup. In the first round on Saturday, 12th December, they achieved a sensational 7-2 win over Northern Nomads at College Road, producing their best form of the season. The team was:

Drury; Kelly, Rankin; Duffy, Worsley, King; O'Donnell, Morgan, Constantine, Garvey, Davies.

Constantine scored five goals, while *"Kelly played an outstanding game at full-back…, and he had a splendid if more robust partner in Rankin."* (15) According to Cantab in his Local Sports and News column in the Waterloo and Crosby Herald, the match was *"an example of Marine's ability to rise to the occasion."* He added, *"It was a magnificent victory and confounded all opinions of the rather poor standard the team had been showing since the commencement of the season."*

In the second round, on Saturday, 14th January, Marine faced South Bank from Middlesbrough, who they had eliminated on the way to the final the previous year. They could not repeat that success, however, losing 1-0 at home. South Bank just about deserved their win though Marine could easily have secured a result if their forwards had taken advantage of the scoring opportunities presented to them.

The club started its defence of the Lancashire Amateur Cup on Saturday, 3rd December, against The Pemblians, who had waived ground advantage. In rather a dull game, The Pemblians rarely looked as if they would make a fight of it. In fact, the game was effectively over by the interval, with Marine three goals up. Marine's team was:

Drury; Platt, Rankin; Worsley, McCough, King; Morgan, Walmsley, Constantine, Garvey, Davies.

In the second round, on Saturday, 7th January, 1933, a goal by Constantine, midway through the second half, gave Marine victory in Manchester over South Salford, one of the strongest sides in the competition. Billy was at left-back.

Three weeks later, on a frostbound College Road, Marine beat Blackburn Technical College 3-0 to reach the semi-final. They fielded the following side:

Drury; Kerr, Rankin; Worsley, Kelly, King; O'Donnell, Morgan, Constantine, Garvey, Glynn Davies.

Just before half-time, the Blackburn goalkeeper was injured and had to leave the field following a collision with his right-half Fisher and Marine's Constantine. He was still off when Marine took the lead through Garvey, almost on the interval. Although the keeper was able to resume in goal for the second half, he could not prevent Marine scoring a further two goals. Blackburn tried hard to get something from the game, but *"could rarely penetrate the alert Marine defence, in which Worsley and Rankin were outstanding."* (16)

The semi-final was played at Orrell on Saturday, 18th February; Marine's opponents were Formby. The side showed two changes from the previous round – Duffy replaced Worsley at left-half, while George Davies came in at inside-right for Morgan. Formby were ahead within three minutes. Marine equalised soon afterwards but, despite having the strong wind behind their backs and almost incessant pressure on the Formby goal, they could not score again before the interval. Facing the elements in the second half, Marine were thought to be a beaten side, but they dominated the game sufficiently to snatch the winner. Full-backs, Kerr and Billy, had to be at their best after the break and the latter had to kick-off the line with Drury beaten.

On Wednesday evening, 12th April, Marine won the Lancashire Amateur Cup for the third year in succession, when they defeated Cadby Hall 2-0 at Anfield. Marine's team was:

Drury; Kerr, Rankin; Worsley, Kelly, King; George Davies, Garvey, Roberts, Talon Jones, Glynn Davies.

Marine were two up at the interval. Cadby rallied strongly in the second half, but *"found Kerr and Rankin a brilliant pair of full-backs."* (17) In winning the Lancashire Amateur Cup for the third successive time, Marine equalled a long-standing record established by Liverpool City Police.

The day after their Lancashire Cup victory, a party of 25 players and officials, including Billy, embarked on the club's first Easter tour for 40 years. The party left Lime Street Station for London on the 5.25pm train, reaching the Regent Hotel, Piccadilly, about 9pm.

On the following morning, Good Friday, the party took a stroll through Whitehall and St James Park, before travelling by underground to Wimbledon's ground, where they gained an impressive 2-2 draw against the Isthmian League champions. Everyone was hugely impressed with the ground, which had a 25,000 capacity, and had dressing rooms, billiard and table tennis rooms, ladies rooms and a dance room. In terms of the game itself, Marine took the lead through Garvey, but Wimbledon equalised before half-time. After 15 minutes of the second half, Wimbledon went ahead, but Roberts equalised for Marine. Two minutes from time, Roberts was fouled in the penalty area; Garvey failed with his spot kick.

Saturday morning was spent walking to Hyde Park and, in the afternoon, the team faced their old rivals Leyton, whom they had eliminated in the quarter-final of the FA Amateur Cup the previous season. The game ended 0-0, although Roberts almost won it for Marine when his shot struck the crossbar.

Sunday was spent at leisure up the Thames and at Hampton Court and then, on Easter Monday, the team had another goalless draw, this time against Enfield, who, like Leyton, were members of the Athenian League. After the match, the party returned to Liverpool by train. According to the Waterloo and Crosby Herald, the tour was *"a complete success, happy in spirit both on and off the field and reciprocated to the highest extent by their several hosts".*

For the second season in succession, Marine were eliminated from the Liverpool Amateur Cup in one of the early rounds. Having beaten Liverpool Trams

3-1 in the first round at home, they were then knocked out of the competition by Costains, in what the Waterloo and Crosby Herald described as a "*first class sensation*", on a frozen College Road pitch on Saturday, 21st January 1933. The score was 3-0 and two of the goals were own goals. The Marine team was:

Drury; Kerr, Rankin; Worsley, Kelly, King; O'Donnell, Garvey, Constantine, George Davies, Glynn Davies.

There was another sensation in the final game of the season at College Road. It was a first round replay in the Lord Wavertree Cup on Saturday, 6th May. In the first game, Marine had earned a 2-2 draw after extra time against Liverpool A, the cup holders for the previous two seasons. The match report in the Waterloo and Crosby Herald, appeared under the headline, "*Rankin Brilliance*" and he was adjudged by the match reporter to have "*rarely played a finer game. His tackling and positioning, as (centre-forward) Bush discovered, was invincible.*" (18)

The replayed match was a thrilling finale to the season with extra time, ten goals and a game that see-sawed until the very end. The Marine team was:

Drury; Hunter, Rankin; Worsley, Kelly, King; White, Constantine, George Davies, Garvey, Glynn Davies.

Marine were two down at half-time. Immediately after the restart, Liverpool struck the upright and, fortunately, the ball eluded the Liverpool forwards. The pitch was very slippery at this stage because of the torrential rain but, somehow, Marine battled through the deluge to draw level with goals from Constantine and Garvey. Within a few minutes, however, Liverpool regained their lead and held on until the final seconds when George Davies equalised. Five minutes into the first period of extra time, Marine took the lead for the first time through an own goal but, with a minute or so to go before the second interval, Marine conceded an own goal to make the score 4-4. The final 15 minutes were very much in Marine's favour, showing surprising stamina they scored twice to put the result beyond doubt. A remarkable victory!

On 1ˢᵗ April, Marine had beaten Peasley Cross Athletic 1-0 in the semi-final of R E Lythgoe Memorial Cup, which is played between the four best clubs in Merseyside by invitation. By virtue of their Lancashire Amateur Cup successes, Marine had been invited for the past three seasons. Completion of the Memorial Cup and the Lord Wavertree Cup were delayed until the next season because some ties, including the Everton-Liverpool semi-final of the Memorial Cup had still to be decided.

It is interesting to note that Everton created a record that season by winning the Second Division and First Division titles and then the FA Cup in consecutive seasons.

1933-34 Season

Marine entertained league newcomers, Northern Nomads, in the first league game of the season at College Road on Saturday, 26ᵗʰ August. The Nomads had decided to enter the Liverpool County Combination for the first time since their inauguration 32 years earlier. A 5-1 victory for Marine ensured a promising start to the season. The Marine team was:

Drury; Kerr, Rankin; Worsley, Fletcher, King; White, Morgan, George Davies, Garvey, Glynn Davies.

The following Saturday, Marine won their second league game at Hoylake by two goals to one, but only just managed to preserve their unbeaten record at Whiston on Saturday, 23ʳᵈ September. They led deservedly by the only goal at half-time but, just before the whistle, Billy received a knock and, after treatment, resumed at outside-left, little more than a passenger. Marine went 2-0 up through George Davies, who injured himself scoring and had to leave the field, but Marine continued to play extremely well and actually scored two further goals to lead 4-1. Then, outside-right White was injured and looked shaky when he resumed. Whiston took advantage to reduce the arrears to 4-3 and equalised with a few minutes to go when Drury misjudged a long shot, following relentless Whiston pressure. Under the circumstances, Marine did extremely well to get a draw.

Marine played their fourth league game on Saturday, 7th October, beating Ellesmere Port 3-0 at home. At this stage, they were third in the league behind Everton A and Liverpool A, both of whom had played two games more than Marine.

Billy did not play against Ellesmere Port as he had not recovered from the injury that he received in the Whiston game. However, he returned to the team the following week for an FA Cup qualifying round match and took his place at left-back in the league game against Hoylake the next Saturday when Marine strolled to an easy 7-2 win.

Billy must have aggravated the injury that he received at Whiston because he did not play again until February the following year and various reports in the Waterloo and Crosby Herald stated that he was unfit to play.

In the meantime, by the end of the year, Marine had lost only one League game, by two goals to one at home to Whiston. On the last Saturday of the year, they beat Everton A 4-3 away from home, which put them at the top of the table with the same number of points as Everton A, but with a better goal average.

After many weeks absence through injury, Billy returned to first team duties in the League against Northern Nomads away on Saturday, 17th February. Marine were without Drury, Garvey, King and Worsley, who were all playing for Liverpool County against Cheshire in the Northern Counties Amateur championship, semi-final, and the team struggled to beat the Nomads by two goals to one.

Marine's championship hopes suffered a severe setback when they were defeated 2-1 at home by Skelmersdale on Saturday, 3rd March. Marine's team was:

Drury; Kerr, Rankin; Quine, Worsley, Farmer; White, Morgan, Davies, Garvey, Barlett.

Marine went ahead early in the first half, but were 2-1 down by the interval. The Skelmersdale defence stood firm to deny Marine the equaliser, although they were unlucky when a shot from Garvey smacked the crossbar.

Marine then had a run of six victories to win the League championship for the third time in the nine years since joining the Liverpool County Combination. Everton A were runners-up, three points behind Marine.

The game that probably did most to secure the title was the 1-0 defeat of Everton A on Easter Monday, 2nd April, at College Road. The result was in doubt until three minutes from time when Garvey scored from a through pass by Fradley. Marine were the better team by far on the day, to such an extent that it was reported that "*it might easily have been six in the favour of Marine, so great was the pressure asserted throughout*". The match report went on, "*In the Marine ranks, one noticed the excellent work of Drury, Rankin, Kerr and Worsley.*" (19)

Another game that brightened Marine's championship prospects was the 8-1 defeat of Prescot Cables at home on Saturday, 14th April. Marine were in dominant form, taking a 5-0 lead by the interval. Prescot scored from the penalty spot when the score was 6-0. The Marine team was:

Drury; Kerr, Rankin; Worsley, King, Fradley; White, Morgan, Davies, Redfearn, Garvey.

In the FA Cup, Marine almost made it through the qualifying rounds to the first round proper. They beat Northern Nomads 2-0 at College Road on Saturday, 16th September 1933; Billy was left-back. The Nomads must surely have considered Marine to be their bogey team, failing to register a win against them since the 1924-25 season. For this game, they arrived with a formidable team, most of them with County honours, and quite a sprinkling of international talent, but they could not prevent Marine from gaining their third victory in consecutive seasons, the previous two of which were in the FA Amateur Cup.

In the next qualifying round, two weeks later, Marine faced Ashton National from the Cheshire League, who had caused a sensation when they signed Alec Jackson, the Scottish international winger the previous season. That game ended in a draw. In the replay at College Road on Wednesday, 4th October, Marine were a goal behind with 15 minutes to go and, ten minutes later, they led 3-1, snatching victory when the match seemed lost.

Billy missed both games through injury. However, he was back in the team for the next tie at home to Glossop on Saturday, 14th October. Glossop were virtually beaten by ten men as Marine lost the services of Davies, when he was carried off with a leg injury and, on his return, he was merely a passenger on the right wing. Marine were leading 2-0 just after the interval, Glossop pulled one back and were unlucky in the last few minutes not to get an equaliser as they pressed Marine's goal.

The Divisional Final, which decided which team would progress into the first round proper of the FA Cup, was played a fortnight later at Blackburn. Injuries prevented both Davies and Billy appearing for Marine against Manchester North End. They were three down at half-time; pulled back to 4-3; had the ball in the net for what the players thought was the equaliser, only for the goal to be disallowed; and then conceded a fifth goal. So, their interest in the FA Cup ended earlier than they had hoped.

Marine's interest in the FA Amateur Cup was also short-lived. After beating Cockfield 2-1 at College Road on Saturday, 9th December, they were defeated, but not disgraced, by South Bank in the next round. Billy missed both games through injury.

However, Marine did have cup success, winning the Liverpool Amateur Cup for the sixth time. In the first round, they beat Linacre Gas Works on Saturday, 20th January 1934. Billy played his first game for three months, but he was clearly not fully fit, and did not appear again for another three weeks, this time in a League game.

He was able to play in the second round of the Liverpool Amateur Cup on Saturday 24th February at home to Olympic. The team was:

Drury; Kerr, Rankin; Fradley, Kelly, Farmer; White, Davies, Redfearn, Garvey, Barlett.

The highlight of the game was a remarkable revival by Marine. They turned a 3-1 deficit at half-time into a 4-3 victory. Two minutes into the game, the Olympic inside-right struck a shot which deflected off Billy into the net to give Olympic the lead. From the restart, a first time shot from an Olympic forward beat Drury to put Olympic 2-0 up after three minutes. Marine reduced the arrears, but just when it seemed that they were set for a revival, Olympic scored a third goal against the run of play. After the interval, the visitors were never in the game.

Marine gave one of their best displays of the season in the next round on Saturday, 24th March, to beat West Derby Union 5-1. In the quarter-final, two weeks later, Marine struggled somewhat to win 3-0 at home against Kirkdale, a side that had been beaten 8-1 by Marine's A team a week earlier. Billy was at left-back in both those cup-ties.

The semi-final was played at Formby on Saturday, 21st April; Marine's opponents were Liverpool Cables. The half-time score was 1-1 but, after the interval, Billy missed his kick completely, allowing Cables right winger to score an easy goal. However, Marine levelled the score and won the game in the second half of extra time with a third goal. This was Marine's twelfth appearance in the Liverpool Amateur Cup Final.

Billy did not play in the final at Goodison on Saturday, 12th May, when Marine defeated Garston Protestant Reformers; he was probably injured. Farmer was at left-back.

Marine were unable to repeat the previous season's success in the Lancashire Amateur Cup, being eliminated at the quarter-final stage by Collegiate Old Boys, losing 3-2. They had had difficulties in selecting a team as a number of regular players, including Billy, were injured and Webb and King had been called up by the Wales and England teams respectively.

Marine also lost in the final of the RE Lythgoe Memorial Cup to the Everton Central League team.

On Saturday, 1st September, it was announced in the Waterloo and Crosby Herald that Marine had re-signed all of the previous season's successful team and, in addition, had signed several prominent new players. However, Billy did not appear in the team during the remainder of 1934 and he was not mentioned in the account of that season in "The Mighty Mariners". He may well have retired from playing football, as he had obviously suffered a serious injury, missing all but two of Marine's games between 23rd September 1933 and 17th February 1934. He had also missed a number of matches in the first half of the previous season because of injury.

In Billy's time at Marine, the Club was FA Amateur Cup finalists, twice winners of the Lancashire Amateur Cup, winners of the Liverpool Amateur Cup on one occasion and also champions of the First Division of the Liverpool County Combination. So, he had had a very successful time there. He was clearly a hard-tackling full-back, and had received many glowing reports in the local newspapers.

References:

1. Waterloo and Crosby Herald, 19th December 1931

2. The Mighty Mariners by David Wotherspoon (1997)

3. Liverpool Echo, 22nd February 1932

4. Waterloo and Crosby Herald, 12th March 1932

5. This brief pen-picture must have been put together for the book, "The Mighty Mariners", because Billy did not represent England at baseball until 1935, three years after the final.

6. Liverpool Daily Post, 18th April 1932

7. Waterloo and Crosby Herald, 23rd April 1932

8. Waterloo and Crosby Herald, 30th January 1932

9. Waterloo and Crosby Herald, 26th September 1931

10. Waterloo and Crosby Herald, 17th September 1932

11. Waterloo and Crosby Herald, 19th November 1932

12. Waterloo and Crosby Herald, 31st December 1932

13. Waterloo and Crosby Herald, 18th March 1932

14. Waterloo and Crosby Herald, 29th April 1932

15. Waterloo and Crosby Herald, 19th December 1932

16. Waterloo and Crosby Herald, 4th February 1933

17. Waterloo and Crosby Herald, 13th April 1933

18. Waterloo and Crosby Herald, 13th April 1933

19. Waterloo and Crosby Herald, 7th April 1934

4

BILLY AND BASEBALL (1932-60s)

Billy Rankin's pen-picture in "The Mighty Mariners" mentions that he was an international baseball player. Then, baseball in Britain was effectively confined to Cardiff and Newport in South Wales and Liverpool in the North West of England. The English game was run by the English Baseball Association (EBA), although a rival organisation, the English Baseball Union (EBU), emerged in the early 1930s, and also organised an English League competition.

The rules of the English version of the game varied in a number of ways from its American counterpart:

Delivery of the ball - The ball is thrown underarm and known as bowling, while in the American version, it is delivered overhand or sidearm and called pitching.

Number of players - There are 11 players in a team with no substitutions allowed. American baseball is played by nine players at a time and, while substitutions are allowed, a player who leaves the game may not re-enter it.

Number of innings - Each team has two innings. An innings ends when all 11 players are either dismissed or stranded on base. American baseball consists of nine innings, and each team's half of an inning ends when there have been three dismissals.

Bases – The bases are poles rather than cushions.

Bat – The bat has a flat striking surface, while the American bat is entirely round.

The Scoring System - In British baseball, a player scores a run for every base he reaches after hitting the ball. He will not subsequently score when moving around the bases on another player's hit. The equivalent of a home run scores four runs. As in cricket, a bonus run can be awarded for excessively-wide deliveries. In America, a player scores a run only on a successful circuit of all four bases, whether on his own or another player's hit. (1)

British baseball players wore football or rugby-type shirts and shorts. In the 1930s, a number of League footballers played baseball to maintain their fitness during the summer months.

The first reports of Billy Rankin playing baseball appear in the 1932 season, which ran from May to August. He was a member of the St. Margaret's team in the English League run by the EBA – the other eight teams were: British Enka, Cowley, Crawford's Athletic, Crystal, New Brighton, North Western, Oakfield Social and Oakmere. In the previous season, 1931, St Margaret's had swept the board of trophies, winning the league, the English Cup, the Lewis Cup and the Robert Marks' Cup.

1932 Season

1932 proved to be much less successful for St Margaret's. They lost the league title to Crystal, who also beat them in the final of the Robert Marks' Cup; they were beaten in the second round of the Lewis Cup by the eventual winners, Oakmere; but, they did win the English Cup.

Billy was one of the backstops for St. Margaret's; the other was Cyril Roche, the club captain and an England international. Billy normally batted at number eight or lower.

One of the most exciting of St. Margaret's League games that season was against North Western on Saturday, 28th May at Pirie Park, Walton Hall Avenue in Liverpool. North Western only managed to score 70 runs in reply to St Margaret's impressive total of 106 and so had to follow on. They reached 73 runs in their second innings. Towards the end of their second innings, St. Margaret's only required four runs to win with three men standing. Somehow, they managed to lose by one run. Billy scored seven runs in the first innings, but failed to score in the second.

St. Margaret's progressed through the earlier rounds of the English Cup to the semi-final on Saturday, 23rd July at Green Lane, Liverpool, where they met Crystal, who had beaten them by five runs a week earlier in the Robert Marks' Cup Final. On this occasion, it was St Margaret's who triumphed, by five runs with three men still to bat. The scores were St Margaret's 120 (49 and 71), Crystal 115 (50 and 65). Billy scored nine runs in the first innings, followed by six in the second.

The final was played at the North Western Ground on Saturday, 6th August. St. Margaret's had held the trophy for the previous two years, whilst their opponents, Oakmere, had never won it. Despite this, Oakmere were probably the favourites, as they had won two of the three meetings between the teams that season. But, St Margaret's emerged as Cup winners for the third consecutive year. The extent of the victory, 58 runs, was rather surprising in view of Oakmere's previous good form. There were ten runs between the teams at the halfway stage, St Margaret's scoring 67 against Oakmere's 57. The holders consolidated their position in the second innings by making 85, whereas Oakmere failed at the critical time, being dismissed for 37. Billy only scored one run in the first innings and failed to score in the second.

In their last match of the season, New Brighton's team included Nel Tarleton, the famous Liverpool boxer.

1933 Season

St. Margaret's started off the season in good form, winning their first four league games, including a two-run victory over League champions, Crystal. At half-time, it looked as if St Margaret's would win easily as they had scored 119 runs to Crystal's 64, a lead of 55 runs. However, they only managed a total of 23 in their second innings, while Crystal responded with 76 runs, falling just two short of St Margaret's overall total. Billy, batting at number 10, scored five and four in his two innings.

Their next four games were a complete contrast – two defeats in the league by Oakmere and British Enka and losses in the Robert Marks' and Lewis Cups at the hands of Oakmere and North Western.

They did get back to their winning ways in the League, but the champions, Crystal, were going strongly. A victory for Crystal over North Western on Saturday, 12th August would secure the League title for them, but North Western were surprise winners. As a result of Crystal's defeat, there was the unusual possibility of three clubs – Crystal, St. Margaret's and British Enka - tying for the championship, thereby requiring a play-off.

In the end, a play-off was necessary, but it did not involve Crystal, who were beaten by New Brighton in their final game of the season. St. Margaret's and British Enka both won their matches and met in the play-off over two evenings, Monday and Tuesday, 4th and 5th September, at the North Western Recreation Ground, Green Lane. St Margaret's went in first, batting with only nine men, as Roberts was playing for Liverpool FC and Billy Rankin was missing; he may have been training with Marine FC, as their season had started too. St Margaret's reached 48 with their nine players; British Enka replied with 69. On the Tuesday evening, St. Margaret's scored 57, with eleven men – Roberts had turned up, but Billy was still missing. This left Enka with 37 runs to get to win the championship, which they accomplished for the loss of only four men. Enka had last won the championship in 1930.

Earlier in the season, on Saturday, 8th July, St Margaret's had easily beaten New Brighton by an innings and 39 runs in the semi-final of the English Cup. Billy scored 11 runs, batting at number 10.

They faced North Western in the Final on Saturday, 29th July, watched by about 2,000 spectators. When North Western were set 114 to win in their second innings, it looked as though they would be easily beaten. They started badly by losing eight men for 28 runs, but they rallied to reach 79, still 34 runs short of the required total. This meant that St. Margaret's had won the English Cup for the fourth year in succession. Mr Robert Gladstone, President of the EBA, presented the Cup to the winning team.

1934 Season

This was St. Margaret's poorest season for some years, as they did not win a single trophy. They were joint runners-up in the League, four points behind champions, Oakmere; they were defeated in the semi-final of the Lewis Cup and the second round of the English Cup by Oakmere on both occasions; and they lost to Crystal in the quarter-final of the Robert Marks' Cup. Oakmere were certainly St. Margaret's bogey team that season, beating them in two cup-ties and in both League games.

St Margaret's had signed Jim Sullivan, captain of the Wigan Rugby Football Club, to play for them, whilst Hanson, the Liverpool FC winger, was a member of the Oakmere team.

Hanson played a key role in Oakmere's victory over St Margaret's in the second round of the English Cup on Thursday, 14th June, when he scored 31 runs in their first innings. St Margaret's had scored 84 runs. In reply, Oakmere lost five men for 12 runs, but somehow managed to total 101, due mainly to Hanson's brilliant batting. As a result of a poor batting display in their second innings, St Margaret's were eliminated from the Cup by 10 runs with eight men to bat, thereby denying them the opportunity to win the trophy for a fifth successive year.

Billy's best batting displays that season were all in the League. The first was on Saturday, 9th June in the defeat by British Enka, when he notched nine and eight runs batting at number 11. A week later, in another defeat, this time by Oakmere, he was batting at number nine and scored five and 17 runs. And then, on Saturday, 30th June, he scored one and ten runs in an unexpected victory over North Western.

1935 Season

The biggest surprise of the season occurred before it had begun. Oakmere, the previous season's champions, withdrew from the league because they did not have a first class bowler. They had lost Arthur Rice and Alex Scott, both of whom had signed for St. Margaret's. In addition to their baseball talents, Rice was a half-back with Manchester United and Scott, who was the fastest bowler in the league, was the Burnley goalkeeper. St. Margaret's had also signed J. Roberts, the Wigan centre-forward. This meant that St. Margaret's now had eight players who had gained international baseball honours.

St Margaret's enjoyed a far more successful season this year. They were undefeated in the League, winning the title by six points from runners-up Crystal.

On Saturday, 22nd June, St Margaret's had a decisive away League victory over Crawford Athletic by 103 runs, after being only 21 runs in front at the halfway stage. St. Margaret's reached 71 in the first innings, whilst Crawfords scored 50 and were far from out of it. In their second innings, the Saints declared at 105 for eight, but their opponents then failed miserably, scoring only 23 runs. Billy scored eight and nought in his two innings.

The outstanding League game the following Saturday was the one between St. Margaret's and Liverpool Amateurs, which produced 280 runs. The Amateurs scored 76 and 60 runs, with St Margaret's amassing 124 in their first innings and then scoring 20 for four, to win by eight runs with seven men to bat. Billy scored only one run in the first innings batting at number nine.

St. Margaret's did not have it all their own way in every encounter for there were two matches in which they achieved victory by the narrowest of margins, a single run. The first of those was on Saturday, 13th July against Crystal. The scores were 39 and 41 for Crystal and 46 and 35 for St. Margaret's. "*The bowling and fielding on both sides was excellent. Alex Scott bowled unchanged for St Margaret's in both innings of Crystal and was excellently supported by W. Rankin at backstop.*" (3) Billy scored five runs and then one batting as last man. In the second of those games, on Wednesday, 24th July, St. Margaret's opponents were Crawford Athletic.

St Margaret's were also successful in two of the three Cup competitions. Probably their most satisfying achievement was winning the English Cup for the fifth time in six years. They beat Crawford Athletic, St. Oswald's and Windsor to reach the final, against Crystal at the Liverpool Police Athletic ground, Prescot Road, Liverpool, on Saturday, 3rd August. Crystal had won the Cup in 1922, 1923 and 1926, and were defeated in the 1930 final by St Margaret's in a replay; they were also losing finalists in 1934. Their record did not quite match St. Margaret's, who first won the Cup in 1928 and then created a record by winning it four years in succession, 1930-1933.

League form suggested a victory for St. Margaret's as they had won both fixtures. And so it turned out, with St Margaret's winning by two runs and two men to bat. The Saints won the toss and, batting first, scored 92. Crystal were dismissed for 38, leaving them 54 runs behind and having to follow on. They scored 102 runs, setting St. Margaret's 49 runs to win, which seemed an easy task. However, St. Margaret's lost nine men in scoring 51 runs, which secured them the English Cup for the fifth time in six years. Billy scored three and one batting at number 11.

St. Margaret's also won the Lewis Cup that season, but not without controversy it should be said. Their semi-final against North Western ended on an unhappy note, when their opponents left the field with St. Margaret's requiring eight runs for victory and with three batsmen not out. The reason for North Western's early departure was not reported but, according to the competition rules, the tie had to be awarded to St. Margaret's. The scores were - North Western 104 (49 & 55), St Margaret's 97 (24 & 73 for 8). Billy scored four and three batting last man.

The final was played on the Bank Holiday Monday, 5th August. Going in first, St. Margaret's scored 60 runs, and then dismissed Crystal for 25. The St. Margaret's captain decided not to enforce the follow-on and batted again. This time, St. Margaret's were dismissed for 37, leaving Crystal to get 73 to win. However, they were dismissed for only 47, falling short of the required total by 25 runs. Billy scored six runs in his first innings, but failed to score in the second. It was St. Margaret's fourth win over Crystal that season.

St. Margaret's were unable to make a clean sweep of all the competitions, despite reaching the final of the remaining trophy, the Robert Marks' Cup. Again, their opponents were Crystal, holders of the Cup for the previous three seasons. The final was played on the North Western ground, Green Lane, Liverpool, on Saturday 20th July, before a large crowd; the gate receipts of £34 were a record for the competition. St. Margaret's only managed 30 runs in their first innings; Crystal replied with 70. Going in a second time, the Saints scored 54, leaving Crystal to get 14 runs to retain the trophy. They reached the required total for the loss of four men. The fielding of St. Margaret's was well below their usual standard and several lapses in the field cost many runs. Billy, batting at number five, failed to score in both his innings.

Despite the failure to win the Robert Marks' Cup, the Saints had had a very successful season winning the English League and the English and Lewis Cups.

The showcase baseball event each year was the international game between England (effectively Liverpool) and Wales (drawn from players in Cardiff and Newport), which alternated between venues in the two countries. The team for the 1935 international to be played at Breck Park Greyhound Track, Townsend Lane, Anfield, on Saturday, 6th July, was:

R. A. Scott (St. Margaret's), bowler; C. Hobson (North Western), No 2 base and reserve bowler; T. Davies (Crystal), backstop; W. Rankin (St. Margaret's), No 3 base and second backstop; C. Davidson (North Western), No 1 base; A. Rice (St. Margaret's), longstop; J. Deegan (Crystal); J. Roberts (St. Margaret's), captain; E. Jones and J. Clegg (both British Enka); H. Griffiths (Liverpool Amateurs); Reserve J. Shacklady (Crawford Athletic); Trainer Mr A C Wright (St. Margaret's).

Hobson, Davies, Davidson, Clegg and Billy were new caps. Griffiths was the former Liverpool winger, who had signed for Port Vale.

England had only beaten Wales on three occasions - 1914, 1923 and 1933 - whilst Wales had triumphed on 13 occasions, four times by an innings. Against the odds, however, and watched by Liverpool's Lord Mayor and Lady Mayoress, England defeated Wales comprehensively by an innings and 68 runs. England scored 162, while Wales only managed 41 and 53. Batting at number 11, Billy scored four runs.

This was Billy's most successful season in baseball; his selection for the England team that beat Wales was the icing on the cake.

1936 Season

St. Margaret's lost Alex Scott, their main bowler, when he went over to the American code, signing for Liverpool Giants, along with H.S. Griffiths, his fellow international from Liverpool Amateurs.

St. Margaret's started their defence of the League title with two wins, beating newly promoted Windsor by an innings and 27 runs on Saturday, 9th May, and then getting the better of Crawford's Athletic a week later with a 45 run victory. Billy played in both matches, but only managed to score four runs in his three innings, batting at number 11.

On Saturday, 23rd May, the surprise of the day was the defeat of St. Margaret's at home by British Enka in a high scoring game, in which 323 runs were scored. St. Margaret's scored 38 and 121 in their two innings, whilst Enka replied with 116 in their first innings and 48 for 5 in their second, to win by five runs with six men to bat. Billy did not play in this game, leaving St Margaret's with only ten men, something of a handicap.

Britsh Enka were the only undefeated team in the League at this stage, and they remained unbeaten for the rest of the season, securing the League title with two games to spare. St. Margaret's and Crystal shared second place.

British Enka had achieved the double over St Margaret's in the League, but the Saints gained their revenge in the final of the English Cup on Saturday, 25th July. They overwhelmed Enka by the astonishing margin of an innings and 61 runs. St. Margaret's scored 127, with Enka managing only 24 and 42 runs in their two innings. Billy scored three at number 11. This victory meant that St. Margaret's had won the Cup seven times in the previous nine years.

Crystal had also completed the double over the Saints in the League, and again, St. Margaret's obtained their revenge in a Cup Final. This time it was the Lewis Cup and they emerged victorious by 41 runs. The scores were 118 and 52 for St. Margaret's and 69 and 60 for Crystal. Billy failed to score in his first innings and managed only a single run in his second. This was the second successive season that Saints had won the cup and on both occasions they had beaten Crystal.

The EBA held an exhibition trial match on behalf of Tranmere Rovers FC Supporters Club at Prenton Park, the Rovers' ground, on Wednesday, 1st July. Billy was selected as one of the backstops in the B team, which was beaten by 67 runs. Billy scored a total of seven runs in his two innings, batting at number eight.

Despite being on the losing side in the trial, Billy was selected for the international match against Wales at Cardiff Arms Park on Saturday, 11th July. The team was:

Bowlers: Hobson (North Western), Roberts (Crystal);

Backstops: Corner (Crawford Athletic), Rankin (St. Margaret's);

No 1 base: Jones (St. Margaret's); Longstop: Winter (British Enka);

Fielders: Thomas (Crystal), Roberts (St. Margaret's, captain), Herbert (Church Road), Deegan (Crystal), McQueen (British Enka).

Unfortunately, Billy had to withdraw from the team at the last minute because of an injured hand, Shacklady of Crawford Athletic replacing him. The late change had no effect on the team, for they beat Wales for the first time in Wales by an innings and six runs. It was a fairly low-scoring match with England reaching 82 runs in their only innings and Wales replying with 34 and 42.

1937 Season

St. Margaret's started off their League season badly, losing three of their first four games. On the opening day, Saturday, 8th May, they lost to North Western by six runs and three men to bat. The Saints scored 29 and 74 runs in their two innings, whilst North Western made 38 runs in their first innings, and then 71 for eight to win the match. Billy scored three and four batting at number 11.

In their next game, at home to Windsor, St. Margaret's won fairly easily by 16 runs and eight men to bat. Batting at number 11 again, Billy made four runs in his first innings, but failed to score in his second. He played well at backstop when St. Margaret's were fielding.

The outstanding game in Division 1 on Saturday, 22nd May, was between Crystal and St Margaret's at the Sefton rugby ground, Leyfield Road, West Derby. Crystal won by five runs and seven men to bat. St. Margaret's managed to score 46 and 42 in their two innings, with Billy, batting at 11, contributing six runs in the first and failing to score in the second. Crystal scored 61 in their first innings and then reached a winning total of 32 for the loss of four men when batting for the second time. After four games, Crystal and North Western were undefeated.

North Western lost their unbeaten record to St Margaret's on Saturday, 5th June, when they were beaten by 60 runs. The Saints continued to lack consistency, beating Crawford's Athletic twice, once by an innings and 78 runs, but losing to

British Enka by an innings and 13 runs. They gained their revenge over British Enka a few weeks later, with a surprise victory by 12 runs.

On 31st July, the Saints lost again in the League, this time to Crystal by 10 runs and six men to bat. Billy scored 14 of the Saints 59 runs in the first innings. Crystal replied with 62, but then St. Margaret's collapsed to 35 all out when batting for the second time. Crystal scored the 33 runs necessary for victory with the loss of 5 men. St. Margaret's only fielded nine men, but had they had a full team, Crystal would have had a hard fight to win.

Following the defeat of St Margaret's, Crystal only needed one point from their match with British Enka on Saturday, 14th August to secure the championship. In fact, they gained both points with a victory by an innings and 43 runs. St Margaret's also won in the League that day, beating Windsor by six runs, despite fielding only eight men.

The surprise of the day in the first round of the English Cup on Saturday, 29th May, was the defeat of St Margaret's by Crystal. The Saints had won the trophy seven times in the previous nine seasons, including the last two. Crystal went on to win the Cup for the first time since 1926.

The final of the Robert Marks' trophy, between Crystal and St. Margaret's, was scheduled for Saturday, 24th July, at the North Western ground, Green Lane. It was postponed to Wednesday, 11th August, however, because of a wet pitch.

In the re-scheduled game, Crystal were dismissed for 29 runs. Hall, the St. Margaret's bowler, bowled six men, including a hat-trick, which he recorded by dismissing the first three batsmen without conceding a run. St. Margaret's made 55 in their first innings, with Billy scoring nine. Batting a second time, Crystal reached 67, leaving St. Margaret's to get 42 runs for victory the following evening, Thursday, 12th August. The Saints must have been fairly confident of reaching that total to record their first win of the season over Crystal and lifting the Robert Marks' Cup for the third time. But, it was not to be. St Margaret's were dismissed for 19 runs with only four players scoring runs; Billy was not one of them.

That season, Crystal also won the Lewis Cup, which meant that they had a clean sweep of the four trophies available, equalling the record set by St Margaret's in 1931.

Although his club had had a poor season by their standards, Billy was again selected for the English team to play Wales in the 20th international between the two countries on Saturday, 10th July. The venue was the Stanley Greyhound Track, Prescot Road, Fairfield. The England team was:

S. Roberts, R. Thomas (both Crystal), T. Davies (Windsor), W. Rankin (St Margaret's), J. Deegan (Crystal), C. Davidson (North Western), A. Rice, J. Roberts, captain (both St. Margaret's), H. Blake, J. Clegg (both British Enka), W. Lynch (North Western).
Reserve: H. Marsh (Scarisbrick United).

The previous year, the England team won for the first time in Wales, by an innings and six runs. Two players created records in that game, both reaching 100 runs in international matches. Jack Roberts of St. Margaret's, the England captain, was the first to achieve the milestone as England batted first, and he went on to reach 108. Davies of Wales then got to 102.

England beat Wales for the third time in succession, creating another record in winning by an innings for the third time in a row. In Wales' most successful period, when they won nine games on the trot, they did not win by an innings in two successive games.

Wales won the toss and, batting first, scored 54 runs. England then replied with 99 runs, giving them a lead of 45 at the interval. Wales' second innings was closed at 37 runs, leaving England winners by an innings and eight runs. Billy Rankin scored four, batting as last man and starred at backstop: "*Rankin, at backstop for England, was in great form. He never wears gloves of any description when backstopping.*" (4)

Having donated the new international trophy, Mr Robert Gladstone, President of the EBA, then presented it to the English captain, Roberts. After the match, the teams and officials dined at the Victoria Hotel, St John's Lane, Liverpool.

1938 Season

St. Margaret's were more successful this year, winning the League and the Robert Marks' Cup, and finishing runners-up in the English Cup. They were undefeated in the League until Saturday, 13th August, when they lost surprisingly to British Enka, who fielded five reserves. However, two of the Saints star players, J. Roberts and A. Rice, were missing as they had to take part in practice matches for their respective football clubs. St. Margaret's scored 31 and 36 in their two innings, whilst Enka replied with 33 and 38 for six, to win by four runs with five men to bat. Despite this defeat, the Saints still led the table by two points from Crystal; British Enka were third, four points behind St. Margaret's, having played a game more.

St. Margaret's began the season on Saturday, 21st May, with an emphatic victory away from home over Windsor by an innings and 33 runs. They had made the highest score of the day when they declared at 132 for the loss of six men. Windsor were out for 34 in their first innings and, then, following on, made 65. Billy was the top scorer for St. Margaret's with 32.

In their next League game, two weeks later, they defeated British Enka by five runs and four men to bat. Batting first, Enka scored 25, whilst, in reply, St Margaret's reached 77 to lead by 52 runs. In their second innings, Enka gave a vastly improved performance, scoring 87. The Saints, requiring 36 runs, lost seven men in reaching a winning total. The leading batsmen for St. Margaret's were Burnham with 19 and Corner and Billy with 13 each.

The outstanding game on Saturday, 18th June, was the meeting between the two unbeaten teams Crystal and St Margaret's at Leyfield Road, West Derby. Surprisingly, the Saints ran out easy winners by an innings and 24 runs. St. Margaret's scored 72 and then dismissed Crystal for 30. Following on 42 runs behind, Crystal were all out a second time for 18. Billy only managed to score one run batting at number 11.

Other victories in the League included the defeat of Croxteth Albion by 43 runs and seven men to bat – leading scorers for the Saints were Jones, Corner and Billy with 15, 14 and 11 respectively; an away win over Church Road Social Club by 34 runs, despite being seven runs behind after the first innings; success against Windsor by 15 runs and ten men to bat, a match in which Billy was the leading scorer for St Margaret's with 18 in his first innings and two not out in the second; a rout of Croxteth Albion by an innings and 33 runs; and completion of the double over the previous year's champions, Crystal, by eight runs.

In the first round of the Robert Marks' Cup, St. Margaret's had an easy victory over Church Road Social Club by an innings and 70 runs. The Saints scored 149 in their innings with brilliant batting from Jones (38 runs), Shacklady (28) and Billy (17). They faced a tougher game in the semi-final, beating Windsor by eight runs and eight men to bat. Billy scored six runs in the first innings, but failed to score in the second.

The final was played at the North Western Ground, Green Lane, on Saturday, 16th July, when the Saints faced the holders, Crystal. In what proved to be a low scoring game, Crystal, batting first, could only make 26 runs. Hoping to gain a large first innings lead, St. Margaret's were disappointed to find themselves with eight men down for only 20 runs. However, a great effort by the last three batsmen, the Rice brothers and Jones, took the score to 63 all out, a lead of 37 runs. Batting a second time, Crystal were dismissed for 34 runs, which meant that the Saints did not have to bat again. Billy scored one run at number 11.

In the semi-final of the English Cup in mid-July, St. Margaret's overcame Church Road Social Club in a particularly low-scoring game by six runs and three men to bat. Church Road scored 23 in their first innings, whilst the Saints only managed three more runs than their opponents in reply. In their second innings, Church Road made 26 runs. St Margaret's reached a winning total of 27 with the loss of eight batsmen. Billy failed to score in both innings. Crystal defeated Windsor in the other semi-final.

The final was played over two evenings, Monday and Tuesday, 16th and 17th August. St. Margaret's won the toss, elected to bat and scored 74 in their first innings. Billy contributed four runs to their total, batting at number 11. Crystal replied with 86, including 22 extras. On the second evening, St Margaret's only made 31 runs and Crystal lost five men in scoring the required 22 runs to retain the trophy. Billy failed to score in the Saints' second innings.

The highlight of the season, of course, was the international against Wales at Cardiff Arms Park on Saturday, 30th July. The England team was:

S. Roberts (St. Margaret's), bowler; J. Burke (Crystal), second bowler; T. Davies (Windsor), first base and third base; R. Corner (St. Margaret's), backstop and captain; W. Rankin (St Margaret's), second backstop; A. Rice (St Margaret's), longstop; J. Deegan (Crystal); E. Jones (St. Margaret's); D. Burnham (Croxteth Albion); H. Marsh (Windsor), fielders.

Reserve: W. Lynch (Crystal). Burke and Burnham were new caps.

More than 2,000 spectators watched England win a most exciting game by two runs with two men to bat. Winning the toss, England batted first, scoring 85 runs. Jones of St. Margaret's made 11, which meant that he had reached 100 runs in these internationals. The other main scorers were Burke with 13, Corner 11, and Davies and Billy making nine each. In their first innings, Wales started badly, losing six men for 25 runs, and then eight for 31, before making a mini-recovery to reach 43. Following on, they reached 88, with several mistakes in the field and two dropped catches proving costly for England. Left with 47 runs to get to win, England collapsed to 21 for eight. Rice and Davies then scored 15 not out and 12 not out respectively to secure a great victory, which looked impossible at one stage. This was England's fourth successive and narrowest win over Wales. Billy failed to score in both innings.

1939 Season

St. Margaret's opened their bid to retain the league championship on Saturday, 13th May with an away game against Rootes Securities, who had been promoted to the First Division as champions of Division Two. They won comprehensively by an innings and five runs. Rootes were all out for 21 and 66, a combined total of 87, which failed to beat the Saints' first innings score of 92, in which Billy was the highest scorer with 16 runs. The following Saturday, St. Margaret's had another easy win, this time by an innings and 41 runs over Windsor.

On Saturday, 3rd June, the Saints recorded their third successive victory by an innings when they beat Crystal, who were also undefeated in the league, by an innings and 28 runs at Aigburth. St. Margaret's then beat Croxteth Albion by 14 runs and seven men to bat and followed this up on Saturday, 17th June, with a fairly easy home win over British Enka by 18 runs and eight men to bat. Batting first, Enka scored 78. St. Margaret's lost seven men for 35 runs, but excellent batting by E. Jones (26), R. Rice (22) and Billy (12) took the score to 93, a lead of 15 runs. In their second innings, British Enka were all out for 42 runs, leaving the Saints requiring 28 runs to win. They passed the required total with the loss of only three men. So, after five games, St. Margaret's were undefeated and top of the league, two points ahead of Crystal and four ahead of Rootes Securities.

St Margaret's achieved the double over British Enka on Saturday, 24th June, winning by 45 runs at Ormskirk Road, Aintree. The Saints scored 66 and 50, a total of 116 runs, whilst Enka could only muster a total of 71 from their two innings. Billy scored five and three. The following Saturday, St. Margaret's retained their unbeaten record, winning by two runs against Rootes Securities in an exciting finish. The Saints now led the league table by six points from Crystal, who had played a game fewer.

St. Margaret's assured themselves of the league championship for the second successive season on Saturday, 15th July, with an easy victory over Windsor by an innings and 60 runs. St Margaret's scored 93 in their only innings, whilst Windsor could only manage 19 and 14 in their two innings.

St Margaret's could not repeat their outstanding league form in any of the three cup competitions, finding themselves eliminated in the first round of each. On Saturday, 27th May, they were beaten by Crystal by 16 runs in the Robert Marks' Cup, of which they were the holders. Four days later, British Enka defeated them by five runs and two men to bat in the Lewis Cup. Billy scored 16 runs in that game. Finally, in a match played over two evenings, 6th and 7th June, they found themselves knocked out of the English Cup when Windsor beat them by an innings and 21 runs.

That season, Billy was selected for his fourth, and what proved to be his final, international appearance for England against Wales. The game was played at the Stanley Greyhound Track, Fairfield, Liverpool, on Saturday, 8th July. The team was:

S. Roberts (St. Margaret's), bowler; R. G. Thomas (Rootes Securities), bowler; J. Burke (Crystal), bowler and first base; R. Corner (St. Margaret's), backstop and captain; Billy Rankin (St. Margaret's), backstop; A. Rice (St. Margaret's), longstop; E. Jones (St. Margaret's); J. Deegan (British Enka); W. Lynch (Crystal); H. Marsh (Windsor). Reserves were: B. Byrne (Rootes Securities) and E. O'Brien (Croxteth Albion). The trainer was Mr. A. L. Wright (St. Margaret's).

John Peel previewed the match in his Daily Post column "World of Sport": *"The English team is strong in every department, and if the players strike their best batting form, and with the bowlers of the calibre of Stan Roberts, R. Thomas, J. Burke and a sound fielding side to support them with backstops like R. Corner and W. Rankin, they should win their fifth successive match and retain the Robert Gladstone International Cup for the third successive year."* (5)

In torrential rain, England did gain their fifth successive win over Wales, and their eighth overall in the 22 matches played between the two countries. Wales won the toss and put England into bat first. England scored 65 runs and, in reply, Wales could only manage 32; only 19 of those runs came off the bat, the rest were extras. England made 71 in their second innings, leaving Wales to score 105 to win. They fell short by 45 runs.

Despite the appalling conditions, the players maintained a very good standard of play throughout the match. The fielding of both sides was excellent, while the bowlers worked under the handicap of a soft and treacherous bowling box. Coupled with the wet ball, this accounted for the large number of extras in the game – 34 conceded by Wales and 33 by England.

Billy batted at number 11, scoring five and four in his two innings. However, the feature of the match was the batting feat of Deegan of England. He scored 20 in the game, reaching the record total of 110 in 10 matches, beating the previous record in the international series of 108 runs by J. Roberts, also of England.

At the conclusion of the match, Mr Manley, vice-chairman of the Welsh Baseball Union, presented the Robert Gladstone Cup to Corner, the English captain. Later, the officers of the two baseball organisations, players and friends were entertained to dinner at the Cattle Market Hotel, Prescot Road.

1940 Season and beyond

Some reports of baseball matches did appear in the local papers in 1940, including those involving St. Margaret's. They did not feature every week and did not include a team listing. So, it is not known if Billy Rankin continued to play that season. Because of the Second World War, however, competitive baseball ceased for six years, until it was revived in 1947.

It would appear that Billy did not begin playing again after the war because his name is not included in any team listings in the local papers. However, according to Colin Williams, the EBA historian, his name re-appeared in the Spring of 1956 but, this time, as a referee. Williams was himself a baseball player, starting out in 1959, and he remembers Billy refereeing, and he considered him to be *"a good referee, very fair minded"*.

Billy refereed for a number of years and was appointed referee for the England v Wales International, played at Edinburgh Park, otherwise known as the Dockers Club, in Townsend Lane, Liverpool, on 29th July 1961.

Some years ago, Colin Williams interviewed a George McIllwrath, whose father was one of the founder members of the St. Margaret's baseball team. According to McIllwrath, Billy Rankin never wore a face-mask or gloves when playing backstop; he considered it unmanly. Although the ball was bowled under-arm over a distance of 50 feet, it reached a speed of between 50 and 60 mph and the backstop stood less than a yard behind the batsman. Therefore, it could be quite dangerous for the backstop. So, it proved for Billy one day. Playing in a final for St. Margaret's against Oakmere, the batsman failed to strike the ball cleanly; it snicked off the bat and broke Billy's nose. He then condescended to wear a mask, but gloves were still for cissies. Indeed, two of his sisters, Elsie and Teeny, thought that Billy was nicknamed, *"The Man with the Iron Hands"* because of his refusal to wear gloves. According to Colin Williams, Les Annett was the only other backstop, at that time, who did not wear a mask or gloves.

Colin Williams never saw Billy Rankin play, but in his conversations with the older generation of players *"his name was always broached as one of the better backstops of yesteryear"*.

Post-sport

As a young man, Billy served his time as an armature winder and, for some years, worked at Plesseys in Liverpool. Later, he was employed by the Liverpool Corporation as a turncock or waterman, and lived with his family at 1 Brook Road, Crosby, a house owned by the Corporation, which went with Billy's job. His job was a protected occupation, so he was not called up during the Second World War.

Billy Rankin had the reputation of being a hard man in sport. He was a tough-tackling full-back in football and, in baseball, he refused to wear a protective face-mask and gloves when playing backstop. It was only when a glancing ball off the bat hit him in the face and broke his nose that he deigned to wear a mask.

Billy's hobby was electronics. His son, Billy, recalled his father building a 9" television, which *"was the first TV ever seen in Waterloo"*. He also built a radio in a cabinet as a wedding present for Billy junior and his wife, Wyn. His daughter Marjory also remembered her father repairing wireless sets and making electric motors for toy trains when he retired.

His two eldest sons, George and Billy, followed their father into sport. George was the more successful, playing football professionally with Everton and Southport for some ten years. Billy signed for Everton as a youth and then played for Southport for two seasons. He did not make the first team but, on several occasions, played with his brother, George, in the Reserves. Both of them were good golfers.

Andy, his youngest son, did not take an interest in sport in general and football in particular because, *"I got too much football and I could never compete with my father."*

One of Billy's happiest memories about his father was when *"Dad and my brothers, George and Andy and me got together one sunny evening and went to Victoria Park in Waterloo and had a game of crown green bowls. We played for a penny an end. The "fat git" (his term of endearment for his father) did not tell us about bias on the bowls and was winning all the money. We got our own back by ganging up on him and demolishing his beautifully placed bowls around the jack with "cannonballs" at 60 miles per hour."* They had some great times after that.

Billy was married twice. He married Florence, known as Florrie, Dolphin in 1926 when he was 22 years of age. They had six children, four boys and two girls. Following Florrie's death in 1960, he married for a second time some two years later; there were no children as a result of this marriage. Billy died on 13th May 1980 in Fazakerley Hospital at the age of 75 from bronchopneumonia and senile dementia; his occupation was recorded as "Water Board Inspector (Retired)". Frances survived him by some two years.

Billy Rankin (second from left) and his wife Florrie (third from left) at the wedding of his daughter Marjory (sixth from left) at St Peter and Paul's Church in Crosby in 1952. His sister Winnie is fourth from the right with Billy's youngest son, Andrew, standing in front of her.

References:

1.   wikipedia.org/wiki/British_baseball. The detailed rules can be found at englishbaseball.weebly.com

2.   Liverpool Daily Post, 1935

3.   Liverpool Daily Post, 12th July 1937

4.   Liverpool Daily Post, 8th July 1939

5

George Rankin at Everton (1946-56)

Introduction

George Rankin was born in Liverpool on 29 January 1930. His father was Billy Rankin, Bruce's son. According to George's younger brother, Billy, their father took a lot of interest in George in his early years, "*no doubt because he was his first son to reach sporting age,*" and encouraged him with his football skills. Apparently, George preferred cricket to football at first. But, after an unsuccessful Lancashire trial when he was about 15 years of age, he concentrated on football and never lifted a cricket bat again. "*That was how George was,*" his brother Billy said, "*it was all or nothing.*"

Youth Football

George signed for Everton as an amateur at 16 years of age in April 1946, becoming a part-time professional 2½ years later in August 1948. During those 2½ years, he played for the Everton Colts and A, B and C teams, winning at least two medals with the B team in the Bootle JOC League – the Warburton Cup and First Division championship.

George represented England Youth (Under 18) in the 1947-48 season. Firstly, he played in what was then known as the International Youth Championship, a competition involving the four home countries. He did not take part in England's first game on 25th October 1947 against Scotland at Doncaster, a 4-2 victory for the home side. However, he did play at left-back in the two remaining fixtures – against Wales at Wycombe Wanderers' ground on 28th February 1948 (a 4-3 win for England) and against Ireland in Belfast on 15th May (a 2-2 draw).

George also played for England in the inaugural International Youth Tournament, which was the brainchild of Sir Stanley Rous, Secretary of the Football Association from 1934 to 61 and the President of FIFA from 1961 until 1974. The tournament later became the European Youth Championship, and is now organised by UEFA as the UEFA Under-19 Championship, the age level being raised in 2001.

England hosted the inaugural tournament, which involved teams from Austria, Belgium, Eire, Holland, Northern Ireland, Italy and Wales. It was a knockout competition, involving a total of eleven games from 15th to 17th April 1948. The matches were played at the grounds of Queens Park Rangers, Crystal Palace, Watford, West Ham United and Tottenham Hotspur.

England were the winners, beating Wales (4-0) at Queens Park Rangers' ground in the first round; Belgium (3-1) in the semi-final at Upton Park; and Holland (3-2) in the final at White Hart Lane. George played in all three games. The team for the tournament was:

The England team in the International Youth Tournament.
Left to right, back row: G. Rankin, M. Leather, K. Burkhill, M. Moorcroft, T.
Brown, J. Macdonald, A. Leake. Front row: D. Brickley, N. Darwin, H. Dodkins, R.
Saunders, D. Toase, K. Bannister (capt), E. Morris, T.R. Giles. Courtesy of The FA.

M. Moorcroft (Sheffield and Hallamshire); D. Toase (Durham), G. Rankin (Liverpool); R. Saunders (East Riding), A. Leake (Staffordshire), H. Dodkins (Essex); D. Brickley (West Riding), E. Morris (Cheshire), N. Darwin (Durham), K. Bannister, captain (Sheffield and Hallamshire), T.R. Giles (Staffordshire). The reserves were: M. Leather (Hampshire), T. Brown (Liverpool), J. Macdonald (Wiltshire), K. Burkhill (Liverpool).

George's badge presented for representing England Youth v Ireland Youth on 15th May 1948 and his plaque for appearing for England Youth in the International Youth Tournament from 15-17th April 1948. Inscription reads: Association Football International Youth Tournament

George also represented the Liverpool County FA Youth side in the National Youth Championship in the 1947-48 season. Liverpool reached the final by beating Lancashire (5-2), Cheshire (10-2), West Riding (8-1), Durham (3-2) and Staffordshire (2-0).

Before the Durham game on Saturday, 13th March, Ranger wrote in the Liverpool Echo *"the players leave on Friday evening, staying overnight at York and the match is in the Horden Colliery Ground near West Hartlepool. The Liverpool lads have been going great guns this season, and though this is their stiffest job so far, they are hopeful of pulling off another victory. The team is: R. Pitman (Southport Leyland Road); R. Pringle (South Liverpool) and G. Rankin (Everton); W. G. Morrey (St Domingo's), T. H. Brown (Milner's) and W. R. Gregory (Southport Trinity); E. Burkhill (Bromborough Pool), J. Lawton (Prescot Celtic), D. Hickson (Shell Mex and Everton), T. Cronin (St Matthew's) and K. Gardner (Liverpool)."* (1) Hickson would later become a team-mate of George's at Everton, as would T. E. Jones, who had played at right-back in the third round game against West Riding.

Liverpool lost the first leg of the final against Essex 3-0 on Saturday, 1st May in London; George had to leave the field injured. The Liverpool side had had the major share of the attacks, according to Stork writing in the Liverpool Echo. He went on: *"The Merseysiders must hold a bright chance playing before their own spectators. All that they needed ... was a little more steadiness in front of goal. The chances were there but they were not accepted."* (2)

George was fit for the second game at Goodison a week later, when a hopeful crowd of nearly 10,000 turned up. Despite taking the lead in the 22nd minute, Liverpool were unable to overcome the three goal deficit, only managing to draw 2-2. After the game, the Lord Mayor of Liverpool presented the trophy to the champions Essex.

George also represented Liverpool Schoolboys whilst at Finch Hall Senior School for Boys where, according to his sister Marjory, he was head boy.

Clearly, having been capped at England Youth level and having been signed by Everton, he had made the sort of start to his football career that would have been the envy of most young men of his age. Things looked very promising indeed.

Everton FC

1950-51 Season

When George was 18 years of age, Everton wanted him to sign as a full-time professional. However, his father would not sign the necessary papers as he wanted George to complete his apprenticeship as a toolmaker before becoming a full-time sportsman.(3) A compromise was agreed and George signed as a part-time professional in August 1948, which enabled him to continue with his apprenticeship.

According to George's brother Billy, "*George never forgot that and bore a grudge with Dad over that*". Dave Hickson, who had played with George in the Liverpool County FA Youth team the previous season, signed professional terms at the same time as George.

Although the maximum weekly wage for a footballer at that time was £12, George's wages were just £3. However, he would have received the same signing-on fee as his grandfather had been paid 47 years earlier; it had remained at £10 since 1901.

According to a newspaper report, George was the fourth member of the Rankin family to wear Everton's colours - his grandfather, Bruce Rankin, was at Goodison as a winger for several seasons in the early 1900s; his father Billy, was an amateur full-back there, later moving to Marine, and appearing in their Amateur Cup Final team of 1932; and his uncle, George, also a full-back, had a short spell with the Club, although George's son, Terry, did not believe his father had played football. But, of course, there was a fifth member of the family to wear the blue of Everton if the article is correct – Bruce's brother, George, played several times for the Reserves in 1905 and later appeared for Tranmere Rovers.

As a part-time professional, George turned out for Everton's A side in the Liverpool County league, winning runners-up medals in the 1948-49 season in the Challenge Cup and the First Division championship.

His first significant appearance for Everton was in the public trial at Goodison Park on Saturday, 12th August 1950. He appeared for the Whites (the Reserves) against the Blues (the senior side). The teams were:

Blues: Burnett; Moore, Saunders; Grant, Falder, Farrell; Buckle, Wainwright, Catterick, Fielding, Eglington.
Whites: O'Neil; Clinton, Rankin; Lindley, Humphreys, Melville; Harris, Donovan, Reid, Hampson, Parker.

The Blues won 4-0. Harry Catterick, who was centre-forward for the Blues, became Everton's manager from 1961 to 1973, leading the Club to two First Division Championships and winning the FA Cup.

Following the trial, George was a regular at left-back for the Reserves in the Central League, missing only one or two games. His big chance came on the 9th December, when he was called into the first team to play against Derby County at Goodison Park. His debut was announced in the local press: *"Everton introduce another debutant to senior football tomorrow, when George Rankin comes into the side against Derby County, the fourth Goodison player under 21 to receive his first team baptism this season. Wainwright is also included, due to Potts being unfit. Rankin, who is aged 20, joined Everton straight from school in 1944 and signed professional just over two years ago. He played with Tommy Jones, the present Everton centre-half, in the Liverpool Schoolboys side, and in representative Youth teams. Rankin gets his chance owing to Clinton being unfit. His inclusion allows Moore to cross over to right-back, which is undoubtedly his best position. Rankin has been playing extremely well in the Central League eleven all season and has earned his big chance."* (4)

Marjory, his sister, recalls, *"I came in for my tea and there were two photographers from the Liverpool Echo taking George's photograph because he had been picked for Everton."*

George's debut did not turn out as well as he might have hoped. Everton lost 2-1 to Derby before a crowd of 37,757 and his performance was mixed:

> *"George Rankin ... seemed a little overawed by the occasion, and did not distinguish himself quite as much as he might have done had he been less anxious. On the other hand, he did nothing very wrong and improved as time went on. He will come "to head" in due course. It is asking a lot of a young part-timer to hit the high spots right away."* (5)

Wainwright scored a consolation goal for Everton with four minutes left. McIntosh, the Everton centre-forward, had missed a penalty earlier. Just before the final whistle, Wainwright, one of Everton's forwards, was carried off with two broken bones in his right leg and missed the rest of the season.

At a meeting of the Club's Board of Directors on Tuesday, 12th December, one of the Directors, Jack Sharp, reported that Stevenson, the left-back of Rhyl, *"was an excellent kicker with both feet and a good header, but was not a good positional player"*. (6) It was agreed that Cliff Britton, Everton's manager, should watch him the following day against South Liverpool. This was the very same Jack Sharp, who had been George's grandfather's main rival for the outside-right position at Everton almost fifty years earlier. Britton reported at the next Board meeting on Monday, 19th December, that, having seen Stevenson play against South Liverpool, he thought that George was *"a better proposition"*. Jack Sharp agreed.

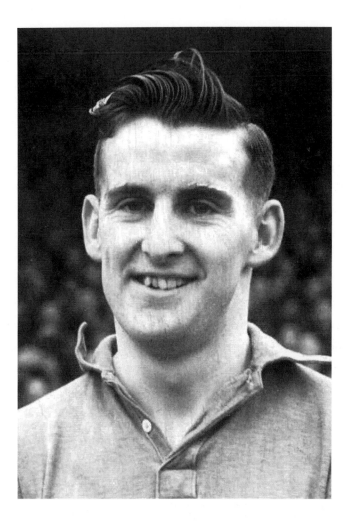

George Rankin about the time that he made his
debut for the Everton first team.

George then played eight consecutive games at left-back in the first team, beginning with Huddersfield, away on Saturday, 16th December. George would seem to have made a better impression in his second game. According to the match report, *"Rankin was playing with all the confidence in the world against McKenna (Huddersfield's right winger)"* (7)

Everton's 2-1 win got them off the foot of the table with 14 points from 22 games, one point above Sheffield Wednesday, who had played a game less. Chelsea were third from bottom, with the same number of points as Everton, but with a better goal average and having played two games less. Coming into a side that was fighting to get clear of the relegation zone was hardly the best time for George to try to establish himself in the first team.

Everton claimed a much-needed 3-1 victory over Newcastle at Goodison Park in George's next game on Saturday, 23rd December before 40,000 spectators. They then took three points out of four in back-to-back games against Burnley, with George at left-back in both matches. They beat Burnley 1-0 at Goodison Park on Christmas Day, giving the home crowd of 40,000 much to cheer about, and then drew 1-1 at Turf Moor on Boxing Day before another large crowd of more than 38,000.

Their fourth game in seven days, against West Bromwich Albion at the Hawthorns, on Saturday, 30th December, brought another 1-0 victory. The pitch was hard underneath, and covered by an inch of snow – today, games are not played under such treacherous conditions. Players found it difficult to keep their feet and to gauge their passes as the snow held the ball up, and *"there were times when Jones and Rankin were beaten by the eccentric bounce of the ball."* (8)

George was beginning to find his feet in the first team. He *"was having a good game (against West Bromwich Albion), and that he was determined to place the ball to advantage was well demonstrated by his display of annoyance when passing it inaccurately for once."*

In his "Notes" in the Liverpool Echo on Wednesday, 3rd January 1951, Ranger was full of praise for George. He wrote, *"Rankin is the only Evertonian who is not training with the rest of the staff. A part-time player only – he is serving an apprenticeship to engineering – Rankin does his training in the evenings. It says much for his ability and stamina that he has put up such splendid performances under the circumstances but football, of course, is in his blood, handed down by his grandfather and father. Should he take to the game full-time, he has obviously a great future ahead."*

Everton's nine points from a possible ten saw them climb to 16th in the league of 22 teams. They had 21 points from 26 games, whilst the bottom two, Sheffield and Chelsea each had 17 points, although they had only played 25 and 23 games respectively. George must have been feeling fairly pleased with himself – he was beginning to get positive reviews and his team was climbing away from the danger of relegation.

The third round of the FA Cup was the focus of Everton's attention on Saturday, 6th January. Another win would give a further boost to their confidence, but it was not to be. Hull beat them by two goals to nil at Boothferry Park. Raich Carter, one of football's all-time greats appeared for Hull at inside-right. Apparently, for the very first time, a white ball was used in a cup-tie. The Cup defeat meant that Everton could now devote all their efforts to trying to secure their place in the First Division for another season.

George played in the next League game the following Saturday, against Stoke City at Goodison Park. Everton were outplayed before 40,000 anxious spectators, losing 3-0.

Arch-rivals Liverpool were Everton's next opponents in the League, at Anfield. For only the second time in ten post-war games, Everton came out on top, winning 2-0 and pleasing their supporters in the large crowd of almost 49,000. According to the match report, *"... Rankin and Moore had stood steadfast to the calls that had been made on them".* (9)

George was again included in the team for the next league game against Portsmouth at Fratton Park on 3rd February. Portsmouth included their Belgian signing, Gaillard, from Crystal Palace at outside-left. Despite a 6-3 defeat, Ranger commented in his Monday "Notes" that Rankin had played well.

Everton got back to their winning ways on Saturday, 17th February, with a 3-0 victory over Chelsea at Goodison Park before some 31,000 spectators. It would seem that George had posed the biggest threat to the Everton goalkeeper. He gave *"a passback which swerved almost out of Sagar's reach, (giving) his side a heart attack"*. (10) Sagar had celebrated his 41st birthday just eleven days earlier, having been with Everton for 22 years.

Another home victory followed in midweek, on Wednesday 28th February, when Everton defeated Fulham 1-0. George played a key role in this win, making two goal line clearances.

He played in the next league game against Bolton at Burnden Park on Saturday, 3rd March. Everton were beaten 2-0 before a crowd of 32,782. Despite that defeat, Everton looked well-placed to avoid relegation. They lay 16th in the table with 27 points from 32 games, whilst Sheffield Wednesday and Aston Villa were in the relegation spots, with 19 points from 31 games and 20 points from 30 games respectively.

On Saturday, 10th March, George turned out in his final game for Everton before being called up the following Thursday for his National Service. The team managed a 0-0 draw against Charlton at Goodison Park, watched by 31,066 spectators.

According to his brother, Billy, George had born a grudge against his father for refusing to sign the papers in 1948 to allow him to become a full-time professional. Having carried out his father's wishes and completed his apprenticeship, he was far from happy when, seemingly having established himself in Everton's first team, he was then called up for his National Service.

It was reported in the Liverpool Echo on Tuesday, 13th March that Everton's manager, Cliff Britton, had been watching Jock Lindsay, the left-back for Glasgow Rangers. In fact, they signed him later that week for £9500, in time to take George's place for the next two games, a 3-0 defeat by Manchester United at Old Trafford and a loss to Blackpool at Goodison Park by two goals to nil.

However, George, now based at Blandford in Dorset, was released by the Army to take his place for Everton in their next League game, against Spurs at White Hart Lane on 31st March. Watched by a large crowd of 46,615, he could not prevent Everton's third defeat in a row, by a 3-0 scoreline. George was injured when he was hit on the side of his face by the heavy ball, but was able to resume after treatment.

He played in the next three games, the first of which was a 1-1 draw against Wolves at Goodison Park on 7th April, when Everton scored their first goal for seven games. In the next fixture, Everton lost 4-0 to Sunderland at Roker Park; this was followed by a 2-1 defeat by Aston Villa at Goodison Park on 21st April. From looking a fairly safe bet to avoid the drop just over a month earlier, Everton were now next to bottom of the league with two games left. They had 30 points from 40 games, whilst Chelsea were bottom with 26 points from 39 games and Sheffield Wednesday were immediately above Everton with a better goal average, having played the same number of games.

Everton had to win their two remaining games, both of which were away from home, to have any chance of avoiding relegation. George was not given the chance to help them stay up as he was dropped for both matches and replaced by Jock Lindsay, the recent signing from Glasgow Rangers.

In their penultimate game, Everton went some way to saving themselves with a 1-0 win over Derby County before a very small crowd of just over 9,000. The final game on Saturday, 5th May, was against one of their fellow-strugglers, Sheffield Wednesday. More than 41,303 spectators witnessed Everton's heaviest defeat of the season, a 6-0 thrashing. The result doomed Everton to relegation to the Second Division, but the win was not enough to save Sheffield Wednesday from the drop. Chelsea scraped home with the same number of points as the two relegated clubs, but had a superior goal average.

It was a season of ups and downs for George. He had played 19 League and Cup games for the first team. He started off with some average performances, but then settled down and received a number of excellent reviews, only to be dropped for the last two games of the season and see his team relegated to Division Two. However, he could still be well-pleased with himself. He had just turned 21 years of age and he had broken into the first team whilst still a part-time professional, training in the evenings. It would remain to be seen, however, just how much his football career would be interrupted by his National Service.

1951-52 Season

The Everton players reported back for training on 18th July to prepare themselves for what was hoped to be an immediate return to the First Division. The Club's public practice match took place at Goodison Park three weeks later on Saturday afternoon, 11th August 1951. George was not included in either team for the kick-off, but did make an appearance in the second half for the Whites. The teams were:

Blues: Sagar; Moore, Lindsay; Grant, Jones, Farrell; Fielding, Potts, Catterick, Parker, Eglington.

Whites: O'Neill; Clinton, Saunders; Donovan, Falder, Lello; McNamara, Hampson, McIntosh, Buckle, Easthope.

The first half, which ended 0-0, provided little excitement for the crowd of just over 4,000 supporters. Several changes were made at the interval. For the Whites (the Reserves), Leyland took the place of O'Neill, George came on for Saunders, Forshaw for Folder and Hickson for McIntosh. In the Blues team, Lindley replaced Jones at centre-half and Gibson came in for Fielding. The final score was 1-0 for the Blues.

At the Board of Directors' meeting on 18th September, the manager, Cliff Britton, expressed his honest opinion that the team was not good enough to win promotion that season. As a result, it was his intention to experiment with junior players. The Board agreed to this, but did not rule out the acquisition of new players if the opportunity arose.

George appeared in only two first team games that season. The first occasion was away to Swansea on Saturday, 10th November, when he came in for Lindsay, who was suffering from a pulled muscle and had failed a fitness test on the Friday morning. Everton won 2-0 and George received two mentions in the match report:

"A temporary threat by Eglington was disposed off, then Rankin conceded a corner which Jones cleared."

"Neither side had produced play of the first half quality, but matters livened up when Rankin blocked a Turnbull shot, and from his clearance Eglington and Hickson raced through for Eglington to shoot badly with a difficult chance." (11)

His second game was on 22nd March 1952 against Bury at Gigg Lane, when Everton had *"to make a last minute alteration owing to the indisposition of Lindsay, the left full-back, who was down with a heavy cold. He arrived at the ground, but it was obvious he was unfit, so that the manager Cliff Britton had to make a quick journey to pick up George Rankin to take Lindsay's place."* (12) Everton lost 1-0.

Unfortunately, manager Britton's assessment at the beginning of the season proved to be correct. Everton were not promoted, finishing in seventh place in the league with 44 points, nine and seven points behind Sheffield Wednesday and Cardiff City respectively, the two promoted sides.

Despite his National Service, George still managed to play in more than half of the Central League fixtures. The mini-derby at Anfield on 9th February 1952, was watched by 17,800 spectators, most of whom had turned up to see the Liverpool centre-forward Albert Stubbins, who was returning from injury. The game was drawn 1-1 and it was reported that *"Rankin and Saunders were two splendid defenders".*(13) Everton Reserves finished runners-up in the Central League behind Wolves.

George also played against Liverpool in a strong Everton team in the Liverpool Senior Cup Final at Goodison Park on Tuesday, 29th April. Everton lost to an 89th minute goal before a crowd of 44,000. The teams were:

Everton: O'Neill; Moore, Rankin; Farrell, Jones, Lello; McNamara, Fielding, Hickson, Parker, Eglington.
Liverpool: Ashcroft, Williams, Lambert; Heyden, W. H. Jones, Brierley; Payne, Baron, Stubbins, Smith, J. M. Jones.

In addition, George represented the British Army that season. One of their games, in October 1951 at Aldershot, was an annual fixture against Everton.

The Army team, which consisted entirely of young players with Football League experience, was:

Anderson (Leicester); Banks (Bolton), Rankin (Everton); Glen (Aberdeen), Twentyman (Carlisle), Fenton (Blackpool); Jackson (Leyton), Taylor (Barnsley), Smith (Chelsea), Cameron (QPR), Parry (Derby).

A number of these players went on to have illustrious football careers. Archie Glen became captain of Aberdeen and was capped twice by Scotland; Ewan Fenton made 195 League and Cup appearances for Blackpool and was a member of the famous 1953 FA Cup winning team; Tommy Taylor, claimed by some to be England's greatest ever centre-forward, was one of the eight Manchester United players, who died in the 1958 Munich air disaster; and Bobby Smith, also an England international, left Chelsea for Spurs in 1958 and was a member of the Spurs' double winning team in the early 1960s.

George also represented the Army in a 2-2 draw against Ireland at Windsor Park on 12th September 1951, watched by a crowd of 14,000. The teams were:

Ireland: Russell (Linfield); Graham (Doncaster Rovers), McMichael (Newcastle United); Dickson (Chelsea), McCabe, capt. (Leeds United), Cush (Glenavon); Hughes (Bolton Wanderers), McGarry (Cliftonville), Smyth (Wolverhampton Wanderers), Harris (Blackburn Rovers).
British Army: Anderson (Leicester City); Banks (Bolton Wanderers), Rankin (Everton); Glen, capt. (Aberdeen), Marchi (Tottenham Hotspur), Fenton (Blackpool); Jackson (Leyton Orient), Uphill (Tottenham Hotspur), Smith (Chelsea), Taylor (Barnsley), Hooper (West Ham United).

George's son, Mark, recalled his father telling him about playing for the British Army against the French Army, "*I know he nearly got lynched. The Brits had been warned to go easy on the French as they didn't like the physical challenges. So, what did Dad do, a hard tackle!*"

Despite being called up for his National Service towards the end of the previous season, George would probably have expected to play more than two first team games. It was not to be as Jock Lindsay had made the left-back position his own. Perhaps, representing the Army was some consolation!

At the beginning of that season, Jack Peart took "a peep into the future" in his article in an August 1951 edition of the Sunday Pictorial. Reviewing the careers of 12 players who had broken into their club's first team the year before, Peart wrote the following of George: *"Fourth member of the Rankin family to play for Everton and, at twenty, this talented full-back looks likely to develop into the best. Grandfather Bruce was a winger, father Bill and uncle George were bucks."* Others included in the list of 12 future stars were Jeff Whitefoot and Mark Jones of Manchester United, Bobby Robson of Fulham and Peter Broadbent of Wolves.

1952-53 Season

Everton were again hoping for promotion to the First Division and were eager to get off to a good start.

The Club's public trial was held on Saturday, 16th August 1952 at Goodison Park. George, who was still in the Army, was included at left-back in the Whites, the probable Central League side. The teams were:

Blues: O'Neill; Clinton, Lindsay; Farrell, Jones, Lello; Harris, Fielding, Hickson, Parker, Eglington.
Whites: Leyland; Moore, Rankin; Donovan, Woods, Grant; Gibson, Potts, Lewis, Cummins, Buckle.

There was a sensational start to the game. Inside two minutes, the Whites took the lead through Buckle, who picked up a short pass and smashed it into the net. The Blues got the equaliser one minute from the interval and scored three more in the second half to win by four goals to one; Fielding scored a hat-trick.

George started off in the Reserves that season. The side took seven points from a possible ten in their first five games, including a victory over a Manchester United Reserve team that contained a number of players who would later become household names – Ray Wood, Bill Foulkes, Jackie Blanchflower, Dennis Viollet and David Pegg – as a result of the Munich air disaster.

On 6th February 1958, an airliner carrying players and backroom staff of Manchester United, plus a number of journalists and supporters, crashed in a blizzard on its third attempt to take off from Munich airport. United were returning from Belgrade where they had just beaten Red Star Belgrade in the European Cup and had stopped off at Munich for re-fuelling. Twenty-three of the forty-four passengers on board the aircraft lost their lives, including David Pegg, but Wood, Foulkes, Blanchflower and Viollet all survived.

Everton team 1952-53

Left to right, back row: A. McNamara, E. Moore, D. Hickson, J. O'Neill, J.W. Parker, T. J. Clinton, G. Rankin, T.E. Jones. Front row: J.S. Lindsay, J.A. Grant, A.W. Fielding, C.P. Lello, P.D. Farrell, E.W. Buckle, T.J. Eglington, D. Donovan, H. Cooke (Trainer) © Mirrorpix

George's first appearance that season for the full Everton team was against Doncaster at Goodison Park on 27th September. He replaced Lindsay who had failed a fitness test. Everton won 7-1, with Eglington scoring five of the goals and Parker getting the other two. That was the first time an Everton winger had scored five in a Football League game. The last occasion Everton had scored seven times in a League match was on 3rd March 1937, when they defeated Leeds United 7-1 at Goodison Park.

Lindsay was still unfit the following Saturday, so George kept his place against Swansea away from home. Swansea had never beaten Everton, so the players and fans were anticipating another victory. But, with three minutes of the game to go, Everton were down 2-1, and then centre-forward, Dave Hickson, secured a welcome draw with a well-taken goal.

George returned to the Reserves on Saturday, 11th October against Bury Reserves at Gigg Lane, as Lindsay was fit again. The Reserves beat Bury 3-1, but George had to leave the field for some minutes with a head injury.

On Wednesday, 22nd October, George turned out against Everton for the Army's Western Command side at Goodison Park. The teams were:

Everton: Leyland; Clinton, Anderton; Donovan, Woods, Melville; Hampson, Farrell, Hickson, Cummins, Buckle.

Western Command: Webster (Derby County); Banks (Bolton Wanderers), Rankin (Everton); Newman (Birmingham), Twentyman (Carlisle), Clayton (Blackburn Rovers); Bevans (Stoke City), Cameron (QPR), Meadows (Manchester City), Hodgkisson (WBA), Nutt (Coventry City).

Everton won 3-0. Heavy rain kept the crowd to less than 2,000, but in the Liverpool Echo, Ranger wrote that the game was *"one of the most entertaining exhibitions I have seen this season"*. (14)

George returned to the first team on Saturday, 8th November, as Lindsay was unfit once more. Everton were lying in ninth place in the Second Division with 15 points from 14 games and were hopeful of improving their position. The game, played at Goodison Park before almost 40,000 spectators, looked to be heading for a goalless draw, when Rotherham deservedly took the lead in the 84th min-ute. A free kick, given against George for obstruction, was crossed into the box and headed goalwards by one of the Rotherham forwards. Everton's goalkeeper, O'Neill, could only push the header into the path of Rotherham's inside-right Shaw, who smashed the ball into the net from six yards.

In the match report, there was criticism of Everton's failure to last the whole 90 minutes: *"Against West Ham, they were well on top for 45 minutes and struggling desperately in the second half. The same thing happened at Fulham. Against Rother-ham on Saturday it was a similar story."* And, on the performance of individual players, the report continued: *"Only O'Neill, Jones, Grant and Farrell played up to anything like their best form. Jones was outstanding. Clinton was the best of the backs, but Rankin had a bad day."* (15)

Everton had had a run of eight games without defeat at the beginning of the season, but had now taken only two points from the last four matches and were slipping down the table. Whilst it was still early days, some reports were already pessimistic about Everton's possible return to the First Division.

Despite his *"bad day"*, George played the following Saturday against Plym-outh Argyle at Home Park. Everton had been the first club to play at Home Park following Plymouth's entry into the Second Division 22 years earlier. Everton's goalkeeper Ted Sagar had played in that game in 1930. A few weeks earlier, on Sunday, 26th October, Sagar broke the league record of service with one club. He had signed for Everton on 26th March 1929, and was still a player more than 23 years later. The record had previously been held by Robert Crompton of Black-burn Rovers. Everton's directors resolved that Sagar's service should be suitably and substantially rewarded at the conclusion of the football season.

Everton had beaten Plymouth 3-2 in 1930, but history was not to repeat itself; on this occasion they lost 1-0. It would seem that contentious refereeing decisions are not just a feature of the modern game. The Liverpool Echo's match reporter laid the blame for Everton's defeat at the door of the referee: *"And to think that this grand side should be beaten by that remarkable goal five minutes from time. Referee Jackson had blown his whistle for a foul several seconds before Neil Dougall netted with that bow-at-a-venture shot from fully 40 yards. Having heard the whistle, the*

Everton defenders made no move to tackle Dougall but the referee refused to listen to their protests. Plymouth directors agreed after the match they were equally as surprised by the goal award as the Everton players." (16)

However, the match could have been saved; the Everton full-back Tommy Clinton missed a penalty. George obviously had a much better game that weekend. The match report went on: *"Clinton and Rankin had a formidable job on hand against the speedy Plymouth wingers but they stood up to the test manfully."*

Lindsay was still injured the following week, so George retained his place against Leeds United at Goodison Park on 22nd November. John Charles, who became one of the best-known footballers of his era, was centre-forward for Leeds. In the first half, Williams, the Leeds left winger, was carried off on a stretcher following a tackle by Everton's right-back Clinton, with what proved to be a broken leg. The score at that time was 2-2 and, as replacements were not allowed in those days, Leeds had to carry on with ten men. However, Everton failed to take advantage of their numerical superiority in the second half, the game ending in a draw.

Lindsay was fit the following week, so George was consigned to the Reserve team once again.

On Wednesday, 3rd December, he represented the Army's Western Command against the Northern Command in the Inter-Command final. The teams were:

Western Command: Webster (Derby); Banks (Bolton), Rankin (Everton); Newman (Birmingham), Twentyman (Carlisle), Clayton (Blackburn); Len Allchurch (Swansea), Cameron (QPR), Meadows (Manchester City), Simpson (Huddersfield), Nutt (Coventry City).
Northern Command: Middleton (Newcastle); Barnard (Middlesbrough), Cameron (Dumbarton); Rawlings (WBA), Porteous (Hull City), Fenton (Blackpool); Kay (Barnsley), Wood (Barnsley), Anderson (Scottish amateur international), Waldock (Coventry City), Frear (Huddersfield).

Western Command won 4-1. They had scored three goals by the interval, decided to rest on their laurels and allowed the North to come into the game. The stars of the Western Command side were Twentyman, Banks, Allchurch and Nutt.

George did not appear again for the Everton first team until 21st February, when Everton's opponents at Goodison Park were Swansea City. Everton were 13th in the League, with Swansea two places below them.

Everton were on the attack for 80 percent of the game, but they just could not score. They did have the ball in the net twice but neither was allowed to count. Everton had so many opportunities that they should have won the game easily despite these two disallowed goals. However, tempers flared towards the end of the game. Cummins, the Everton inside-right, and Thomas of Swansea became involved in a wresting match, with Farrell and Buckle of Everton trying to separate them. Both Cummins and Thomas were sent off with twelve minutes of the game left. The 39,608 spectators were not very pleased with Everton's performance or with the referee and there was a lot of booing at the end of the match.

George did not play in the FA Cup quarter-final on the following Saturday, the 28th February, when Everton beat Aston Villa 1-0 at Goodison Park. Everton were drawn against Bolton in the semi-final, to be played at Maine Road on 21st March.

It would seem that the players, in those days, had quite a say in their training, for Cup-ties at least. The Liverpool Echo of 5th March reported that: *"Whether Everton will undertake special training for the semi-final against Bolton depends entirely on the players themselves. They will vote on the matter and if in favour the board and manager are certain to add their blessing to the proposal."*

Two days later, according to the paper: *"Everton players have voted for a week's seaside training and relaxation prior to the semi-final. They will go to Brighton after the home game against Leicester on Saturday and remain there until next Saturday morning, when they journey to London for the game against West Ham. The last week before the Maine Road game will be spent in normal training."* (17) George was not included in the party to travel to Brighton.

On 21st March, Everton lost the FA Cup semi-final by four goals to three in a game of two halves. Everton were down 4-0 after 41 minutes, during which time Everton's centre-forward, Dave Hickson, had been off the field injured for 15 minutes after a heavy blow to the face and he was dazed to some extent for the rest of the game. Just before half-time, Everton had the chance to get a goal back, when they were awarded a penalty for a handball; Clinton shot wide of the goal. Things looked a little brighter within a minute of the re-start when Parker made it 4-1. With about ten minutes of the game to go, Everton had pulled two further goals back, through Farrell and a second by Parker. Bolton were then an anxious and worried team, reduced to kicking the ball anywhere. The final whistle went with Bolton hanging on for grim death. But for the penalty miss, the Blues would have been on level terms and would have achieved one of the greatest fight backs in cup history. So near and yet so far!

The semi-final had clearly taken a great deal out of both the supporters and the players. For the game against Fulham at Goodison Park just four days later, only 10,474 spectators, the lowest home crowd for many years, turned up to watch and only five of the Cup team turned out. George was included at left-back. Both teams came out slowly, side by side, wearing black armbands and stood in silence to the memory of Queen Mary, who had died the day before, on 24th March 1953. Although Everton scored first, they had then to come back twice from a goal behind to earn a 3-3 draw, which was not too bad a performance in the circumstances.

George, who had signed as a full-time player earlier in the week following completion of his National Service, kept his place in the first team for the game on Saturday, 28th March, away to Rotherham. Everton were missing four of their semi-final team – goalkeeper O'Neill and both fullbacks through injury and inside-forward Cummins, who was suspended following his dismissal against Swansea on 21st February. As at Goodison on Wednesday, the teams wore black armbands and stood in silence in memory of Queen Mary.

Everton were sixth from bottom of the Second Division; Rotherham, with four points more than Everton, were five places higher, but had played two games more. The game ended 2-2 and George seemed to have had a decent game. According to the match report, *"Everton's defence was very steady and the three lads who filled the rearguard positions all did extremely well,"* and *"Donovan and Rankin stuck to their guns well during Rotherham's heaviest pressure"*. (18)

Everton then had back-to-back games against Huddersfield Town over the

Easter holiday. Huddersfield, who were 2-1 victors at Goodison Park on Saturday, 4th April, then suffered one of their heaviest defeats, by eight goals to two, on Easter Monday.

George did not appear in either of those games. However, he was selected to play against Leeds United at Elland Road on Saturday, 11th April. Everton, playing in an uncharacteristic black and white strip, lost 2-0. Writing in the Liverpool Echo on Monday, 13th April, Ranger commented that the *"Everton-Leeds game was as tame as a game of croquet"*.

George played in Everton's final game of the season on Saturday, 25th April against Birmingham City at St Andrews before a crowd of 17,000. Everton played in black and white again. Just before the interval, with the score 1-1, Everton's right-back, Clinton, was struck in the head with a vicious drive and had to leave the field. When he returned 20 minutes later, taking up the outside-right position, Everton were leading 2-1. However, they eventually succumbed 4-2. It was a hard game with plenty of incidents; Everton never gave up and had City worried at times. On Monday, 27th April, Stork summed up, *"a grand game to send people away regretting that the season was at an end"*. (19)

Everton finished 16th in the League. Sheffield United were champions and promoted with Huddersfield Town.

On 30th April, Everton announced that they were retaining 30 full-time professionals, including George.

Two days later, Bolton and Blackpool met in an all-Lancashire FA Cup Final at Wembley, in what is one of the most famous finals of all time. Blackpool won 4-3, scoring two goals in the last two minutes to snatch victory from Bolton, victors over Everton by a similar score in the semi-final.

Ted Sagar finished his playing career at the end of the season, taking up an offer to work with the ground staff. He was presented with an inscribed gold watch at the Club's AGM to mark his long and successful playing career, and he received a cheque for £1000 at the following season's public practice match.

1953-54 Season

George, a keen golfer, was one of 13 Everton players participating in the North West Regional competition of the Professional Footballers' Golf Championship on Monday, 10th August at the Old Links, St Anne's, near Blackpool. Altogether, 82 competitors took part and those returning the 14 best gross scores went through to the final. George was not among them.

Everton's public trial took place at Goodison Park on Wednesday evening, 12th August. It was a case of the senior side v the Reserves and the teams were:

Blues: O'Neill; Clinton, Donovan; Farrell, Jones, Lello; Buckle, Cummins, Hickson, Parker, Eglington.
Whites: Leyland; Moore, Rankin; Grant, Forshaw, Melville; McNamara, Potts, Saunders, Stewart, Easthope.

Lindsay, who was nursing a slight ankle injury, was the only absentee from the senior side. Donovan took his place in the Blues team, so it was quite clear that George had slipped down the "pecking order". The Blues won, but it was obvious they were not playing all out with the start of the season only days away.

Two days after the public trial, Everton, somewhat surprisingly, transferred George Cummins, their 22 year old Irish inside forward, to Luton Town for a fee of over £10,000. He had been included in the Blues team for the trial, and had made 29 senior appearances during the previous season, albeit without scoring.

Everton's first three games of the season were away from home against Nottingham Forrest, Luton Town and Hull City. With two draws and a win in those games and a home victory against Hull on Tuesday, 25th August, Everton had taken six points from a possible eight. Not a bad start!

The next game was at Goodison Park against Oldham Athletic, promoted from the Third Division, on Saturday, 29th August. Jones was unfit, so Donovan moved from left-back to centre-half, with George filling in at left-back in what proved to be his only first team appearance of the season.

After 52 minutes, Oldham went in front through a goal scored by Adams, the Oldham right-winger. However, Adams *"should never have been allowed by*

Rankin to get his shot in, but having managed that, it should have been saved by Leyland, who seemed taken by surprise and had hardly moved when it was in the net." (20) However, George later made amends for his partial mistake *"by heading away off the line and then breasting another ball down when a goal seemed certain".* (21) Parker equalised three minutes after Adams' goal, and then completed his hat trick within nine minutes to give Everton a 3-1 victory. A crowd of 49,523, much larger than for most First Division fixtures, watched the game in damp and depressing conditions.

Jones was fit to take his place at centre-half for the next League game against Bury, with Donovan reverting to left-back in place of George, who returned to play in the Reserves. One of his first games was the mini-derby at Goodison Park on Wednesday evening, 7th September, with kick-off at 6pm. The Everton team was:

O'Neill; Tansey, Rankin; Grant, Woods, Melville; Mayers, Potts, Wainwright, Stewart and Easthope.

Everton won 2-0 and *"were good value for their victory over their rivals from across the park in a Central League game, which attracted close on 9000 spectators".* (22) Easthope scored two headed goals for Everton.

That October, Torquay bid £2000 for the transfer of George, despite being told that the asking price was £2500 following their initial enquiry. Everton accepted Torquay's offer provided the Club received 50% of any fee over £2000 if George was subsequently transferred, otherwise the fee would be £2500. Torquay agreed to the transfer terms, but George refused to move. (23)

On Saturday, 16th January 1954, Everton Reserves won a needle game against Derby Country Reserves at the Baseball Ground by two goals to one. Before the game, Derby were top of the Central League, Everton were in third place with two points less, whilst Burnley had a point more than Everton in second position.

A few weeks later, the Liverpool Echo included an analysis of the performance of the Everton Reserve side, which was making just as strong a bid for the Central League championship as the senior team was for promotion. At that time,

Everton Reserves were second in the League, level on points with Wolves, but with a slightly inferior goal average.

> *"While sustained League and Cup interest in the senior eleven has tended to push the central league team out of the limelight, the latter is an extremely important part of the Club's organisation. Obviously, it is upon these players that Everton will rely – almost exclusively if their determination not to go into the transfer market remains – for future reinforcements for the first team. For that reason, it is encouraging to see the reserves justifying the long term policy to which Everton have been devoting themselves over recent years.*
>
> *Considering that the Central League side has been very largely used by manager Britton as an experimental avenue – no fewer than 36 players have been utilised to fill 30 fixtures – this record is all the more praiseworthy for the players have not had anything like the same chance to become as thoroughly acquainted with one another as the seniors."* (24)

The average age of the players used in the Reserve team was around 21, with the youngest at 17 and a number of 18 and 19 year olds. Many were in their early 20s and had nearly five years professional service so were not lacking experience if called upon for the senior side.

To secure the Central League Championship, Everton Reserves just needed one point from their final two games, against Manchester United Reserves away on 24th April and Newcastle Reserves at home two days later. They did it with a game to spare, managing a 1-1 draw against the Manchester side.

The first team was promoted to the First Division as runners-up, losing out as champions to Leicester on goal average, and beating Blackburn Rovers to second place by a single point. Local rivals Liverpool were relegated to the Second Division.

George was among the 21 players used by Everton in their fight for promotion, but he would have been very disappointed to have played only the one game.

On Tuesday evening, 30th March 1954, Everton played Southport at Haig Avenue in the semi-final of the Liverpool Senior Cup. While Southport fielded their full League team, Everton sent their strongest Central League side, which included eight men with first team experience. George was among them and he and his full-back partner, Moore, *"took the eye"*. (25) Everton just proved to be too good for Southport, reaching the final of the Cup with a 2-1 win. They put out their first team in the final on Monday, 3rd May, overcoming Liverpool 2-0.

The Everton Reserve team with the Central League Championship Cup won for Season 1953-54. Left to right, back row: T.G. Watson (Assistant Trainer), E. Moore, J. Tansey, M. Woods, H.K. Leyland, I. Melville, T.J. Clinton, H. Potts. Front row: A. McNamara, R. Saunders, J.A. Grant, G. Lewis, J. Harris, G. Rankin. Courtesy of The Everton Collection Charitable Trust, Reference 796EFC/26/1/250.

On the day of the Liverpool Senior Cup-Final, Everton announced their retained list of 24 full-time professionals, six part-time professionals and eight players who were on National Service. George was among the full-time players.

George, along with Hickson, Parker, Moore, Lewis and Jim Tansey, was awarded a benefit payment in recognition of his loyalty, having spent five years at the Club. The maximum benefit payable was £750. George was awarded £600, which, after tax had been deducted, amounted to £421, worth more than £14,000 today. (26)

1954-55 Season

The usual public trial took place at Goodison Park on Saturday, 14th August 1954, before 10,751 spectators. The teams were:

> **Blues:** O'Neill, Moore, Clinton; Farrell, Jones, Lello; Wainwright, Fielding, Hickson, Parker, Eglington.
>
> **Whites:** Leyland; Tansey, Rankin; Grant, Woods, Melville; McNamara, Potts, Saunders, Lewis, Buckle.

Lindsay, one of George's rivals for the left-back position, had broken his leg towards the end of the previous season and was unable to take part in the trial. The break was a severe one and his leg was still in plaster. The Blues won 3-0, but in his report on the match, Ranger wrote: *"It was an entertaining game, productive of some nice football when the ball was kept on the ground, but as a guide to Everton's future possibilities it was no more informative than the usual run of such games. The acid test will come later.* (27)

The 1954 World Cup had been played in Switzerland during the summer. West Germany emerged as world champions with a 3-2 victory over Hungary in the final. Cliff Britton, the Everton manager, was not sure whether the English fans would appreciate the type of football, *"sometimes played almost farcically at a standstill"* seen at the competition. He was of the opinion that, *"the cut-and-thrust excitements of a good League match or cup-tie will still compel capacity attendances, irrespective of whether games contain the pattern-weavings of such sides as Hungary and the Austrians. The incisive tackling of British half-backs, adds charm to the British way and purpose. The public will follow a team which plays attractively, whether they win the championship or not".* (28)

Everton got off to a flying start on their return to the First Division. After four games, they were top of the League, equal with Sunderland, with four wins from their first five games.

Having won the Central League Championship the previous season, Everton Reserves played in the annual match between the Central League champions and a Central League representative side at Goodison Park on Wednesday, 22nd September 1954. Everton Reserves were playing great football and had made a strong start to the season. The teams selected for the challenge match were:

Everton Reserves: Leyland, Tansey, Rankin; Grant, Woods, Melville; Gibson, Potts, Saunders, Lewis, Buckle.

Central League representative side: Dwyer (Wolves); Bourne (Stoke), Batty (Newcastle Utd); Gibson (Manchester Utd), Mattinson (PNE), Crowe (Aston Villa); Stephenson (Burnley), McAnearney (Sheffield Wednesday), Carter (WBA), Stevens (Bolton), Acourt (Liverpool).

On the eve of the game, Stork wrote: *"Outside the First and Second Divisions, the Central League is recognised as one of the best in the country and so it should be for it is the "nursery" for the senior sides."* (29)

Today's managers do not see the Central League in the same light. They tend to loan promising young players to other clubs to gain first team experience and further encourage their development. The Central League does not provide the challenge that it did in the 1950s.

The game did not live up to Stork's expectations. In his match report, he wrote: *"Many managers and club officials were present to see if there was anyone who would interest them, but there were few shining stars. At times, there were dull and unattractive moments and one reason was an injury to Potts, who carried on to the interval although under a handicap."* (30)

Ever since the inauguration of the match between a Central League representative XI and the Central League champions, it had always been won by the title holders. That season's game was an exception. Everton were beaten by a solitary goal scored by inside forward McAnearney a minute from the interval. Everton had been the better side before the Rest scored, twice hitting the woodwork. Potts, who had been injured, did not appear after the break, Eddie Thomas taking his place.

Stork thought George *"had an excellent first half when he practically blotted little Anders out of the game, despite the fact that the Manchester City winger was full of tricks and pace".* Anders must have replaced Stephenson of Burnley, who was the original choice on the right wing.

Medal presented to George Rankin for playing in the Everton Reserve team against the Central League representative side on 22nd September 1954.

The senior side had adapted exceptionally well in their first weeks in the First Division, losing only two of their first nine games. According to Peter Farrell, Everton's captain, *"the main difference between the First and Second Divisions is that whereas the pace is a shade faster in the top sphere, the tackling is a bit keener in the lower division".* (31)

At a pre-match kick about before Everton's game against Leicester at Goodison Park on 11th September, a young boy had gone on to the pitch and approached an un-named Everton player for his autograph. The player in question refused and the incident was brought to the attention of the Club by one of its supporters as the player's action was thought to be in bad taste. In his Liverpool Echo column on 23rd September, Peter Farrell answered the supporter's criticism, pointing out that in most clubs' *"pavilions"* there is a notice asking players to refrain from signing autographs on the playing field. In his view, this was *"a good idea"* as there would be chaos if hundreds of enthusiastic youngsters were to swarm across the field looking for players' signatures.

Meanwhile, George was a regular at left-back in the Reserves until Saturday, 6th November when he got his chance in the senior side once again, against Portsmouth at Fratton Park. Everton had released four first team players – O'Neill, Donovan, Farrell and Eglington – to play for Eire against Norway that same day. This meant that, for the first time for 21 consecutive games, Everton had to make changes to their defence. Leyland came in for O'Neill in goal, Moore moved over to right-back to make way for George, and Grant replaced Farrell at right-half.

Portsmouth were unbeaten at home, dropping only two points in draws against Wolves and Sunderland. Portsmouth's main threats were Harris and Gordon on the right flank; they had scored 14 of Portsmouth's 24 goals between them. So, George was warned. Everton paid the penalty for releasing their four Eire internationals, losing 5-0. Ranger wrote: *"Even had the Blues been at full strength, it is doubtful whether they would have saved a point against this speedy and talented side. Portsmouth on this showing are one of the most effective sides I have seen this year. Their forward line has punch and power in every link."* He went on to say that *"it would be unfair to criticise any of the reserves unduly for they all tried hard"*, and added *"it is asking a lot of any side to bring in four reserves, particularly against a team which is playing with such confidence"*. Certainly, George did not have a good game. In the first half, he had not been able to cope with the speed of Harris, and was at fault for at least one goal, the first, when he held off tackling Harris, allowing him to cross for Gordon to score with a brilliant header. However, he *"had a fair second half without ever looking likely to fathom the puzzle which Harris presented him with"*. (32)

Everton were still a commendable seventh in the League at this point of the season; Portsmouth were in fourth.

Whilst George turned out for the first team at Portsmouth, the Reserves played Bolton Reserves at Goodison Park in what turned out to be a game of incidents of an unwanted nature. When two of Everton's players, Potts and Birch, were ordered off in separate incidents, the crowd were so incensed that they stopped the game temporarily by invading the pitch. As a result, Everton were ordered to post warning notices in prominent positions at Goodison Park for a month starting on Monday, 13th December. A similar warning had also to be included in the club's programme.

Arising out of the sending off incidents, an FA Commission, sitting at Manchester on 6th December, heard the evidence of both Potts and Birch. The Commission agreed that Potts was guilty of showing dissent and decided that he be severely warned as to his future conduct. They were satisfied that Birch did not deliberately kick an opponent and decided to take no further action. In addition, Everton were ordered to pay £10 and Potts £5 towards the cost of the Commission.

By the beginning of December, the Central League side had completed 18 fixtures. But, like the first team, it had not maintained its brilliant start of 11 wins from the first 13 games. The five subsequent matches brought only four points and the side had dropped to second place, a point behind Preston North End Reserves. Bolton were in third place, with a point less than Everton, but having played a game more. The club was hopeful, at this stage of the season, of a second Central League championship.

Since being top of the League after four games, the senior side had slipped to eighth place after 21 games. Despite this, the team had done better in the first half of that campaign than in any other season since the end of the Second World War.

George was unfit for some of November at least, because it was reported at the meeting of the Board of Directors on 30th November that he was to have an X-ray for a pain in his thigh. A week later, the Board were informed on 7th December that he was still unfit.

However, George returned to the first team on New Year's Day 1955 against Preston at Deepdale because Donovan had pulled a groin muscle against Wolves over the Christmas period. The Blues had defeated Preston 2-0 at Goodison in August before a crowd of 76,839, just short of the ground record of 78,299. The attendance for the game at Deepdale was 33,881. Although the final score was 0-0, Ranger wrote in his Monday column *"I don't think one single person left the ground dissatisfied with what they saw for there was always a spice of uncertainty as to what would happen."* According to him, *"Rankin played very well against Finney, until the winger started to wander, realising that if he did not do something, there was no one else to do it."* (33)

The following Saturday saw Everton take on Southend United in the Third Round of the FA Cup at Goodison Park. At the corresponding stage of the competition in the 1946-47 season, Everton had emerged 4-2 victors over Southend and expected no less again. There was one survivor in the Southend side from that occasion – Sibley, their right winger. For Everton, Eglington had featured in every FA Cup tie since the 1946/47 season, a total of 25 games, the only Everton player to do so.

George kept his place for this game as Donovan had still not recovered from his injury. A crowd of 53,043 turned up, and must have wondered if the match would go ahead. Half-an-hour before the start, heavy fog descended on Goodison, preventing spectators from seeing the opposite touch line. Fortunately, a light breeze dispelled the fog before the start, though conditions were dull and the visibility was still not good.

Southend surprised everyone by taking the lead in three minutes through an own goal by full-back Moore. Seven minutes later, their outside-left, Bainbridge, pulled a muscle and was a passenger for the rest of the game. It took Everton until the 23rd minute to get back on level terms with a headed goal by Potts. By this time, the fog had come down again, but not as heavily as before. Despite virtually playing with ten men, Southend were unlucky to find themselves a goal down a minute before half-time, and then Hickson made the game safe with a third goal in the 66th minute. *"Rankin shaped well"* (34) over the 90 minutes.

Unlike the preparations for the FA Cup semi-final against Bolton two seasons earlier, Everton had no special training before the Southend match. In his weekly article in the Liverpool Echo on Saturday, 8th January, Peter Farrell, the Everton captain, argued that from his own experiences of going on special training, he found it had many advantages. Firstly, players were housed in a first class hotel with every convenience and no personal expense; secondly, there was a complete change from the general routine of training; and finally, training and living together helped foster team spirit. There were drawbacks, however, he added. Hotel meals, despite their excellent quality, could hardly be compared to the good old home cooking; whilst he was a good sleeper, he would far rather sleep in his own bed than in a strange one in a hotel in order to get the maximum rest necessary to keep in peak condition; and, following a week's special training, he had always found himself a little sluggish the next Saturday during the game. He was not against the idea of special training, he claimed, only that he felt it to be more beneficial to go away a fortnight before the game, and then players really felt the benefit of the change. At Everton, he was happy to say, the players always had an input regarding any decision whether they would like to go or not.

Most of the Everton side had a day's golf at Hillside Golf Club, near Southport, the Wednesday before the Southend game. Some people might ask "How can golf be good for football?" To Farrell's way of thinking, apart from the exercise and fresh air, it gave the players a break from the strenuous training and all returned to Goodison the following day raring to go.

Following the cup-tie victory, Everton's next League game, against Burnley at Goodison Park, ended in a 1-1 draw. The team was unchanged, so George appeared for the first team for the third consecutive week. It was Peter Farrell's 350th League and Cup game for Everton and, when he led the team on to the field, the crowd showed their appreciation. Harry Potts was appearing against his old club, having been transferred from Burnley to Everton for £20,000 in 1950, and Britton, Everton's manager, had once been in charge at Burnley, leading them to the FA Cup-Final and promotion to the First Division.

Goodison was covered with two inches of snow and the ground was hard underneath. However, the referee had no hesitation in pronouncing the pitch fit for play. The match would certainly not have been played today in those conditions, although the undersoil heating that the top clubs have now would probably have prevented the surface from becoming frost-ridden. Despite the top cushion of snow, the ground underneath was treacherous and, in the early minutes, the players skidded about. Everton took the lead in the 7th minute when Eglington put the ball through the middle and one of the Burnley defenders missed his kick. Fielding accepted the chance of a first time shot and the ball was in the back of the net before goalkeeper McDonald could do anything about it. It was Fielding's second goal of the season. Soon afterwards, a storm of booing arose behind the Goodison Avenue goal when Hickson fell to the ground just outside the penalty area while the ball was over on the left wing. The match reporter had not seen what happened but, from then on, the crowd booed Burnley's left-back Winton. It was obvious that he had done something to Hickson, who had picked himself up and carried on without requiring attention from the trainer. The next time Winton went to the corner flag half-a-dozen snowballs were aimed at him. He was roundly booed as he left the field at half-time.

As in the first half, the 7th minute after the break saw a goal. The referee adjudged Jones, the Everton centre-half, to have handled a cross in the penalty area. McIlroy scored from the spot. The Everton goal then had a narrow escape when a clearance by George struck Gray, but the Burnley player shot behind when he was well placed. Players continued to find it difficult to maintain their footing when they tried to turn or run with the ball. Despite the difficult conditions, George would appear to have played well. According to the match report, *"The Everton wing-halves did all that could be expected as also did Rankin, who seems now to be settling down well and to have increased in confidence."* (35)

George was selected to play in an unchanged team at Leicester the following Saturday, but the game was postponed because of the weather. The match referee travelled 4½ hours from Scunthorpe to Leicester, leaving at 6am, and took only a few minutes to decide that the game was out of the question. Large stretches of the pitch were covered with ice, some of it more than half an inch thick. The Everton team had stayed the night at a Derby hotel and received a telephone call there from the Leicester club as soon as the referee had made his decision. Altogether, 26 games were postponed. The previous Saturday 41 of the 62 fixtures in the English and Scottish Leagues had to be postponed and another three abandoned.

The fourth round cup-tie between Everton and Liverpool at Goodison Park on 29th January was an all-ticket affair with a limit of 72,000 spectators, more than 6,000 below the capacity. The decision to restrict the size of the crowd was taken in order that everyone attending could see the game without crushing and discomfort.

The early edition of the Liverpool Echo on the day of the match had a profile of each player. George's profile read:

"George Rankin, left-back – Don Donovan's recent injury has given George Rankin another senior chance, which he has grabbed avidly. Liverpool born and bred, George first came into the team at a difficult time, when relegation was a threat. National Service did not help his football career, but now that he is back in full-time training, his form is improving rapidly. He has been with the Blues as an amateur and professional for over six years. His father, grandfather and an uncle all played for Everton." (36) The teams were:

Everton: O'Neill; Moore, Rankin; Farrell, Jones, Lello; Wainwright, Fielding, Hickson, Potts, Eglington.
Liverpool: Rudham; Lambert, Moran; Saunders, Hughes, Twentyman; Jackson, Anderson, Liddell, Evans, Acourt.

Liverpool were unexpected, but worthy, winners by four goals to nil. They were two up at half-time through Liddell and Acourt, although Everton did have the ball in the net on two occasions, both efforts being disallowed. Evans scored Liverpool's third in the 57th minute, *"but much of the credit goes to Jackson, who beat Rankin and then fired a tremendously powerful oblique shot from 20 yards or so, which O'Neill caught, but could not hold, so that the inrushing Evans had the simplest of chances to put it into the net and thus maintain his record of having scored in all three Liverpool cup ties this season"*. (37) Evans headed in his second goal of the game in the 75th minute, from a *"peach of a centre"* by Jackson, *"who had a splendid day against the uncertain Rankin"*. (38)

In his column on Monday, 31st January, Ranger, who had predicted an Everton win, was clearly puzzled, *"The most mystifying thing about the game was that here was a lowly Second Division side which had not won an away match of any description for close on a year and only six out of the last 50 or more, making one of the leading First Division sides look so ordinary. Football can be a funny game."*

What made the loss harder to bear for Everton fans was that Hughes, the Liverpool centre-half, was injured seven minutes into the second half. Twenty-man took Hughes' position and Liddell moved to left-half. Though Hughes had a certain amount of nuisance value, Liverpool were clearly handicapped in attack by the enforced re-shuffle, yet still scored two goals. In the second half, the referee stopped play, while he took a bottle that had been thrown on the field to a police sergeant.

Liverpool did not progress any further in the Cup, losing 2-0 at home to Huddersfield Town on 19th February.

Everton players training at Goodison Park in preparation for an FA Cup match against Liverpool on 29th January 1955. Left to right: Eric Moore, Tommy Jones, Cyril Lello, Wally Fielding, Eddie Wainright, John Parker, Dave Hickson, Tommy Eglington, Peter Farrell, Jimmy O'Neill, George Rankin and Harry Potts.

© Mirrorpix

Donovan returned to Everton's first team against Chelsea at Goodison Park on 5th February. Everton restored some normality to their season, drawing 1-1. Everton's first team finished a respectable 11th in their first season back in Division One.

George played in just over half of the remaining Reserve games following the Liverpool Cup-tie. However, the side did not win its second successive Central League title; Manchester United Reserves were the champions.

Everton retained all its staff for the following season, with the exception of two lesser known young players, Eric Rabone and George Tansey, both of whom were given free transfers. This meant that the Club had 49 players on its books – 32 full-time, four part-time and 13 in the Armed forces. George was only offered, and accepted, a part-time contract.

Everton left on 6th May, the day before Cup-Final, for a close-season tour of Denmark, Germany and Belgium. George was not included in the party; the full-backs were Moore, Donovan and Jim Tansey.

1955-56 Season

Although George was now a part-time professional, he participated from the start in Everton's public trial on Saturday, 13th August 1955. Donovan had a groin strain and was rested in the hope that he would be fit for the first game of the season. Tansey took his place in the Blues, which was effectively the first team. The teams for the trial were:

Blues: Leyland; Moore, Tansey; Farrell, Jones, Lello; Wainwright, Fielding, Hickson, Parker, Eglington.
Whites: O'Neill; Sutherland, Rankin; Grant, Woods, Melville; B Harris, Thomas, J Harris, Lewis, E Canavan.

Everton's Reserves gave the Blues plenty to think about in the early stages of the game. They took the lead in the 22nd minute through Brian Harris, but 15 minutes later the Blues were awarded a penalty when Woods had instinctively punched away a header by Fielding, saving a certain goal. Jones scored from the spot. For the second half, the Whites forward line saw four changes and read - Harris, Far-rall, Saunders, Potts and Mayers – and Birch took Grant's place at right-half. The only goal after the interval was scored by Wainwright in the 89th minute to give the Blues a 2-1 victory.

The Liverpool Echo on Saturday, 20th August included details of all the Everton staff. The entry for George read: *"Date signed: 23/8/1948; Status: professional; Height: 5' 7¾"; Weight: 10st 8 lbs; Where born: Liverpool; Previous club: Amateur."*

In his column on Saturday, 20th August, Ranger thought that *"Everton would have a more difficult time this season"*. Although the side had started off well the previous year and, at the half-way stage, were only two points behind the leaders, they only took 14 points from the last 18 matches. If that average had been spread over the season, then Everton would have been fighting to avoid relegation. Ranger was also concerned with the fact that no newcomers had been brought in, that the senior players were one year nearer the end of their careers and that 14 of the young professionals were in the forces. His doubts seemed justified when Everton lost the first two games of the season but, following the introduction of Brian and Jimmy Harris into the side, the Club won the next two.

Dave Hickson was clearly unhappy at losing his place to Jimmy Harris. He asked to be placed on the transfer list and was immediately signed by Aston Villa for £20,000. He had signed for Everton as an amateur almost 12 years earlier and had played 151 League and Cup games, scoring 69 goals.

In the meantime, George had been playing at left-back for the Reserves. After seven games unbeaten, they faced Manchester United Reserves at Goodison Park on Wednesday evening, 21st September. United included two players who would later be in the Munich Air Crash - Billy Whelan, who was killed, and Bobby Charlton, who survived. Grant, the Everton half-back, was reduced to little more than a passenger following an injury, handicapping Everton to such an extent that they lost the game 2-1.

Grant was later chosen for the Central League representative side against the previous season's champions Manchester United, but had to withdraw because of his injury.

George continued to be a regular in the Reserves, but was called into the first team against Birmingham City at Goodison Park on Tuesday, 27th December, replacing the injured Tansey. Birmingham had beaten Everton the previous day at St Andrews by six goals to two, so the fans feared another heavy defeat. Everton, however, excelled themselves with a 5-1 victory.

George kept his place for the next match, against Luton away, on New Year's Eve as Tansey had still not recovered from his calf injury. Luton were third in the League, two points ahead of Everton, who lay in 7th place. Despite *"the pitch being inches deep in mud"* (39), Everton were leading 2-0 at half-time but allowed their lead to slip away, just managing to hold on for a 2-2 draw.

This proved to be George's final first team game for Everton, but he continued to play regularly at left-back for the Reserves. By mid-January 1956, Manchester United Reserves had a five point lead over Liverpool Reserves, who were in second place, with Everton in third position, a further two points behind Liverpool.

Early in 1956, arrangements had been made for Everton to tour the United States of America during the summer and, at the Board meeting on 7th February, *"it was resolved that Mr. H. R. Pickering be appointed Acting Manager during the absence of the Manager"* for the duration of the tour. That decision led to one of the most traumatic situations at the Club for many a year.

At the Board meeting the following week, Manager Britton informed the Directors that, following legal advice, he was seeking termination of his contract and claiming two years' salary as compensation for breach of his contract by the appointment of an acting manager, during his absence on the summer tour, without prior consultation with himself. He went on to say that he objected to the appointment of Mr. Pickering as acting manager and requested that he be relieved of his duties until the matter was settled. The Directors refused to agree to his demands.

On 23rd February, the Board sent a letter to Britton informing him that it intended to overturn the decision to appoint Pickering as acting manager at its meeting the following day. The letter also made it clear that the appointment of an acting manager was no reflection on Britton himself but, as he would be out of the country for six weeks, there was clearly a need for someone to deputise for him and deal with matters that would normally have been handled by him. Finally, the Board asked for any suggestions that he might make regarding the temporary arrangements.

At the following day's meeting, Britton told the Board *"that he could walk out of the meeting and could ruin the reputation of every Director and referred to them as despicable men".* (40) He then left the meeting.

Immediately after Britton left the meeting, a solicitor advised the Board that, in his opinion, *"the rescinding of the minute removed the allegation of Breach of Contract and that if Mr. Britton walked out, he thought that it would be a breach of contract on his part".* Mr. Green, the Chairman of the Board, then went to see Britton and explain the solicitor's views, but returned soon afterwards to tell the members that Britton wanted to leave the Club.

The Board later issued a press statement outlining the above facts. The statement went on to explain that Britton had threatened to resign unless the Board agreed to a number of terms set out in a document, one of which was that he and his family should have occupancy of his club house for a period of 40 years.

In the end, Britton left Everton after confirming in writing that he would not claim compensation for loss of contract. He was allowed to buy his club house in Southport Road for £3500.

Britton joined Preston North End as manager in August 1956 and finished third and runners-up in his first two seasons there. However, they were relegated at the end of the 1960-61 season prompting Britton's resignation. He joined Hull soon afterwards, remaining manager until November 1969, when he was appointed general manager of the club. He died on 1st December 1975.

Ian Buchan was appointed as chief coach following Britton's departure, but was never given the title of manager. He was a Scottish amateur international, but had never played professional football. Following six straight defeats at the start of the 1958-59 season, he resigned and was replaced by Johnny Carey. Buchan returned to Scotland and died tragically in a car crash in 1965 at the age of 45.

Everton's senior side failed to maintain the early season form, finishing 15th in the First Division. Manchester United were champions, whilst Huddersfield and Sheffield United were relegated. Liverpool missed out on promotion from Division Two, with Sheffield Wednesday and Leeds United making the step up.

Jock Lindsay and Willie John Parker were placed on the open-to-transfer list by Everton and both were transferred to Bury in mid-May for fees said to be reasonably substantial. Lindsay, of course, had been signed from Rangers in 1951 and had kept George out of the first team. He was considered to be one of the best full-backs in the League, but had never managed to regain his place in the senior side following his broken leg two years' earlier. He had made 117 senior appearances.

George was also placed on the transfer list and signed for Southport FC in August for a reported fee of £500 as a part-time professional. In his six seasons as a professional at Everton, he had made only 36 League and three FA Cup appearances, almost half of those having been made during the 1950-51 season, his first as a professional. Being called up for National Service during the latter half of that season may well have hindered his progress. But, having been an England Youth international and making a great start to his professional career, it must have been extremely disappointing to find himself only on the fringes of first team selection for five years, often as third choice left-back.

References:

1.   Liverpool Echo, 10th March 1948

2.   Liverpool Echo, 4th May 1948

3.   At that time, because George was under 21 years of age, he required the permission of his father before signing a professional contract.

4.   Liverpool Echo, 8th December 1950

5.   Liverpool Echo, 11th December 1950

6.   Minutes of Meeting of Everton's Board of Directors, 12th September 1950

7.   Liverpool Echo, 16th December 1950

8.   Liverpool Echo, 30th December 1950

9.   Liverpool Echo, 20th January 1951

10. Liverpool Echo 17th February 1951

11. Liverpool Echo, 10th November 1951

12. Liverpool Echo, 22nd March 1952

13. Liverpool Echo , 9th February 1952

14. Liverpool Echo, 23rd October 1952

15. Liverpool Echo, 10th November 1952

16. Liverpool Echo, 17th November 1952

17. Liverpool Echo, 7th March 1953

18. Liverpool Echo, 30th March 1953

19. Liverpool Echo, 27th April 1953

20. Liverpool Echo, 31st August 1953

21. Liverpool Echo, 29th August 1953

22. Liverpool Echo, 10th September 1953

23. Minutes of the Meetings of Everton's Board of Directors, October and November 1953

24. Liverpool Echo, 16th February 1954

25. Liverpool Echo, 31st March 1954

26. Minutes of the Meeting of the Everton Board of Directors, 8th December 1953

27. Liverpool Daily Post, 16th August 1954

28. Liverpool Daily Post, 19th August 1954

29. Liverpool Echo, 21st September 1954

30. Liverpool Echo, 23rd September 1954

31. Liverpool Echo, 23rd September 1954

32. Liverpool Echo, 8th November 1954

33. Liverpool Echo, 3rd January 1955

34. Liverpool Echo, 10th January 1955

35. Liverpool Echo, 17th January 1955

36. Liverpool Echo (Cup Tie Special), 29th January 1955

37. Liverpool Echo, 29th January 1955

38. Liverpool Echo, 31st January 1955

39. Liverpool Echo, 31st December 1955

40. Minutes of the Meeting of the Everton FC Board of Directors, 24th February 1956

6

GEORGE AT SOUTHPORT FC (1956-60)

Introduction

In May 1920, it was decided to form a Third Division in the Football League, with Northern and Southern Sections. The Southern Section was established in time for the 1920-21 season, but the Northern Section was not set up until the following year. Southport were founder members of the Northern Section along with 19 other clubs – Accrington Stanley; Ashington; Barrow; Chesterfield; Crewe Alexandra; Darlington; Durham City; Grimsby Town, who transferred from the Southern Section; Halifax Town; Hartlepool United; Lincoln City; Nelson; Rochdale; Stalybridge Celtic; Stockport County, who had been relegated from the Second Division; Tranmere Rovers; Walsall; Wigan Borough; and Wrexham.

When George joined Southport in 1956, the club was still in the Northern Section of the Third Division, and had just finished in 5th place, nine points behind the leaders, in a record breaking season. The club was looking to build on that success.

1956-57 Season

George played in the public trial at Haig Avenue on Saturday, 11th August, along with five other professionals signed by the club during the close season. The teams were:

Old Golds (Probables): Minshull; A. Parkinson, Rankin; Hunter, Taylor, Charlton; Miles, Gryba, Birkett (signed from Manchester United), Walsh (Oldham), McDermott.

Black and Whites (Possibles): Richardson (Canterbury); Lomas, Gradwell; E. Parkinson (Preston), Henderson, Simms; Lawrenson, Bloomfield (Carlisle), Forsyth, Woodcock, R. Rimmer

The Old Golds were down 1-0 at the interval but, as expected, won 6-1. George *"was not unduly pressed at left-back (and) he was more than equal to the calls and should prove a safe defender".*(1)

The Old Gold team that won the Southport F.C. trial on 11th August 1956. Left to right, back row: Don Hunter, Allan Parkinson, Ray Minshull, Wally Taylor, Wilf Charlton, George Rankin, Bob Jones (trainer). Front row: Dennis Miles, Ray Gryba, Cliff Birkett, Kevin Walsh, Tommy Lawrenson. Courtesy of Trinity Mirror.

In the first league game of the season, on Saturday, 18th August, Southport faced Bradford City away from home. There were two newcomers in the Southport team – George at left-back and Bert Mitchell at outside-left. Mitchell had only been signed from Middlesbrough the day before the game *"for a substantial fee"*. He was an experienced player, having made 50 first team appearances for Middlesbrough in two seasons, scoring five goals. He had previously played for Stoke, Blackburn, Northampton, and Luton, for whom he made 104 Second Division appearances in three seasons, scoring 46 goals. The Southport team was:

Minshull; Parkinson, Rankin; Hunter, Taylor, Charlton; Miles, Gryba, Bromilow, McDermott, Mitchell.

One player of particular interest in the team was centre-forward George Bromilow. Southport born, he was a teacher in a local school, and was an amateur during his time with the club, from 1955 to 1959, making 84 first team appearances and scoring 37 goals. He was one of only three amateurs to top the scoring charts of any Football League club since 1919. He was an England Youth International, represented the full English Amateur side on more than a dozen occasions, and represented Great Britain at football in the 1956 Olympic Games in Melbourne.

Two goals by Bradford within a space of three minutes midway through the second half dashed Southport's hopes of any points, having fought back from a goal down after 14 minutes. *"Newcomer Rankin had a grand game at left-back after recovering from a shaky start. The former Everton player soon got into his stride. His anticipation and positioning was good and there were two occasions in the second half when he raced across to the right to make timely interventions and so bring in a successful conclusion to what looked like developing into nasty situations."*(2)

Southport's other debutant, Mitchell, scored their only goal and looked to be a good buy. However, Bradford City deserved their success in a game played before a crowd of 10,000 in heavy rain.

For their first home game, against Scunthorpe on Tuesday, 21st August, close-season signing Cliff Birkett from Manchester United replaced Gryba at inside-right. Almost 7,000 spectators went home disappointed with Southport's inability to gain a victory after twice being in the lead. The final score was 2-2, which meant that Southport had only gained one point from their first two games.

According to the local press report of the game, *"It was newcomer, George Rankin from Everton who took the eye most in the home rearguard. He never put a foot wrong throughout, always positioning himself well and giving effective cover, while his distribution was first class throughout."*(3)

Southport lost their next two games by one goal to nil - at home to Stockport County, their first home defeat for almost 12 months, with goalkeeper Ray Minshull making his 200th appearance for the club; and then away to Scunthorpe.

One point from four games was not the sort of start envisaged by the club and its supporters.

Things improved, however, on Saturday, 1st September when they gained their first win of the season with a 2-1 victory at Carlisle, even though they fell behind to a brilliant 30 yard goal by former England international, Ivor Broadis.

Despite the encouragement offered by that win at Carlisle, Southport suffered heavy defeats in their next three games. On Tuesday evening, 4th September, they lost 6-1 at home to Hartlepool United. This was Southport's biggest defeat since Rochdale won 7-1 in the 1925-26 season. Surprisingly, there were no goals in the first half, when the home defence had proved more than equal to its task, but it simply fell to pieces following Hartlepool's first goal in the 54th minute.

Saturday, 8th September, saw another home game, this time against Accrington Stanley, one of the founders of the Football League. Southport were hopeful of their first home win of the season, as they had not been beaten by Accrington Stanley at Haig Avenue since the first season after the war, winning five and drawing four of the nine games played. That elusive home victory seemed a certainty when they ran into a 3-1 lead but, for the second game running, the defence cracked and Accrington Stanley hit the back of the net four times to give them a clear-cut win before a crowd of 7,375 spectators.

The return fixture with Hartlepool United on Monday evening, 10th September, saw Southport's third heavy defeat in a row and Hartlepool complete the double. As in the two previous games, the half-time score gave little indication of what was to follow. Southport went in at half-time with the score at 1-1, following an equaliser from the penalty spot just before the interval. However, the 57th minute was a tragedy for Southport and George. *"The full-back tried to put the ball back to Minshull, but the keeper had moved forward and both of them could only watch the ball roll inside the post."*(4) The defence went on to concede another three goals, to give Hartlepool a resounding 5-2 win.

So, after conceding 16 goals in three games in six days, it was perhaps surprising that there were only two changes in defence for the next fixture, away to Tranmere Rovers, on Saturday, 15th September. Out went right-back Parkinson and left-half Charlton. The team was:

Minshull; Forsyth, Rankin; Hunter, Taylor, Walsh; Lawrenson, McDermott, Gryba, McIlvenney, Mitchell.

Southport gained a welcome point from a 1-1 draw but, until Tranmere equalised with only four minutes left, it looked as if they would get maximum points. George had a hand in the Southport goal:

"... in the 32nd minute, Southport took the lead. Lawrenson got away from a Rankin clearance and passed inside to McDermott who transferred to McIlvenney over on the left. When the inside-left centred, there was Gryba to head into the net. A good goal this, and it resulted from the best move to date."(5)

On Tuesday, 18th September, Southport gained another point, drawing 1-1 at home against Mansfield Town. However, they should have won as Mansfield were handicapped for virtually the whole game. Their left-back and captain had to leave the field in the third minute when he was struck in the face by the ball. After receiving treatment for 12 minutes, he returned to play the rest of the game on the wing. Worse was to follow for Mansfield. With 30 minutes to go, their centre-half dislocated his shoulder in a fall and was taken to Southport Infirmary, taking no further part in the game.

The home game against York on Saturday, 22nd September, saw the third 1-1 draw in succession. It began to look as if York would steal both points as a result of their penalty goal in 32 minutes but, eight minutes from time, Southport were awarded a spot kick themselves and inside-right Charlton equalised. Southport had sufficient chances to win the game quite comfortably, but the opportunities were not taken. *"There was only one occasion in the second half when things looked bad for Southport. This was when Minshull, a little late in coming out, was beaten to the ball by Fenton. Fenton diverted the ball goalwards, but Rankin kicked clear."(6)* Southport's crowd of 4,019 was the lowest attendance in the Football League.

After their run of three draws, Southport lost 2-1 at Oldham the following

Saturday, watched by almost 10,000 spectators. With minutes of the game to go, it looked as if Southport were going to secure their fourth 1-1 draw in a row but, in the 86th minute, one of the Oldham forwards *"decided to try a shot and it looked harmless enough as it speeded towards the waiting arms of Minshull. But, alas it struck Rankin in flight and was deflected away from the keeper."*(7)

A 1-0 home defeat to Rochdale on Saturday, 6th October, meant that Southport were the only team in the Football League without a home win. The following Saturday they slumped to their ninth defeat of the season, against Halifax. With only six points from 14 games, Southport were bracketed with Chester, Tranmere and Crewe at the foot of the table.

George suffered an Achilles tendon injury in the Halifax game and had not recovered for the home game against Wrexham on Saturday, 20th October, thereby losing his ever-present record. The match ended 1-1.

However, he regained his left-back spot for the away game against Hull City the following Saturday, having recovered from his injury. The team was:

Minshull; Lomas, Rankin; Hunter, Taylor, Charlton; Lawrenson, Prescott, Birkett, McIlvenney, McDermott.

Hull's captain, Stan Mortenson, the former Blackpool and England star, scored the only goal of the first half and then got a second in the 57th minute. Birkett scored a consolation goal for Southport almost immediately afterwards. The defeat consigned Southport to third from bottom on goal average, only a point above Crewe, who were at the foot of the table.

Luck was against Southport in their goalless draw at home against Barrow on Saturday, 3rd November. They had a goal disallowed for offside after 65 minutes and two opportunities were cleared off the line with the goalkeeper beaten. Southport's problem was a failure in front of goal; they had only scored seven goals in nine games.

Southport continued to struggle, losing their next five games, scoring only two goals and conceding 12 in the process. George played in all of those games. On Christmas Day, however, they managed to gain a point in a drab goalless draw away to Crewe. The return game with Crewe on Boxing Day was postponed because of a heavy snowfall.

Southport's last chance in 1956 to gain their first home win of the season was against Carlisle on Saturday, 29th December. Their only victory of the season had been at Carlisle almost four months earlier, and they had failed to win any of the 18 League games since. The team was:

Richardson; Parkinson, Rankin; Hunter, Lomas, Charlton; Miles, Evans, Bromilow, McIlvenney, McDermott.

Bromilow had only got back from his 13,000 mile round trip to Australia, where he had played for the Great Britain football team in the Olympics. His return to the team made all the difference for he had a hand in three of the goals scored by Southport in their 4-1 win. Southport had been the only club in the Football League without a home win.

George was dropped for the New Year's Day game at Haig Avenue against Bradford, in which Southport romped home 5-1 for their second home victory of the season. This brought their goals tally for two games to nine, after scoring only nine in their previous 15 games. It also meant five points from the previous three games as against five in the last 14. Certainly a change in fortune!

George returned to the first team for the next League game away to Accrington Stanley on Saturday, 12th January. Right-back Alan Parkinson had been called up to join the RAF the previous week, so Wally Taylor, who had replaced George for the match on New Year's Day, moved to right-back with George regaining his place at left-back. Southport lost 4-2 to Accrington in atrocious conditions. There were pools of water on the pitch to start with and, after the game had been in progress for only a few minutes, the pitch had been turned into a sea of mud. George had an *"uncomfortable afternoon"* against Accrington's right-winger, Scott.

Defeat at Accrington meant that Southport were now next to bottom in the League. It looked as if the fight to avoid re-election to the Third Division, Northern Section was down to four teams – Chester, Tranmere, Southport and Crewe.

Southport still had to entertain all their companions in distress, so it was essential that they collected all the points at stake in those vital games.

The first of those critical games was against Tranmere on Saturday, 19th January, which Southport won 1-0 as a result of a penalty in the 52nd minute. George was dropped to the Reserves for this game as Alan Parkinson had obtained his discharge from the RAF.

George continued in the Reserves for the next two Saturdays, when Southport suffered two very heavy defeats away from home: 6-0 at Chesterfield and 9-1 at York. York's win was their biggest ever in the Football League and, as far as Southport were concerned, their heaviest defeat since they went down 10-1 at Hull in the 1937-38 season. Southport were affected in both defeats by an injury to one of their defenders. In the Chesterfield match, right-back Parkinson badly sprained an ankle with the game just over half-an-hour old and had to move to the right wing where he was no more than a passenger. Against York, they lost the services of Lomas, who had replaced the injured Parkinson, after a quarter of an hour with a leg injury and he did not take any further part in the game.

On Saturday, 2nd February 1957, the Southport Visitor published a letter from P.A.L. from Birkdale in which he criticised the Southport selectors. He complained of men being played out of position and others being dropped without justification and went on to say that he, along with another 12 regular supporters, considered that the strongest available team with Parkinson missing was:

Richardson; Forsyth, Rankin; Gryba, Taylor, Charlton; Birkett, Evans, Bromilow, McIlvenney, McDermott.

It is doubtful that this letter swayed the selectors' team choice, but George was recalled to the first team for the match against Oldham Athletic at Haig Avenue on the Saturday following the letter's publication, albeit at left-half. The team was:

Minshull; Forsyth, Hunter; Gryba, Taylor, Rankin; Miles, Prescott, Bromilow, McIlvenney, McDermott.

Southport won 2-0 and while victory maintained Southport's unbeaten home record for 1957, it was not enough to get them away from next to bottom place in the League.

The talking point that Saturday was not the team's victory over Oldham, but the announcement of Southport's biggest signing in their history. On the day before the game, Stan Mortenson, a former England international, and still remembered for his Cup-Final hat-trick for Blackpool against Bolton in 1953, agreed to join the club from Hull City. He had scored both goals for Hull in October when they beat Southport 2-1.

George had sustained a knock against Oldham and failed a late fitness test on the morning of the away game against Rochdale on Saturday, 16th February. His place at left-half was taken by Charlton. The game ended in a 6-1 win for Rochdale, a crushing blow for Southport's hopes of escaping re-election.

Only four of the team that had faced Rochdale were retained for the home game against Halifax Town. They were Minshull, Taylor, Charlton and McDermott. In came Parkinson, George and McIlvenney, who had both recovered from injury, Bromilow, who had missed the previous game because he had been playing for Lancashire in the Northern Counties Amateur Championships, and, of course, Stan Mortenson, making his first appearance for Southport. The team was:

Minshull; Parkinson, Rankin; Hunter, Taylor, Charlton; Lawrenson, Mortenson, Bromilow, McIlvenney, McDermott.

The match was played in atrocious conditions, *"a glue-pot ground"* with rain, sleet and snow throughout, requiring the players to change their strip at half-time. Halifax had won five successive matches so, in the circumstances, Southport were probably relieved to get a point. Halifax went ahead with the last kick of the first half, *"when Hutchinson outpaced Rankin and went in to score, the ball entering the net on the far side of Minshull, who had gone down to try to save."*(8) Southport equalised in the 63rd minute through Bromilow and, while he did not score, Stan Mortenson had a big influence on the attack.

Southport's next game, away against Wrexham, was their second successive

1-1 draw. It was also their luckiest point of the season, according to the South-port Visitor match reporter, for Wrexham were on top for at least 80 percent of the game and squandered chances galore. Wrexham went ahead after 33 min-utes, when they scored from the penalty spot, but Mortenson scored his first goal for Southport with a header to earn them a valuable point. George was at left-back.

On Saturday, 9th March, Hull City made their first appearance at Haig Ave-nue since the 1948-49 season. They had scored 31 goals on their travels, only Stockport County with 35 goals had scored more. But, Southport, with George again at left-back, beat Hull 1-0 on a muddy pitch. Bromilow scored the only goal of the game.

The following Saturday, Southport created a club record for the season when they extended their unbeaten run to four consecutive games with a 1-1 draw at Barrow. Southport scored five minutes before the interval and it seemed that they would hold out for both points, but Barrow scored the equaliser with two minutes of the match remaining. George played in the left-back position. Southport were now out of the re-election places, third from bottom and three points ahead of Tranmere Rovers, the team immediately below them.

Southport, unbeaten at home since 15th December, faced Darlington at Haig Avenue on Saturday, 23rd March. A 1-0 win, through Mortenson's first goal at home, extended their unbeaten run at home to seven games – six wins and a draw. It also gave them a seven-point lead over Tranmere Rovers, which looked suffi-cient to prevent them having to apply for re-election.

Southport entertained Chesterfield at Haig Avenue the following Tuesday. Chesterfield were lucky to get a point in a scoreless draw, although they did come near to scoring: *"Ground was made by the visitors and Rankin saved a certain goal by dropping back on the line and clearing as Richardson had missed the ball when Lewis sent in an oblique shot."*(9)

Southport achieved their first away win and the double over Bradford the following Saturday with a 3-2 victory. It was also Southport's seventh game with-out a defeat since the signing of Mortenson. In the first half, Bradford were the better side and were leading 2-1 at the interval, but, in the second- half, it was

Southport's turn to take the initiative with goals from McDermott and McIlven-ney and, long before the final whistle, Bradford looked a well-beaten side. Accord-ing to the match report, *"Rankin was the better of the full-backs, as Parkinson found a tricky customer in Kendall, the former Rochdale winger."*(10)

On Saturday, 6th April, Southport failed to extend their unbeaten run to eight games when they lost 3-2 to Gateshead at Haig Avenue. Despite the defeat, they were in 21st position in the league. Crewe were certain to have to apply for re-elec-tion as they only had 13 points. Above them were Tranmere Rovers with 23 points, Chester with 26 points and Southport, who had 27. Southport had played one game less than their rivals, but their remaining fixtures looked tougher, so there was still plenty to play for. In the 16 days to the end of the season, Southport had no fewer than seven league games and two cup-ties.

Workington became the seventh team to complete the double over Southport when they won 2-0 at Workington on Saturday, 13th April. Workington had gone ahead in the 12th minute and 13 minutes later Minshull was beaten again *"to the dismay of Rankin, who made a frantic effort to palm the ball away."*(11)

Southport's Easter programme began the following Friday with a 1-1 draw at home with Chester. Then, the following day, Saturday, 20th April, they beat pro-motion hopefuls Derby County 3-2 in an exciting struggle at Haig Avenue. In the 78th minute, the crowd was silenced when Derby equalised with a penalty after Hunter was adjudged to have handled the ball. But, their disappointment turned to cheers in the next minute, as Mortenson netted in a goalmouth scramble. They were beaten 2-0 by Chester in their final Easter game on the Monday.

Tranmere Rovers had only got one point from the three Easter games, while Southport had earned three and could not, therefore, be overtaken. Consequently, it was Tranmere and Crewe that had to apply for re-election.

Southport's final home game of the season, against Crewe Alexandra, on Wednesday, 24th April, proved to be a great disappointment. Crewe scored the only goal of the game in the third minute and, in losing the game, Southport allowed Crewe Alexandra to register not only their first away win of the season, but their first away win since Christmas Day 1954.

Derby County beat Southport 2-0 on the last Saturday of the season to clinch the League championship before a crowd of almost 26,000. Then, on Monday, 30th April, Southport ended the season on a happy note by beating Mansfield 2-1 to earn their third away win of the season.

The final placings at the foot of the table were Crewe 21 points, Tranmere 27, Southport 32 and Chester 33. Although Southport had avoided re-election, there were still some disappointing aspects to the season. Their goals against - 94 - was the highest in the club's history, beating the old record of 92 set in 1925-26, and their gates were the second lowest in the Football League. Gateshead's were the lowest with an average of 3,768; Southport's average was 4,415.

In terms of Cup games, Southport went out of the FA Cup in the first round. Following a scoreless draw at home against York City on Saturday, 17th November 1956, before a crowd of 5,560, they were beaten 2-1 in the replay at York four days later. George played in both games.

Southport reached the semi-final of the Lancashire Senior Cup, but were beaten 1-0 by Burnley at Turf Moor on Wednesday, 17th April, during a period when they were required to play nine games in 16 days. George was at left-back.

However, they proved to be more successful in the Liverpool Senior Cup, which was contested by Everton, Liverpool, Southport and Tranmere Rovers. In the semi-final on Monday, 15th April, Southport beat Liverpool 3-2 at Haig Avenue before a paltry crowd of 2,272. The teams were:

Southport: Richardson, Parkinson, Rankin; Hunter, Taylor, Charlton; Prescott, Mortenson, Gryba, McIlvenney, McDermott.
Liverpool: Rudham; McNulty, Byrne; Burkinshaw, Whyte, Campbell; Bimpson, Wheatley, Arnell, Rowley, Lockey.

Twice Southport went in front, only for Liverpool to draw level and when they were ahead for the third time in the 82nd minute, they had to fight to hold on to their lead. Gryba, a former Liverpool player, who was made captain for the game, scored two of Southport's goals, while Mortenson got the other.

The final, against Everton, was played at Anfield on Saturday 11th May. South-port were bidding to win the cup for the fourth time. They first won it in 1931, retained it the following year but did not win it again until 1949. Eight of the side fielded by Everton were first team regulars. The teams were:

Southport: Richardson; Parkinson, Rankin; Hunter, Taylor, Charlton; McDermott, McIlvenney, Bromilow, Mortenson, Mitchell.
Everton: Dunlop; Donovan, Sutherland; Birch, Sanders, Rea; J Harris, Gauld, Hood, Haughey, Eglington.

Southport were by no means disgraced in a game that ended 2-1 in Everton's favour. Mortenson opened the scoring in the 4th minute for Southport when he headed the ball into the net from a McDermott corner, and then Donovan headed a Bromilow shot off the line, with Dunlop beaten, to prevent a certain second goal for Southport. Everton equalised from the penalty spot in the 38th minute, after Parkinson had brought down Eglington. Donovan was the scorer. Everton's winner was scored in the 65th minute by Rea. "*Rankin tied with Donovan as the outstanding defender.*"(12)

Southport had announced their retained list at the end of April It was: Minshull and Richardson (goalkeepers); Alan Parkinson and George (full-backs); Hunter, Taylor, Charlton and Gryba (half backs); Miles, Prescott, Mortenson, Bradnell, McIlvenney and McDermott (forwards). Forsyth and Lomas (defenders) and Mitchell and Evans (forwards) were placed on the transfer list, while Eric Parkinson (defender) and Lawrenson and Birkett (forwards) were given free transfers.

Southport did receive one piece of good news in April, when the Chancellor abolished entertainment tax in sport. The tax had cost Southport £2,455 the previous year. It did not mean cheaper admission prices, however, although it was suggested that cheaper admission charges would mean larger crowds.

1957-58 Season

During the close season, Stan Mortenson was appointed as first team "supervisor" with responsibility for coaching, practice policy and tactics.

George had signed for the season on a part-time basis, receiving £9 a week during the season and £8 in the summer. At that time, the maximum weekly wage for a footballer was £17, so George was in a fortunate position of receiving £9 a week from Southport, whilst being allowed to continue other employment.

There was some surprise expressed in the local press when Southport disclosed at the end of July that George was to be played at wing half. He had only previously played once for the first team in that position, against Oldham.

9. In consideration of the observance by the said player of the terms, provisions and conditions of this Agreement, the said........C. G.................... ....Hunt........................on behalf of the Club hereby agrees that the said Club shall pay to the said Player the sum of £ 8. 0. 0. per week from 1st July 1957   to   3rd August 1957 3rd May 1958 .... to ....30th June 1958 and £ 9. 0. 0. .... per week from ....3rd August 1957 to........3rd May 1958.

10. This Agreement (subject to the Rules of The Football Association) shall cease and determine on....................30th June 1958 unless the same shall have been previously determined in accordance with the provisions hereinbefore set forth.

Fill in any other provisions required

Player allowed to follow present employment.

Player to attend training as instructed (including Tuesday afternoons for practice.)

As Witness the hands of the said parties the day and year first aforesaid

Signed by the said........C. G. Hunt........................ ....and   George ....Rankin

In the presence of

(Signature) ....

(Occupation) ....Clerk.

(Address) Haig Avenue, Southport.

(Player)

(Secretary)

George Rankin's contract with Southport FC for the 1957-8 season.

The usual public trial was held at Haig Avenue on Saturday, 17th August, when 12 newcomers were on display, including three full-backs. The game ended in a 2-2 draw and was watched by 1,728 spectators. The teams were:

> **Old Golds:** Richardson; A. Parkinson, McCredie (signed from Accrington Stanley); Dunne (Shrewsbury), Taylor, McCallum (Hartlepool); McKenna (Blackpool), Mortenson, Bromilow, Alexander (Burnley), McDermott.
> **Black and Whites:** Minshull; Whitfield (Carlisle), Dodd (Shrewsbury); E. Parkinson, Wassall (Coventry), Rankin; Phillips (Liverpool), Hazledine (Boston), Gryba, McCoy (Burnley), McManus (Bury).

Southport lost their first league game of the season 1-0 at Barrow; the full-backs were Dodd and McCredie. George was at left-half in the Reserves, who drew 4-4 with Chorley at home.

George was not selected for the first team for the next four games, in which Southport lost to Workington twice and Bury once; their sole victory was 2-1 at home to Oldham. After the first two defeats, the Southport Visitor's view on Saturday, 31st August was that it was hardly surprising as there were only three players from the previous season in the team – Minshull, Taylor and Mortenson.

During that time, George played for the Reserves. In the game on Wednesday, 4th September against Bacup at Haig Avenue, Southport were handicapped *"when the heads of Halstead and Rankin clashed before the interval and Rankin was led from the field with his head covered in blood. He returned after 28 minutes in the second half"*. (13) Southport won 3-0.

On Saturday, 7th September, the Reserves entertained Wigan Athletic at Haig Avenue. Both teams were unbeaten, Wigan had seven points from four games, while Southport had five points from three. For this game, George reverted to left-back. The team was:

> Richardson; Wilkinson, Rankin; E. Parkinson, Whitfield, McManus; Phillips, Hough, Hazledine, Phoenix, Rimmer.

There were three former Southport players in the Wigan side – Hitchen, Prescott and Forsyth. The game was watched by just over 2,000 spectators and ended in a 1-1 draw, both teams preserving their unbeaten record. According to the Southport Visitor of 10th September, *"the game showed that Rankin is much more a full-back than he is a wing half. Playing with a plaster over his right eye following the injury he sustained against Bacup in midweek, he played a strong game throughout, and often came to his side's rescue with timely interventions."*

And yet, when George was called upon for his first appearance of the season in the senior side on Wednesday, 11th September, it was at left-half. The team to face Bradford City at Haig Avenue was:

Minshull; Parkinson, McCredie; McCallum, Taylor, Rankin; McKenna, Mortenson, Bromilow, Alexander, McDermott.

Southport suffered their fifth defeat in six games, by two goals to nil. According to the Southport Visitor on Thursday, 12th September, there could *"be few grumbles at the result"* and *"neither of the wing halves looked happy and both looked out of position"*. The defeat by Bradford City meant that Southport were bottom of the league with just two points, having made a worse start than the previous season when they only just escaped re-election.

For the home game against Accrington Stanley on Saturday, 14th September, Southport selected a defence that included five players, who at one time or another had played at full-back. The team was:

Minshull; Parkinson, Rankin; Wassall, Taylor, McCredie; McKenna, Mortenson, Bromilow, Gryba, McDermott.

Almost 5,500 spectators turned up to see a game with plenty of goals and thrills. Three times Accrington took the lead and each time Southport fought back to level matters, showing a fighting quality that had been missing from the previous games and scoring as many goals as they had in the previous six games. *"Rankin looked much more at home than at left-half."* (14)

George retained his place in the team beaten 2-0 by Bradford City at Bradford the following Wednesday, and was again in the senior team at Chester on the Saturday. Southport made six changes to the team beaten at Bradford, including three positional, which meant that they had already called upon 21 players, when they had only used 23 for the whole of the season just gone. The team was:

Richardson; Dodd, Rankin; Dunne, Taylor, McCredie; McKenna, Gryba, Mortenson, McCoy, McManus.

Southport picked up their first away point of the season in a 1-1 draw, but only just made it. George conceded a penalty when he brought down Foulkes, Chester's ex-Welsh international. Jepson, tried to place the spot kick to the left of Richardson, who anticipated the direction and moved sharply across his goal to save. A goal at this point of the game, just before the interval, would have put Chester two up. Mortenson gained a point for Southport when he equalised in the 82nd minute. According to the match reporter, "*no great blame attaches to him (Rankin) for the penalty incident, which was of a mild and possibly accidental nature, although the referee was right in his decision.*"(15)

Southport were at home for the next two games and won both, defeating Carlisle 2-0 and Chesterfield 5-2. The win against Chesterfield, their biggest victory since they beat Bradford 5-1 on New Year's Day, was all the more surprising as ten of their professionals and six amateurs were either injured or had flu. In fact, they had to postpone their second team game against Accrington Stanley. In the Chesterfield game, "*Rankin gave another polished display at left-back, this time against Tomlinson, a former Everton teammate. As usual, he tried to use his clearances to advantage and once or twice he was seen to move up with his attack.*"(16)

On Tuesday, 1st October, Southport had the chance to complete their first double of the season and extend their unbeaten run to four games. Instead, they suffered their heaviest defeat of the season when Carlisle beat them 4-0 at Brunton Park.

The next game was a local derby against Tranmere at Prenton Park on Saturday afternoon, 5th October. A crowd of almost 11,000 spectators watched Tranmere win 2-1, a score that flattered Southport and did not reflect the territorial advantage enjoyed by Tranmere. Rovers had two of George's former Everton colleagues in their side – Tommy Eglington and Peter Farrell, who had only been signed the day before the match. Eglington was too good for right-back Dodd and often beat him for speed. *"Rankin also had a speedy winger to cope with in Davies, but he had more success than Dodd and came out with honours even. In the second half, Rankin saved Southport from being three goals down when he headed off the line a header from McDonnell following a corner."*(17) Southport were now in 23rd position, only a point better off than Crewe, who were bottom.

For the game against Stockport County at home the following Saturday, Southport called upon their 22nd player of the season, Eric Parkinson, who was making his debut at right-half in his second season at Haig Avenue. Parkinson had actually been given a free transfer at the end of the 1956-57 season, but eventually re-signed for the club. The team was:

Richardson; Dodd, Rankin; E Parkinson, Taylor, McCredie; McKenna, Alexander, Mortenson, Gryba, McDermott.

More than 5,500 people turned up to see Southport beat Stockport 1-0 and gain their third successive home win.

Southport fielded an unchanged side for the game against Gateshead at Redheugh Park, only the second time that the same team had been fielded two matches running that season. However, they did not improve on their dismal away record of one point from a possible 14, the worst in the Northern Section, as they were beaten 2-1. Southport actually scored first in the 12th minute, Gateshead equalised six minutes later and it looked as if Southport would hold on for their second away point of the season, only for Gateshead to score the winner three minutes from time.

Despite fielding the same team for the third game running, Southport lost 3-0 at home to Darlington on Saturday, 26th October, slipping up on the opportunity to extend their unbeaten run at Haig Avenue to four games.

The following Wednesday, Wally Taylor, Southport's centre-half, had an impressive debut for the Northern Section against the Southern Section in the Third Division representative game at Crystal Palace. The game was watched by some 15,000 people and Taylor was generally regarded as the outstanding man in a sound Northern defence. The South equalised six minutes from time to earn a 2-2 draw. He was only the third Southport player to represent the Northern Section at that time, the other two were Minshull (twice) and Prescott (once).

For the second away match running, Southport were beaten by a late goal, losing 1-0 to Scunthorpe United before a crowd of more than 9,000. It was the old story of the defence having to shoulder the burden, as the attack was very seldom in the picture. As Scunthorpe were the most prolific scorers in the four Divisions of the Football League, the Southport rearguard did well to keep the goals against tally down to one. This defeat pushed them to the bottom of the table on goal average.

The next visitors to Haig Avenue in the league were Wrexham, whose away record was almost as bad as Southport's, having collected only three points as opposed to Southport's one. Surprisingly, they beat Southport 3-1, despite being a goal behind until the 76th minute, when they equalised. Two further goals in six minutes ended any hopes Southport had of a home win.

On Saturday, 23rd November, Southport suffered their fifth successive league defeat, three of them at home, and were firmly fixed at the bottom of the table. Rochdale not only won 2-0, but also missed a penalty. They took the lead in the 38th minute, after which *"Southport were unlucky not to score when the free kick taken by Rankin was tipped over the bar by Jones."*(18) Rochdale did not score again until 85th minute when they profited from a slip by George.

Only three players retained their positions for the away game at Halifax the following Saturday – George, Dunne and Taylor – although there were three positional changes. The team was:

Richardson; Dodd, Rankin; Dunne, Taylor, Gryba; Phillips, Alexander, Bromilow, McDermott, McCredie.

These sweeping changes did not prevent Southport losing their sixth successive League game, thereby equalling an unenviable club record set in 1948. The score was 4-1 to Halifax. "*Rankin had to come up against two wingers, as at half-time Kelly and Sharp changed places. Having dealt quite well with Kelly, he was given the run-round by the midget Sharp, who was the best of the Halifax forwards.*"(19) Conditions could not have been much gloomier. There was a mist all over Halifax, though it was fortunate that it did not get worse in the later stages of the game.

On Thursday, 5th December, the Southport Visitor announced that Stan Mortenson had been relieved of his duties as Southport's coach and team supervisor at his own request and that he would concentrate on playing. The club had no plans to appoint another coach, it was reported, and it was likely that Gordon Hunt, secretary-manager from 1937, who had been concentrating on administration duties, would again take full charge of the playing and training side, with the directors selecting the team for the most part. Mortenson told the Southport Visitor: "*My reason for the request was that in view of the fact that my team suggestions and recommendations had from time to time been amended by the board of directors. I therefore felt I could be of more service to the club as a player only.*"

The Visitor announced another surprise on Saturday, 7th December, when it stated that Ray Minshull, Southport's long-serving goalkeeper, had been placed on the transfer list at his own request, apparently because of heckling by some of the crowd behind the goal. Minshull had been at Anfield for five years, making a number of first team appearances, and had joined Southport on a free transfer. He was in his seventh season at the club, having made his 218th league appearance against Rochdale two weeks earlier. His departure would mean that there was only one professional goalkeeper, Jack Richardson, on the books.

Against Hull City away on Saturday, 14th December, Southport were three goals down at one stage, but managed to get two back to make the final score more respectable. This was Southport's eighth successive league defeat, establishing a new record, beating the old one that had stood since the 1946-47 season. It was also the first time Southport had scored two goals that season in an away match, and it was the first time since 28th September that Southport had scored more than one goal in a game – a run of 11 games. George had missed the Lancashire Senior cup-tie against Liverpool the previous week as he was suffering from flu, but he was fit enough to travel to Hull as reserve.

George did not play again for the first team until 15th February 1958, missing nine first team matches in which Southport won two, drew three and lost four games and found themselves in one of the two re-election spots.

During that time, George played in the Reserves. He featured at right-back, alongside his younger brother Billy, on Saturday, 21st December in a 5-1 defeat at Chorley.

They played together again the following Saturday at Haig Avenue against Prescot Cables, losing 3-0. The team was:

Grundy; A. Parkinson, G. Rankin; E. Parkinson, Gradwell, Ogden; Hollis, Scott, Barker, Wilkinson, W. Rankin.

Grundy, the goalkeeper, was a new amateur signing. The report in the Southport Visitor of Tuesday, 31st December, stated that, "*there was little right with the experimental side. Alan Parkinson was not his usual safe self, and while George Rankin tried to urge his wing brother into action, there were times when he left plenty of space for the opposition to work in,*" adding that "*the wingers Hollis and W. Rankin would have done better had they got the ball across oftener, instead of trying to beat the Prescot defenders by dribbling a way through and losing the ball in the process.*"

George again appeared for the Reserves at left-back in the Liverpool Combination Cup replay against South Liverpool on Wednesday, 1st January, 1958. Their hopes of a win were high after an earlier 2-2 draw at South Liverpool's ground. However, they suffered a humiliating 9-2 defeat. George scored Southport's first goal when they were down 7-0. Billy Rankin did not play, he was replaced at outside-left by Rimmer.

On Thursday, 23rd January, it was announced that Angus Alexander had been placed on the transfer list at his own request. The Scotsman had come to Southport in the summer after four seasons with Burnley, making 13 league appearances and scoring one goal. He was dissatisfied with having to play in the Lancashire

Combination. Alexander was the fourth player to request a transfer – Minshull had been transferred to Bradford; George Rankin had been placed on the list; but Jimmy McDermott's transfer request had been refused.

George returned to the first team against Tranmere Rovers at Haig Avenue on Saturday, 15th February. He took the place of Norman McCredie, who was suffering from a bout of flu. The team was:

Richardson; Taylor, Rankin; Dunne, Gryba, Hazledine; Phillips, Dodd, Phoenix, Schofield, McDermott.

Tranmere were two up within six minutes and ended the game 3-0 winners, their inside-right Williams scoring a hat-trick.

For the away game against Rochdale the following Saturday, George moved over to right-back replacing the injured Taylor; McCredie returned at left-back having recovered from flu. Rochdale won 2-0. "*Full-backs Rankin and McCredie had all their work cut out in trying to stop Lockhart and Vizard. Both defenders put in creditable performances, however, with Rankin, perhaps, a little steadier of the two.*"(20)

Southport faced Gateshead at Haig Avenue on Saturday, 1st March with two newcomers in the team. Walter Hughes, signed from Bradford Park Avenue a week earlier was making his home debut, whilst Tommy Kinloch, just signed from Workington, was making his first appearance at right-half and was appointed captain. Angus Alexander went to Workington in an exchange deal for Kinloch, who had had six seasons with Carlisle, making 164 league appearances for them, before signing for Workington prior to the end of the 1956-57 season. Rankin and McCredie continued at full-back. Southport had a rare victory, defeating Gateshead 1-0, for their first win since Boxing Day and only their second clean sheet of the year. Kinloch had a steadying influence on the defence, but the match reporter, "*made George Rankin one of the best Southport defenders. Although in the unaccustomed position of right-back – the vast majority of his games have been on the left flank – he hardly put a foot wrong, getting through his work in a cool and quiet manner.*" (21)

With four inches of snow on the pitch, the away game against Darlington on Saturday, 8th March, was postponed. Southport did not learn of the postponement until they reached Darlington.

Scunthorpe came to Haig Avenue as league leaders the following Saturday and scored all three goals in a 2-1 win, their centre-half putting through his own goal to give Southport the lead. Scunthorpe scored either side of half-time.

The postponed game at Darlington was played on Wednesday, 19th March. Southport were the slightly better of two poor sides and gained a rare away victory by two goals to one. George returned to his usual position of left-back.

On the Saturday, Southport not only gained their second away victory in three days by beating Stockport County 2-1, but their third win in the last four games. It also meant that Southport had completed their second double of the season. The defence, with George again at left-back, looked much sounder than it had done for a long time.

Crewe Alexandra, with the joint worst away record in the Football League and bottom of the Northern Section table, were the visitors to Haig Avenue on Saturday, 29th March. Southport recorded their third successive win, by two goals to nil.

Two days later, Southport won again, when they beat Mansfield Town 4-1 at Haig Avenue, with George continuing at left-back. That victory meant five wins from six games and gave Southport hope that they could escape the two re-election places.

However, the Easter programme was a disaster for them. They lost all three games, including 1-0 defeats home and away to York City, who were only one place above them in the league; the other defeat was at the hands of Mansfield. They also failed to find the net in 270 minutes of play. George was left-back in all three games.

Crewe Alexandra were firmly rooted at the bottom of the league with only 17 points from 41 games. Next was Southport with 27 points from the same number of games, four points behind Bradford, but with a game in hand.

On Saturday, 12th April, Southport suffered their fourth successive defeat without scoring a goal but, according to the match report, "*Halifax should have been beaten hands down but while Southport frittered away chances and dawdled on the touchline, Halifax shot away and finished with power".* (22)

The midweek 0-0 draw away to Chesterfield was Southport's fifth successive match without a goal but, at least, it broke the bad run of defeats after they had promised so much in March. Only two of Southport's 12 close season signings were in the team at Chesterfield, Dodd and Hazeldine; five had been at the club the previous season – George, Richardson, Gryba, McDermott and Bromilow. The other four had been signed during the season.

To keep their faint hopes of avoiding re-election alive, Southport had to win their last three games and, at the same time, Bradford would have to lose their last two. But, it was not to be. Southport were beaten 1-0 away to Wrexham. Wrexham scored after 35 minutes. *"It came when Rankin allowed the ball to trickle over the dead-line, thinking it was only going to be a goal-kick, but the referee awarded Wrexham a corner. From Jones' flag kick, Bernard Evans headed the ball first time past an unsighted Richardson."*(23) In any case, Bradford won at Rochdale so a victory for Southport would not have saved from having to apply for re-election. Southport lost their last two games, 3-2 away to Crewe and 2-1 at home to Hull. George played in both games.

New National Third and Fourth Divisions were to come into operation for the 1958-59 season. The top eleven clubs in the Northern and Southern Sections, together with the two clubs relegated from the Second Division were to form the Third Division, with the bottom 12 clubs from the two Sections comprising the new Fourth Division, with a promotion system of four up from the Fourth Division and four down from the Third. Clubs forming the new Fourth Division were York City, Gateshead, Oldham Athletic, Carlisle United, Hartlepool United, Barrow, Workington, Darlington, Chester City, Bradford Park Avenue, Southport, Crewe Alexandra, Northampton Town, Crystal Palace, Port Vale, Watford, Shrewsbury Town, Aldershot, Coventry City, Walsall, Torquay United, Gillingham, Millwall and Exeter City. The only derby matches for Southport would be against Oldham, Chester and Crewe, so the club would have greater expenditure on travel and possible overnight stays.

Southport's retained list was announced at the end of April. The players retained were: Richardson, Dodd, Rankin, Kinloch, Gryba, Hazledine, McDermott, Schofield, Barker, Phoenix and Alan Parkinson.

Hughes, McKenna and Taylor, who had been at Southport for seven seasons, making 277 league appearances, were placed on the transfer list. Oldham Athletic subsequently signed Taylor for a fee of £500. Free transfers were given to Dunne, McCredie, Eric Parkinson, Phillips and Les Wood, a goalkeeper. McCredie's inclusion in the free transfer list was a surprise, as he had replaced George at the beginning of the season at left-back and he had been an ever-present in the first team until mid-February. Stan Mortenson retired.

As in the previous season, the Liverpool Senior Cup was Southport's most successful competition. On Saturday, 26th April, they beat Tranmere Rovers 2-1 at Prenton Park in the semi-final, although the winning goal only came two minutes from time. Tranmere had been awarded a penalty after 20 minutes when George was adjudged to have pulled inside-right Green back, but the spot kick went straight at Richardson, who saved easily. The Southport team was:

Richardson; Dodd, Rankin; Kinloch, Taylor, Hazledine; McDermott, Gryba, Bromilow, Barker, Phoenix.

In the final at Haig Avenue, on Saturday, 10th May, Southport and Everton drew 0-0 after extra time in heavy rain, and so both clubs were joint holders of the Cup. The teams were:

Southport: Richardson; Dodd, Rankin; Kinloch, Taylor, A. Parkinson; McDermott, Gryba, Bromilow, Barker, A. Lee.
Everton: Dunlop; Saunders, Tansey; King, Labone, Meagan; J. Harris, Thomas, Hickson, Ashworth, B. Harris.

In the first round of the FA Cup, Southport. were drawn against Wigan Athletic, a non-league side. Wigan had five former Southport players on their books, including their player-manager Trevor Hitchen, full-back Bill Forsyth and inside-left Jimmy Prescott. Before the game, Stan Mortenson, Southport's coach, said, "*If we can't beat a Lancashire Combination side we don't deserve to be in the Cup.*"(24)

The match was played on Saturday, 16th November, watched by Southport's biggest crowd for some time – 14,170. Southport flopped in front of their own supporters, losing 2-1 to a side that played in the same league as their reserve team. They seemed to have the measure of Wigan before the interval, so it came as a big surprise when Wigan Athletic scored twice in six minutes early in the second half. Southport did not get their consolation goal until the 85th minute. The teams were:

Southport: Minshull; A Parkinson, Rankin; Dunne, Taylor, McCredie; McKenna, Mortenson, Bromilow, Gryba, Phoenix.

Wigan Athletic: Arkwright; Whyte, Forsyth; Hitchen, Whitfield, Bramwell; Harrison, Banks, McLaren, Prescott, Buckle.

In December, Southport's "*makeshift team*", which did not include George, was knocked out of the Lancashire Senior Cup by Liverpool.

1958-59 Season

In early June, Trevor Hitchen was appointed as Southport's manager. He had signed for Southport as a player on 31st December 1948 from Wellington for a four-figure fee. In seven and a half seasons with the club, he made 275 first team appearances. He then moved to Oldham for two seasons before joining Wigan Athletic as player-manager 12 months before returning to Southport as manager. He was captain of the Wigan side that had knocked Southport out of the FA Cup in November 1957. Two weeks after Hitchen joined Southport, the Club sacked its trainers, Birkett and Jones, replacing them with Jack Tait, who had held a similar position at Wigan Athletic.

In July, wing-half Geoff Hazledine, who had been retained by the club, was given a free transfer. He had been married a few months earlier in Nottingham and would not agree to Southport's stipulation that all full-time professionals should live in the town in the coming season.

George re-signed for the club in mid-July, the last of the retained players to do so.

The usual public trial was held on Saturday, 16th August at Haig Avenue. As the previous season, George found himself replaced in the probable first team by a close season signing. The teams were:

Old Golds: Richardson; Dodd, Lawless (signed from Aldershot); Kinloch, Darvell (Gillingham), Morgans (Wrexham); McDermott, Kerr (Liverpool), Schofield, Davies (Chester), Cunliffe (Chesterfield).

Black & Whites: Wood (Burscough); Parkinson, Rankin; Greenwood, Ogden, Williams (Tranmere); B. Lee, Booth, Phoenix, Barker, A. Lee.

Eight new signings appeared in the trial, which the Old Golds won 3-0. "*The two best defenders were Dodd for the Probables and Rankin for the Possibles.*"(25)

The Old Golds team was chosen for the first game of the season, against Watford away, on Saturday, 23rd August 1958. This was the first meeting of the two clubs in the league, with Watford emerging as worthy winners by five goals to one.

George played for the Reserves in the 4-2 defeat by Netherfield at home. Southport were two up with a third of the game to go, but then conceded four goals.

George remained in the Reserves until Tuesday, 9th September when he appeared against Bradford at Haig Avenue. Schofield, who had been chosen to lead the first team attack, failed to arrive at the ground, so Trevor Hitchen called in George from the Reserves to play at left-back. Dodd, the side's right-back, was switched to centre-forward, while left-back Lawless moved over to the right. The team was:

Richardson; Lawless, Rankin; Kinloch, Darvell, Morgans; McDermott, Kerr, Dodd, Barker, Cunliffe.

Southport secured their second victory of the season with a 1-0 win, although Bradford were reduced to nine men for the last 20 minutes when two of their forwards collided and had to be taken to hospital with cut faces.

Southport fielded the same team in the away game against Torquay the following Saturday, when they were unlucky to be beaten 1-0. Poor finishing lost them the game.

In the next game on Monday, 15th September, Bradford gained revenge for their defeat of the previous week when they won 3-0 and inflicted a fifth successive away defeat on Southport. Southport had not scored on an opponent's ground since their goal at Watford on the opening day of the season. However, luck was against them in the Bradford game, as they struck the woodwork three times. George was at left-back again.

The only change to the team against Crewe Alexandra at Haig Avenue was the inclusion of new signing Ray Smith, Wigan's 22 years old centre-forward, for Bromilow, who was unavailable. Southport gained their third home success of the season with a 3-0 win; debutant Smith scored one of the goals. "*There was an interesting tussle throughout between two former Everton players, Southport's Rankin and Crewe's McNamara. The visiting outside-right was his side's best forward ... Taking the duel between the two former Goodison Park men as a whole, honours were about even. On the other flank, Lawless was not quite as steady as Rankin.*"(26) It was the first time Southport had scored more than once in a game that season; it was also the first time they had scored more than two in a match since 31st March.

In their next game, against Port Vale at Haig Avenue on Tuesday evening, 23rd September, Southport seemed certain to surrender their unbeaten home record when they found themselves two goals behind with less than a third of the game left. However, they drew level with a McDermott goal and an own goal five minutes from the end. "*Southport were troubled by Port Vale's tricky wingers and yet in Rankin they had one of the best defenders on view.*"(27)

Southport had made their worst start away from home since the War, losing their first five games on opponents' grounds. Results did not improve in their next two away games, in which they were beaten 3-1 by Northampton Town on

Saturday, 27th September, and 4-1 by Port Vale two days later. George played at left-back in both games.

At home, however, they maintained their unbeaten record with 3-0 and 2-0 victories over Workington and Darlington respectively. In between those two Saturday games, they travelled to London on Wednesday morning, 8th October, where they were beaten 1-0 by Crystal Palace in an evening game watched by almost 14,000 spectators. The team stayed in London overnight after the match, travelling back to Southport on Thursday morning.

Southport maintained an unchanged team for the away game against Walsall on Saturday, 18th October, the third game in a row. It was:

Richardson; Dodd, Rankin; Kinloch, Darvell, Morgans; McDermott, Kerr, Smith, Barker, Cunliffe.

Walsall scored after 25 seconds, the day's quickest goal, and went on to score four more, with Southport managing only one in return. That was Southport's ninth away defeat of the season, and 25 of the 28 goals scored against them had been in those nine away games.

However, the following Saturday, Southport preserved their unbeaten home record with a 2-1 win over Millwall watched by almost 4,700 spectators. Millwall's outside-right, Broadfoot, *"was as fast a winger as has been seen on the ground this season, but it was seldom that he got the better of Rankin, and towards the end of the game, he wandered inside to get more sight of the ball."* (28)

Southport fielded the same team for the fifth successive game in a 3-2 defeat on their first ever visit to Aldershot. It was the first time in the season that South-port had scored more than one goal away from home and it brought their tally to six, losing their tag of scoring fewer goals away than any other side in the League. Southport should have earned at least a draw, but they paid dearly for their failure to accept chances.

As a result of a last-minute equaliser against bottom-placed Gateshead the following Saturday, Southport ensured that they maintained their unbeaten home record.

The draw against Gateshead saw Southport in 20th position, just one place above the danger zone and only one point better off than the club immediately below. Southport entertained Barrow, two places above them on Saturday, 22nd November. A penalty save by goalkeeper Richardson earned a point for Southport in a 0-0 draw, watched by Southport's lowest gate of the season, a mere 2,500, with receipts of £223.

A 5-0 defeat at Carlisle the following Saturday, equalled a 30-year old record for Southport – 11 consecutive away defeats. It was also Southport's heaviest loss of the season and the third time that campaign that they had conceded five goals away from home. Carlisle took the lead in 10th minute. *"When the ball came over from the right, it should have been cut out. Rankin unfortunately deflected the ball on to Mooney, whose centre found Ackerman and he netted from close range."* The half-time score was 2-0 and then Carlisle scored three goals in ten minutes. The first came after 53 minutes. *"Six minutes later, Rankin was adjudged to have brought down Mooney (outside-right) – it was a harsh decision as it looked as though the players collided – and Troop made no mistake from the spot."*(29)

Following the game against Gateshead, goalkeeper Richardson asked for a transfer as he felt that he was worth a better class of football than the Fourth Division. His request was granted.

Exeter and Southport were the only two teams in the Fourth Division unbeaten at home and they met on Saturday, 13th December at Exeter. Left-half Williams pulled a muscle in midweek training and it was decided that manager Trevor Hitchen should play in his first competitive game of the season. The team was:

Richardson; Dodd, Rankin; Parkinson, Darvell, Hitchen; Schofield, Kinloch, Smith, Morgans, McDermott.

Southport were only a goal down at the interval. However, they drew level 20 minutes into the second half when Dodd scored from the penalty spot after Schofield had been brought down in the box. Shortly afterwards, Southport took the lead through McDermott, but two late goals, including a 35 yard drive that Richardson could only push into his net, secured victory for Exeter. Southport set a club record by losing their first twelve away games. They had 16 points from 22 games, which was actually better than the previous two years when they had eight points from the same number of games in the 1956-57 season and ten points in 1957-58. Despite the improvement in the number of points gained, they were still in the bottom two in the league table, just as they had been at the same time in the two previous seasons.

Southport's lost their unbeaten home record to Watford, who were 3-0 winners on Saturday, 20th December. George did not play as he had not recovered from a knock that he received in midweek training. He also missed the Christmas Day and Boxing Day games against Shrewsbury, which Southport lost 1-0 and 6-2 respectively.

Barely 2,000 had watched the home defeat by Shrewsbury Town, Southport's last ever Christmas Day game. A significant counter-attraction had arrived in October of that season with the first transmission of BBC TV's Saturday afternoon Grandstand programme offering a variety of sports. Football was clearly going to have to work harder to attract spectators.

George recovered from his injury in time to feature in the New Year's Day game at home against Crystal Palace. The team was:

Richardson; Dodd, Rankin; Parkinson, Darvell, Williams; McDermott, Kerr, Smith, Barker, Lee.

Palace scored twice in the opening minutes of the second half to make it an unhappy start to 1959 for Southport and consigned them to bottom place in the league.

George missed the next game away to Hartlepool United as he was injured again. Southport gained a 1-1 draw, ending a run of 15 away games without a point. In fact, it was the first point Southport had gained on an opponent's ground since they took part in a goalless draw at Chesterfield on 16th April 1958. Despite that point, Southport were still bottom of the league.

On Saturday, 10th January 1959, the Southport Visitor reported that "*George*

Rankin has received medical advice to rest. Rankin has been dogged by bad luck just lately. After gaining his place in the team in September, Rankin played 18 successive senior games. He was forced to miss the games with Watford and the two matches with Shrewsbury, but came back for the New Year's Day game with Crystal Palace, only to break down again and he was not able to play against Hartlepool. It is hoped that he will soon be in action again, as Southport need the services of this classy defender."

Five days later, Southport signed Wally Fielding as their new player-manager on a three-year contract. Fielding had lost his place in Everton's first team following the arrival of Bobby Collins, the Scottish international. His transfer from Everton was reported to have involved a four-figure fee. He was to make his debut against Coventry City, the league leaders, on Saturday, 17th January, but the game was postponed because of snow.

The news of Fielding's appointment came as a big surprise to Trevor Hitchen, Southport's team manager since the beginning of the season. The way in which the signing of Fielding was handled by the club caused a furore. In the Southport Visitor on Saturday, 17th January, the "Last Word in Sport" column asked why the local press was ignored in the announcement of Fielding as manager. Also, according to "Last Word in Sport", the club chairman, Mr Thornley, admitted to the Daily Express that Trevor Hitchen *"knew nothing about the negotiations"*, and added that *"he is not on the phone so I can't tell him."* (30) Yet, on finding out that he was no longer the manager, the unassuming Hitchen agreed to cooperate with his successor and became his assistant, stating, *"I bear no malice, it isn't in my nature to do so. Naturally, the news came as a shock to me, but the Directors have done what they thought best."* (31)

"Last Word in Sport" went on, *"I understand a number of directors were rather upset when they read the news. They have every right to be because as directors they have every right to know what is going on, particularly when a four-figured amount of money is involved."*

The Southport Visitor also published a number of letters about the matter. In one, three shareholders wrote, *"This latest development is another instance of how ruthless the present board is. Just look at some of the events since the present set-up took charge. Their first action was to make it so some of their colleagues*

– *five in fact – had to retire. Then, they chased away the President… On the playing side, they relieved Mr G Hunt of his managerial duties and Stan Mortenson was appointed team supervisor. But they made it impossible for Mortenson to carry on and so Mr Hunt became secretary-manager again. Then for this season, Mr Hunt reverted to secretary again and Mr Hitchen was appointed team manager and loyal servants, who were previously told they would stay with the Club, were sacked. But after six months, Mr Hitchen has been demoted and a new player-manager has been appointed. To us this seems a strange way to foster team spirit and how does it tie up with the chairman's statement at the beginning of the season that the club's policy would be economy with efficiency. We are not fast losing confidence in the chairman and directors of Southport, we have lost it."*

Negotiations about the transfer of Fielding took place at Everton on Monday morning. Another letter posed the question, *"Has the phone been taken out at Haig Avenue where Mr Hitchen would surely be in the afternoon?"*

Yet another letter was published under the heading *"New players, not new manager is needed."* The author asked, *"If you take Richardson, Darvell, Rankin and McDermott out of the team, what is there left? – nothing in my opinion,."* and added that it was time that the club had a new board of directors, not a new manager.

"Last Word in Sport" concluded his column, *"Whilst the Wally Fielding story has been the talking point in town this week, it is obvious from the letters I have received that the manner in which the news broke has been talked about just as much as the signing itself."*

After all the fuss about Fielding's appointment, it was back to the football itself. George was to have a try-out following his injury and was named at left-back in the Reserve team to play Ashton United away on Saturday, 24th January. However, he did not play as he was still unfit.

That same Saturday, Wally Fielding made his first appearance in the 2-1 home win against Gillingham. It coincided with the debut of another ex-Evertonian, Jackie Grant, who had signed from Rochdale a few hours before the game.

George missed four league games as a result of his injury, four games in which Southport remained unbeaten with three draws and a win, taking five points out of a possible eight.

George finally resumed in the first team at left-back on Saturday, 14th February against Northampton Town at Haig Avenue. Since joining Southport, George had been a part-time professional, but in the week before the Northampton game, he signed a full-time professional contract. The Southport team was:

Richardson; Dodd, Rankin; Kinloch, Parkinson, Grant; McDermott, Fielding, Darvell, Barker, Woodhead.

Northampton claimed a double over Southport with a last second 2-1 victory. *"Woan restored Northampton's lead in the closing seconds of the game, heading through a pass pushed forward by an opponent as Rankin was leisurely holding the ball until dispossessed."*(32)

The defeat by Northampton Town started a run of 16 games to the end of the season without a win – five draws and eleven defeats, including defeats in the final six games. George appeared in all of those matches.

It is interesting to note that the trip to Barrow for the away game on Saturday, 11th April, did not cost the club a penny. The cost of the coach and the players' meals, lunch and dinner after the game at Morecambe, were paid for by a supporters' outing. It did not improve the team's performance, however, as they lost 3-0 to the team with the poorest home record in the Football league – five wins, five draws, and ten losses. That result made Southport firm favourites for the wooden spoon and, after losing their five remaining games, finished bottom of the league for the very first time. They also failed to win an away game in a season for the first time. Clearly, the lack of goals was a contributory factor as the 46 league games yielded only 41 of them.

In the penultimate game of the season against Gillingham, on 25th April 1959, Southport fielded a side with six players, who had turned 30 years of age – George 30, Grant 35, Robinson 31, Fielding 40, Rutherford 30 and Harrison 32. Previously, Ashe, who was 34 had been playing at right-back and Darvell at centre-half was 29. Clearly, Fielding was putting his faith in experience and that team must have been one of the oldest sides Southport had ever put out.

The attendance for the 23 home league games was 78,000, a drop of 10,000 on the previous season, which in turn was 14,000 down on the campaign before that. The average attendance of 3,400 made Southport one of the worst supported clubs in the country. And another record of the wrong kind set up during the campaign was one of not having at least one 5,000 gate for a league game – the highest was 4,693 against Millwall on 25th October 1958. The club also sustained a record loss of £7,756.10s.9d for the season, making the club's total deficit £27,237.

Twenty-seven players were called on for league duty during the season. Only Richardson and Darvell were ever-present, while George played in 34 of the 46 league games.

Southport fared no better in their Cup games that season. On Saturday, 15th November 1958, they were knocked out of the FA Cup in the first round at Haig Avenue by Halifax Town, who scored twice through errors by goalkeeper Richardson. Watched by 6,331 spectators, Southport failed to reply. The Southport team was:

Richardson; Dodd, Rankin; Kinloch, Darvell, Williams; McDermott, Davies, Smith, Kerr, Cunliffe.

A few weeks before, they had lost 1-0 away to Barrow in the first round of the Lancashire Senior Cup and, in March the following year, Everton beat them 3-2 at Haig Avenue in the semi-final of the Liverpool Senior Cup. Southport's team included three former Evertonians – Fielding, Grant and George – whilst Everton fielded pretty much their Central League side:

O'Neill; Parkes, Tansey; Sanders, Labone, Rea; Bonar, MacKay, Wignall, Ashworth, Godfrey.

At the end of the season, Southport announced that they had retained ten players. They were: Darvell, Fielding, Grant, McDermott, Parkinson, Rankin, Richardson, Robinson and Wood plus Beadnell, who had not played for the club for two years owing to illness. Barker, Dodd, Kerr, Kinloch, Stokes and Gryba were placed on the open-to-transfer list, while Cunliffe, Lawless, Morgans and Williams were given free-transfers. Trevor Hitchin's contract finished at the end of June, but he left in May to become manager of Formby.

In March, Roy Smith, who had led the Southport attack on 23 occasions the previous season, left to join Morecambe. Three months later, on Wednesday, 3rd June, he was killed in an underground colliery accident at Haydock. He was not a regular underground worker, but went down from time to time as part of his job as a Coal Board surveyor.

Season 1959-60

Before the season started, Southport reached the final of one competition – the Heading Tennis tournament organised by the Everton Supporters' Club at the Old Coliseum in City Road, the proceeds being donated to charity.

Heading tennis was something of a misnomer as each team of two players was able to kick, knee or head a football to each other or over a net in an attempt to beat their opponents. The net was fixed at the height of a badminton net and the game was played on a court somewhat smaller than that used for lawn tennis. Some of the rallies lasted as long as any at Wimbledon and each match was the best of three games at 21 up.

Liverpool, Everton, Tranmere Rovers and Southport had each entered two teams and on the afternoon of Saturday, 8th August, Southport met Tranmere in the final. Southport's squad for the final was Fielding, Grant and George, who had all played in the earlier rounds. The result of the final is not known.

Southport were re-elected to the Fourth Division and in their public trial on Saturday, 15th August, included 12 new professionals signed by Wally Fielding, two professional trialists and a new amateur. The Probables won 3-2 and the teams were:

Probables: Richardson, Ashe (signed from Gateshead), Rankin; Clayton (Everton), Darvell, Robinson (Bradford); Taylor (Bolton), Moss (Liverpool), Green, Reeson (Doncaster), Harrison (Reading).
Possibles: A N Other; Leath, Bruce; Rutherford (Darlington), Parker

(Shelbourne), Grant; Newman, Baker (Halifax), Blakeman (Workington), Harris (Preston), Norcross.

Southport's first game of the season was on Saturday, 22nd August, at home to Rochdale, who had been relegated from the Third Division. Seven newcomers were selected, with Richardson, Rankin, Darvell and Green the only players from the previous season to retain their places. The team was:

Richardson; Ashe, Rankin; Clayton, Darvell, Robinson; Taylor, Moss, Green, Reeson, Harris.

A crowd of 6,000 people saw Rochdale go two goals up in the 60th minute, before Southport fought back to level the scores to gain a point.

There was one change for their first away game, against Workington, in mid-week. Peter Harrison, signed from Reading, replaced Harris at outside-left. Green equalised 18 minutes from the end for Southport and Workington were glad to hold on in the last 10 minutes for a point in a 1-1 draw.

Southport lost their next game, away to Gateshead on Saturday, 29th August, by a goal to nil. A bad defensive error in the 58th minute cost Southport a point. *"There was absolutely no danger as a pass from Lumley to Kirtley failed to reach the target. Rankin gained possession and from about 20 yards decided to pass back. Richardson was out of his goal and the ball sailed over the goalkeeper's head and into the net."*(33)

Another defensive blunder cost Southport a point in their next game. With four minutes to go in the home match against Workington on Tuesday 1st September, Southport were leading, but goalkeeper Richardson failed to hold a shot and Workington were presented with the easiest of chances to equalise. George was later forced to kick-off the line with Richardson well beaten.

Following Richardson's poor performance in his 50th consecutive game, Southport signed a new goalkeeper for the Saturday fixture against Darlington at Haig Avenue. He was 26 year old Arthur Barnard, who had been with Stockport County for three seasons and previously at Bolton. Two weeks later,

Richardson left the club to join Wigan Athletic, after making 103 appearances for Southport.

Unfortunately, in his first game, an error by Barnard allowed Darlington to score the only goal of the game in the 57th minute. Their left-winger, Redfearn, crossed the ball from near the touchline and saw it sail between the arms of Barnard into the net. It was Southport's first home defeat of the season. The Southport team was:

Barnard; Ashe, Rankin; Clayton, Darvell, Robinson; Taylor, Fielding, Green, Reeson, Harrison.

A 4-0 loss at Torquay in midweek sent Southport to the bottom of the table with only three points out of a possible 12.

On Saturday, 12th September, they visited Aldershot, and were forced to make several changes through injury. The team was:

Barnard; Leath, Rankin; Rutherford, Darvell, Robinson; Taylor, Moss, Clayton, Reeson, Harrison.

Aldershot had a 100% home record, so Southport did well to earn a 0-0 draw. It was their first clean sheet of the season but, unfortunately, the attack failed to find the net for the third game running.

Southport lost their home game to Torquay the following Tuesday, fielding the same team that opposed Aldershot but, on Saturday, 19th September, they deservedly beat Barrow 1-0 at Haig Avenue to record their first win for 27 games. Their last victory was almost 12 months earlier, when they overcame Millwall by two goals to one at home on the 25th October 1958. The team against Aldershot was unchanged for the third time running, and "*Rankin gave a better all-round display and once, early in the second half went close to scoring. Harrison had forced a corner and when the ball was beaten out, Rankin gained possession and his fierce drive flashed inches wide of the post.*"(34)

The win against Barrow gave the Southport players their first £4 bonus of the season. At that time, the maximum weekly wage paid to a part-time or full-time professional over 20 years of age was £20 in the winter and £17 in the summer; the minimum for a full-timer was £8 in summer and winter, whilst the minimum for a part-timer was £5. For the 1957/58 season, when George was a part-timer, he was paid £9 per week during the winter and £8 per week in the summer.

Following their victory over Barrow, Southport then suffered two heavy defeats within three days, 5-0 by Doncaster and 4-1 by Gillingham. On Tuesday, 29th September, the Southport Visitor reported that far too many Southport players had an off day against Gillingham and went on to say that, "*In fact, only three players really lived up to their reputations, and they were left-back George Rankin, centre-forward Johnny Clayton and inside-left Tony Reeson.*"

After fielding the same team for five matches, Southport made one change for the home game against Crystal Palace on Saturday, 3rd October. Grant came in for Rutherford at right-half. Southport won 3-1 and moved away from bottom place. Two nights later, Southport were within three minutes of wrecking Millwall's unbeaten record and ending their own run of 34 away games without a win, only to concede a second goal to Millwall, which earned them a draw. The Millwall game was watched by 17,773 spectators. The match receipts were over £1,900, so Southport's 20% cut was more than their share of the gate for their home game against Crystal Palace.

In the Southport Visitor on Saturday, 10th October, "Last Word in Sport" wrote about the Club's recent national press. The theme had been the same – Southport are in a false position in the league table. After the victory over Crystal Palace, Noel Stanley wrote the following in the Daily Express under the headline "*Don't worry, you'll climb Southport: My second visit in a fortnight to Haig Avenue convinced me of one thing – Southport won't have to seek re-election this season.*" The News Chronicle headline after the Millwall game was "*Greatest show this season*" and its reporter Ian Wooldridge wrote, "*…while 17000 Londoners looked on with dropping jaws, they (Southport) turned this into the greatest soccer entertainment I've seen this season.*" In the Daily Herald, Sam Leitch wrote, "*…pardon me while I wipe away a tear for the gallant souls of Southport.*" The Liverpool Daily Post's headline was "*Ovation Deserved*".

The positive press failed to stir Southport to even better things. They lost their next away game to Stockport by the only goal, when a draw would have been a fairer result. The Sports Editor of the Southport Visitor claimed that he had never seen a ground in worse condition than Stockport's and went on to add, *"Both full-backs showed good positional skill and this particularly applied to Rankin on one occasion in the second half when, from his position almost on the goal line, he was able to clear a shot which might have beaten Barnard."*(35)

Southport recorded their third successive home win on Saturday, 17th October, when they beat Exeter 3-2 before a crowd of just over 4,000 spectators. Winning three home games in a row was something they had not done for 12 months. However, the win still left them next to bottom place in the league. *"The most harassed defender on the home side was Rankin, who was never comfortable against the quick moving right winger Stiffle, the best of the visiting forwards, who had a part in both the visitors' goals."*(36)

After a 2-1 away defeat at Watford on Saturday, 24th October, Southport beat Oldham 1-0 at Haig Avenue the following weekend to record their fourth straight home win. Before Southport scored the only goal of the game, Oldham had the ball in the net after 30 minutes, but the goal was disallowed. *"Southport had been awarded a free-kick, and Rankin intended to tap the ball to the goalkeeper, but Buzley (the Oldham outside-right) intervened and the ball finished in the net. The referee ruled that the Oldham player was not the required distance from the ball when the free-kick was taken and waved aside the Oldham appeals for a goal."*(37) The win moved Southport up the table by two places.

The following Saturday, Southport, still without an away win, visited Carlisle, who were in fourth place. The side was unchanged for the seventh game in a row, with the same attack for the 13th game on the run. Fielding's policy was one of making as few changes as possible. In the 16 games since the season started, only 12 changes had been made, one or two of them enforced and 18 players had been called on. There were still six ever-presents: George, Darvell, Robinson, Taylor, Clayton and Reeson. For the third consecutive away game, all against clubs in the top half of the table, Southport were beaten 1-0. Southport matched Carlisle when it came to football skill and were within five minutes of a deserved point. Barnard saved a late penalty to deny Carlisle a second goal.

Southport faced league-leaders Walsall on the 21st November with a new centre-forward – Barry Jepson, who was signed from Chester only the day before the game. Twenty-seven year old Jepson cost a three-figure fee and had had a good scoring record with both Chester and Mansfield. With Green, Clayton and Parker all injured, Southport were desperate for a recognised centre-forward. The team against Walsall was:

Barnard; Rutherford, Rankin; Grant, Darvell, Robinson; Taylor, Moss, Jepson, Reeson, Harrison.

In losing 8-0, Southport suffered their heaviest defeat for 2½ years, and Walsall achieved their biggest home win since the turn of the century. Southport conceded the first goal after 12 seconds and the third in the 63rd minute. But, in the last 18 minutes, Southport's defence went to pieces, giving away five goals. Jepson must have wondered about his decision to join Southport.

Without a win in November, Southport badly needed the two points they gained by beating Hartlepool United 2-1 for their fifth successive home league win. Hartlepool went ahead in the eighth minute, but goals from Southport in the 44th and 70th minutes secured the two points.

They followed the victory over Hartlepool with another home win, this time against Chester by three goals to one. The team was:

Barnard; Rutherford, Rankin; Grant, Parker, Robinson; Taylor, Moss, Jepson, Reeson, Harrison.

Jepson scored twice against his old club for his first goals for Southport. "*The visitors had a clever winger in 17 year old Jimmy Cooper, and George Rankin revealed the wiliness of experience as he struck blow after blow at the machinations of the youngster. But when he switched from the right wing to the left, he found the going easier and was the scorer of the Chester goal.*"(38)

That win put Southport ahead of the previous season's return from the same number of games. Twelve months before, they had 16 points from 21 games, the win against Chester put them on 17 points and lifted them away from the last four in the league table. Although the gate was the smallest of the season, Southport were still better supported than the previous season. Ten league matches at Haig Avenue had been watched by an average of 4206 a game, against 3,567 at the same time in 1958. Receipts were up by £1,080.

Manager Fielding had hoped to name the same team for the game against Rochdale at Spotland the following Saturday. However, Grant needed a cartilage operation, so Bill Parker moved to right-half and Roger Darvell returned to centre-half after missing two games. Rochdale had not been beaten in their last 12 home games, whilst Southport had the worst away record in the four divisions, so they were desperately unlucky to lose 1-0 as a result of an own goal and a lack of punch in attack. As far as the match reporter was concerned, *"the honours in defence were taken by George Rankin. Seldom has he played better. Time and again his covering and quick interceptions nipped home raids in the bud, and right winger Barnes was practically played out of the game."*(39)

Boxing Day was the last chance Southport had of winning their first away game of 1959. They had not won away from home for 40 league games, and in those 40 games, which had yielded eight draws, only 22 goals had been scored, while 99 had been conceded. Clearly, there was a lack of scoring power away from home. In the previous season at this stage, Southport were pointless away from home, so their three draws was an improvement. Indeed, one more point on tour would equal the return from all of the previous season's away matches. But, it was not to be. Southport lost 3-0 to Bradford.

The return match at Haig Avenue on Monday, 28th December ended in a 1-1 draw. Left-winger Harrison scored for Southport after ten minutes, whilst Bradford equalised two minutes before the interval. Five minutes from the end, Harrison was brought down in the penalty area, but he shot over from the spot, denying Southport their seventh successive home league win. The team was:

Barnard; Rutherford, Rankin; Clayton, Parker, Robinson; Keeley, Moss, Jepson, Reeson, Harrison.

Southport were now back in the re-election places, fourth from bottom, on the same number of points as Doncaster Rovers but with an inferior goal average.

Southport's first game of 1960 was at home to Gateshead on Saturday, 2nd January. George had broken a foot in the Bradford game, so Rutherford moved to left-back and Leath came in at right-back for his first senior game since October. A 67th minute goal for Southport was enough to secure both points and move them to fifth from bottom in the league. It was their seventh win of the season, equalling the previous season's number of successes.

The following Saturday, Southport were at home again, this time to Notts County, who were the second most prolific scorers in the Football League. George was still unfit so Leath continued at right-back. Southport were beaten 2-1, but two missed penalties cost them the points. With the score at 1-1, Southport were awarded a penalty for handball. The County goalkeeper pushed Parker's spot kick on to the upright, the ball went back to Parker who shot again, but the keeper saved the ball with his body to knock it clear of goal. Southport were awarded a second penalty 15 minutes later when Reeson was brought down in the box. Parker again took the kick but, this time, completely missed the goal. Notts County later had a penalty saved by Barnard, but went on to score the winner six minutes from time when Southport were looking the more likely victors.

George missed two more games – 5-0 and 4-0 defeats by Darlington and Aldershot respectively – before returning to the first team at left-back for the away game against Barrow on Saturday, 6th February. The team was:

Barnard; Leath, Rankin; Rutherford, Darvell, Robinson; Taylor, Moss, Jepson, Reeson, Harrison.

Despite scoring their first away goal since 24th October, Southport lost 3-1.

Southport signed two new players in an effort to strengthen the team – Jimmy Blain, a 19 year old forward, who had played in a number of games in Everton's

Central League side and Tom Finley, an experienced wing half from Workington. Both went straight into the team for the home game against Gillingham on Saturday, 13th February. The team was:

> Barnard; Rutherford, Rankin; Finley, Darvell, Robinson; Blain, Moss, Jepson, Reeson, Harrison.

Southport ended their run of four successive defeats by gaining a point with a 1-1 draw, with the debutant Blain scoring Southport's goal. The gate of 2,551 was the lowest of the season.

The surprise result of the day the following Saturday was Southport's 2-2 draw at promotion seeking Crystal Palace. Southport went in at the interval with a 2-0 lead, but Palace scored in the 66th and 74th minutes to level the scores. Southport came close to recording their first away victory for 22 months, but were lucky to have "*Rankin on hand when Sexton shot hard and beat Barnard only to have the ball kicked off the line by the back.*"(40)

In their next game, Southport recorded their biggest win of the season when they beat Stockport County 3-0 at Haig Avenue, despite injuries to Moss and Reeson, which left them with only three effective forwards in the second half.

Southport gained a point from each of their next two games, both of which ended 1-1. The first was away to Exeter. It was their fifth away point of the season, thereby bettering their away record of the previous season when they only had four points to show from 23 games. The second 1-1 draw was at home to Watford, two of whose forwards had scored 63 goals between them that season. Southport were ahead within 30 seconds, and just before Watford got the equaliser, in the 58th minute, George cleared off the line with goalkeeper Barnard beaten.

On Wednesday, 16th March, Southport were well and truly beaten 5-1 by Crewe Alexandra away from home. Crewe were five goals up before their goalkeeper was called upon to make a save. However, the following Saturday, the 19th March, was a day to remember in the history of Southport Football Club. The club ended a two-year and 47 game run without an away victory, when they defeated Oldham by a goal to nil at Boundary Park. It was also their first double of the season. Following the win at Oldham, Southport had 28 points, which beat the previous season's total by two The Southport team against Oldham was:

Barnard; Ashe, Rankin; Rutherford, Darvell, Grant; Taylor, Moss, Jepson, Blain, Harrison.

Southport's home game against Carlisle on Saturday, 26th March was watched by the lowest gate of the season so far – 2,385. The match was in direct competition with the very first televised screening of the Grand National. Carlisle had agreed to a 4.15pm kick-off to avoid the clash, but Southport directors decided to go ahead with the 3pm kick-off. The television coverage of the National undoubtedly affected attendance. Southport were unhappy with the 1-1 draw against Carlisle. They went ahead after 32 minutes but nine minutes into the second half, Carlisle got a lucky equaliser and went away with a point. The linesman flagged for off-side against Carlisle's left-half Thompson and the home defence eased up. But, the referee ignored the signal and Thompson went on to score. Moreover, the referee turned down three reasonable claims for a penalty by Southport. However, Southport had little excuse for not getting a win, Harrison and Jepson failed with simple chances.

Falling attendances were a problem for all clubs at this time, although the decline was less marked in the First Division. When George started out with Everton, football crowds had reached their peak with more than 41m people watching the games during the 1948/49 season. Attendances had fallen gradually over the years and by the end of the current season - 1959/60 - just under 28m fans had turned up to watch their teams. Whilst alternative attractions such as television and live commentary on radio undoubtedly had an impact, other reasons put forward included the increase in admission prices, unattractive football – the number of goals scored were at their lowest, and the poor facilities at most grounds. The facilities at grounds had changed little since the pre-war period with three sides of most grounds providing no cover and the catering services and toilet facilities provided were derisory.

Southport suffered heavy defeats in their next three games – 4-1 away to

Notts County; 4-1 in their first home defeat since 23rd January to league leaders Walsall; and 4-0 away to Northampton Town. At this stage, it looked certain that Southport would have to apply for re-election for the third season running.

There were sweeping changes after the defeat at the hands of Northampton. Out went George, Wally Fielding and Bill Norcross and there were four positional changes. The team to face Hartlepool United on Saturday 16th April was:

Barnard; Ashe, Rutherford; Grant, Darvell, Robinson; Blain, Moss, Jepson, Reeson, Harrison.

Unfortunately, the changes did not affect Southport's fortunes as they lost 3-2.

George had been an ever-present since his return from injury on 6th February. After being dropped from the first team, he appeared for the Reserves at Haig Avenue on Saturday, 16th April, against Wigan Athletic, facing two former Southport colleagues - Jack Richardson in goal and Jimmy McDermott on the right wing. McDermott, directly opposed to George, got both Wigan's goals in their 2-0 win.

He also played at left-half for the Reserves on Wednesday, 20th April, when they defeated Ashton United 3-0 at Haig Avenue to progress to the semi-final of the Lancashire Combination Cup.

George was then recalled to the first team for the home game against Millwall on Monday evening, 25th April, which Southport won 1-0, ending Millwall's promotion chances. The victory was too late to prevent Southport having to apply for re-election once again.

George played in the last two games of the season – a 2-2 draw away to Chester and a 1-1 draw at home to Doncaster Rovers. He had made 39 league and six Cup appearances during the season. Only Barnard, Darvell, Harrison, Rutherford and Reeson had played more games than him.

The two draws meant that Southport finished in 21st place in the league, five points behind Chester, who escaped the need to seek re-election. Southport's total of 34 points was their best since the 1955-56 season, when they finished fifth in the Northern Section of the Third Division. Their home games were better attended than the previous season. The average attendance for league matches was up by over 200, while the receipts were £9,100 compared with £7,410.

Like their senior counterparts, Southport Reserves had not had a good season; they had only a slender chance of avoiding relegation in the Lancashire Combination. For that to happen, they had to win their last two games by quite convincing margins and Darwin had to lose their remaining match. George played in those last two games, along with several other first team players. They slipped at the first hurdle, only managing a 1-1 draw at home to Marine, but beat Rossendale United 5-3 in the next game to end the season with a victory.

Southport's luck of the draw for the first round of the FA Cup held good when they were drawn at home for the fifth successive time. Their opponents at Haig Avenue on 14th November 1959 were Workington Town, the club that they had met more than any other in the FA Cup. It was their ninth meeting since Workington gained League status, with six wins out of eight to Southport. After a 2-2 draw at Haig Avenue before a crowd of over 5,500, Southport lost the replay on Wednesday evening, 18th November by three goals to nil. Southport's team was:

Barnard; Rutherford, Rankin; Grant, Darvell, Robinson; Taylor, Moss, Parker, Fielding, Harrison.

Southport were under a severe handicap from the 15th minute when Parker sustained a bad cut to his head, leaving the field for the wound to be stitched. After returning 15 minutes later, he re-opened the wound upon heading the ball and had to play with a sponge, which he used constantly to wipe the blood from his face.

Southport also went out of the Lancashire Senior Cup in the first round, this time after two replays. They drew 1-1 with Blackburn Rovers at Ewood Park in October. The replay at Haig Avenue on Tuesday, 24th November, also ended in a 1-1 draw, after extra time. George almost won the game for Southport in extra time when his shot struck the bar. Southport won the toss to stage the second replay at Haig Avenue on Tuesday, 1st December, but were deservedly beaten 4-0. George also played in the second replay.

A week later, they were knocked out of the only other cup competition in which they had an interest, the Liverpool Senior Cup. Tranmere Rovers beat them 1-0 at Prenton Park, in a match that showed little difference between the Third and Fourth Division. "*The duel of the match was between two former Evertonians – George Rankin and Tommy Eglington. Rankin often brought about the displeasure of the crowd with some hard tackling of his former colleague, but honours were just about even by the end.*" (41)

George was placed on the open-to-transfer list at the end of the season, along with inside-forward Tony Reeson and centre-forward Barry Jepson. Eight of the 22 professionals were retained – Leath (full-back); Darvell, Rutherford, Clayton, and Grant (half-backs); and Moss, Blain and Harrison (forwards). Free transfers were given to Barnard, Wood, and Walton (goalkeepers); Ashe (full-back); Parker, Finley, and Robinson (half-backs); Taylor, Green, Baker, and Harris (forwards).

Joe Moore expressed surprise in his "Spotlight on Sport" column in the Southport Visitor on Saturday, 7th May, at the decision to place George on the transfer list, and added, "*Since coming here from Everton prior to the start of the 1956-57 season, Rankin has given grand service to the club. His record speaks for itself as in the four seasons he has been at Southport he has made 144 league appearances. A stylish player, he has had his critics - but who hasn't – but nevertheless his coolness and positional play has often stood the team in good stead, and I think the club will be very lucky indeed to get a replacement as good without paying a fee.*"

A letter from J.E. Bosler appeared in the same edition. He was shocked to find the name of Barnard was not in the 'retained' list, and he went on to say, "*George Rankin is another who has been given the wrong treatment. At the beginning of nearly every season at Southport, he has played in the Reserves, losing his place to a newcomer, only to regain the number 3 shirt within a few weeks and he has always played well for the club and given his best service.*"

George had just completed his fourth season with Southport, making 144 league and 6 FA cup appearances. Maybe his entitlement to a benefit the following season had something to do with Southport's decision to release him.

George was working as a draughtsman for a Southport firm and joined Borough United in the Welsh League, and later moving to Dolgellau also of the Welsh

League. At this stage, George was going through a difficult period, according to his brother Billy. He was having a stressful time at work where he was experiencing *"some bullying"*, he and his wife had bought a busy newsagents in Liverpool, and his marriage was going through a bad patch. It all got too much for him and he suffered a breakdown on his way to play for Dolgellau one Saturday and did not know where he was. The police contacted his father and asked him to collect George from Dolgellau. George was admitted to Ormskirk Hospital, diagnosed as suffering from schizophrenia, and remained there for six weeks or so. He was never the same after that. His marriage failed, he lost his job and his football career was finished.

Life after Football

George eventually started work again as a toolmaker for Delco Electronics in Liverpool. George Allen, one of his colleagues in the 1970s, recalled that *"George was a quiet chap when I knew him, he was a toolmaker and you would always find him at his bench in a far corner of the toolroom. Apart from going to the toilet or to get water for his "brew" he was always at his work place. He didn't socialise or converse much with anyone, he preferred to be left alone to get on with what he was doing, people generally left him to himself, which is what he seemed to prefer. New starters were quite surprised that he was once left-back for Everton because he didn't come across as someone who was once quite famous locally."*

George had been a keen golfer during his football career, playing in a number of the Professional Footballers' Golf Championships over the years. His last appearance was in the 1959 competition when he was among the fifteen players who qualified from the north-west for the final held in London. He did not win the competition but Wally Burnett, who had been at Everton with George, thought that George would have been a better golfer than a footballer.

After his football career was finished, George found solace in his golf. He was a member of Hesketh Golf Club, near Southport, for many years and won numerous trophies. Alan Deutsch, one of his playing partners, described George as *"a quiet well-mannered man,"* and added that George was *"a keen golfer off a handicap of four when he played with me around local courses on summer evenings in the late 1960s/early 1970s. I was a reasonably steady 18 handicapper and our combination usually won us the meal after the match. He was a typical professional sportsman – always wanting to win and he played to the principle that you do not relax one iota until the game is definitely won or lost."* Another member of the Golf Club also remembered him as *"a quiet man",* but indicated that *"some of the Club members looked down on George because he had been a professional footballer."*

George in later life with a golf trophy he had won.

Former team-mates and family all described George as a quiet man. Jack Richardson, the Southport goalkeeper remembered George as *"a nice man, a quiet man, but a helluva a footballer. Being part-time, he didn't socialise with the full-time players."* According to Wally Burnett, *"George was a nice man, but he also kept himself to himself."* Jimmy Tansey, who partnered George at full-back for Everton, enjoyed playing with him. He thought that George was a good man to have in your side but he always seemed to have something on his mind. Another Everton contemporary, Dave Hickson, said that George minded his own business and did not socialise a great deal with the other players. Indeed, his aunt, Alice (Teeny) Rankin, said, "*George did not smoke, drink or bother with women and this meant that he was teased by the other players*".

However, George Allen, his colleague at Delco Electronics remembered an incident that perhaps revealed another side of George's character. "*He had a short fuse when he felt that someone was being funny with him. Once, when George switched off someone's radio so that he could plug in his kettle there was an argument. The younger chap told George that he would meet him in the car park and sort him out. Anyway, after work, George was in the car park waiting for this younger chap, teeth out and not prepared to back down. People gathered round to prevent anything happening but everyone was generally more careful with George after that*".

George must have also been quite a modest man. His brother, Billy, who had played with him several times for Southport Reserves did not know that George had played for England Youth until he was interviewed about George for this book.

Billy himself had been on Everton's books as a 15 year old, playing for the Colts. He was devastated after two years or so to be told that he was being released as he was not good enough.

George was eight years older than Billy and was "*an inspiration*" to his younger brother. When George was playing for Everton, he would always take Billy along to the game and sit him in the stands. Getting the autographs of stars such as Stanley Matthews was no problem for Billy and he would "*take orders from the lads at school for two bob a signature.*"

George retired early from Delco Electronics but did not enjoy a long retirement. He died unexpectedly at the age of 59 years, on 22nd September 1989, in Fazakerley Hospital from a blood clot, following a hip replacement operation.

George's son Mark had a trial for Aston Villa, but was rejected in Mark's own words "*as being too slow*". George and Mark shared an interest in golf and went on a number of golfing holidays to Ireland; they also went to watch football matches together. Unfortunately, Mark died in 2008 from cancer at 50 years of age.

References:

1. Southport Visitor, 14th August 1956

2. Southport Visitor, 21st August 1956

3. Southport Visitor, 23rd August 1956

4. Southport Visitor, 11th September 1956

5. Southport Visitor, 18th September 1956

6. Southport Visitor, 25th September 1956

7. Southport Visitor, 2nd October 1956

8. Southport Visitor, 26th February, 1957

9. Southport Visitor, 28th March 1957

10. Southport Visitor, 2nd April 1957

11. Southport Visitor, 16th April, 1957

12. Liverpool Daily Post, 13th May 1957

13. Southport Visitor, 5th September 1957

14. Southport Visitor, 17th September 1957

15. Southport Visitor, 24th September 1957

16. Southport Visitor, 1st October 1957

17. Southport Visitor, 8th October 1957

18. Southport Visitor, 26th November 1957

19. Southport Visitor, 3rd December 1957

20. Southport Visitor, 25th February 1958

21. Southport Visitor, 4th March 1958

22. Southport Visitor, 15th April 1958

23. Southport Visitor, 22nd April 1958

24. Southport Visitor, 14th November 1957

25. Southport Visitor, 19th August 1958

26. Southport Visitor, 23rd September 1958

27. Southport Visitor, 25th September 1958

28. Southport Visitor, 28th October 1958

29. Southport Visitor, 2nd December 1958

30. Southport Visitor, 17th January 1959

31. The Sandgrounders: The Complete History of Southport FC by Geoff Wilde and Michael Braham; Palatine Books; 1995

32. Southport Visitor, 17th February 1959

33. Southport Visitor, 1st September 1959

34. Southport Visitor, 22nd September 1959

35. Southport Visitor, 13th October 1959

36. Southport Visitor, 20th October 1959

37. Southport Visitor, 3rd November 1939

38. Southport Visitor, 15th December 1959

39. Southport Visitor, 22nd December 1959

40. Southport Visitor, 23rd February 1960

41. Southport Visitor, 10th December 1959

7

Andy Rankin at Everton (1961-71)

Introduction

Andrew George Rankin was born in Bootle, Lancashire on 11ᵗʰ May 1944 and was the grandson of Bruce. He was the eldest of three brothers. His father George was said to have been on Everton's books at one time (1), although Andy's brother, Terry, was not aware of his father ever playing football.

Andy attended Bootle Grammar School and played for a successful local junior football team, Galcap United. On leaving school, he worked for a time at a cable factory in Bootle as a machine operator.

1961–62 Season

Andy signed for Everton as an amateur in May 1961 when he was 17 years old. Shortly afterwards, he joined the Liverpool City Police Cadets as Cadet 114. Numbers were assigned alphabetically and Keith Ranford, who was Cadet 113 (extreme left on the next to back row in the photograph on Page 239), was allocated the bedroom next to Andy during their stay at the Police Training School in Mather Avenue, Liverpool. Keith recalls, "*Andy was popular and one of the lads. He seemed more mature than most, especially me. We had plenty of laughs, none more so than having to do each others collars in the mornings. Getting the hang of those collar studs was a problem for both of us. In the short time I knew Andy, it was obvious to me he would have made a great copper, and gone a long way*."

He left the Cadets when he signed professional forms for Everton in October of that year. His signing was reported in the local press:

"Everton, at last, have signed a goalkeeper. It is a fact that they have con-tacted several clubs to ask whether or not they could release a player and always they have been sent away empty-handed. With their vast army of scouts, which goes into operation every weekend, they have scoured England, Wales and Scotland pretty thoroughly, and yet, where do you think they eventually found their man? – Liverpool, on their own doorstep.

He is Andrew Rankin, eighteen years old, 5ft 11ins tall, who has been with Everton as an amateur since the start of the season.

It was one day recently Mr Catterick was busying himself in the train-ing programme at Goodison that he saw this youngster in goal. His eyes popped at the promise in the boy. He promptly withdrew him and gave him a personal workout. The lad responded by answering every requirement asked of him. The manager's mind was made up. This could be the lad to solve the difficulties about a deputy for Albert Dunlop.

Rankin was a police cadet and Mr Catterick promptly discussed the position with the boy and his parents, with the result that the police force has lost a recruit and Everton have gained a new full-time professional. "He is a player of tremendous promise, full of ability and enthusiasm," Mr Catterick told me.

With his acceptance of his new career, Rankin's job will be to keep them out instead of running them in."(2)

Just months before Andy had signed for Everton, the Football League, under the threat of a players' strike, abolished the maximum wage, which was £20 a week at that time. Soon afterwards, Johnny Haynes, of Fulham and the England captain, became the first £100 a week footballer. However, few were paid such sums. The average weekly wage of First Division players that year was £25 and did not break through the £50, £100 and £1000 barriers until 1967, 1974 and 1985 respectively. (3)

Andy's first appearance in the Reserves was in a Lancashire Senior cup-tie game at Rochdale on Wednesday, 25th October 1961, which Rochdale won with a goal just 30 seconds before the final whistle. Everton's team was:

Rankin; Parnell, Green; Sharples, Gerrie, Meagan; Tyrer, Jarvis, Webber, Temple, Ring.

Andy Rankin (extreme left on front row) as Liverpool City
Police Cadet 114 in 1961.

Andy played in almost every Reserve game during the remainder of the season, receiving some excellent reviews in the local sporting pages. After one match, however, the report may not have been quite what he wanted. Everton Reserves were two up against Chesterfield Reserves at Chesterfield on Saturday, 10th February 1962 when, midway through the first half, Everton's centre-forward, Wignall, was carried off on a stretcher after he had fallen over the wall surrounding the pitch. Seizing the advantage against ten men, Chesterfield went straight onto the attack and their centre-forward Poole charged Andy and the ball into the net to reduce the arrears. Two minutes later, they were level but, in scoring the equaliser, their outside-right Duncan collided with Andy. A fight immediately broke out between the two players, and it took more than a dozen players three minutes to break it up. The referee perhaps took a lenient view of the altercation, as he only booked both players. That behaviour seems to have been out of character as there were no similar incidents or bookings involving Andy reported whilst at Everton.

Andy was probably rather surprised and disappointed a few weeks later to learn that Everton had signed Blackpool's keeper, Gordon West, who was only a few months older than him. On his first appearance, against Hibs from the Scottish First Division in a friendly on Saturday 10th March, West saved a penalty in the 1-1 draw.

West was drafted into the first team for the remaining League games at the expense of the regular keeper, Albert Dunlop. It was Dunlop, however, not Andy, who deputised for West when he was injured.

1962-63 Season

Andy shared the goalkeeping duties in the Reserves with Albert Dunlop that season. However, when West badly injured his shoulder against Arsenal in April, Dunlop stepped in for the remaining four League games.

That winter was one of the worst for many a year and there was no football on Merseyside for six or seven weeks. Because so many games had been postponed, Everton played their first team against Derby Reserves in the Central League on Saturday, 16th February, to give the players some match practice. West was in goal.

Everton were League Champions for the first time since the war. The partnership of Alex Young and Roy Vernon was crucial to the club's success. Between them, they scored 46 goals, more than half of the team's total for the season. However, Gordon West played a key role, helping Everton to have the best defensive record by far that season.

1963-64 Season

Andy started off in the Reserves again. For the opening Central League match against Preston North End Reserves at Deepdale on Saturday, 24th August, which Everton won 1-0. The team was:

Rankin; Parnell, Thomson; Sharples, Heslop, Harris; Humphries, Harvey, Rees, Hurst, McKenzie.

Albert Dunlop left Everton during the first week of November for Wrexham. He had joined Everton in 1949 as a 17 year old, but had to wait seven years for his league debut. It was against Manchester United at Old Trafford in front of more than 50,000 people. Everton claimed the shock result of the season by ending United's unbeaten run of 26 League games with a conclusive 5-2 victory. Dunlop made a total of 231 League and Cup appearances between 1956 and 1963. After he had given up football in the late 1960s, his personal life became something of a disaster and in 1979 he was placed on probation for two years after being found guilty of three charges of deception.

Everton football squad August 1964: Left to right, back row: Johnny Morrissey, Jimmy Harris, Sandy Brown, Brian Labone, Gordon West, Andy Rankin, Jimmy Gabriel, Fred Pickering, Colin Harvey and Jimmy Hill. Front row: Alex Parker, Alex Scott, Dennis Stevens, Derek Temple, Roy Vernon, Tony Kay, Alex Young and Ray Wilson. © Mirrorpix

Andy got his chance in the first team on Saturday, 16th November 1963, against Nottingham Forest at The City Ground. Gordon West was dropped, having been the first choice keeper since he joined the club from Blackpool eighteen months earlier. He had played in all the league matches during their championship win the previous season, except for the final four games, which he missed through injury.

Before the game, Harry Catterick, the Everton Manager said of Andy, *"He is a mild mannered boy and if he repeats his reserve team form he should do very well."*(4) The Everton team was:

Rankin; Parker, Meagan; Harris, Labone, Kay; Scott, Stevens, Young, Vernon, Temple.

Nottingham Forest made former Everton centre-forward, Frank Wignall, captain for the day against his old side. Forest might have been a couple of goals in front within the first half-hour, but only fine goalkeeping by Andy and some rather lucky interceptions prevented it. And then, completely against the run of play, Everton took the lead after 39 minutes when Brian Harris diverted a Temple free-kick into the net. Five minutes after the break, Everton increased their lead with an excellent goal from Vernon and began to control the game. But, with 20 minutes to go, Brian Labone limped off with an injured leg. He returned on the right wing, with Stevens dropping back to left-half, and Harris moving to centre-half. With ten minutes left, Alex Parker pulled a thigh muscle and had to go off, so Everton were now down to ten men, one of whom, Labone, was a passenger. After 81 minutes, Forest pulled a goal back and a minute later levelled the score. An Everton victory seemed inevitable until they suffered injuries to two key defenders.

In his weekly column the following Saturday, Alex Young wrote that Andy Rankin *"can look back on his debut with great satisfaction. Considering his size, I am amazed at the speed with which Andy manages to get down for ground shots."*(5)

Andy kept his place for the home fixture against Stoke on Saturday, 23rd November. However, Parker and Labone had still not recovered from their injuries, so Sandy Brown deputised for Parker, whilst Labone's replacement was

George Heslop, who was making only his second appearance for the club. Everton were 2-0 winners in a disappointing game watched by a crowd of just over 47,000. Stanley Matthews played at outside-right for Stoke following a ten-week absence through injury, and he was applauded off the field as he had thrilled the crowd every time he got the ball.

Everton fielded an unchanged team for the midweek game against Rangers, the Scottish League champions, at Ibrox, in the first leg of the "unofficial" British championship. They were three up before the interval through goals from Alex Young, Alex Scott, who was captain for the occasion in recognition of his first appearance against his former club, and Derek Temple. Rangers scored a consolation goal late in the second half when an error by Andy allowed John Greig to score.

After the match, Rangers' chairman, Mr John Lawrence, told the Liverpool Echo reporter, "*If this is Everton's reserve goalkeeper, do us a favour on Monday by playing your first team man. He was out of this world. Even when we were awarded a penalty I knew we would not score – and we didn't.*"(6)

The paper's football correspondent, Horace Yates, wrote: "*This was my first sight of Andy Rankin as a goalkeeper. While experience has taught me never to be swayed by first impressions, I am confident I am on the safest of sound ground by predicting for Rankin a highly successful career. He is a discovery beyond price, ripe and able to add something to the first team scene. Once or twice only was his handling at fault but in the course of an evening which kept him fully employed, he displayed the all-round qualities that bore the stamp of a first class craftsman. West was there to see his successor seize his opportunity, I say his successor advisedly for unless Rankin slips or West dramatically hits top form, I cannot see how the former police cadet can be displaced.*"

Everton and Wolves drew 0-0 at Molyneux on Saturday, 30th November. Despite the lack of goals, the match was full of thrills at both ends. Andy was injured making one save, but was able to resume after treatment.

The second-leg of the unofficial British Championship was played at Goodison Park on Monday, 2nd December. It ended in a 1-1 draw, which gave the "title" of British champions to Everton with an aggregate score of 4-2. Just as in the first game, Andy's goalkeeping performance broke the hearts of the Rangers' players and fans:

"Everything hinged midway through the first half on two fantastic saves by young Andy Rankin, the Bootle boy, whose goalkeeping dynamics make him the find of the season. To put it shortly, Rankin broke Rangers' hearts in two minutes of goalkeeping magic even a Scott, a Hardy, or a Sagar could not have bettered. Ritchie, in his goal, had punched a long clearance from hand plumb down the centre of the field, three parts of its length. Heslop, misjudging the arc of the ball as it dropped, let in Millar and that hefty bundle of football skill, hit his shot on the volley with all the considerable power at his command. Somehow, Rankin saw this one coming, somehow he got his hands to it and turned it to Brand on the left whose gallop with the ball was suddenly stopped. The murmurs of wonderment at such a save (which if it had not been made would have taken the aggregate score to 3-2) had scarcely died when little Henderson, roaming to outside-left made a glorious jinking run which enabled him to shoot, at point blank range and still found those trusty hands of Rankin reaching out to make contact in yet another stupendous save."(7)

Everton supporters were clearly not impressed by the Scottish fans. A number of letters were published in the Echo on Thursday, 5th December, complaining about their behaviour. One from L. Grayson of Stand Road catalogued instances of appalling behaviour and the writer finished up:

"I thoroughly enjoyed the football played by both sides. The referee and his officials did an excellent job. The Liverpool City Police did a grand job and I take my hat off to them. But these Rangers supporters – they're a disgrace to a great team. The impression I had of them before seeing them was that they were fair-minded yet loyal supporters. My impression now of the bad ones among them is of foul-mouthed, drunken, fanatical louts."

Another letter ended: *"Please Mr Moores, let's have no more visiting Rangers' supporters."*

Maybe the behaviour of the Rangers fans was a contributory factor, but the Everton v Rangers contest is the only occasion on which the unofficial "British Championship" has been contested.

On the Saturday, Everton were held to another 1-1 draw, this time by Chelsea. There was one change to the team that had faced Rangers, with Sharples coming in for Gabriel, who had left the field injured in the first half. Although Chelsea looked the better team before the interval, Everton took the lead through Vernon in the 41st minute. The major incident of the second half came with 15 minutes left, when the referee was knocked out in a collision with Blunstone, the Chelsea left winger, and had to be carried off on a stretcher. One of the linesmen took over, whilst his replacement was someone from the Everton dugout. Chelsea equalised with eight minutes to go.

Everton were thrashed 6-0 in their next game by Arsenal at Highbury on Tuesday, 10th December. Arsenal were 5-0 up after 47 minutes and their, centre-forward, Baker, scored a hat-trick in 18 minutes. Horace Yates wrote:

"I hope these six goals will not be held against the young goalkeeper. Maybe not everybody shares my opinion that he was blameless in the concession of such a score, but nothing that happened in this Everton travesty destroyed my impression that here is a first class goalkeeping discovery."(8)

After a 2-2 draw with Fulham at Craven Cottage on the Saturday, Everton faced Manchester United at Goodison Park the following week in a match, which was billed as a "Champions v Cup-Winners clash". The teams were:

Everton: Rankin; Brown, Meagan; Gabriel, Heslop, Harris; Scott, Stevens, Young, Vernon, Temple.

Manchester United: Gaskell; Dunne, Cantwell; Crerand, Foulkes, Setters; Muir, Moore, Sadler, Herd, Charlton.

After a goalless first half watched by a crowd of just over 48,000 spectators, Everton began to play their best football of the season. Brown hit the bar from 30 yards soon after the restart and, then, in the 55th minute, Everton got the goal they deserved when Temple hit a fierce shot into the roof of the net from six yards. They increased their lead seven minutes later through Vernon and, in the 66th minute, Harris scored a third. Ten minutes from the end, Stevens made it 4-0. It was sweet revenge for their 5-1 defeat at Old Trafford earlier in the season.

Everton were now 5th in the League, four points behind leaders Blackburn. Liverpool were two points ahead of Everton having played a game fewer.

Earlier that week, the Everton players were presented with championship plaques. When Alex Young had been at Hearts, the Club had won the Scottish League championship and the Scottish FA and League Cups. The Club was of the opinion that most footballers tended to put their championship and cup medals in a drawer and forget them after the novelty had worn off. So, it was decided to present the players with plaques, inscribed with the team's record, and with the appropriate medal in the centre. When Young mentioned this to Harry Catterick following Everton's championship success, the manager liked the idea. Young then had an Everton plaque to go alongside his Scottish ones.

Andy played in both defeats to Leicester over the Christmas period – a 2-0 defeat away on Boxing Day and a 3-0 defeat at home on Saturday, 28th December. These defeats saw Everton slip to 10th in the League, whilst Liverpool remained third.

Everton's first game in the New Year was away to Hull in the Third Round of the FA Cup. The team was:

Rankin; Brown, Meagan; Gabriel, Heslop, Harris; Scott, Stevens, Young, Vernon, Temple.

Before 36,748 spectators, Vernon had the ball in the net after five minutes, but the linesman flagged for offside and the effort was disallowed. Gabriel had damaged his nose the previous week against Leicester and, after hurting it again, he had to come off the pitch with almost 10 minutes of the game gone, blood streaming down his face. Almost immediately, Hull took the lead with a header from inside-right Wilkinson, which flew into the corner of the net. Immediately after the restart, a back-heel from Young crossed the goal-line before a Hull defender cleared. Despite protests from the Everton players, and despite consultation with the linesman, the referee did not allow it. Five minutes later, however, Everton equalised with a magnificent goal from Scott.

In the Liverpool Echo on Monday, 6th January, Michael Charters wrote, "*this was one of Everton's bad days. There were brilliant performances from a few, notably Temple, Scott and Rankin, but the general standard of team work left much to be desired."*

The Everton team for the replay at Goodison Park the following Tuesday showed one change, Brian Labone returning at the expense of Heslop. Everton were 1-0 down at the interval, but two goals in the second half secured a Fourth Round trip to Leeds. Hull from the Third Division emerged with most credit from an exciting game, which was watched by 56,000 spectators.

In his weekly column, Alex Young wrote about the Hull game: *"I feel that we might not have lived to fight another day, but for the fine goalkeeping of young Andy Rankin. Andy made three brilliant saves when the score was 1-1, one of them a point blank Wilkinson shot, having to be seen to be believed."*(9)

Everton faced Burnley in the League at Turf Moor on the Saturday. Catterick dropped Young and Vernon, who were out of form, and replaced them with Hill and Morrissey, the former Liverpool player. Gabriel captained the side in the absence of Vernon. The team was:

Rankin; Brown, Meagan; Gabriel, Labone, Harris; Scott, Stevens, Temple, Hill, Morrissey.

Burnley took the lead after 22 minutes against the run of play. Brown cleared straight to O'Neill, who played the ball to Connelly, the left-winger, and he slipped Brown's tackle before floating the ball over Andy into the corner of the net. Burnley increased their lead in the 41st minute. Again, it was caused by an Everton defensive error. Gabriel made a mess of a back pass to Andy, who was left stranded as the unmarked Connelly once more stepped into score. A minute before half-time, Everton got a goal back through a penalty by Scott after Temple had been brought down from behind. Everton then equalised in the 56th minute, when Gabriel shot into the net through a ruck of players from 25 yards out. Eight minutes later, Everton scored what proved to be the winner just when a draw seemed to be the likely outcome.

Young and Vernon were omitted again from the team that faced Ipswich at

Goodison Park the following Saturday. Ipswich took the lead two minutes before the interval. Midway through the second half, with Everton still behind, there was slow-handclapping followed by a tremendous chant of "We want Alex Young". With quarter of an hour to go, many Evertonians were leaving the ground, missing their team's equaliser in the 87th minute when Scott scored from the penalty spot after an Ipswich defender had knocked the ball away with his hand.

Following a shoulder injury going down for a ball at the Bellfield training ground on Wednesday, 22nd January, Andy had to have his arm immobilised. As a result, he missed the next seven first team games; Gordon West deputised.

During that period, Everton defeated Leeds, captained by Bobby Collins, the former Everton player, in the FA Cup Fourth Round tie at Goodison, after a 1-1 draw at Elland Road. However, Sunderland then knocked Everton out in the next round by three goals to one. In between the cup-ties, Everton comprehensively overcame their arch-rivals Liverpool at Goodison Park 3-1; drew 0-0 at Sheffield United; and defeated both Aston Villa at Goodison and Spurs at White Hart Lane by four goals to two.

After three games for the Reserves, Andy regained his place for the home fixture against Nottingham Forest on Saturday, 14th March, which also featured the debut of Fred Pickering, who had signed for Everton earlier that week from Blackburn Rovers for a reported fee of £80,000. The team was:

Rankin; Brown, Harris; Gabriel, Labone, Kay; Scott, Stevens, Pickering, Vernon, Temple.

More than 50,000 spectators turned up to see Pickering make his debut, and they were not disappointed. The home side were 3-0 up at half-time, Pickering netting two of the goals and Stevens scoring the other. Vernon made it 4-0 in the 59th minute. Ten minutes from the end, Pickering got his hat-trick, the first for an Everton player that season, and four minutes later, Stevens made certain of Everton's biggest victory of the season with a splendid individual goal. Just before the final whistle, Forest got a consolation goal when Andy failed to hold a shot, the ball bouncing off his chest to allow one of the Forest forwards to score. All the

Everton players stood back at the end and applauded Pickering off the pitch; the crowd joined in to give him a warm welcome to Goodison.

The following Saturday, Everton faced Blackburn at Ewood Park. The only change to the team was the introduction of Colin Harvey for his debut in place of Roy Vernon; Jimmy Gabriel was captain. Everton came out in a new strip – yellow jerseys with black cuffs and black around the neck.

Everton were lucky not to go a goal down in the first half. Pickering's intended pass back to Andy went straight to Blackburn's inside-left, Douglas, who had a great chance to score. However, Andy came out of his goal quickly to block Douglas' shot with his legs. Blackburn failed to capitalise on other chances but, eventually, did take the lead three minutes after half-time when Douglas beat Andy from ten yards. Minutes later, Blackburn again had the ball in the net but the referee ruled that Andy had been fouled by Douglas. After 59 minutes, Everton equalised through a wonderful shot by Scott. Everton were beginning to play much better and, with only seconds left, Temple scored the winner after a magnificent 50 yards run. Michael Charters wrote: "*Rankin with his startlingly quick reactions made many fine saves.*"(10)

As a result of the victory over Blackburn, Everton were now top of the league, two points ahead of Liverpool and Spurs with the former having played a game fewer.

Everton dropped three points from a possible six over the Easter programme. They drew 1-1 with West Bromwich Albion at home on Good Friday, 27th March. Everton did not look like champions and, after the game, some of the crowd demonstrated in front of the director's box chanting, "We want Young. We want Young." Along with Vernon, he had been dropped from the first team in January.

On the Saturday, for the home match against Blackpool, Temple moved from the left-wing to the right in place of the injured Scott, Morrissey came in at outside-left, and Young was selected at inside-left in preference to Harvey. One can only guess if the demonstration by the fans the previous day influenced Young's selection, but there was a great roar of appreciation when his name was announced over the loudspeaker. The team was:

Rankin; Brown, Meagan; Gabriel, Labone, Harris; Temple, Stevens, Pickering, Young, Morrissey.

Everton took the lead in the 5th minute with a brilliant Pickering header from a cross by Morrissey. Five minutes later, Pickering extended the lead with another headed goal. With ten minutes of the match remaining, Blackpool reduced the deficit, but Young got the greatest applause of the day when he restored Everton's two-goal lead three minutes before the final whistle.

A 4-2 defeat in the return fixture with West Brom on Easter Monday all but ended Everton's hopes of retaining the championship. They were now second with 49 points from 38 games; Liverpool were top with 50 points from 36 games; whilst Manchester United lay in third place with 47 points from 37 games.

Everton slumped to their second defeat in succession on Saturday, 4th April, when they lost 3-2 away to Stoke. *"Of the Everton defence, Kay, early on, Labone, who had to do a lot of covering, and Rankin alone came out with credit."* (11) Everton's championships hopes had well and truly gone now.

On Tuesday evening, 7th April, a much belated testimonial match was played at Goodison Park for Dixie Dean, one of Everton's greatest players. His best known achievement is the record-breaking 60 League goals that he scored for Everton during the 1927/28 season when Everton were champions. That record still stands today and is never likely to be broken. As the match programme pointed out, these were not the only goals scored by Dean that season: *"On top of these he scored 35 in cup-ties and other matches, and five scored on the Swiss tour at the end of the season plus two international matches in Belgium and France bring his aggregate for the season to the fantastic total of 100 goals."*

The testimonial featured a team of English players and a team of Scottish players drawn from Liverpool and Everton:

English Players: Rankin; Byrne, Lawler; Harris, Labone, Kay; Callaghan, Stevens, Pickering, Temple, Morrissey.
Scottish Players: Lawrence; Brown, Thompson; Gabriel, Yeats, Stevenson; Scott, Young, Graham, Hill, Wallace. (Hill was an Irishman)

Liverpool were top of the league with five matches left, Everton were in third place with three games to play. So, both sets of players treated the testimonial as an exhibition game and it was played in a light-hearted manner. Even the fans joined in, booing Brian Labone because he had the affrontary to half-heartedly charge Alex Young. Scotland came out on top with a 3-1 victory watched by 36,870 spectators who paid some £7,000.

On the Saturday, 11th April, a thrilling match at Goodison saw Everton and Wolves draw 3-3. Everton were two up within eleven minutes, but Wolves got a goal back just past the half-hour mark. Two minutes after the interval, Wolves were level. Andy dived for a first-time shot from the Wolves' left- winger Wharton and seemed to have the ball safely in his grasp, only to let it squirm away from him to centre-forward, Crawford, who slid the ball over the line. In the 54th minute, Wolves found themselves ahead, when Wharton scored following a slip by Gabriel. The crowd was becoming restless, but a minute from the end, Temple got the equaliser following an error by the Wolves' goalkeeper.

The Wolves game proved to be Tony Kay's final appearance for Everton because on the Monday after the match, Everton announced that they had suspended him pending an investigation into allegations that he had been involved in match "fixing" when a Sheffield Wednesday player. Kay's name was linked with that of two other Wednesday players – centre-forward David Layne and centre-half Peter Swan, both of whom had also been suspended by their club. The allegation concerned a match on 1st December 1962 when Ipswich Town won 2-0 against Sheffield Wednesday at Ipswich. The matter was being investigated by the police.

The following day, it was reported that Everton had agreed to a transfer request from Alex Young, who had not been selected for the Wolves game.

Everton faced Chelsea at Stamford Bridge on Saturday, 18th April, before a crowd of almost 38,000. The team was:

Rankin; Brown, Meagan; Gabriel, Labone, Harris; Scott, Stevens, Pickering, Vernon, Temple

Before the kick-off, Chelsea's forward, Frank Blunstone, was presented with a cheque for £5,000, the proceeds of a testimonial. He was Chelsea's longest serving player at the time, having been signed by them ten years earlier from Crewe Alexandra when the Everton manager, Harry Catterick, was in charge at Gresty Road.

The only goal of the game came when Chelsea were awarded a penalty in the 37th minute as a result of what Michael Charters described as *"quite the most amazing decision I have seen this season".*(12) Blunstone pushed the ball too far in front of him; Andy came out quickly and picked the ball up. Continuing his run, Blunstone collided with Andy and fell over. A penalty the referee decided and outside-right Murray scored from the spot. The game was spoiled by niggling fouls and unnecessary obstruction by Chelsea and Ron Harris in particular, who was booked when he appeared to strike Roy Vernon. In his column in the Echo on Monday, 20th April, Michael Charters wrote: *"Rankin made several good saves, notably two from Venables and Tambling, and the rest of the defence were hard pressed at times…"*

Liverpool secured the championship that weekend when they defeated Arsenal 5-0 at Anfield. Everton were to finish third, five points behind their local rivals.

The team for the final game of the season against West Ham at Goodison the following Saturday was:

Rankin; Brown, Meagan; Gabriel, Labone, Harris; Scott, Stevens, Pickering, Vernon, Temple.

Before the match began, a man carrying a board bearing the words "Sack Catterick – Keep Young" was escorted from the ground by a police officer. The game itself was typical end of the season stuff between two teams with nothing to lose. Pickering scored twice to give Everton victory.

An Everton party was soon off for a tour of Australia. The first game was against New South Wales on Saturday, 2nd May, before a crowd of 52,000, a record for a soccer match in Sydney. The hosts gave their fans something to shout about when they took an early lead but, by the finish, Everton ran out easy winners by 4-1. The Everton team was:

Rankin; Brown, Meagan; Gabriel, Labone, Harris; Scott, Stevens, Temple, Vernon, Morrissey.

Two days later, Everton overran Queensland 5-0 in Brisbane and then flew to Melbourne. On the Saturday, some of the tour party went to watch an Australian Rules football match, whilst others attended a race meeting.

The following day, Sunday 10th May, Everton beat Australia 8-2 before a crowd of 32,000 at Flemington, Australia's most famous racecourse. The Australian side was made up of players from England, Scotland, Wales, Poland, Germany, Yugoslavia and Austria, as well as two native-born players. Vernon and Gabriel both scored hat-tricks, with two goals from Temple. Andy was a lonely figure in his goal.

Everton won their next two games, beating South Australia in Adelaide on Wednesday, 13th May and overwhelming West Australia 14-1 in Perth a week later.

A second game against the Australian national side was played at the Sydney Showground on 16th May. With Andy in goal once more, Everton had another easy victory by five goals to one.

A few days later, they had a much stiffer test in a 3-1 victory over Victoria in Melbourne. The Everton team was:

Rankin; Brown, Meagan; Stevens, Labone, Harris; Scott, Temple, Gabriel, Vernon, Morrissey.

They ended their eight-match tour undefeated with an 8-1 win over New South Wales in Newcastle on Wednesday, 27th May, watched by a crowd of 13,000 spectators. Gordon West was in goal.

The Everton party flew out of Sydney Airport on the Saturday. Before boarding the plane, the players linked arms on the tarmac, and sang Waltzing Matilda.

1964-65 Season

1964 saw the end of the "Retain and Transfer" system, which had existed since the 1890s. It meant that a player could not leave a club without its agreement. Bruce Rankin was able to move from Everton to West Bromwich Albion in 1906 because the Everton Directors were willing to release him and West Bromwich Albion were willing to pay the transfer fee requested. However, if Albion had not been willing to pay that fee and Bruce had pursued a transfer request, then, when his contract had finished, Everton would have placed him on the transfer list without wages until another club agreed to pay the required transfer fee or until Bruce caved in and signed a new contract.

Following the George Eastham case, the system changed. Eastham had asked Newcastle United for a transfer during the 1959/60 season. They refused and stopped his wages when he refused to re-sign. Some months later they relented and sold him to Arsenal. In the meantime, however, Eastham had pursued his case through the courts for "unlawful restraint of trade", with financial support from the Professional Footballers Association. In 1963, his case reached the High Court, which ruled that the "Retain and Transfer" system was unlawful and that clubs should no longer keep a player's registration and refuse to pay him if he asked for a transfer. The result was that if a player's club did not wish to renew his contract on the same terms, then his club could offer him a free transfer.

In 1978, the system was amended further to allow players to decline new terms offered and join a club of their choice. If the two clubs could not agree the transfer fee, the case was to be referred to a transfer tribunal.

The rules changed again in 1995. Jean-Marc Bosman, a player with FC Liege of Belgium wanted to move to a French club upon the expiry of his contract. However, Liege demanded a transfer fee, which the French could not or would not pay. As a result, Bosman took his case to the European Court of Justice, which decided that clubs could not demand transfer fees for out of contract players who were moving to another club within the European Union. So, now players can leave for nothing when they are out of contract, although the bigger clubs now tend to offer their best players longer term and more lucrative contracts.

Everton signed Ray Wilson, the England full-back, during the close season, for £25,000. As part of the deal, Mick Meagan went to Huddersfield. Perhaps even more satisfying for the Everton fans was the news that Alex Young had been taken off the transfer list at his own request.

Everton had their first public practice match for five years on the evening of Friday, 14th August. Fifteen thousand fans turned out to see the first team face two other sides during the 90 minutes – first, the potential reserve side (Whites) and then, in the second half, the club's youth eleven (Ambers). The teams were:

Blues: Rankin; Parker, Wilson; Gabriel, Labone, Stevens; Scott, Young, Pickering, Vernon, Temple.

Whites: West; D'Arcy, Brown; Sharples, Heslop, Rees; Shaw, Harvey, Hill, Humphreys, Morrissey.

Ambers: Barnett; Wright, Curwen; Clark, Smith, Grant; Roberts, Glover, Hurst, Husband, Veall.

The first half, between the Blues and the Whites ended 1-1 whilst, in the second half, the Blues scored five against the Youth side, which included some future Everton stars, in particular Tommy Wright, John Hurst and Jimmy Husband.

In the first game of the season, on Saturday, 22nd August, Everton defeated Stoke 2-0 in the Potteries. Everton played excellent football but did not take all their chances. The team was:

Rankin; Parker, Wilson; Stevens, Labone, Harris; Scott, Young, Pickering, Vernon, Temple. Parker had been named as club captain.

That same day, the very first edition of Match of the Day was screened on BBC2, featuring Liverpool v Arsenal at Anfield. The programme moved to BBC1 the following year.

On the following Tuesday, with an unchanged team, Everton recorded their second victory, beating Nottingham Forest 1-0 at Goodison Park. But for a series of outstanding saves by Andy, Forest would have been at least three goals in front at the interval. And then, "*not long after the crowd had shown their gratitude (and weren't they right) to Rankin as he took his place for the second half, than Forest's Wilson thumped the ball against the bar with Rankin, for once, not within reach of the ball.*"(13) Pickering got the only goal of the game after 55 minutes. Everton's Wilson was injured and went to outside-left, but left the field with seven minutes remaining. The Echo's headline was "*Rankin, then Pickering won this match*".

A crowd of 55,000 spectators turned up at Goodison on Saturday, 29th August, to watch Everton face Spurs. The team showed only one change – Brown at left-back for the injured Wilson. Everton took the lead against the run of play after 25 minutes through Pickering when goalkeeper Jennings deflected the ball into the corner of his own net. Andy made a number of excellent saves before Young headed Everton's second goal in the 59th minute. Eight minutes later, Everton conceded their first goal of the season, but two further goals from Pickering, in the 73rd and 80th minutes, gave him his hat-trick and ensured a comfortable victory for Everton. After three games, Everton were top of the League with maximum points, along with Chelsea and Leeds.

In their next game, the return fixture with Forest on Tuesday evening, 1st September, Everton suffered extremely bad luck within the first few minutes. Pickering strained a muscle in his left thigh and had to move to the left-wing. Despite having Everton on the defensive following Pickering's injury, it took Forest 30 minutes to score, due largely to some brilliant goalkeeping by Andy. Then, in their first attack, Everton got themselves back into the game with a goal from Sandy Brown. Two Forest goals after the interval settled the game in Forest's favour. "*Rankin was Everton's great performer. He is in brilliant form at the moment and some of his first half saves were breathtaking.*"(14)

Everton were 1-0 down at the interval in their Saturday game, against Burnley at Turf Moor, due to a disputed penalty. However, a minute after the restart, Everton were awarded a free-kick. With everybody expecting Brian Harris to lob the ball into the goalmouth, he merely tapped it two yards to his right for Brown to hit a great drive past Blacklaw, the Burnley keeper. Pickering should have won the game for Everton in the 71st minute when, unmarked in front of goal, he simply struck the ball straight at the goalkeeper. In the Echo on Monday, 7th September,

Horace Yates wrote: "*Andy Rankin in making one of the most courageous dives of the afternoon at the feet of Towers was badly scarred about the neck. It speaks much for his toughness and willingness to get on with the game that he made light of his disability when others were going down for trivialities.*"

In an exciting, hard-fought match on Tuesday evening, 8th September, Everton drew 3-3 with Manchester United before 63,000 spectators. A share of the points was a good result for Everton, having been 2-0 down at the interval and 3-2 down with 20 minutes to go. Andy put on another excellent performance with a number of fine saves. According to Leslie Edwards, "*Rankin's most superb save was his catch from Charlton's free-kick. This drive flew like a bullet, but it was not too fast for handy Andy Rankin.*"(15) The teams were:

Everton: Rankin; Parker, Brown; Gabriel, Labone, Harris; Scott, Young, Pickering, Vernon, Temple.

Manchester United: P. Dunne; Brennan, A. Dunne; Crerand, Foulkes, Stiles; Connolly, Charlton, Herd, Law, Best.

There was another home draw on the Saturday, this time 1-1 with Sheffield United. Everton were unchanged and took the lead four minutes into the second half through Brown, his third goal in four matches. It came from a free-kick outside the penalty area, which Harris touched to one side for Brown, as he had in the game with Burnley. Brown's shot took a slight deflection before going into the corner of the net. With only seconds to go, centre-forward Jones equalised for United with a scrambled goal. Chelsea were now top of the League, undefeated after seven games with 11 points; Blackpool were second with 10 points; whilst Everton were third, together with three other clubs, all on nine points.

That Saturday evening, the Liverpool Football Echo published a statement by the Everton Board in response to allegations by former Everton player, Albert Dunlop, that were to be published in a Sunday newspaper, accusing some of the club's leading players of taking drugs during the 1962-63 championship season. There were further claims that Tommy Eggleston, the Everton chief coach, had offered money to the Fulham centre-forward, Maurice Cook, to lose the game, which won Everton the title, and that there had been a collection on the Everton coach to bribe an opponent.

In the statement, the Board admitted that players were given the opportunity to take a mild stimulant before a game and that it was entirely a matter of personal choice. Brian Harris, Everton's longest serving player, and Gordon Watson, second team trainer, who had been with the club as player and trainer for 30 years, were both quoted in the Liverpool Echo on Tuesday, 15th September, explaining that mild stimulants had been available to Everton players all the years they had been at Goodison, not just since the arrival of Catterick and Eggleston as had been inferred. Indeed, as reporter Michael Charters pointed out in the same paper, it was not against the laws of the game to take a mild pick-me-up.

With regard to the allegation that players took purple-hearts, the Board stated that it was satisfied that the claims of wholesale drug taking were unfounded and, in any case, it would not attempt to control the private activities of its players, unless it clearly affected their playing ability.

The Board also mentioned that a remark in jest by Eggleston to his friend, Maurice Cook, about the payment of £10 for losing the game was made in the presence and hearing of quite a number of other people and had been magnified out of all proportions. The allegation of a collection on the team bus was denied.

Everton faced Manchester United in the League for the second time in eight days – this time at Old Trafford on Wednesday, 16th September. Their team was:

Rankin; Harris, Brown; Gabriel, Labone, Stevens; Scott, Young, Pickering, Harvey, Temple.

Best and Law put United two up before Pickering pulled a goal back eight minutes before the interval. That was the end of the scoring and the end of the football. The rough stuff started in the second half, with four players being booked. Ten minutes from the final whistle, the referee called the 20 outfield players together to lay down the law. In the Liverpool Echo the following day, Michael Charters commented that the referee had the power to end the players' bad behaviour by sending one or two players off, but he did not use it. In terms of players' football performances, he wrote, *"Had it not been for Brown and Labone, who both played brilliantly all through, with Rankin's aid as the last line, United might have been four up in no time."*

Some 52,600 spectators turned out to see the first Liverpool derby of the season at Anfield on Saturday, 19th September. The teams were:

Everton: Rankin; Harris, Brown; Gabriel, Labone, Stevens; Scott, Harvey, Pickering, Temple, Morrissey.
Liverpool: Lawrence; Byrne, Moran; Milne, Yeats, Stevenson; Callaghan, Hunt, St John, Wallace, Thompson.

It was Andy's first derby match, and there was a sensational opening with Everton taking the lead in the first minute. Yeats miskicked a Morrissey centre, sending the ball straight to Temple, who hit it instantly into the corner of the net. Almost immediately, Hunt hit the bar with Andy beaten. After 34 minutes, Everton increased their lead through a fine individual effort by Pickering and Harvey got a third before half-time. In the second half, the referee was speaking to Stevens and Thompson in front of the Kemlyn Road stand when a spectator ran on to the pitch and aimed a punch at Stevens. He missed and was chased by several policemen into the stand before disappearing down a tunnel. Morrissey then hit a magnificent goal against his old club in the 64th minute to make it 4-0 for Everton. Soon afterwards, Andy was injured when Ron Yeats fell on top of him as they both went for a corner. Following treatment for a couple of minutes, he was able to continue in goal and, in the final minutes, foiled St John when he turned his shot away with a brilliant save. In fact, according to Michael Charters, Andy *"had a superb game once more, (and) saved in breathtaking style from Wallace and St John..."*(16)

Almost fifty years later, in an interview with Greg O'Keeffe, the Everton Reporter for the Liverpool Echo, Derek Temple reflected on that derby win:

"The derby that stands out was in 1964 when we went to Anfield and won 4-0. It always a difficult place to go and get a result but that day we did and our man of the match was stand in keeper Andy Rankin. Westy was injured and Andy was

superb – not a big lad but a great shot-stopper and he stopped a lot that day. It could have been 6-4 to them."(17)

Everton were now fifth in the league with 11 points, four behind leaders Chelsea; Liverpool were next to bottom with five points from eight games.

The following week, Everton travelled to Oslo to play amateur team Valerengen in the Inter-Cities Fairs Cup on Wednesday, 23rd September. The team was:

Rankin; Harris, Brown; Gabriel, Labone, Stevens; Scott, Harvey, Pickering, Temple, Morrissey.

As expected, Everton dominated for most of the game, but were not particularly impressive in the 5-2 win. Indeed, they were behind twice, did not gain the lead until the 78th minute, and it was only in the last ten minutes that their superior stamina told with goals from Temple and Scott.

Viking boat presented to Everton on occasion of the game against Valerengens IFV in Oslo on 23rd September 1964. Courtesy of The Everton Collection Charitable Trust, Reference 796EFC/51/36

There was a glut of goals in the league at St Andrews on the Saturday, with Everton emerging as 5-3 winners after a fight back by Birmingham. Everton played the same team that had won in Norway in midweek. They went ahead in the 26th minute with a goal from Harvey, increased their lead seven minutes later through a Pickering header and, a minute before half-time, Pickering scored his second with a right foot shot into the top corner of the net. They started the second half as they had finished the first, with a goal from Morrissey two minutes after the restart. A minute later, Birmingham pulled one back, only to see Scott score Everton's fifth in the 52nd minute. Birmingham scored again three minutes later and got their third and final goal 18 minutes from time.

Everton's next two home games were disappointing 1-1 draws – the first against West Ham on Saturday, 3rd October, and the second with Sheffield Wednesday a week later. That meant four home draws in succession, certainly not championship winning form. Sandwiched between those two home matches was a 2-1 midweek victory over Aston Villa at Villa Park. Andy played in all of those games.

The home leg of the Inter-Cities Fairs Cup tie with Valerengen was played at Goodison on Wednesday, 14th October. The visitors were leading 2-1 until the 60th minute, after which Everton scored three times. But for their opponents' goalkeeper Sorlie, Everton would have won by a far greater margin. He was applauded off the field at the end of the game by the Everton fans. Leslie Edwards wrote of the game, *"The sordid niggling and fouling of League matches was absent. There was scarcely a foul, scarcely a moment when we were not being entertained."*(18)

Blackpool's largest crowd of the season - 37,855, including 10,000 visiting fans – was at Bloomfield Road on Saturday, 17th October, to witness another Everton draw. The Everton team was:

Rankin; Wright, Brown; Gabriel, Labone, Stevens; Scott, Harris, Pickering, Young, Temple.

Alan Ball, who was later to become a great Everton favourite, was at inside-forward for Blackpool. Everton were ahead in the 6th minute through Scott but, just over 28 minutes later, Wright's under-hit back pass allowed centre-forward, Charnley, to reach the ball first and place it beyond Andy into the net. Ball then went on a 50 yard dribble before passing to Horne, whose shot was brilliantly saved by Andy, who hurt his left leg in the process; he recovered after attention.

During the following week, Andy received the news that he had been selected for the England Under-23 team to meet Wales at Wrexham on Wednesday, 4th November.

On Saturday, 24th October, Everton were two up against Blackburn Rovers within ten minutes of the kick-off. However, three goals from the visitors – one before the interval and two in the second half – saw Everton slip to their first home defeat of the season.

Everton tripped up again the next Saturday, losing 3-1 to Arsenal at Highbury. In his report of the game, Horace Yates wrote: *"Only a few days before he is to wear the England Under-23 jersey for the first time, Andy Rankin fell from grace in a way I have not seen him fall before. His and his alone was the responsibility for Baker's first goal, after Armstrong had opened the scoring, for he allowed a header directed right at him to pass through his hands and he could not have been happy about his part in Baker's second goal."*(19)

There was an interesting letter in the Echo from Everton fan, J.A. Morgan of 19 North Linkside Road, Woolton, Liverpool, on Wednesday, 4th November, the day of the Under-23 International. He wrote endorsing Harry Catterick's condemnation of the barracking of younger players by a certain section of the Goodison crowd. In particular, Mr Morgan highlighted the attitude to Colin Harvey, who was being jeered every time he made an error and, he added, *"the attitude is further evidenced by the shouts of derision which greet Andy Rankin's thrown passes to his half-backs and inside-forwards – moves which are far more likely to start the forward line moving than the long ball up the middle which nine times out of ten is cleared by a tall centre-half."*

The teams that appeared in the Under-23 International at Wrexham were:

England: Rankin (Everton); Badger (Sheffield United), Knowles (Spurs); Hollins (Chelsea), Mobley (Sheffield Wed), Hunter (Leeds); Wilson (Preston), Bennett (Rotherham), Chivers (Southampton), Ball (Blackpool), Sissons (West Ham).

Wales: Sprake (Leeds United); Barton (Newcastle United), Rodrigues (Cardiff City); England (Blackburn), James (Blackpool), Hennessey (Birmingham); Rees (Coventry City), Draper (Swansea), Ryan (Charlton Athletic), Blore (Blackburn Rovers), Evans (Swansea).

A crowd of just over 15,000 turned up to see the game. Tambling of Chelsea, who came on as a substitute for the injured Bennett, ten minutes before half-time, scored two late goals for England to give them a 3-2 victory they hardly deserved; Wales were worth at least a draw. In his match report, Michael Charters wrote: *"Our only representative, Everton's Andy Rankin, did not do his representative chances much good, I fear. He looked nervous, uncertain in his handling, and was fortunate not to concede more than two goals. He was at fault with the first goal scored by Blore, the former Liverpool and Southport inside-forward. Rankin caught a free-kick from the left, dropped the ball, and Blore slammed it back in the net. Again, Rankin was out of position when Blore made a good header in the second half, but full-back Knowles cleared off the line. Altogether, a rather unhappy international debut for Rankin, who has played so brilliantly for Everton this season."*(20) Indeed, this was to be Andy's first and last international recognition.

It was back to League football on the Saturday for Andy, when he faced Leeds at Goodison Park. Full-backs Parker and Wilson and outside-right Scott were all unfit. The teams were:

Everton: Rankin; Rees, Brown; Gabriel, Labone, Stevens; Temple, Young, Pickering, Vernon, Morrissey.
Leeds: Sprake; Reaney, Bell; Bremner, Charlton, Hunter; Giles, Storrie, Belfitt, Collins, Johanneson.

Everton lost 1-0 in a match that Leslie Edwards described *"as a crime against football and against sportsmanship and good sense."*(21) There was a sensational start to the game. Full-back Brown was sent off after five minutes for punching Giles, in retaliation for a gash to his stomach, he later claimed. As a result, Stevens dropped to left-back, with Morrissey moving to half-back. Worse was to follow for Everton nine minutes later when Leeds took the lead with a header by Bell from a free-kick floated in by Bobby Collins.

Fouls continued to be committed by both sides, and there was a running battle between Vernon and Bremner. Then, a collision between Bell and Temple, ended with the Everton player having to be taken from the field on a stretcher. The Everton players surrounded the referee demanding that Bell be sent off. Instead, the referee left the field for the dressing room, followed by all the players. Many in the crowd thought that he had abandoned the game but, about five minutes later, an announcement was made that the game would be abandoned unless the crowd stopped throwing missiles on to the pitch, despite the fact that it was later reported in the Press that no dangerous or solid missiles had been seen.

Play resumed after eleven minutes. The Leeds players were first out and, before the Everton team appeared, the crowd started a chant of "Dirty Leeds". Temple returned four minutes after play restarted. There was more football in the second half, but there was still a considerable number of fouls committed by both sides, with twice as many free-kicks being awarded to Leeds. Everton failed to score for the first time that season and they had not won at home since 29th August.

Sandy Brown was later suspended for 14 days from Monday, 14th December, for his sending off and Everton were fined £250. The Club was also ordered to post warning notices in prominent positions in their ground for one month from Monday, 14th December, and to print a warning to their spectators in their club programme for the same period.

Following the "battle" with Leeds, Everton's next game was away to Kilmarnock in the Inter-Cities Fairs Cup on Wednesday, 11th November. Their opponents were unbeaten so far that season and were undefeated in 26 previous home games. Everton emerged worthy 2-0 winners, with Andy keeping a clean sheet.

On the following Saturday, Everton faced Chelsea at Stamford Bridge. The teams were:

Everton: Rankin; Stevens, Brown; Gabriel, Labone, B. Harris; Temple, Young, Pickering, Harvey, Morrissey.
Chelsea: Bonetti; Hinton, McCreadie; Hollins, Mortimore, R. Harris; Murray, Graham, Bridges, Venables, Tambling.

Brian Harris had to leave the field within minutes of the start with a pulled thigh muscle and was a mere passenger when he returned. Chelsea took the lead in the 9th minute when a shot by Graham was deflected over Andy's head into the net. Graham scored again after 16 minutes and Chelsea were three up two minutes later with a goal from Hollins. In contrast to the Leeds game, the first foul came after 30 minutes when Labone brought down Hollins just outside the penalty area. Gabriel pulled a goal back for Everton just before half-time, but Chelsea scored two further goals late in the second half. Everton were well beaten, but they did at least do their reputation a power of good and were applauded off the field at the end of the game.

Everton failed to win again at home the next Saturday, only drawing 2-2 with Leicester, despite playing their best football for weeks. Everton took the lead through Pickering after seven minutes. Soon afterwards, Andy made a fine save, touching a shot from the Leicester centre-forward over the bar. Within minutes, Everton had to thank him again when he saved magnificently, finger-tipping Goodfellow's shot round the post. Seven minutes into the second half, Everton went two up when Gabriel scored a glorious goal from 25 yards. Andy then let a shot slip through his legs, but as one of the Leicester forwards was about to put the ball into an empty net, Wright came to his rescue, clearing the ball from the goalmouth. By this time, Scott was clearly limping and, playing against only ten fit men, Leicester were able to rescue a point with two goals in the last ten minutes. Andy was at fault for the second. He came out too far to meet a cross from the Leicester right-back, Sjoberg, only to see the ball drop over his head into the net.

Everton went through to the next round of the Inter-Cities Fairs Cup with a 4-1 victory at Goodison Park in the second leg of their tie with Kilmarnock, giving them an aggregate score of 6-1. Kilmarnock were still unbeaten in the Scottish League.

Sunderland scored an emphatic 4-0 victory over Everton at Roker Park on Saturday, 28th November. Michael Charters summed up Everton's performance in the Echo on the Monday following the game: "*This was the poorest form of the season by Everton. Not one Everton player approached his best standard, although there were creditable displays by Young, Labone and Morrissey in the first half. Generally, the team lacked combination and drive. An off-form Rankin did not inspire confi-dence and this feeling of uncertainty spread right through the defence, which was under heavy pressure from a lively, clever Sunderland attack."*

Everton recorded their first home win since 29ᵗʰ August on the first Saturday in December when they thrashed Wolves 5-0. The incessant fine rain until 30 min-utes before kick-off may have had something to do with the smallest crowd of the season - 27,533. Everton's team was:

Rankin; Wright, Brown; Gabriel, Labone, Harris; Temple, Harvey, Pickering, Vernon, Morrissey.

The former Liverpool player, Jimmy Melia, was at inside-right for Wolves, who were unbeaten for four games. *"The most testing moment for Everton came when the game was goalless. Rankin was out of position and partly unsighted when Melia from about 18 yards out, cracked the ball towards goal with the best shot he can have delivered for seasons. It was long odds on Everton going a goal down, but Rankin leaped acrobatically and somehow contrived to fling a hand at the ball to deflect it for a corner."*(22) Eleven minutes into the game, Pickering put Everton ahead. Despite some brilliant football from Everton, they did not get their second goal until a minute into the second half, when a long clearance from Andy was knocked into the path of Temple, whose shot was deflected into the net by a Wolves defender. Everton's dominance was rewarded with further goals from Temple, Pickering and Brown.

Ray Wilson returned to Everton's side for the home game against Stoke on Saturday, 12ᵗʰ December, after an absence of nearly four months through injury. The team was:

Rankin; Brown, Wilson; Gabriel, Labone, Harris; Scott, Harvey, Pickering, Vernon, Temple.

The ground was very heavy after hours of rain but, despite the difficult conditions, Everton played some fine football and went ahead after 16 minutes with a goal from Pickering. Andy made several good saves in the first half and then, seven minutes after the interval, he was injured diving to save at the feet of the Stoke inside-left Skeels. He had to leave the field for treatment and Brown went into goal, Harris moved to full-back and Harvey to left-half. Ten minutes after being taken off, Andy returned with a bandage on his left forearm and went to the left-wing. Brown made several good saves before he was beaten with 13 minutes to go.

The following Friday, Everton issued a statement that *"Roy Vernon has been omitted from the team as a disciplinary measure for a breach of club and training regulations."* Even with Kay still suspended by the Club, Brown suspended by the F.A. for being sent off against Leeds in early November, Rankin and Stevens injured and Harris ill with flu, Everton still sent out a strong side to play Spurs at White Hart Lane on Saturday, 19th December:

West; Wright, Wilson; Gabriel, Labone, Harvey; Scott, Young, Pickering, Temple, Morrissey.

Spurs included Alan Gilzean, who had been signed from Dundee earlier in the week for £72,000, at centre-forward. Pickering scored twice for Everton to earn a 2-2 draw.

After being suspended, Roy Vernon asked for a transfer and was placed on the transfer list. Although he made a further four appearances for Everton, he was signed by Stoke three months later, in March 1965.

Andy was out for two months following the injury to his left arm against Stoke on 12th December, returning for the Reserves against Newcastle Reserves at Goodison Park on Saturday, 13th February, 1965.

With Gordon West playing well in goal for Everton, Andy remained in the Reserves for the rest of the season. Along with Peter Bonetti of Chelsea, West was selected as goalkeeper in the England Under-23 squad to tour Europe during late May and early June.

Of the 12 League games missed by Andy through injury, Everton lost only one, 4-1 away to Leeds; they drew three and won eight, including a 2-1 victory over Liverpool at Goodison Park to complete the double over their great rivals.

They finished fourth in the League; Liverpool were seventh but did win the FA Cup for the first time.

Everton were knocked out of the FA Cup by Leeds, who seemed to be becoming something of a bogey team for them, in a fourth round replay at Goodison and were defeated in the Inter-Cities Fairs Cup by Manchester United after drawing the first leg at Old Trafford.

Looking back on the season, Andy would have had mixed emotions. He would have been happy with a number of splendid performances and extremely positive press reports during his run of 26 consecutive appearances for the first team. He would also have been pleased with his selection for the England Under-23 side. However, he was at fault for the two Welsh goals in the international and his subsequent displays for Everton did not set the world alight. His injury half-way through the season ended his run in the first team and he would have been extremely disappointed to see his replacement, Gordon West, selected ahead of him in the England Under-23 squad to tour Europe during the close season.

As mentioned earlier, Everton's Tony Kay had been suspended by the Club on 13th April 1964, following allegations of corruption when he had been a Sheffield Wednesday player. Kay, and nine other footballers - James Gauld, 35 (ex-Mansfield Town and former Everton player); John Fountain, 32 (ex-York City); Richard Beattie, 27 (Portsmouth); Samuel Chapman, 26 (ex-Mansfield); Brian Phillips, 32 (ex-Mansfield); Kenneth Thompson, 34 (Hartlepools United); Ronald Howells, 29 (Walsall); David Layne, 25 (Sheffield Wednesday); and Peter Swan, 28 (Sheffield Wednesday) – were sentenced to varying terms of imprisonment for conspiring to defraud people accepting bets by fixing the results of certain League matches. Gauld received the longest sentence of imprisonment, four years, whilst Kay, Layne and Swan each received four months.

1965-66 Season

A major change to the rules was introduced that season when substitutes were allowed in League games for the first time, one by each side for an injured player.

On Sunday, 8th August, Harry Catterick flew from Liverpool Airport with a party of 17 players for a two match pre-season tour of Norway. The players were: West and Rankin; Wilson, Brown and Wright; Gabriel, Stevens, Labone and Harris; Scott, Shaw, Young, Harvey, Pickering, Husband, Temple and Morrissey. Everton won both games – 7-3 against an Oslo Select and 3-1 against Rogaland Combination, a team drawn from the district around Stavanger. Andy did not play in either of the games. The party arrived back in Liverpool on the following Thursday.

Everton's public trial was held on Saturday, 14th August, watched by 10,000 spectators. Temple and Gabriel were missing – the former through injury, the latter because of illness. The teams were:

Blues: West; Wright, Wilson; Hurst, Labone, Harris; Scott, Harvey, Pickering, Young, Morrissey.

Whites: Rankin; Parker, Brown; Glover, Heslop, Stevens; Shaw, Humphreys, Hill, Husband, Maher.

The game ended 1-1, and Barnett replaced Andy in the second half.

Everton's first opponents of the season were Northampton Town at Goodison Park the Saturday after the public trial. Northampton had climbed from the Fourth Division to the First Division in only five years, without financial backing and only small crowds. Their initial experience of the First Division was a 5-2 defeat.

Andy was in the Reserve team that drew 1-1 away to Preston Reserves on the first Saturday of the season. The Everton Reserve team was:

Rankin; Curwen, Brown; Stevens, Heslop, Clark; Shaw, Glover, Hill, Husband, Morrissey.

He appeared in goal in five of the next six Reserve games, Barnett substituting for him in the other. Saturday, 25th September, saw the first team and Central League derby games. The Reserves were at home. The teams were:

Everton Reserves: Rankin; Curwen, Darcy; Hurst, Brown, Stevens; Shaw, Royle, Hill, Husband, Morrissey.

Liverpool Reserves: Ogston; Parsley, Hignett; Evans, Moran, Bennett; Graham, Wallace, Sealey, Chisnall, Walker.

Eleven of the players taking the field were Merseysiders, a far cry from the football of today, when some clubs fail to field an English player, never mind a local one, in their first team.

Liverpool were in front in the 13th minute, when Andy misjudged a cross leaving the unmarked Graham to put the ball into an empty net. Four minutes later, the Liverpool centre-forward ran through on goal, with the Everton defenders appealing for offside. He was brought down by Andy in the penalty area and Chisnall converted the penalty. Husband pulled a goal back for Everton two minutes before the interval, but Liverpool secured the win with another goal in the second half.

In the first team derby, Liverpool won easily by five goals to nil. Everton were mid-table, with Liverpool lying in sixth place.

Everton drew 1-1 with Nuremberg in West Germany on Tuesday, 28th September in what Michael Charters of the Liverpool Echo described as a disgrace to football and made him wonder if European competitions were worth it. He went on, *"Different interpretation of the rules, poor refereeing by our standards, obstructive tactics, vicious tackling, provocation and retaliation, foul and counter-foul – all ran riot here last night."*(23) After the game, Harry Catterick said, *"I'm no softie, but Nuremberg are the dirtiest side I have ever seen, so far as they are concerned the war is still on."*

Eggleston, the Everton trainer, ran on to the pitch when both Morrissey and Harvey were lying on the pitch injured, but was sent off by the referee for coming on to the pitch without his permission. Later, when Wright was injured, Andy had to attend to him in place of Eggleston. The Everton team was:

West; Wright, Wilson; Gabriel, Brown, Harris; Temple, Stevens, Pickering, Harvey, Morrissey.

Everton got their revenge at Goodison Park two weeks later when they won the second-leg 2-0, knocking Nuremberg out of the competition. There was little or no violent conduct in the game, which was well-handled by the French referee.

Andy was called into the first team against Fulham at Craven Cottage on Saturday, 16th October, as Gordon West had broken his collar-bone in the Nuremberg game. The team was:

Rankin; Wright, Wilson; Gabriel, Brown, Harris; Scott, Harvey, Pickering, Temple, Morrissey. Young was substitute.

The Fulham team included Johnny Haynes, George Cohen and Bobby Robson.

Everton were ahead in the second minute when Pickering scored after Morrissey's shot rebounded off the bar. A quarter of an hour later, however, Fulham were on level terms when Harris brought down Marsh in the penalty area and Dyson converted the subsequent penalty. Fulham were leading 2-1 at half-time, but Everton drew level seven minutes into the second half, when Macedo, the Fulham goalkeeper, could only push a Harris shot into the path of Pickering, who immediately hit the ball into the net. After Fulham had gone ahead again, Gabriel had the ball in the net, but was ruled offside. Ten minutes from the end, Harvey was sent off for retaliation when he was brought down from behind. It looked a harsh decision, according to Horace Yates, the Liverpool Echo reporter. Harvey was the 10th Everton player to be sent off in League football in the post-war period. Only Swansea Town (12) and Halifax Town (11) had had more dismissals in League football.

In their away game, against Blackpool at Bloomfield Road the following Saturday, Everton played delightful football and should have been six or seven goals up at the interval. However, the half-time score was 0-0 and both teams failed to score in the second half, despite the fact that Andy rolled the ball to Charnley, the Blackpool forward, who fortunately hit the ball over the crossbar. Everton fielded the team that lost to Fulham, while Blackpool included Tony Waiters, Jimmy Armfield and Alan Ball.

Everton recorded their first away victory of the season at Ewood Park on Saturday, 30th October, when they beat Blackburn Rovers by two goals to one.

On the Wednesday, they lost 3-0 to Upjesti Dozsa in Hungary in the Inter-Cit-ies Fairs Cup. The team was:

Rankin; Wright, Wilson; Stevens, Labone, Harris; Scott, Harvey, Pickering, Temple, Morrissey.

There were only 5,000 people in a stadium that held 100,000. According to Michael Charters, the Yugoslavian referee allowed the Hungarians to get away with obstruction that would anger an English crowd but, even so, "*Everton were beaten by a vastly superior side whose ball skill, accurate passing and smooth switch-ing of defence into attack was on a far higher level than their own.*"(24) Charters added, "*Rankin must share some of the blame for the first two goals, but otherwise he handled everything that came his way in a competent fashion. The rest of them were well below form.*"

Everton were unchanged from the Upjesti Dozsa game for their home fixture against Leicester City three days later, which they lost 2-1. In his column in the Echo, Leslie Edwards wrote, "*Rankin's propensity for leaving his line and his giving Leicester forwards the opportunity to float the ball over his head was only one weak-ness in an Everton defence, which degenerated as the match progressed. Yet, it was the attack and its lack of understanding and inaccuracy in passing which caused the crowd so much concern.*"

Young was substitute for the Leicester match and when the game was stopped to allow Derek Temple to receive treatment, the fans started to shout, "We want Alex, We want Alex…". Then, over the public address system came the message, "Here is an SOS for Mr Young of 30 …" The rest was lost in a roar of laughter, which broke out afresh when the voice was heard urging Mr Young to come to the Everton office immediately.

Everton lost again on Saturday, 13th November, this time away to Sheffield United by two goals to nil. Andy was at fault for the second goal, seven minutes from the end, when he missed his punch to a cross from right-back Badger and allowed centre-forward Jones to head the ball into the net.

Everton were now 13th with 16 points from 17 games, seven points behind leaders Burnley, having played a game more, and seven points ahead of the bottom club Blackburn Rovers.

Pickering was dropped for the first time since joining from Blackburn Rovers in March 1964 when Everton faced Upjesti Dozsa at Goodison in the second-leg of their Inter-Cities tie. Although Everton won 2-1, they went out of the competition on aggregate by 4-2. The team was:

Rankin; Wright, Wilson; Harvey, Labone, Harris; Temple, Gabriel, Young, Husband, Morrissey.

Andy played in the next two League games, a 0-0 draw at home with Leeds and then a 3-0 defeat by West Ham at Upton Park. However, he was dropped in favour of 18 year-old Geoff Barnett, for the home game against Sunderland, which Everton won 2-0. It was Barnett's first team debut.

Barnett kept his place for the next eight games, of which Everton won two, drew two and lost four. The last of those games was a 2-0 defeat by Blackpool at Bloomfield Road on Saturday, 15th January, 1966, a defeat for which Barnett was blamed.

West was recalled to the first team the following Saturday for the Third Round FA Cup tie at Goodison Park against Sunderland, which Everton won 3-0. Andy was in the Reserves, although he was replaced by Barnett for the next two Reserve games.

On 8th February, it was reported by the local press that Andy had suffered a hairline fracture of the cheekbone in an accident at home. Someone had opened the door in the room where he had been laying linoleum and the door had smacked him on the side of the face.

Andy did not play again until the Reserve game at Goodison Park on Saturday, 12th March, which Everton won 1-0. The following week was the first team and Reserve team derby games. The Reserves were at Anfield and the teams were:

Everton Reserves: Rankin; Pearson, Darcy; Hurst, Smith, Glover; Shaw, Humphreys, Husband, Trebilcock, Maher.

Liverpool Reserves: Molyneux; Ross, Lowey; Strong, Marsh, Moran; Hall, Chisnall, Sealey, McDougall, Long.

Everton Reserves won 4-0 with two goals from Trebilcock and one each from Humphreys and Husband. Andy was forced to make two brilliant saves. The first team game at Goodison ended in a 0-0 stalemate. Gordon West was in goal.

Everton drew both their 6th round FA Cup tie and the replay with Manchester City. The second replay was to be at Blackburn on Monday, 4th April, so Harry Catterick made a number of changes for the league game at Leicester, on the Saturday before the second replay, including the recall of Andy in goal. Heavy snowfalls and blizzards in the North and Midlands caused the Leicester game and the second replay with Manchester City to be postponed.

The City game was eventually played on the Wednesday. Everton won 2-0 to progress to the semi-finals to face the other half of Manchester on 23rd April.

During that week, Alf Ramsay named four Everton players and seven from Anfield in his squad of 40 players for the World Cup, which was being hosted by England that summer. The players were West, Wilson, Pickering and Temple from Everton; Lawler, Byrne, Smith, Milne, Callaghan, Hunt and Thompson from Liverpool; the final 22 were to be nominated to FIFA on 3rd July.

Before the FA Cup semi-final, Everton had three League games. They lost 3-1 to Sheffield United and beat Newcastle United 1-0, both games being played at Goodison. The third game was against Leeds United at Elland Road, the Saturday before the semi-final. Everton played a team of reserves, showing eleven changes from the printed programme. Harry Catterick said all the changes were due to injuries. The teams were:

Everton: Rankin; Brown, Darcy; Hurst, Smith, Glover; Husband, Humphreys, Royle, Trebilcock, Morrissey.

Leeds: Harvey; Bell, Cooper; Bremner, Charlton, Hunter; Greenhoff, Lorimer, Storrie, Giles, Johanneson.

Darcy, Humphreys and Smith were making their debuts for Everton. Leeds were one up at the interval, and just minutes before the whistle, Lorimer had been spoken to by the referee for running straight into Andy, who was on the ground with the ball firmly in his grasp. Within a minute of the restart, Everton were on level terms with a goal from Trebilcock. But, Leeds went ahead again five minutes later, when Charlton headed in a free-kick from just outside the penalty area. Leeds scored a third in the 57th minute. A slip by Darcy allowed Lorimer to run on goal. Andy could only push out his shot and Johanneson ran in to slot the ball home. Six minutes later, Lorimer scored Leeds' fourth, when Andy punched a Bremner cross straight to him, and he hit a great shot just inside the post.

English League Division One match at Elland Road on 16th April 1966 – Everton keeper Andy Rankin dives to save from Leeds Jimmy Greenhoff as Peter Storrie comes in. © Mirrorpix

According to a Football League official, there had been many complaints from Yorkshire fans about Everton playing a reserve team against Leeds, and the club was to be asked for an explanation. It was against Football League regulations for a club to fail to field its full strength team unless there was a satisfactory reason. Everton failed to convince the Football League that there were good grounds and were fined £2000. Everton's fine was double the highest imposed previously for the offence - Burnley were fined £1000 in March 1961 for not fielding their strongest available side in a League match against Chelsea at Turf Moor.

Everton beat Manchester United 1-0 in the FA Cup semi-final on 23rd April and were the first club in "modern" times to reach the final of the FA Cup without conceding a goal. United had played Partizan Belgrade in the European Cup the Wednesday before the tie, whilst Everton had had no midweek commitment. Sheffield Wednesday beat Chelsea 2-0 at Villa Park in the other semi-final.

Everton went on to win the Cup three weeks later for the first time since 1933 with one of the greatest fight-backs in Cup history. Two goals down after 54 minutes, Trebilcock, who had only played eight first team games for Everton, scored twice and Derek Temple got the winner with sixteen minutes of the game remaining. West was in goal.

Goodison was to host five World Cup games starting in July. So, Liverpool allowed Everton to play their Central League fixture against Sheffield United at Anfield on 4th May to give their ground staff as much time as possible to prepare the pitch.

England won the World Cup by beating West Germany 4-2 at Wembley on 30th July. Liverpool's Roger Hunt and Everton's Ray Wilson were members of the winning team.

It was a disappointing season for Andy. Recalled to the first team in October to replace the injured Gordon West, he was blamed for a number of goals in the nine games that he played, and was then replaced by Geoff Barnett, the third choice keeper.

1966-67 Season

The first Liverpool derby of the season was the Charity Shield game at Goodison Park on Saturday, 13th August. Before the kick-off, the teams did a lap of honour led by Roger Hunt and Ray Wilson, captains for the day, carrying the World Cup between them. Brian Labone and Ron Yeats followed with the FA Cup and League Championship trophy respectively. Just over 63,000 spectators saw Liverpool win 1-0 with a Roger Hunt goal. Gordon West was in goal for Everton.

In the week before the League competition started, Everton signed World Cup hero, Alan Ball, from Blackpool for £110,000, a record fee for English clubs. A transfer request from Fred Pickering was rejected by the club.

Ball made his debut the following, Saturday, 20th August, at Fulham and scored the only goal of the game. Andy played for the Reserves in the 7-1 victory over Bury Reserves at Goodison Park . The Reserve team was:

Rankin; Turner, Darcy; Hurst, Smith, Glover; Wallace, Humphreys, Royle, Husband, Morrissey.

Andy did not make an appearance in the first team during the remainder of 1966, but was a regular for the Central League team. Probably the most important Reserve games were the two mini-Liverpool derbies. The first was at Anfield on Saturday, 27th August. The teams were:

Liverpool: Ogston; Carroll, Moran; Chisnall, Ross, Evans, Graham, Livermore, McDougall, G. Wallace, Walker.
Everton: Rankin; Pearson, Darcy; Hurst, Smith, Harris; Wallace, Humphreys, Royle, Trebilcock, Husband.

Everton were beaten 2-1 in front of a crowd of 4,000. Liverpool should have scored early in the game, but McDougall shot tamely at Andy from only three yards out. However, they did go ahead in the 25th minute with a goal from Graham. Almost from the restart, Andy made a magnificent save when he threw himself across the goal to push a deflected shot for a corner. Royle equalised six minutes into the second half. Liverpool were pressing for the winner, but Andy brought off another good save from Chisnall. However, he was unable to prevent McDougall scoring the winner with a minute to go.

The Everton senior side beat Liverpool 3-1 at Goodison, watched by 64,318 spectators.

The second mini-derby was played on New Year's Eve at Goodison Park. Everton Reserves lost 2-1 again. On this occasion, the teams were:

Everton: Rankin; Turner, Darcy; Smith, Kenyon, Brindle; Wallace, Glover, Royle, Trebilcock, Maher.

Liverpool: Ogston; Wall, Byrne; Chisnall, Marsh, Evans; Graham, Livermore, McDougall, Arrowsmith, Moran.

Liverpool nearly scored in the first minute, but Andy got his foot to an Evans shot to deflect the ball just past the upright. Almost immediately, Trebilcock beat Ogston with a shot, only to see Byrne clear the ball off the line for a corner. Liverpool did go ahead in the 14th minute when Arrowsmith scored following hesitation in the Everton defence. Wallace equalised for Everton when he scored against the run of play in the 61st minute, but Arrowsmith scored his second to win the game for Liverpool.

The first teams played out a goalless draw at Anfield.

In the first week in January 1967, Everton signed 17 years old Terry Owen, one of the apprentices, on full-time professional terms. An outside-right, he had come to them from Crosby Boys. He managed only two appearances in the senior side before moving to Bradford City, the first of his five clubs in the lower divisions. He has achieved greater fame as the father of Michael Owen, the former Liverpool and England centre-forward.

On Friday, 10th March, Everton announced the signing of Howard Kendall for £80,000 from Preston North End. Kendall was, at that time, the youngest player to appear in an FA Cup Final when he turned out for Preston against West Ham in 1964. Kendall went on to play more than 230 games for Everton and is their most successful manager, winning two league championships, the FA Cup and the European Cup Winners' Cup.

The following evening, Everton beat Liverpool 1-0 at Goodison in the 5th round of the FA Cup. Alan Ball scored the only goal. The game was televised and relayed to watching fans in the Anfield ground. Everton were to face Nottingham Forest in the semi-final on Saturday, 8th April.

Andy continued in the Reserves until Saturday, 1st April, when he was called into the first team for the home game against Aston Villa in place of the injured Gordon West. West's hand had been broken when Gilzean of Spurs collided with him in the 2-0 defeat at White Hart Lane in midweek. Before the Villa match, Michael Charters wrote: "*Great interest will centre today on how Andy Rankin plays on his recall because of West's injury. It is more than two years since Rankin held the job down on merit and since then West's form has been so good that Rankin has soldiered on in the Reserves playing well but knowing that he would not push West out of the first team spot. Rankin's big test, of course, will be in the Cup-tie, but he should take the chance today of getting back into the big-time atmosphere instead of the placid temperature of the Central League. On form, he could hold his place in any First Division team and Everton are fortunate to have reserves of his quality and also a man like Sandy Brown, coming in for Wilson, who may still be all right for the Cup.*"(25)

Everton were three up at half-time, but Villa got a consolation goal in the 58th minute when Anderson, their right winger, hit a powerful shot, which Andy could only parry. The ball ran loose to the other Villa winger, who prodded it into the net. The Everton team was:

Rankin; Wright, Brown; Hurst, Labone, Harvey; Scott, Ball, Husband, Young, Morrissey. Sub Temple.

Everton were now 7th in the League with 38 points from 35 games. Aston Villa were third from bottom.

The following Saturday was the FA Cup 6th round tie with Nottingham Forest at The City Ground. The teams were:

Everton: Rankin; Wright, Wilson; Hurst, Labone, Harvey; Young, Ball, Husband, Brown, Morrissey. Substitute: Temple.
Forest: Grummitt; Hindley, Whitfield; Hennessey, McKinlay, Newton; Lyons, Barnwell, Baker, Wignall, Moore. Substitute: Hinton.

Forest's former England centre-forward, Baker, was injured in the first minute when he collided with Labone. He left the pitch for attention and returned a few minutes later. However, he had to be replaced by Hinton on the half-hour.

Everton went ahead after 36 minutes with a glorious goal by Jimmy Husband and, going in at half-time with a one goal lead, looked the better team and had made Forest look mediocre. After the interval, however, it was Forest that was pressing for a goal. It came in the 67th minute when Wignall hit a fine shot from 20 yards. Andy saved, but then lost the ball, which bounced out to Moore, who had a simple job of turning it over the line. Two minutes later, Moore scored a second with an excellent shot from inside the area. Somehow, Everton managed to get themselves back into the game with an equaliser and second goal from Husband. But, with only seconds to go before the final whistle, Moore completed his hat-trick in what Michael Charters described as *"one of the greatest FA Cup ties I've seen, a match packed full of incident and drama bordering on the sensational, a match that will be talked about as long as Everton play in the Cup."*(26)

FA Cup Quarter Final at the City Ground. Nottingham on 8th April 1967 - The last-gasp winner! Having seen his first shot blocked by a defender and his second saved by keeper Andy Rankin, Forest winger Ian Storey-Moore has headed against the Everton crossbar and is about to nod the rebound into the empty net to claim a place in the FA Cup semi-final as the City Ground explodes with excitement. © *Mirrorpix*

Following the cup defeat, Andy appeared in the next five League matches, which included three wins, a draw and a defeat. Gordon West returned for the final two games, a 1-1 draw with Burnley at Turf Moor and a 4-1 win over Sunderland at Goodison Park.

Manchester United were League champions and Spurs won the Cup. Everton were 6th in the League, three points behind Liverpool, who were 5th; the Central League team were runners-up.

Glasgow Celtic became the first British Club to win the European Cup when they beat Inter-Milan 2-1 in Lisbon. All eleven players in the Celtic side had been born within a 30 mile radius of Glasgow. A far cry from today's multi-national sides in the Premier League.

1967-68 Season

A change to the substitution rule was introduced for the new season. Whilst a team was still only permitted to use one substitute, that substitute could now be introduced for tactical reasons rather than only as a replacement for an injured player.

West's injury at Spurs at the end of March had presented Andy with an opportunity to re-establish himself as the first choice keeper. But, a number of errors, particularly in the FA Cup tie with Nottingham Forest, cost him that chance. Perhaps, then, it was no surprise to him when he found that he had effectively slipped to third choice keeper for he was not selected for the pre-season tours to Dublin and Holland, or the public trial at Goodison on Saturday, 12th August. Gordon West and Geoff Barnett were the keepers on each occasion. Andy played for the A team, with only rare appearances for the Reserves.

A number of players had left Everton for other clubs during the pre-season period. Jimmy Gabriel signed for Southampton for £50,000; Fred Pickering returned to Blackburn for a similar fee; Derek Temple was transferred to Preston for £40,000; and Alex Scott moved back to Scotland with Hibs.

On Friday 15th March 1968, the Liverpool Echo broke the news that Andy Rankin had signed for Huddersfield for £25,000 and that he was to keep goal for them in their home match with Derby County at Leeds Road the following day. But four days later, the same newspaper reported that he was still an Everton player and according to reporter, Chris James, the clubs had agreed terms, but the deal had broken down *because of a problem over medical examination.*

1968-69 Season

Andy was clearly still third choice keeper as Gordon West and Geoff Barnett were again selected for the pre-season trip to Dublin. He and Barnett shared the goal-keeping duties for the Reserves during the season.

1969-70 Season

Andy and Barnett continued to share the goalkeeper's jersey in the Reserves. When West was injured and likely to miss the Aston Villa game on Saturday 27th September, it was Barnett, however, who was called into the squad as cover. In the end, West recovered sufficiently to take his place in goal.

A few days later, Barnett moved to Arsenal for a fee in the region of £30,000. Their first choice keeper, Bob Wilson, had broken his arm and they quickly needed a replacement. Barnett had joined Everton with Hurst, Glover and Maher, after all four had been capped by England Schoolboys at the same time and he had played ten League games for the Club. At Arsenal, he was always second choice behind Bob Wilson and later Jimmy Rimmer. He left Arsenal in 1976 for Minnesota Kicks in the United States, having appeared in 49 League games for them and with an FA Cup runners-up medal from 1972 when Leeds United beat them 1-0.

Everton won the First Division championship that season when they finished nine points clear of runners-up Leeds United.

1970-71 Season

Ten days before the start of season, Andy had an appendix operation so he missed the public trial on Wednesday, 5th August 1970. Clarke was in goal for the Reserves. However, he recovered sufficiently to play for the Reserves in September and was named as a reserve for the European Cup-tie against Keflavik, a team of amateurs from Iceland, at Goodison Park on Wednesday, 16th September.

Keflavik caused a sensation when they scored in the 11th minute and led

Everton until six minutes before the interval. Everton eventually won 6-2. Both Keflavik's goals resulted from mistakes by Gordon West, who was jeered by the Everton fans during the game.

Manager Harry Catterick dropped West for the Saturday League game against Blackpool at Bloomfield Road, explaining that West had *"lost his confidence and form. I have decided to rest him until he gets them back"*.(27) Andy was promoted from the Reserves to take West's place, his first appearance in the senior team since 6th May 1967 when he played against Aston Villa, an absence of nearly three and a half years. In that time, West had played in 158 League and Cup games, missing only one match, when Geoff Barnett replaced him – a remarkable record.

Andy had little to do in the 2-0 win over Blackpool and kept his place for the home game against Crystal Palace on Saturday, 26th September. Everton's team was:

Rankin; Wright, Newton; Kendall, Kenyon, Harvey; Whittle, Ball, Royle, Hurst Morrissey.

The Palace defence was one of the best in the country, having only conceded five goals in nine games, but Everton thrilled their fans with three goals in the first half. When the game was goalless, Andy made a magnificent save, turning a fierce shot away for a corner and, then, shortly after Everton had gone ahead through Morrissey, he again came to Everton's rescue when he blocked a shot with his legs.

The second leg of the European Cup-tie was played in Iceland on a very muddy pitch on Wednesday, 30th September. Keflavik never threatened Andy's goal, whilst Everton scored three times, to win 9-2 on aggregate.

In their League game the following Saturday, Everton lost 3-1 away to Coventry City, with former player Ernie Hunt scoring two of the goals, one of which became one of the most famous goals in English football as the match was televised on BBC's Match of the Day. Everton lined up to face a Coventry free-kick from just outside their penalty area. Willie Carr gripped the ball between his heels and jumped up releasing the ball behind him for Hunt to volley the ball past Andy into the net. The move was outlawed at the end of the season.

A week later, Everton were at home to Derby County. Wright, Husband and Ball were all injured. The teams were:

Everton: Rankin; Brown, Newton; Kendall, Kenyon, Harvey; Whittle, Jackson, Royle, Hurst, Morrissey.
Derby: Green; Webster, Robson; McGovern, McFarland, Mackay; Gemmill, Carlin, O'Hare, Hector, Hinton.

Tommy Jackson was making his first League appearance of the season for Everton. Morrissey gave Everton a great start when he scored with just over 15 minutes of the game gone. Andy then produced two splendid saves in quick succession. He made his third great save of the day immediately after the interval, when he somehow managed to turn a deflected header from Hinton round the post for a corner. But almost immediately, Derby equalised, when Andy could only parry a header from Hector. McGovern got to the loose ball first and drove it through a ruck of players into the net.

The following week, Everton signed Henry Newton from Nottingham Forest for £150,000, making him the third most expensive player in British football behind Martin Peters (Spurs for £200,000) and Allan Clarke (Leeds for £165,000). Tommy Jackson moved to Forest as part of the deal. Jackson had made 34 first team appearances for Everton, since signing for them 2½ years earlier from Glentoran for £9,000. .

Newton made his debut against Arsenal at Highbury on Saturday, 17th October. He was unable to make any impact in the 4-0 defeat, Everton's heaviest loss of the season. "*But for Rankin, Everton's defeat would have been even heavier.*"(28)

In midweek, Everton drew 1-1 with Borussia Monchengladbach in Germany in the European Cup and then had mixed results in their next two League games, beating Newcastle 3-1 at Goodison on 24th October and losing 3-0 away to West Bromwich Albion a week later. Following the Albion game, Andy had to have four stitches inserted in a cut over his eye.

In an unforgettable and thrilling match at Goodison Park on Wednesday evening, 4th November, Everton reached the quarter-finals of the European Cup.

They won 4-3 on penalties against Borussia Monchengladbach after the game had ended 1-1 (2-2 on aggregate) after extra time. The headline in the Liverpool Echo the following day was "*Heroes all – but Andy Rankin is the king.*" Michael Charters reporting for the Echo wrote: "*… it needed Everton's goalkeeper, Andy Rankin, a spectator for so much of the game to win the match for his side by saving the last penalty from the last kick of 120 minutes of high drama.*" Andy had dived to his right to push away the German defender Muller's well-struck shot and was immediately engulfed by his team-mates wishing to congratulate him. Summing up, Charters wrote: "*It was the greatest European tie I've seen. It had everything and even though Everton won on the penalty system, it would have been, to use that well-known phrase, a travesty of justice, if they had not gone through to the quarter-finals.*"

On the Saturday, Andy was given a great reception by the 40,000 crowd at Goodison as he came out to face Nottingham Forest in the League. It was a scrappy game and Everton seemed to be suffering from a European hangover, although they did scrape home with a 1-0 win, with Alan Whittle scoring the only goal of the game.

The following week, Everton earned a point at the Potteries when they drew 1-1 with Stoke. Towards the end of the game, Andy made the save of the match when he touched a great shot from Stoke's Barnard round the post.

Saturday, 21st November, saw the 103rd local derby. Playing at Anfield, the teams were:

Liverpool: Clemence; Lawler, Lindsay; Smith, Lloyd, Hughes; Hall, McLaughlin, Heighway, Toshack, Ross.
Everton: Rankin; Wright, Newton (H); Kendall, Labone, Harvey; Whittle, Ball, Royle, Hurst, Morrissey.

Despite taking a 2-0 lead after a goalless first half, Everton were beaten 3-2. Whittle and Royle scored to put Everton two up with just over quarter of an hour of the second half gone. Heighway pulled one back for Liverpool in the 69th minute and, then, Toshack equalised eleven minutes later. Five minutes from the end Lawler scored the winner. Watched by almost 54,000 spectators, Everton threw the game away; at 2-0 up they were the better team and seemed to have the game won.

Everton drew their next two games – 0-0 at home to Spurs and 1-1 away to Huddersfield Town – and then at Goodison on Saturday, 12th December, they completely outclassed Southampton, who had Jimmy Gabriel in their side. Everton were four goals up before Southampton got a consolation goal with 12 minutes to go. Royle (2), Whittle and Morrissey were the scorers. Andy's only save came three minutes from the end.

The following Saturday, Everton had another home game, against League leaders Leeds United on this occasion. The teams were:

Everton: Rankin; Wright, Newton (H); Kendall, Kenyon, Harvey; Whittle, Ball, Royle, Hurst, Morrissey. Sub: Brown

Leeds: Sprake; Reaney, Cooper; Bremner, Charlton, Hunter; Lorimer, Clarke, Jones, Giles, Madeley. Sub: Bates.

Jack Charlton headed the only goal of the game after ten minutes. Everton gave everything they had but it was not enough to breach the Leeds defence. It was a real battle with 43 free-kicks, 22 of which were awarded against Everton. The crowd blamed Leeds for the physical elements of the game, booing and slow-handclapping them off the field at the end.

Everton trained normally on Christmas morning, reporting to Bellfield for a short workout, a discussion on tactics for the Wolves match the following day and the announcement of the squad to travel. Instead of having lunch together, they went home for their Christmas dinner. They met a few hours later for the journey to Wolverhampton, where they stayed the night at a hotel before the game at Molyneux on Boxing Day.

Perhaps they had too much to eat and drink for their Christmas dinner, because they failed for the first time in nine years to beat Wolves at Molyneux. On an icy surface, Wolves scored twice with Everton failing to reply. "*In fact it was Andy Rankin the Everton goalkeeper who saved his team from complete humiliation.*

First when he rather luckily got his body in the way of a powered drive from Hib-bitt, Wolves latest Under-23 international in the 55th minute, and then again when Hibbitt had pushed through a dream ball on the inside of Newton to Bailey. Rankin rushed out to prevent the Wolves captain scoring what seemed a simple goal. In between these two, Hibbitt hammered a shot against the underside of the woodwork for another Everton let off."(29)

Joe Royle heads away an attempt at goal by Liverpool's Larry Lloyd in the Everton/ Liverpool derby on 27th March 1971, watched by Colin Harvey, keeper Andy Rankin, Lloyd and Howard Kendall. Courtesy of The Everton Collection Charitable Trust, Reference 796EFC-26-2-335-0001

The following Saturday, 2nd January 1971, Everton beat Second Division Blackburn Rovers 2-0 in the third round of the FA Cup. Husband scored twice for Everton, whilst Andy was not called into action until the 77th minute.

Whilst Everton were beating Blackburn Rovers, Ibrox Park in Glasgow saw its second major disaster, almost 70 years after the first in 1902 during the England - Scotland fixture. This time, 66 people, including a number of children and one young woman, died in a crush on an exit stairway towards the end of the New Year game between Rangers and Celtic. The inquest into the tragedy concluded that the accident had happened because one or more fans had tripped on their way down the stairs and that the pressure from the supporters behind caused those at the front to fall on those who had collapsed first.

In a civil case brought against Rangers by the widow of one of the casualties, the Sheriff in the Scottish Court severely criticised Rangers, saying that the Club had done little to improve safety on the staircases after previous incidents and awarding the widow more than £26,000. The previous incidents referred to by the Sheriff occurred in 1961 when two people died in a crush on the stairway and in 1967 and 1969 when a number of people were injured in both instances.

Following the 1971 disaster, the Government appointed Lord Wheatley to carry out an inquiry into the safety of British football grounds. His recommendations were embodied within the Safety of Sports Grounds Act of 1975. First and Second Division grounds and those with a capacity of over 10,000 now required safety certificates issued by local authorities.

Between those two Ibrox tragedies, disaster had struck at Burnden Park, Bolton, on 9th March 1946 where the home side faced Stoke City in an FA Cup quarter-final tie. A crowd of some 80,000, many of whom had gained access without payment by various means, was in the ground. Shortly after kick-off, several crush barriers collapsed causing spectators to fall forward, piling on top of each other. The referee, having been told that something was amiss, stopped the game and took the players off the field. About half-an-hour later, the game restarted on police advice so as to avoid panic, with the teams simply swapping ends at half-time to finish the game as quickly as possible. Thirty-three people died and some 500 were injured that day.

After their New Year defeat of Blackburn Rovers, Everton drew their next League fixture, 2-2, with Burnley in ankle-deep mud at Turf Moor. David Johnson scored on his debut for Everton; he had replaced Joe Royle at centre-forward.

Everton faced Chelsea at Goodison on Saturday, 16th January, hoping for

a confidence-boosting win before their fourth round FA Cup tie with Middlesbrough the next week. The teams were:

Everton: Rankin; Wright, Newton H; Kendall, Labone, Harvey; Husband,
Ball, Royle, Hurst, Morrissey.

Chelsea: Bonetti; Boyle, Harris; Hollins, Dempsey, Hinton; Cooke, Baldwin,
Osgood, Hudson, Houseman.

Everton were two up at half-time with goals from Husband in the eighth minute
and another from Newton about 30 minutes later. In between these two goals,
*"Rankin reproduced his "German" save to prevent Chelsea equalising from a penalty
after 19 minutes".*(30) Hurst had handled in the box, Osgood shot low and hard
from the penalty spot but Andy dived to his right and held on to the ball. Royle
added a third for Everton five minutes from time.

Everton fielded the same team against Second Division Middlesbrough in the
FA Cup at Goodison Park and had no trouble despatching them from the competition by three goals to nil. Almost 55,000 fans watched the game.

Everton won their next two League games, both of which were at Goodison
Park. They beat Spurs 2-1 on Saturday, 30th January, a game in which Brian Labone
was carried off on a stretcher after only eight minutes with a muscle injury. The
following week, they defeated newly promoted Huddersfield Town by the same
score.

It was back to the FA Cup on Saturday, 13th February – a 5th round tie at home
to Derby County. West was back in the first team for the first time in five months.
Andy had been injured against Spurs and, although he had played against Huddersfield the following week, he was still feeling the injury in training and it was
decided not to risk him. Johnson scored the only goal of the game to put Everton
through to the next round.

Andy missed the next three games, including the derby match, which finished goalless. However, he was back in the team for the FA Cup quarter-final
against Colchester at Goodison Park on Saturday, 6th March. Manager Harry

Catterick had told reporter Michael Charters: "*Rankin was playing well before he was injured… and he is fully fit now. West is a great goalkeeper, who has lost his confidence because of barracking by the crowd. I feel very sorry for him, as sorry as I have ever been for any player in my experience.*"(31) Everton fielded the following eleven against Colchester:

Rankin; Wright, Newton H; Kendall, Kenyon, Harvey; Husband, Ball, Royle, Hurst, Morrissey.

Colchester had beaten Leeds 3-2 in the fifth round, but there was no giant killing this time. Everton had finished off the game before the interval with four goals in 13 minutes; the scorers were Kendall with two, the first time he had scored twice for Everton in a match, Royle and Husband. Five minutes from the end, Ball added a fifth. Before Everton had scored, Andy had to pull out all the stops to prevent Colchester taking the lead. "*He saved brilliantly from Crawford's header, cut off a dangerous centre from Lewis, and suddenly the drive of Colchester's attacks evaporated like smoke.*"(32) Even Crawford himself applauded the first save.

Liverpool drew 0-0 with Spurs at Anfield in the Cup, but won the replay 2-1. The Cup draw produced the semi-final that no Merseysider wanted – Everton to face Liverpool at Old Trafford on Saturday, 27th March. It was Everton's fourth semi-final in six years.

In the meantime, Everton drew 1-1 with the Greek Champions Panathanaikos, managed by Ferenc Puskas, at Goodison on Tuesday, 9th March in the European Cup. Everton attacked for 95 percent of what Chris James described in the Liverpool Echo as the most one-sided game that he had seen in top-class football. Andy did not have a save to make until the 66th minute but soon afterwards, the Greeks stunned the Everton fans, when they took the lead in only their second attack of the evening. Then, in the final minute, Royle headed down Everton's 17th corner for Johnson to score. That goal meant that he had scored on his League, FA Cup and European Cup debuts in a matter of weeks.

On the Saturday, Everton beat Stoke 2-0 in the League at Goodison. Labone was included in the side for the first time since he had been injured at Spurs six weeks earlier. Whittle and Royle were the Everton scorers. Andy was injured after 20 minutes of the first half but he still managed to make three first class saves. In the Liverpool Echo on Monday, 15th March, Michael Charters wrote: "*Rankin, with much less to do than Banks, looked the more capable goalkeeper in direct contrast to the England Number 1. He made a magnificent save from Ritchie in the first half, hurtling himself across the goal to turn away a header. He had been pulled to the near post to take Conroy's cross, had been beaten by the flight of it, but still recovered to make his save. Later, he pushed headers from Ritchie and Smith over the bar in rare Stoke attacks which invariably looked dangerous, thanks to Conroy's hard running and clever passing, allied to Ritchie's power in the air.*"

Andy's injury to his knee, which he received against Stoke, kept him out of the game away to Newcastle on the following Wednesday. His place was taken by Dai Davies, 22 years of age, who had been signed from Swansea four months earlier for £20,000 after playing some 30 League matches. Although Davies did well on his debut, Everton lost 2-1.

Davies kept goal again for the away fixture against Nottingham Forest on the Saturday, which Everton lost 3-2.

Andy was recalled for the European Cup away leg against Panathanaikos on Wednesday, 24th March. Neither keeper had much to do and the match ended in a goalless draw and 1-1 on aggregate, which meant that the Greek side went through to the semi-finals on the away goal.

There was another important game on the Saturday – the FA Cup semi-final against Liverpool at Old Trafford.

In the Liverpool Echo Semi-Final Special published on the day of the game, Michael Charters assessed each of the Everton players. His assessment of Andy was: "*A completely transformed young man. He lay in the shadows for a long time, but now that his final chance has come he is taking it with both hands. Growing more watchful in each game he plays and reacting to difficult situations quickly. Would like to see him boss his area more, and protect himself when he comes out of his goal against big opponents for high balls.*" The teams on the day were:

Everton: Rankin; Wright, Newton K; Kendall, Labone, Harvey; Whittle, Ball, Royle, Hurst, Morrissey.

Liverpool: Clemence; Lawler, Lindsay; Smith, Lloyd, Hughes; Callaghan, Evans, Heighway, Toshack, Hall.

Sixty-two thousand fans saw Alan Ball give Everton the lead after only ten minutes. Clemence missed a cross and the ball travelled to the far side of the goal where Ball ran in to score. Five minutes after the interval, an injury forced Brian Labone to limp off the field to be replaced by substitute Sandy Brown. This proved to be a turning point in the game for less than ten minutes later, Evans equalised. Liverpool then did most of the attacking, and it was no surprise when they went ahead in the 72nd minute with the final goal of the tie. Heighway centred from the left, and Andy, who had had *"a magnificent game otherwise..."*. let the ball slip from his grasp whereupon Hall pounced to drive the ball into the net for his first senior goal. The headline in the Monday Echo was *"Greatest semi of them all"*. Manager Harry Catterick had missed both Cup games because he was ill in bed with bronchitis and flu.

Everton lost their next two League games – 1-0 to West Ham at Goodison on Tuesday, 27th March and then 3-0 to Manchester City at Maine Road on the Saturday. Against City, *"Rankin had looked far from happy and he was at fault when he came out to the edge of the penalty area trying to get the ball away from Hill. The City player cleverly floated the ball over Rankin's head but it dropped on the top netting."* Andy was also at fault with City first goal. He mispunched a Donachie cross straight to Doyle, who fired the ball into the net. However, he did make a number of fine saves, including the save of the match to deny Francis Lee in the closing minutes.

On Tuesday, 6th April, Everton drew 0-0 away to Ipswich. According to Michael Charters: *"... it was Rankin who played the major role on the field in keeping Ipswich goalless. He made four great saves in the first half – one from Robertson was outstanding – in what I thought was his best display of the season."*(33) Everton had chartered their own plane for the trip to Ipswich – a Dan Air 28-seater. The journey normally involved a train to London Euston, travelling across the city to Liverpool Street to catch another train to Ipswich. Travelling by plane allowed the players to train at Bellfield on the morning of the match, have lunch there and fly from Speke in the afternoon. They returned by plane immediately after the match, arriving in Liverpool about midnight.

Everton were then beaten 2-1 at home by Wolves on Saturday, 10th April, their fourth home defeat of the season; they beat Coventry 3-0 at Goodison in midweek; lost again on Saturday, 17th April, this time 3-1 to Derby County at the Baseball ground; shared a goalless draw with Blackpool at Bloomfield Road on Saturday, 24th April; and then lost their final League game of the season a week later when they were beaten 2-0 by Crystal Palace at Selhurst Park. Andy featured in all of these games.

Since their disastrous 72 hours when they lost their European Cup quarter-final and FA Cup semi-final, Everton had played eight league games - losing five, winning one and drawing the other two. They finished 14th in the League with 37 points from 42 games, their lowest League placing since Harry Catterick became manager. Earlier, he had celebrated ten years as the Everton manager, in which time the team had won two League titles (1962-63 and 1969-70), the FA Cup in 1966 and had been losing FA Cup finalists in 1968.

Everton's final game of the season was the third and fourth FA Cup play off against Stoke City on the evening before the Cup-Final itself. The match was played at Crystal Palace before a crowd of only 5,031. Despite leading 2-0 and playing some of their best football of the season, Everton lost 3-2. The teams were:

Everton: Rankin; Wright, Newton (H); Kendal, Labone, Harvey; Whittle, Ball, Johnson, Lyons, Morrissey.

Stoke: Banks; Marsh, Pejic; Bernard, Skeels, Lees; Hazlegrave, Greenhoff, Ritchie, Mahoney, Burrows.

The following day, Liverpool lost 2-1 to Arsenal after extra time in the FA Cup Final at Wembley, despite taking the lead.

The Everton v Stoke game to determine third and fourth place in the FA Cup was only the second of its kind. The first was in April 1970 when Manchester United defeated Watford 2-0 at Highbury, watched by a crowd of just over 15,000. There was little or no interest in these deciders and they lasted only five years. On the final occasion, in May 1974, Leicester lost 1-0 to Burnley on their home ground, Filbert Street, when less than 6,500 spectators turned up to see the game.

In all, Andy had played in 28 League matches and nine Cup games, the most first team appearances he had made in a season during his years at Everton. He would probably have been fairly satisfied with himself. He would certainly have long-lasting memories of his penalty save against Borussia Monchengladbach that secured a place for Everton in the quarter-finals of the European Cup. He would also have been aware, however, that he had made some errors that had led to crucial goals, not least when he dropped the ball to enable Liverpool to score the goal that sealed their appearance in the FA Cup Final.

In reviewing Everton's season, Michael Charters wrote: "*Goalkeeping was a problem. West faded out of the first team scene, shattered by the mistakes which upset him so much that he was only a shadow of the great goalkeeper who earned England honours. Andy Rankin did a fair job as his replacement but I assess his part no higher than that. He never looked the complete answer.*"(34)

Seventeen players were named for the three-match tour of Israel. They were: Rankin, Davies, Wright, Husband, Newton H, Buckley, Kendall, Darcy, Labone, Kenyon, Harvey, Whittle, Ball, Johnson, Morrissey, Hurst, Royle. The party flew out on Sunday, 16th May without Ball and Harvey, who were in the England squad for the home internationals. They travelled on 22nd May.

The day before Everton were to fly to Israel, Johnny Morrissey appeared before a special court in Ormskirk, Lancashire, charged with dishonestly handling two million cigarettes, worth £22,282, knowing or believing them to be stolen. He was remanded on bail of £200 to appear before the court again on the 4th June, which allowed him to travel with the team. Many years later in an interview for this book, Howard Kendall said, "*No one dare mention the incident to him and he certainly didn't talk to us about it.*"

Everton beat a Combined Tel Aviv XI 2-1 in their first game on the evening of Wednesday, 19th May before a crowd of 10,000. The team was not listed in the match report, nor was there any mention of the goalkeeper in the details of the game. Andy certainly played in the second match of the tour on Monday, 24th May, in which Everton defeated the Israeli champions, Maccabi Netanya, by three goals to one. In the final match, a 4-0 win over a Combined Jerusalem XI, Dai Davies was in goal.

1971-72 Season

Although Andy, was in the squad to play Rangers and the Israeli champions Maccabi Netanya in pre-season matches, Gordon West was selected in goal for both games.

When the season began, West was back in favour and was the first choice goalkeeper from the outset, whilst Andy shared the Reserve team berth with Dai Davies. Two of the most important Reserve games each season were the "mini-derbies". Andy played in the first of the season, at Anfield on Saturday, 13th November. The teams were:

Everton Reserves: Rankin; Newton K, Styles; Smith, Lyons, Darracott; Whittle, Kenny, Wilson, Sergeant, Goodlass.

Liverpool Reserves: Lane; Webb, Evans R; McLaughlin, Rylands, Thompson Phil; Hall, Boersma, Whitham, Johnson, McAuley.

Everton were 2-0 up at half-time and *"Rankin was having a magnificent game"*(35). The final score was 3-0. The senior team were also victors, beating Liverpool 1-0 at Goodison.

The "mini-derby" proved to be Andy's last game for Everton. The following week, he signed for Watford, who were bottom of the Second Division, for a reported fee of £20,000. Manager, Harry Catterick said, *"Rankin did not ask for a transfer but we thought this was an ideal opportunity for him to obtain regular League football. He is obviously worth that. We have two young professional goalkeepers in Dai Davies and Keith Williams and that was why we let Rankin go".*(36)

In his ten years at Everton, Andy made more than 100 first team appearances - 85 League games, seven FA Cup-ties and 11 European matches. He made his League debut against Nottingham Forest in November 1963 and was effectively first choice goalkeeper until December the following year, during which time he made 48 League and Cup appearances, missing only seven matches because of injury. However, following an injured arm against Stoke City on 12th December 1964, West replaced him and his form was so good that Andy could not regain his first team spot. Andy's 19 appearances in the first team during the following two seasons were primarily when West was injured.

Andy then spent more than three years in the wilderness at Everton, playing in the Reserves and sometimes the A team. However, West was dropped following mistakes in a European cup-tie against the Icelandic part-timers Keflavik in September 1970, when he was barracked by his own supporters. Andy seized the opportunity to re-establish himself as first choice goalkeeper, making 24 consecutive first team appearances until injury cost him his place against Derby County in the 5th round FA Cup tie on 13th February 1971. He regained his place from West a month later but, after three matches, missed two games with an injured knee. Following his second recall, one game - the FA Cup semi-final defeat by Liverpool on 27th March - may have sealed his fate at Goodison. He dropped a cross from Steve Heighway with less than 20 minutes of the game remaining, allowing Hall to nip in and score the winning goal. Whilst he kept his place until the end of the season, he was replaced by Gordon West when the new season started and did not appear for the first team again.

So, how were Andy's goalkeeping abilities viewed by his team-mates? In "Still Talking Blue", Gordon West expressed the opinion that *"Andy Rankin, when he took over for a while, was a bit flash, his legs were up in the air and he was launching himself around. A normal keeper would have caught it but he wanted to look the part."*

Not quite the view of Howard Kendall, who told the author in 2010: *"Andy was agile, he had a good pair of hands and he was not flamboyant or loud, he simply got on with the job. No goalkeeper plays as many games in their career as he did without being a good keeper."* Kendall went on: *"The one thing I will always remember about Andy was his penalty save against Monchengladbach to get us through to the quarter-finals of the European Cup. He saved the last penalty when it was 4-3 for us, I think. I seem to remember that he was four or five yards off his line when the kick was taken. And then, everyone was running on to the pitch and he was running to the centre for congratulations. There was no way the referee was going to order the penalty kick to be re-taken."* Probably, that is what most Everton supporters will remember best about Andy too.

References:

1. Liverpool Echo, 17th February 1954

2. Liverpool Daily Post, 27th October 1961

3. http://www.sportingintelligence.com/2011/01/20/from-20-to-33868-per-week-a-quick-history-of-english-footballs-top-flight-wages-200101

4. Liverpool Echo, 15th November 1963

5. Liverpool Echo, 23rd November 1963

6. Liverpool Echo, 28th November 1963

7. Liverpool Echo, 3rd December, 1963

8. Liverpool Echo, 11th December 1963

9. Liverpool Echo, 11th January 1964

10. Liverpool Echo, 23rd March 1964

11. Liverpool Daily Post, 6th April 1964

12. Liverpool Echo, 18th April 1964

13. Liverpool Echo, 26th August 1964

14. Liverpool Echo, 26th August 1964

15. Liverpool Echo, 9th September 1964

16. Liverpool Echo, 21st September 1964

17. Liverpool Echo, 21st November 2013

18. Liverpool Echo, 15th October 1964

19. Liverpool Echo, 2nd November 1964

20. Liverpool Echo, 5th November 1964

21. Liverpool Echo, 9th November 1964

22. Liverpool Echo, 7th December 1964

23. Liverpool Echo, 29th September 1965

24. Liverpool Echo, 4th November 1965

25. Liverpool Echo, 1st April 1967

26. Liverpool Echo, 10th April 1967

27. Liverpool Echo, 18th September 1970

28. Liverpool Echo, 17th October 1970

29. Liverpool Echo, 28th December 1970

30. Liverpool Echo, 16th January 1971

31. Liverpool Echo, 5th March 1971

32. Liverpool Echo, 8th March 1971

33. Liverpool Echo, 7th April 1971

34. Liverpool Echo, 11th May 1971

35. Liverpool Echo, 13th November 1971

36. Liverpool Echo, 17th November 1971

8

ANDY AT WATFORD (1971-76)
– THE SLIDE FROM DIVISION TWO TO DIVISION FOUR

1971-72 Season

Andy's arrival at Watford in mid-November was heralded in the national newspapers as "*the bargain of the century*", with the transfer fee being variably reported as £15,000 to £20,000. When asked about his move, Andy said, "*Frankly, I want first team football. Watford? I know them as a good Cup side and I saw them on television when they beat Liverpool. That was a fine performance.*"(1)

Watford's regular first team keeper, Mike Walker, was shocked by the signing. He said that whilst he had no animosity towards the Club, he would not be prepared to play in the Reserves, as it would affect his chances of playing for Wales. However, he did not leave for 18 months, signing for Colchester United in July 1973 for a fee of £4,000 on the same day as his Watford colleague Mick Packer. Walker went on to play 451 league games for Cochester, including 310 consecutive appearances between February 1977 and January 1983. He was appointed Colchester's manager in 1986 and later managed Norwich City and Everton, lasting only ten months at Goodison Park before being sacked.

Watford were bottom of Division Two when Andy signed, having been promoted at the end of the 1968/69 season. The Club had become members of the Football League 50 years earlier, when the First Division of the Southern League became Division Three of the Football League in 1920. Watford's home ground was Vicarage Road and they were known as "the Hornets".

Andy made his debut at Vicarage Road on Saturday, 20th November against Division Two's most prolific scorers, Burnley. Watford won 2-1 to record their second successive victory for the first time that season and to haul themselves off the foot of the table.

Watford's manager, George Kirby, said that he was satisfied with Andy's debut, while Bert Slater, the coach and former Falkirk, Liverpool, Dundee and Watford goalkeeper praised his performance, adding, *"The save to Fletcher was 75-25 against him. A really superb save."* He also excused Andy's failure to hold on to the ball, which led to Burnley's last minute goal. He said, *"Funnily enough, as a goalkeeper, I made a mental note of the possibilities as the rain started to fall at the end. The ball was very slippery at the end."*(2)

Watford lost their next two games – 2-0 away to Preston North End and 1-0 at home to Orient. Andy was Watford's star performer against Preston, making two brilliant saves and one that was described as world class.

On Saturday, 11th December, Watford drew 1-1 with Norwich City at Carrow Road to end their run of nine successive away defeats. Watford's goal was scored in the last minute by striker Pat Morrissey, who was making his debut, following his recent signing from Chester for £8000. The match reporter wrote: *"Rankin, occasionally brilliant but giving an overall impression of nervousness, played his part in stopping Norwich from running up a large score."*(3)

Watford then had a sequence of nine consecutive defeats, including a 4-1 defeat at Vicarage Road by Notts County in the FA Cup. During that terrible run, they conceded 23 goals, scoring only two in reply. Whilst they suffered some heavy defeats in those nine games, clearly the failure to score goals was the real problem, particularly as three of the defeats were by the only goal.

Andy played in all of those defeats. He was certainly not blamed for the failure to record a victory and actually received some good reviews. For example:

Cardiff City 2 Watford 0 on 18th December 1971: It was Andy Rankin *"who stopped the scoreline from taking on the appearance of a rout."*(4)

Hull City 4 Watford 0 on 29th January 1972: *"At times, only the courage and dexterity of the hobbling Andy Rankin stood between Watford and an even heavier defeat. He made three brilliant saves and in the final assessment only one of Hull's goals could be blamed on the injury he received in the first half."*(5) Andy had collided with Hull's centre-half Knighton in making a save and had twisted his ankle. Following several minutes of treatment, he resumed heavily bandaged.

Watford 0 Middlesbrough 1 on 12th February 1972: *"Only the skill and determination of Andy Rankin kept the score-line down to the solitary goal."*(6)

Following a 2-1 defeat by Sheffield Wednesday at Hillsborough on the 19th February, Andy missed six league games as a result of an injury; Mike Walker replaced him. During Andy's absence, Watford lost four and drew two of their six fixtures.

Andy returned on 3rd April when Watford drew 2-2 with Portsmouth at Fratton Park. He then played in the final six games of the season, in which Watford won one, drew one and lost the remaining four. In those six games, Watford conceded 12 goals, scoring only two in reply.

The 1-0 victory over Preston North End on 15th April was Watford's first win for five months and it was also the first time that Andy had kept a clean sheet since joining the Club. The two points meant that Watford avoided being remembered as the Club with the lowest points total in the history of Division Two.

In the final game of the season, on Saturday, 29th April, Watford earned a 1-1 draw against Norwich at Vicarage Road. The point won by Norwich was enough to clinch the Division Two championship. Watford's team for that final game was:

Rankin; Welbourne, Williams, Lees, Franks, Eddy, Wigg, Kenning, Jennings, Lindsay, Farley.

Watford were relegated to Division Three along with Charlton - Watford had managed only 19 points, whilst Charlton had 33. Of their 42 games, Watford won only five, the lowest ever number of victories in a season in Division Two. They also set the record for the lowest number of goals scored in a season – 24, whilst conceding 75.

Andy had played 19 league games and one FA Cup tie. He must have wondered what he had let himself in for. In twelve months, he had gone from playing for Everton in Division One to facing life in Division Three with Watford.

During the close season, Watford sold their captain and leading goal scorer Keith Eddy to Sheffield United for a club record of £50,000.

1972-73 Season

Watford, hopeful of an immediate return to Division Two, started the new season well with two wins and a draw, including two clean sheets. In the second game, against Bournemouth on Saturday, 26th August, Watford were two down within 32 minutes, but they snatched what seemed then an unlikely victory with a great fight back, scoring three goals without reply. It was the first time Watford had scored more than two goals at Vicarage Road since February 1971 when they defeated Sheffield Wednesday 3-0.

Bournemouth's team included Jimmy Gabriel, Andy's former Everton team-mate; Harry Redknapp, the former manager of Tottenham Hotspur, now manager of Queens Park Rangers; and Ted McDougall, centre-forward, who moved to Manchester United the following month for £200,000 and went on to play for a host of sides including West Ham United, Norwich City and Southampton. The Watford side was:

Rankin; Butler, Williams, Keen, Lees, Franks, McGovern, Wigg, Morrissey, Lindsay, Farley.

Andy distinguished himself in the goalless draw at Shrewsbury on Tuesday evening, 29th August, with a magnificent penalty save in the second half. He dived full-length to his right to turn the ball round for a corner. It was his third penalty save since joining the club. Even former Manchester United goalkeeper Harry Gregg, the Shrewsbury manager, was quick to applaud the save.

After a defeat at Grimsby on 2nd September, Watford had an unbeaten run of five games - two wins and three draws. But their problem of the previous season – a lack of goals – was still apparent. In those five games, Watford scored only four goals, although they did only concede two in the process. It was Andy's excellent goalkeeping that won Watford a point in the goalless draws against Blackburn and York on the 16th and 18th September respectively.

The five match unbeaten run came to an end at The Valley on 30th September when Charlton scored three minutes from time to earn themselves a 2-1 victory. Watford had been a goal behind early in the first half, but equalised with their first away goal of the season, at their fifth attempt.

Following a 1-0 loss in their next game, away to Rochdale, Watford had a sequence of 12 matches between 10th October and 23rd December, in which they suffered only one defeat.

Rotherham were the team that ruined an otherwise unbeaten run on 4th November at Millmoor. Watford looked the better side, created more chances, but just could not score. Rotherham got the only goal of the game in the 57th minute and, afterwards, Andy was called upon to make three full-length saves to keep Watford in with a chance, but the team could not take advantage.

Two of the wins during this period were in the FA Cup. In the first round on 18th November, Watford faced non-League Guildford City at Vicarage Road. Their team was:

Rankin; Butler, Packer, Keen, Lees, Woodfield, McGettigan, Wigg, Wellbourne, Franks, Farley.

Guildford twice took the lead in the first 16 minutes, and were leading 2-1 at the interval. However, Watford scored twice within a minute of the restart and, after that, Guildford never looked like getting back into the game. Watford got a fourth goal from the penalty spot with 16 minutes remaining.

Watford won their second round Cup-tie, beating Aldershot from Division Four 2-0 at Vicarage Road on 9th December.

The week after the win against Guildford, Watford signed 21 year old Ross Jenkins, a 6' 3" striker, from Crystal Palace for £30,000. He made his debut the following Saturday, in the 3-1 away win over Walsall, Watford's first success away from home for 18 months. Jenkins took some time to settle at the club, only managing two goals in his first 28 matches. He was in and out of the team for two or three seasons, and when Watford agreed to sell him to Huddersfield during the 1974-75 season for £12,000, he refused to go. That was Watford's good fortune. By the time he was given a free transfer in 1983, he had made 398 appearances for the club, scoring 142 goals.

Andy put in some good performances during that series of 11 wins and one defeat between the 10th October and 23rd November. In the 1-1 away draw at Chesterfield on 21st October, "*it was left to Andy Rankin to save the day with two great saves*".

The following Saturday, against Bristol Rovers at Vicarage Road, Watford were two goals up when Andy let a shot slip under him into the net 20 minutes before the final whistle. But, "*ironically, it was Rankin who finally preserved the victory with three superb and courageous saves to deny Rovers a point.*" He also played particularly well in Watford's 2-1 win over league leaders Bolton Wanderers at Vicarage Road on 2nd December.

The Boxing Day match, a 1-0 defeat at Notts County, in which Andy won the Man of the Match Award with four first-class saves, was also the start of a sequence of eleven losses. One of the eleven defeats was at the hands of Division One side, Sheffield United, on 13th January 1973, in the third round of the FA Cup. The only goal of the game came in the 67th minute.

Andy actually missed three of these eleven defeats at the end of January and beginning of February when Mike Walker stood in for him. His recently born daughter had a heart complaint and he was left out of the team on compassionate grounds, but then suffered from flu, which delayed his return.

He came back to face Blackburn Rovers at Vicarage Road on 10th February. Blackburn were managed by Ken Furphy, former Watford manager, and were unbeaten for 14 games. Watford's team was:

Rankin; Butler, Williams, Keen, Franks, Woodfield, Packer, Jenkins, Morrissey, Welbourne, Farley.

Furphy triumphed over his former side by three goals to one. Andy was blamed for the second goal, coming off his line too early and allowing one of the Rovers' forwards to chip the ball over him from the edge of the penalty area. However, he had no chance with the other two goals. Watford scored from the penalty spot.

Watford lost their next two games, away to Tranmere Rovers and at home to Swansea, both by the only goal of the game.

In the return game with Swansea on Tuesday evening, 27th February, Watford took the lead in the 25th minute. However, Swansea equalised nine minutes after the break and, later, scored a second from the penalty spot. Andy's faultless handling of crosses and three superb saves won him the Man of the Match Award.

Watford's 11-match run of defeats came to an end on Friday night, 2nd March, in a goalless draw with Rochdale at Vicarage Road. Andy made two first class saves in the opening period, preventing Rochdale from taking a shock early lead. In the end, it was Watford's failure to convert their clear-cut chances that cost them a win.

However, Watford found their shooting boots the following Tuesday evening. Watched by 4,578 spectators at Vicarage Road, their lowest crowd since May 1966, they beat Scunthorpe 5-1. Scunthorpe scored the only goal of the first half, but any hopes they had of an away victory were soon dispelled by two quick goals from Jenkins, who had come on as substitute for Markham at the start of the second-half, and a further three from his team-mates. This was Watford's biggest success since the 1968-69 season. The Watford team was:

Rankin; Butler, Welbourne, Keen, Lees, Franks, Morrissey, Craker, Markham, Wigg, Farley.

Four draws followed the win against Scunthorpe. Three of them were goalless - away to Southend and at home to Wrexham and Chesterfield. In the other, a 1-1 draw away to Brentford on 19th March, there were some fine performances by Watford players. Topping the lot was Andy, who made three incredible saves in the first half. *"Had the last of these saves been made by Gordon Banks, we would have watched television repeats of it until the next century."*(7)

Watford were brought back down to earth by Blackburn Rovers at Ewood Park on 24th March when they were beaten 2-1, with Rovers' winner coming five minutes from the end. Watford did enough to deserve a point, but their poor finishing let them down again. Andy made a string of fine saves throughout the match and was chosen as Man of the Match. However, he suffered from concussion for most of the game and was receiving regular doses of smelling salts from trainer Mike Baxter, who sat behind the goal.

Following two home victories over Halifax and Walsall, Watford travelled to face Bolton, the Division Three leaders, on Saturday, 7th April. The first half was goalless, primarily because Andy brought out *"another string of spectacular saves in the first half from his seemingly bottomless repertoire"*.(8) Watford took the lead in the 69th minute, but Bolton equalised from the penalty spot when Francis Lee sent Andy the wrong way.

Home draws against Brentford and Charlton were followed by a 1-0 defeat away to Scunthorpe United on Saturday, 21st April. According to the match reporter, it was probably Watford's most ineffective performance of the season, and it was the sort of match which made choosing Man of the Match award a simple task. The report continued: *"Andy Rankin was head and shoulders above the rest and it was only his dexterity which kept Watford from suffering a humiliating reversal of their five goal victory over the bottom of the table club. One save in particular would have brought volumes of ecstatic quotes had the header come from Pele and not the urbane United's Rod Fletcher. The forward got up well to a cross and (it) appeared to be heading for the far post. Rankin was off striding across the goal only to have to twist, arch and reach back for the ball as Fletcher seemed to mishead the ball towards the near post. Rankin managed to parry the effort. Then, late in the second half substitute, George Kerr, was all on his own as he received a pass on the edge of the box with Rankin advancing. The forward hit the ball powerfully towards the top corner but Rankin backpedalled and took off to hook the ball down."*(9)

Radio Humber described Andy's save from Fletcher as the best seen on the Scunthorpe ground in 23 years of League football.

In the penultimate game of the season, Watford gained a point from a 1-1 draw away at Plymouth. Their final game, at home to Shrewsbury on Saturday, 28th April, saw them slump to their first home defeat for ten games by the solitary goal of the game. Watford missed 30 chances and, according to the match reporter, even some of Andy's goal kicks had more power in them when they reached their end than many of Watford's shots. Watford's team was:

Rankin; Welbourne, Butler, Keen, Lees, Franks, Craker, Jenkins, Jennings, Morrissey, McGettigan.

Rotherham, Brentford, Swansea and Scunthorpe United were relegated from Division Three. Watford finished 19th out of the 24 teams, escaping relegation as they had a better goal average than their rivals. The team's poor performances impacted on home attendances. In their three years in Division Two, the average crowd at Vicarage Road was 14,100; in their first season in Division Three, attendances plummeted to an average of 6,700. Clearly dissatisfied with this, the Board sacked manager George Kirby. His replacement was first-team captain, Mike Keen.

Andy played in 43 of the 46 league games and the three FA Cup ties. For the first time, the local weekly newspaper, the Watford Observer, introduced a Player of the Season Award, voted on by the fans. Andy won the inaugural Award with 711 votes, beating Colin Franks (677 votes) and Duncan Welbourne (523 votes) into second and third place respectively. Andy received a trophy, along with a cheque and a night out at the Talk of the Town for him and his wife. Watford coach Bert Slater said of Andy,

> *"He's one of the top seven in the League. His displays away from home have been terrific. You could have made a film of his display at Plymouth and used it as the ideal textbook coaching for all aspiring goalkeepers. Most keepers should get high crosses but Andy's handling of the low ones is brilliant. I would rank him among the best. Obviously, you have got to include Pat Jennings, Bryan King, Phil Parkes, Colin Boulton, Bob Wilson and Peter Shilton on that list but I'd put Andy up alongside them."*(10)

In the close season, before Keen's appointment as manager, Colin Franks was transferred to Sheffield United for a new club record of £60,000.

1973-74 Season

Keen's first signing was midfielder Dennis Bond from Charlton for £15,000; he had previously been with Watford.

Watford's opening league fixture of the new season, at home to Huddersfield Town on Saturday, 25th August, ended in a 1-1 draw. Watford had gone in front in the 50th minute, only for Huddersfield to equalise two minutes later. Watford's team was:

Rankin; Butler, Williams, Keen, Lees, Welbourne, Jennings, Bond, Morrissey, Lindsay, Farley.

The following Tuesday evening, Watford met Reading at Elm Park in the first round of the League Cup. After throwing away a one goal lead, Watford fell behind and then had to fight back to earn a replay. It was the first time Watford had scored two goals away since the previous November. When the draw for the next round was made, Andy was pleased to learn that he would face Everton, provided Watford beat Reading in the replay. It was not to be, for a week later, Watford lost 3-2 at Vicarage Road after extra time and after twice being ahead.

Back in the League, Watford beat Southend 3-2 on Friday evening, 31st August, to record their first away win for 13 matches. Billy Jennings scored all three of Watford's goals to become their first player to score a hat-trick since Barry Endean against Gillingham in the winter of 1969.

Watford's next two games were at home. The first was a 1-0 defeat by Oldham, in which Andy won the Man of the Match Award. In the second, the side recorded their first home victory of the season with a 2-0 win over Wrexham.

On Saturday, 15th September, Watford faced Hereford, who were unbeaten at home for 24 games, but they were unable to dent that record, the game ending 1-1. Two days later, Watford thought they had earned another away point, this time against Cambridge, only to concede an injury time goal and lose 3-2.

In their next four games, Watford drew 1-1 at home with York City; beat Brighton 1-0 away from home; got their revenge over Cambridge when they thumped them 3-0 at Vicarage Road, and then earned a goalless draw against Bristol Rovers at home, watched by more than 10,000 fans, Watford's largest crowd for some time.

After three successive clean sheets, however, Watford's defence fell apart on Saturday, 13th October, conceding three goals at Chesterfield. The team was:

Rankin; Butler, Lees, Woodfield, Welbourne, Bond, Keen, Lindsay, Jennings, Jenkins, Morgan.

Ian Morgan had been recently signed on a month's loan from Queens Park Rangers, where his twin brother Roger was also a player. Ian was later signed by Watford for £10,000 on completion of his loan period. Chesterfield took the lead after five minutes when Andy misjudged the flight of the ball, which was later replaced as it had become misshapen. Watford were two goals down when Jennings pulled one back, heading in Butler's cross in the 68th minute, only for Chesterfield to restore their two goal lead soon afterwards.

Watford conceded another three goals the following Saturday to Plymouth Argyle in what was their biggest home defeat for 20 months. After the game, Tony Waiters, the Plymouth manager and former Blackpool and England goalkeeper, defended Andy, saying, "*I would not blame Andy. The goals were well-taken but I thought the organisation of the defence was wrong for both corners.*"(11)

Watford also lost their next two games, away at Wrexham and Bournemouth, and both by the only goal. At Wrexham, where Watford squandered numerous chances, Andy gave "*a faultless display liberally sprinkled with fine saves,*" which earned him the Man of the Match Award. The Bournemouth match was significant for the fact that defender Duncan Welbourne made his 399th League appearance for Watford, breaking a 33 year old record set by Tommy Barnett, and he only needed to play another six first team games to pass Barnett's overall total of appearances. Welbourne had arrived from Grimsby in November 1963 for a fee of £1300 and, from September 1964 until November 1970, he only missed one game - a fantastic record.

Watford returned to winning ways on Saturday, 3rd November, when they defeated Aldershot at Vicarage Road by two goals to one. The Watford team was:

Rankin; Butler, Williams, Craker, Lees, Welbourne, Morgan, Bond, Morrissey, Jenkins, Farley.

Watford triumphed again the following Saturday at Rochdale, winning 3-1 and drew 0-0 with Halifax Town in a dreary home fixture on Monday, 12th November. The only event of significance in the latter game was Halifax's tamely struck penalty, which Andy had no trouble saving down to his right.

On the Saturday, Watford suffered their biggest defeat for 18 months, 5-0 at the hands of Blackburn Rovers at Ewood Park. Despite the score, Andy was awarded the Man of the Match Award and, according to the match report, it was often a case of Rankin v Blackburn as the home side ripped Watford's midfield to shreds.

Saturday, 24th November, was the first round of the FA Cup. Watched by more than 6,500 spectators at Vicarage Road, Watford beat Chelmsford City 1-0 in a poor game. Watford's team was:

Rankin; Butler, Lees, Markham, Welbourne, Bond, Morgan, Lindsay, Jennings, Morrissey, Farley.

Before the kick-off, Duncan Wellbourne was presented with a silver salver to commemorate his 446th game for Watford, breaking the previous record set by Tommy Barnett before the Second World War.

Watford's next game was at home again, when they faced Charlton on Saturday, 8th December. The team included a new face – Stuart Scullion, who had been sold to Sheffield United for £25,000 some 30 months earlier, before being re-signed earlier that week for £15,000. However, he could not prevent Watford being well and truly beaten 3-1.

The following Saturday, Watford were knocked out of the FA Cup at Vicarage Road when Bournemouth scored the only goal of the game in the 56th minute. They then beat Brighton and Hove Albion by the same score in the League on Saturday, 22nd December; Brighton were managed by Brian Clough. That victory moved Watford five points clear of the relegation zone.

Watford's festive programme started badly when they lost 3-2 at Shrewsbury Town, despite recovering from 2-0 down to go in on level terms at half-time. However, they improved to take maximum points from their next two games.

They defeated Oldham Athletic 3-0 at Boundary Park on Saturday, 29th December, recording their biggest away win since beating Blackpool by a similar score in September 1969. Morrissey scored all three goals and *"Rankin, with a series of superlative saves and perfect handling, kept Watford in the picture. He made his contribution at the telling moments...".*(12) Watford had had a nightmare trip to Oldham on the day before the game, when the journey took seven hours after their coach broke down on the motorway.

On New Year's Day, watched by a crowd of 8,195, Jennings scored his 13th goal of the season three minutes from time to give Watford two points against Southend.

Following a 1-1 draw at Southport on Saturday, 5th January, Watford had two wins – 2-1 at home over Hereford and by a similar score-line at Huddersfield. Against Huddersfield, a Morrissey goal gave Watford a 1-0 lead at half-time and Jennings scored a second midway through the second half. Huddersfield's Alan Gowling pulled a goal back just before the end and then Andy ensured victory with a fine save. Watford's defence had to rely on *"a handful of truly superb saves from Andy Rankin. (He) made his saves at the right time – early on; after Watford had gone ahead; after the interval and in the dying minutes."*(13)The win took Watford to 10th place in the League, 12 points behind leaders Bristol Rovers.

On Saturday, 26th January, watched by 7,281 fans at Vicarage Road, Watford lost 3-1 to Walsall. The following week, they were again at home, but this time recorded their highest score at Vicarage Road for ten months, beating Tranmere Rovers 4-2. Billy Jennings scored a hat-trick and became the first Watford player to notch two in the same season since Tony Currie in 1967.

Watford did not have a game the following week, but the next weekend they played their first-ever Sunday fixture on 10th February, away to York City. Their team was:

Rankin; Butler, Williams, Craker, Lees, Keen, Farley, Bond, Jenkins, Scullion, Jennings.

Jenkins was playing his 30th game for Watford, which meant that the club had to pay Crystal Palace another £5000, and it was he who gave Watford a 1-0 lead at the interval. Half-way through the second half, York equalised from an indirect free-kick; the referee ignoring Watford's claims that the ball had gone directly into the net. However, Watford regained their lead in the 71st minute through Jennings, but two minutes later York were back on level terms with a superb goal when Andy was beaten by the sheer pace of the ball. Although a Scullion shot struck the bar ten minutes from the end, Watford were probably pleased with a point against the team second in Division Three and one which had only conceded seven goals at home all season.

There was a scare at training the following Thursday when Andy suffered a gash on his knee. However, the injury was not as serious as first thought and he was able to take his place in goal for the home game against Chesterfield, which Watford won 2-1.

Watford lost their next game 1-0 away to Bristol Rovers. Rovers had 80 per-cent of the play and Watford did not win a corner until two minutes from the end. According to match reporter Oliver Phillips, it was the most one-sided game he had seen. Watford then defeated Shrewsbury by the same score when Stewart Scullion scored his first goal since rejoining the club. This was followed by a 1-1 draw with Bournemouth at Vicarage Road, Jennings scoring his 23rd goal of the season three minutes from time to earn his team a point.

On Saturday, 16th March, Watford lost 2-0 away to Plymouth Argyle. The most memorable moment of the game was when Plymouth defender Hore brought the ball over the half-way line, looked up, saw Andy was standing on his six-yard line and hit the ball over Andy from 35 yards into the net. Andy admitted after the game that he thought that the ball had been going over the crossbar.

Watford won the following two games, both were at home and both were by a margin of 4-0. The first was against Rochdale, the second against Southport. It was the first time Watford had scored eight goals without reply since the 1959-60 season when they beat Oldham 6-0 and Crewe Alexandra 2-0.

Andy then won the Man of the Match award in the 1-0 defeat at Aldershot on Saturday, 30th March, and this was followed by two away draws – 2-2 at Walsall and 0-0 at Halifax. That Watford should fail to score at Halifax was hardly surprising as Halifax had the best home defensive record in the League, having only conceded eleven goals in 16 games.

On Monday evening, 8th April, Watford lost 1-0 to Tranmere Rovers at Prenton Park. Ron Yeats, the former Liverpool player and Tranmere's player-manager, scored the winning goal in the final minute when he headed in from a corner. Until then, Andy had kept Watford in the game with a string of fine saves. It was the fourth time that season that Watford had lost to a last-minute goal.

The 0-0 draw at home with Blackburn Rovers on Monday, 13th April proved to be Andy's final game of the season. He finished the match limping and did not play in the last five games because of his injury. Malcolm Dalrymple stepped in for Andy, his only appearances for the Club, and Watford won three, drew one and lost one of those five games.

Watford finished 7th in the League, 12 points behind the champions Oldham Athletic. Cambridge United, Shrewsbury Town, Southport and Rochdale were relegated.

Billy Jennings scored 29 goals and was named the Watford Observer's Player of the Season. Andy came fifth.

Probably Watford's most important recruit that season was Elton John. He was appointed as a vice-president and a member of the Board. After becoming chairman in 1976, he led the club to its most successful period ever in the 1980s.

1974-75 Season

Watford's team for the opening League game of the season at Colchester on Saturday, 17th August was:

Rankin; Butler, Keen, Goodeve, Williams, Craker, Bond, Scullion, Morrissey, Jennings, Downes. Downes had been signed from Rochdale for £10,000 and Goodeve had arrived from Brighton and Hove Albion.

Colchester fielded three former Watford players – Walker in goal, Packer and Lindsay. The match ended 1-1, after Colchester had taken the lead in the 37th minute and Scullion had equalised twelve minutes after the break.

Almost 10,500 spectators turned up at Vicarage Road the following Wednesday, Watford's biggest crowd for a first round League Cup tie, to witness a 1-1 draw against fellow Third Division side, Crystal Palace. Morrissey gave Watford the lead a minute before half-time, but Watford's failure to convert their chances allowed Palace to snatch a draw and force a replay.

An even bigger crowd – 12,810 - watched the replay at Selhurst Park on Tuesday evening, 27th August. The Watford team was:

Rankin; Butler, Williams, Craker, Keen, Goodeve, Jennings, Bond, Morrissey, Scullion, Downes.

Watford supporters must have wished they had stayed at home for their team was outfought and outplayed, losing 5-1. After the third goal, Watford played on with ten men as Craker had to leave the field injured after Morrissey had already been replaced by Jenkins. Andy had a busy evening and, despite the score, picked up the Man of the Match Award.

On the Saturday sandwiched between the two games with Palace, Watford faced Preston North End, managed by Bobby Charlton, in their first home League fixture of the season. On a beautiful sunny afternoon, Watford quickly established a three-goal lead, only for Preston to pull one back a minute before the interval. Seven minutes into the second half, Preston scored another, but Watford held on to win. It was a superb game and the crowd rose to applaud the players at the interval and at the final whistle.

Watford's next two games were away from home. They lost 3-1 to Huddersfield on Saturday, 31st August, when Andy was again named Man of the Match. The match at Huddersfield proved to be Billy Jennings' last for the Club. He was sold to West Ham for £110,000 that week and won an FA Cup winners' medal with the Hammers at the end of the season when they defeated Fulham 2-0 at Wembley.

On the following Wednesday, Watford beat Hereford with a Jenkins goal scored in the 73rd minute. Andy provided his usual handful of saves to keep Hereford at bay.

Watford faced Halifax at Vicarage Road on Saturday, 7th September, and had to settle for a point, thanks to the performance of their opponent's goalkeeper. Ross Jenkins scored his third goal in three matches to win Man of the Match. Whilst Andy was not at fault with Halifax's first goal, he had to take some of the blame for their second as he allowed the wind to carry an attempted cross over his head into the net.

Despite having at least 13 good chances to score, Watford lost 2-0 at Brighton the following Saturday and, then, three days later drew 2-2 at Grimsby when they fully deserved to win.

On Saturday, 21st September, they met Division Three leaders Southend at Vicarage Road. A crowd of almost 7,000 saw them take the lead sixty seconds after the interval; Jenkins later scored Watford's second, and his fifth goal in six games.

Watford drew their next three games – 0-0 at home to Gillingham; 2-2 away to Swindon Town; and 1-1 at home to Hereford. In the first half of the Swindon game, Andy required treatment *"when he bravely came out to take the ball off the feet of McLean. He was injured when the forward slid into him and he spent the rest of the game limping."*(14) The injury did not prevent him from keeping goal against Hereford.

Watford then beat Bury 2-1 at Vicarage Road on Saturday, 5th October. The team was:

Rankin; Butler, Williams, Keen, Goodeve, Lees, Mercer, Bond, Jenkins, Scullion, Downes.

Seventeen year old Mercer was making his debut and scored the winner in the 70th minute. Butler was injured ten minutes before the interval. His replacement was McGettigan, who had been named substitute for the ninth successive game.

Watford's old weakness in front of goal was apparent in their next two games – a 1-0 defeat at Peterborough and a home win over Bournemouth by the same scoreline.

Then, on Tuesday evening, 22nd October, they were at The Valley, where they were torn to shreds by Charlton, eventually losing 4-1. Andy stood between Watford and an even bigger defeat, with some spectacular saves, and was chosen as Man of the Match. When Charlton were 3-1 up, they *were awarded a penalty. Curtis, scorer of 12 successive penalties, stepped up to send the ball to Rankin's left. The goalkeeper was there to save, however, diving low to parry the ball towards the touchline. He had the right to expect his defenders to clear, but a Charlton player knocked the ball back in to a grateful Curtis, who scored with his second chance.*(15)

Four days later, Watford conceded another four goals away to Chesterfield although, on this occasion, they managed to score four themselves. It was Watford's highest total away from home since Gillingham in 1969. They fought back from two goals down to square the match in the last ten minutes. *"But, at the back of it all was Andy Rankin, who made two amazing saves at the end to preserve the Hornet's point."*(16) Watford's team was:

Rankin; Walsh, Lees, Goodeve, Williams, Scullion, Bond, Keen, Morrissey, Jenkins, Downes.

Andy won the Man of the Match Award in the next two matches, both at home - a 1-1 draw with Aldershot on Saturday, 2nd November and a 2-0 defeat at the hands of Charlton four days later. Against Aldershot, *"while not overworked, (Rankin) did enough that was right to justify the Man of the Match award. He gathered cleanly and made two really good saves and gave a thorough overall display despite the handicap of a greasy ball. The rest were lost in murky mediocrity."*(17)

After the Charlton match, their manager, Andy Nelson, was full of praise for Andy. *"I think the keeper (Rankin) is the best in the Third Division,"* he said, *"He's a really excellent player and had no chance with either of the goals tonight."*

Watford gained an undeserved point in their next outing, away to Plymouth, when the home goalkeeper Furnell's mistake let them in for an equaliser with only 90 seconds to go. Plymouth had 20 shots at goal to Watford's four.

Manager Mike Keen bought two recruits before the home game against Port Vale on Saturday, 16th November. Twenty year old reserve striker Alan Mayes was signed from Queens Park Rangers for £8000 and midfielder Roger Joslyn from Aldershot for £10,000 with Pat Morrissey going to Aldershot as part of the deal. Both players made their debut against Port Vale. The team was:

Rankin; Craker, Lees, Goodeve, Williams, Bond, Joslyn, Keen, McGettigan, Jenkins, Mayes.

Watford's 3-2 win ended Port Vale's run of five games without a defeat. Watford were two up after 58 minutes, with Mayes scoring the second goal on his debut. Port Vale pulled one back a few minutes later, but Jenkins restored Watford's two goal lead before Williams sliced the ball into his own net.

On Saturday, 23rd November, Watford saw their FA Cup hopes ended for another year when Colchester defeated them 1-0 at Vicarage Road.

Their next League game, away to League leaders Blackburn Rovers, ended in a goalless draw, but they then suffered two defeats – 2-1 at home by Crystal Palace and 5-1 away to Wrexham. At Wrexham, they were five down in the first half in what was their heaviest defeat of the season. The last time Watford had conceded five first half goals was in the final game of the 1957-58 season when they had been defeated 6-0 at Brighton.

Watford started their festive programme with a 1-1 draw with Brighton at Vicarage Road on Boxing Day, avoiding a third successive defeat, and drew again on Saturday, 28th December, away to Tranmere Rovers, who were rooted at the bottom of the table. The 2-2 draw was Watford's 12th tie of the season – three more than any other team in Division Three and only Orient and Everton in the whole Football League had drawn more often.

Watford enjoyed their first win in seven games with a 3-2 victory over Grimsby at Vicarage Road on Saturday, 4th January 1975. The team was:

Rankin; Craker, Markham, Goodeve, Williams, Joslyn, Bond, Mayes, Downes, Scullion, Jenkins.

Grimsby had pulled back twice from a goal down to thwart Watford, but Ross Jenkins hit the winner with only three minutes to go. Andy was one of the stars for Watford.

Watford failed to score in their next two games, losing 1-0 to Crystal Palace at Selhurst Park, and deserving more than a 0-0 draw at home to league leaders, Blackburn Rovers.

Laurie Craker broke his leg in the match against Crystal Palace on the 11th January, forcing the club to buy defender Alan Garner from Luton Town for £22,000. Garner went on to make 232 appearances for Watford, scoring 16 goals.

They then slumped to three successive defeats. After the first of those losses, 3-1 at home to Plymouth Argyle on Saturday, 1st February, Tony Waiters, the Plymouth manager said, "*We gave Andy Rankin a lot to do and he showed he is one of the best goalkeepers in Division Three. Rankin stood out for me…*"(18)

A goalless draw with Port Vale away from home was followed by a 1-0 win at Vicarage Road over Huddersfield Town, their first success for two months. Watford's goal came from the penalty spot and three fine saves by Andy, who won the Man of the Match Award, ensured his team got maximum points.

Watford lost eight of their last 13 games of the season, drawing three and winning the other two, a poor run which saw them finish next to bottom in the Third Division. In fact, they only needed seven points from their last 11 games to avoid the drop but they could not even manage what was a very achievable total. In the end, they were relegated to Division Four along with AFC Bournemouth, Tranmere Rovers and Huddersfield Town.

There are a few points in those last 13 games worthy of mention. Watford's lowest crowd for more than a decade - 3,941 - watched the 2-1 home defeat by Colchester on Wednesday, 19th March. Then, on Saturday, 12th April, striker Brian Greenhalgh became the first Watford player to be sent off for six years when he received his marching orders in the second half at Gigg Lane in the 1-0 defeat by Bury. He was seen by the linesman to kick a Bury defender in retaliation and was sent off just when Watford looked like earning a point. Greenhalgh had been signed from Bournemouth in March for £5000. He had played for various clubs, including Aston Villa and Leicester, scoring 76 goals in 229 first team appearances, but only managed one goal in his 12 games for Watford that season.

On Tuesday evening, 22nd April, Watford scored two goals in an away match for the first time in 1975 when they drew 2-2 with Preston North End at Deepdale. The Watford team was:

The triumphant trio in the Watford Observer Player of the Season Awards, pictured with last season's winner Billy Jennings, fresh from his Wembley FA Cup success with West Ham. From left to right: third-placed Roger Joslyn, Winner Andy Rankin, runner-up Ken Goodeve and Jennings, who presented the awards. Courtesy of the Watford Observer

Rankin; How, Garner, Goodeve, Williams, Joslyn, Keen, Bond, Greenhalgh, Scullion, Downes.

The game had *"one outstanding performer...Andy Rankin. One second half save must rank as one of the best anywhere this season. Professionals and fans alike had no quibbles when pressmen voted him man of the match."*(19)

Whilst Andy must have been extremely disappointed to find himself in the lowest of the Football Leagues having played in the top Division only four years earlier, he must have been pleased with his own performances. He was an ever-present in the League and Cup, a total of 49 appearances, and he was voted Watford Observer's Player of the Season for the second time in three years. Ken Goodeve, who was second, said, *"Let's face it. For a number of reasons we've been a bit shaky at the back all season. Andy's had a tremendous job on his hands and he's done really great."*

According to the Watford Observer, when the newspaper announced the awards: *"Father of two, Andy is known as the dry dressing-room wit. A man of few words, he usually makes them count. For many managers, he is too good a goal-keeper to be in Division 4."*

1975-76 Season

Before the new season had started, manager Mike Keen predicted that Watford would finish in the top four and go straight back up to Division Three.

In the close season, Ross Jenkins had been placed on the transfer list for £15,000, but he was still at the Club when the new season opened.

The first match was away to Barnsley on Saturday, 16th August, and the team was:

Rankin; How, Garner, Goodeve, Akers, Bond, Joslyn, Mayes, Greenhalgh, Jenkins, Downes.

But, it was the same old story. Although Watford outplayed Barnsley for much of the game, they could not score. Garner then gifted Barnsley a goal when, instead of clearing the ball, he passed it straight to a Barnsley player, who had no trouble beating Andy for the only goal of the game.

Only 3,368 spectators, Watford's lowest gate for almost 20 years, turned up to watch them beat Northampton Town 2-0 in the League Cup at Vicarage Road on the Monday evening. *"Watford had to place much reliance on Andy Rankin, who capped an evening full of masterful saves, by stopping a penalty 18 minutes from time."*(20) His display won him the Man of the Match Award.

The following Saturday, 23rd August, Watford lost 2-0 at home to Huddersfield Town, with an unchanged team for the third game in succession. The players seemed to concede defeat when Huddersfield went two up six minutes after the interval. The journalists did not bother to vote for the Man of the Match Award. According to the Watford Observer's reporter, *"Bobby Downes and Andy Rankin would have probably tied for the prize had we bothered to vote. Rankin made two or three excellent saves to maintain a fine personal start to the season for last year's Player of the Season."*(21)

In midweek, Watford drew 1-1 at Northampton to go through to the second round of the League Cup 3-1 on aggregate. Andy was again named Man of the Match and had started the season in tremendous form.

A 1-0 defeat away to Darlington on Saturday, 30th August, meant that Watford had lost their first three League games, conceding four goals and failing to score in reply .

However, they managed their first League win the following Saturday at Vicarage Road when they beat Hartlepool United 2-1. It was Hartlepool's first defeat of the season. The game was watched by Watford's lowest League gate for two decades - 3598 - just 200 more than the crowd at the League Cup tie with Northampton eleven days earlier.

Watford's next game was the second round League Cup tie with Spurs at Vicarage Road the following Tuesday evening. The teams were:

Watford: Rankin; Butler, Lees, Goodeve, Akers, Joslyn, Bond, Downes, Scullion, Jenkins, Mercer.

Spurs: Daines, Pratt, Naylor, Chivers, Osgood, McAllister, Neighbour, Perryman, Duncan, Jones, McNab. Sub: Hoddle

The Watford fans in the crowd of almost 15,000 were disappointed when their former favourite, Pat Jennings, was prevented from playing in goal for Spurs because of illness. Watford lost to the only goal of the game, scored by John Duncan, the former Dundee centre-forward, but they were certainly not disgraced.

During the week, Watford signed Arthur Horsfield, a centre-forward cum centre-half, for £17,000 from Charlton Athletic. He went straight into the team as a striker against Reading away on Saturday, 13th September, but he could not prevent his team being well-beaten by three goals to nil.

Horsfield endeared himself to the Watford fans the following Saturday, however, when he scored his team's first goal in the 67th minute of the home game against Doncaster Rovers. Jenkins followed up with his first goal since early January, before Rovers got a late consolation goal. Speaking about Andy's performance after the game, manager Mike Keen said, "*He came out and collected the crosses. That makes a real difference between remaining under pressure or getting the ball in their half.*"(22)

Watford lost their next two games, which were both away from home, 4-1 at Cambridge and 1-0 to Bradford City. It was now 13 months since Watford had recorded an away victory.

The old story of inconsistent form and a failure to put chances away continued to dog Watford. They won four of their next eight games, drew two and lost two, scoring only ten goals, little more than an average of a goal a game, whilst conceding nine.

But things went from bad to worse as they lost four games in succession, conceding ten goals while scoring just one. The second of those defeats was 3-0 at home to Brighton in the FA Cup on Saturday, 22nd November, before a crowd of 9,283. The last of the four defeats was again at Vicarage Road two weeks later, this time by three goals to one at the hands of Lincoln City. "*Only the brilliance of man-of-the-match Andy Rankin kept their (Lincoln's) tally down to three. Rankin was the only man to emerge with real credit from the game…*", wrote the match reporter. (23)

Watford were away from home on Saturday, 12th December and faced a Stockport County team that included George Best of Manchester United fame.

He was just a shadow of his former self, but did score one of Stockport's goals in a 2-2 draw.

Watford opened up their festive programme at home to Newport County on Saturday, 19th December. The team was:

Rankin; How, Lees, Garner, Akers, McCarthy, Joslyn, Scullion, Horsfield, Jenkins, Coffill.

A crowd of 3,271, Watford's lowest League attendance since April 1956, watched them win 3-1, their first victory for seven games. In probably their most entertaining display of the season so far, Jenkins put Watford in front as early as the seventh minute, but Newport were on level terms again before the half-hour. Horsfield restored Watford's lead before the interval and Jenkins made the game safe with five minutes to go to the final whistle. Jenkins became the first Watford player for 66 games to score more than one goal in a first team outing. Watford's three goals were also their highest since the first match of 1975.

On Boxing Day, Watford were twice a goal in front away to Swansea, but ended up losing 4-2. The following day, Saturday, 27th December, they returned to winning ways when they defeated Exeter City 2-0 at Vicarage Road. According to the match reporter, there were two moments in the match that would be long remembered. One was Bond's goal for Watford on the stroke of half-time; the other was *"a save from Andy Rankin who justly received the rare accolade of a standing and lengthy ovation from the crowd during the match."*(24) Unfortunately, perhaps, the goal would not have counted if the ball had gone into the net, as there had been an earlier infringement by an Exeter player. Afterwards, manager Mike Keen said that it was the finest save he had seen Andy make.

It was a forgettable start to 1976 for Watford, losing 1-0 away to Torquay United on Saturday, 3rd January. Only full-back How and Andy emerged from the game with any credit.

But things did get better, for Watford recorded seven wins in their next eight games. Their 1-0 win away to Scunthorpe United on the Tuesday 10th February was their fifth in succession, their longest unbeaten run in the league for 12 seasons.

The result was effectively decided by the two goalkeepers. An error by Scunthorpe's 16 year old apprentice goalkeeper gave Watford a goal they didn't deserve, but the game's talking point, according to the match reporter, "*was undoubtedly Andy Rankin, his exemplary display and two prodigious saves*". The report went on, "*But the premier accolade has to go to Rankin, the dry-humoured doyen of the Watford goal, who admits to a bad memory and remembers little of events and saves. Pat Jennings would have been proud of both Rankin's efforts which closed each half and preserved Watford's unlikely victory.*(25)

A 4-1 defeat the following Saturday away to Bournemouth prevented Watford extending their unbeaten run. However, they did win their next two games, both at Vicarage Road, to equal a post-war record of seven successive home victories. In the first of those games, on Saturday, 21st February, Watford were twice behind, but Downes scored with 20 minutes to go to secure a 3-2 victory. The win was witnessed by 6,223 spectators, Watford's biggest home gate so far that season. Three days later, Watford beat Cambridge 1-0.

For their next match on Wednesday, 3rd March, Watford faced Crewe at Gresty Road, a ground where Watford had won on their last four visits. However, they could only draw 2-2 on this occasion, despite being awarded two penalties. Bond scored both. Crewe had taken the lead after ten minutes when Andy and defender Garner collided as they both went for a free-kick. As a result, Andy miscued his punch to one of the Crewe strikers, who promptly hit the ball into the net.

The season's largest crowd of 7,389 then saw Northampton end Watford's record sequence of home wins three days later. Ten minutes into the game, Andy could only parry a shot and Northampton's forward Hall headed the loose ball into the net for the only goal of the game.

The following Saturday, Watford recorded their fourth double of the season when they defeated Workington away by three goals to one. Jenkins scored two of the goals for his second brace of the season. Andy, who was chosen as Man of the Match, "*produced perhaps two or three saves beyond the normal call of goalkeeping duty. The performance from the goalkeeper, coming as it did after a couple of poor outings and under the handicap of an early injury, earned him the vote. He was the only player who played consistently well throughout the game and excelled in the face of some hefty and crude challenges allowed by a referee, who afforded the goalkeeper little or no protection."*(26)

Jenkins notched another two goals in the 3-0 victory over Rochdale at Vicarage Road on Tuesday, 16th March, taking his tally for the season to 16.

After a 2-2 draw at home with Tranmere Rovers, Watford faced Division Four leaders Lincoln City at Lincoln on Sunday, 26th March. A 5-1 thrashing showed Watford that they were a class below the top sides in the league. Watford's team that day was:

Rankin; How, Garner, Lees, Walsh, McCarthy, Bond, Coffill, Mercer, Horsfield, Downes.

Watford then had a run of three victories without conceding a goal – 2-0 away to Newport County; 1-0 at home to Barnsley, who had lost 11 of their previous 12 matches; and another home win by three goals over Bradford City. In the last of those games, Bond hit Watford's first goal after just 45 seconds, the fastest goal by a Watford player for six seasons. That goal also took him into double figures for the season, the third player that campaign to do so, the others being Jenkins and Horsfield. It was the first time that three Watford players had reached double figures in the same season for 11 years.

Watford's next two fixtures involved a 2-1 defeat away to Hartlepool on Saturday, 10th April and, six days later, a goalless draw at home with Torquay on Good Friday. In the second of those games, Andy pulled a muscle in his rib cage when he was taking a goal kick and, as a result, missed the final three matches of the season, two wins and a defeat. Andy's place in those games was taken by nineteen year old Peter Gibbs.

Unfortunately, manager Mike Keen's prophecy of promotion at the beginning of the season was not fulfilled. Watford finished eighth and it was Lincoln City, Northampton Town, Reading and Tranmere Rovers who moved up a Division.

Andy made the most appearances for the Club that season – 43 League games, three League Cup and one FA Cup ties. He came third in the vote for Player of the Season; Ross Jenkins winning the accolade with his 19 goals.

References:

1. Watford Observer, 19th November 1971
2. Watford Observer, 26th November 1971
3. Watford Observer, 17th December 1971
4. Watford Observer, 24th December 1971
5. Watford Observer, 4th February 1972
6. Watford Observer, 18th February 1972
7. Watford Observer, 23rd March 1973
8. Watford Observer, 13th April 1973
9. Watford Observer, 27th April 1973
10. Watford Observer, 4th May 1973
11. Watford Observer, 26th October 1973
12. Watford Observer, 4th January 1974
13. Watford Observer, 25th January 1974
14. Watford Observer, 4th October 1974
15. Watford Observer, 25th October 1974
16. Watford Observer, 1st November 1974
17. Watford Observer, 8th November 1974
18. Watford Observer, 7th February 1975
19. Watford Observer, 22nd April 1975
20. Watford Observer, 22nd August 1975
21. Watford Observer, 29th August, 1975
22. Watford Observer, 26th September 1975
23. Watford Observer, 12th December 1975
24. Watford Observer, 2nd January 1976
25. Watford Observer, 13th February 1976
26. Watford Observer, 19th March 1976

9

ANDY AT WATFORD (1976-79)
– THE CLIMB BACK TO DIVISION TWO

1976-77 Season

Jim Bonser, chairman of Watford FC for 18 years, was replaced by Elton John. It was to be the start of an incredible football journey that was to take Watford from Division Four to runners-up in Division One of the Football League and to the FA Cup Final in the early 1980s.

Watford's two opening games of the new season were League Cup clashes against Brentford. Their home game on Saturday, 14th August, ended in a 1-1 draw, whilst two goals in the last minute of the second leg tie at Griffin Park saw Watford go through to the second round.

Their league campaign got off to a poor start when they were beaten 2-1 at Southend on Saturday, 21st August. The team was:

Rankin; How, Garner, Walley, Walsh, Joslyn, Bond, McCarthy, Jenkins, Mercer, Downes.

Walley, who had been signed from Orient in the close season was appointed captain. He had previously been with the club from 1966 to 1972 during which time he made 203 league appearances and he played a further 13 games during his second spell before being appointed coach at the club.

Things soon began to look more promising with three wins in succession. In the league, they recorded their biggest win since March 1974, defeating Hartlepool 4-0 at Vicarage Road in a midweek game; Ross Jenkins notched his first ever

League hat-trick. Four days later, on Saturday, 28ᵗʰ August, they beat Scunthorpe United 2-1 in another home fixture.

Andy Rankin at Watford in 1977. Courtesy of Allan Cozzi/Watford FC

Then, on the following Tuesday evening, they faced Crystal Palace from the Third Division at Selhurst Park in the second round of the League Cup. Their 3-1 victory was the upset of the round and the first time Watford had reached the third round for five years. It was "*Andy Rankin, pulling out one of those supreme displays, who deservedly won the Man of the Match Award by a street. It was he who made Watford's honest toil worthwhile and in doing so formed the springboard for Mayes to deliver his killer blows.*"(1)

Palace were leading 1-0 at half-time but, five minutes after the interval, Watford were on level terms with a superb goal by Mayes. Soon afterwards, Andy made a magnificent save from a deflected shot but, as he fell to the ground, Palace's Chatterton crashed into him, injuring him in the face. Andy was able to continue after treatment and went on to make four first-class saves to deny the home team. Just as a draw seemed likely, Joslyn put Watford ahead and Mayes sealed the win in the final seconds when he curled the ball over the Palace keeper from the edge of the penalty area.

Andy suffered a depressed cheekbone in the collision with Chatterton, which prevented him from appearing in the 4-0 league defeat at Cambridge four days later. His replacement, Peter Gibbs, and the rest of the defence, had a nightmare. After the game, Gibbs gave up football saying, "*I am not dedicated enough. Frankly, had I carried on, I would have cheated myself, football and my teammates.*"(2)

Andy was obliged to return the following Saturday for the home game against Colchester despite not being 100 percent fit. Colchester were leading 1-0 when their captain Packer, the former Watford player, was sent off in the 62nd minute. Watford took almost 15 minutes to equalise through Garner, but Mayes made the game safe two minutes later with a diving header. Mike Walker, Andy's predecessor at Watford, had an excellent game for the visitors.

After a 3-1 defeat at Rochdale on Saturday, 18th September, Watford faced Sheffield Wednesday from the Third Division at Hillsborough the following Tuesday in the third round of the League Cup. The team was:

Rankin; How, Garner, Walley, Walsh, Craker, Geidmintis, Joslyn, Bond, Mayes, Poole.

It was Craker's first game for 18 months following a broken leg and a subsequent broken ankle. Watched by a crowd of almost 16,000 spectators, Wednesday were two goals up at half-time. Joslyn pulled one back after the interval but a third Wednesday goal ended Watford's hopes of getting to the fourth round for the first time.

Watford had a convincing 4-1 victory over Exeter at Vicarage Road on 25th

September. The team showed two changes from the side that had lost to Sheffield Wednesday. Walley was replaced by Eades, an on-loan signing from Cambridge United and Mercer came in for Geidmintis, who had joined from Workington Town in the close season. Watford were 2-1 up in the second half when Andy pulled off a superb reflex save to keep Watford's lead intact. In the 73rd minute, Mercer was knocked out in a collision with an Exeter player and had to leave the field. Coffill had just come on for Poole so Watford had to play the final quarter of an hour with ten men. It did not stop them scoring two further goals before the final whistle. After the game, Poole, a 19 year old former Brentford player, signed professional terms until the end of the season, having completed a three-month loan period.

Their next game, on Saturday, 2nd October, was again at home, but this time they could only manage a goalless draw against Halifax, managed by Alan Ball senior, father of the 1966 World Cup star. It was Halifax's first away point of the season, whilst it was the first home point dropped by Watford.

The following Saturday, Watford slumped to their fourth away defeat and their first-ever loss at Gresty Road, where Crewe beat them 2-0. The only players on the Watford side to emerge with any credit were Eades, Garner and Andy.

Watford then had a run of five matches unbeaten, beginning with a home 1-1 draw with Bournemouth and ending with a similar result at home to Aldershot. Sandwiched between those home draws were an away victory over Workington Town, a 2-2 draw away to Huddersfield Town, and a 1-0 home win against Barnsley. According to the Observer's match reporter at the Barnsley game, Geidmintis and Andy, who made several important saves to keep Barnsley at bay, deserved to share the Man of the Match Award.

Watford's unbeaten run ended on Saturday, 6th November when they lost 3-1 at Torquay. Watford included 23 year old, left-back Keith Pritchett, who had signed earlier in the week for £4000 from Brentford. His previous clubs included Wolves, Doncaster Rovers and Queens Park Rangers.

On Saturday, 20th November, Watford faced Gillingham away in the first round of the FA Cup. The team was:

Rankin; Geidmintis, Horsfield, Garner, Pritchett, Bond, Joslyn, Coffill, Mayes, Mercer, Downes.

Although Watford were on top for much of the game, a draw seemed inevitable until the last minute when a poor back pass by a Gillingham defender set Mercer free to slot the ball past the Gillingham keeper.

Watford were away again in the next round of the Cup on Saturday, 11th December, this time to non-League Hillingdon Borough. They fielded the same team that beat Gillingham. Hillingdon caused a shock when they went ahead in the first minute. Pritchett hit a back pass wide of Andy, whose despairing dive only knocked the ball to a Hillingdon player, who gratefully hit it into the empty net. Jenkins came on for Downes at the interval and, within minutes, Watford were back on level terms. They then went ahead in the 72nd minute, only for Hillingdon to surprise their opponents by getting back on level terms. Hillingdon's joy was short-lived, however, as Coffill scored his first goal of the season three minutes from time to put Watford into Round Three.

Although Watford were drawn away for the third time, they must have thought fortune was on their side as their opponents were another non-league side – Northwich Victoria from Cheshire. The tie was played on Saturday 8th January 1977; Watford fielded the following eleven:

Rankin; Geidmintis, Horsfield, Garner, Pritchett, Bond, Joslyn, Downes, Coffill, Mercer, Jenkins.

Watford outplayed Northwich in the first half, going in with a 2-1 lead at the interval, although they could easily have been 4-1 up. Watford were made to pay for their missed chances for, shortly after the interval, Northwich were back on level terms when they scored from the penalty spot and then, minutes from the end, they got the winner to cause one of the shocks of the afternoon.

In the five League games between the cup-ties, Watford were unbeaten with three draws and two wins. On Saturday, 27th November, they achieved a goalless draw away to second-placed Bradford. Andy made two brilliant saves in the second half to win a point for his side. For the first, he dived to save a downward header at the foot of the post; for the second, he had to change direction quickly to save a cross, which had been deflected away from him by Geidmintis.

That week, Watford signed 22 year old, 6'3½", goalkeeper Steve Sherwood for £3000 from Chelsea for whom he had made 82 league appearances.

A 2-0 home win over Swansea moved Watford into the top half of the table, just two points from a promotion place. Andy *"produced his customary telling save when it was needed most."*(3) Two draws followed – 0-0 at Darlington and 1-1 against Stockport Country at Vicarage Road.

On New Year's Day, despite heavy rain, a crowd of 6,824 fans turned up at Vicarage Road to see Watford record their biggest win for five months, a 4-0 defeat of Torquay.

On Tuesday, 11th January, Watford had a welcome win at home after the Cup defeat by Northwich Victoria three days earlier; they beat Newport County 2-0.

The win over Newport meant that Watford had suffered only one League defeat in their previous 12 outings. But that sequence ended the following Saturday, when they failed to score for the third successive away game and were beaten 1-0 at Hartlepool. After 18 minutes, Horsfield was adjudged to have pushed a Hartlepool player in the box and full-back Wiggett scored from the spot. Eighteen minutes later, the same two players went for the ball, only for the referee to award a second penalty against Horsfield. This time, Andy flung himself to his left to save Wiggett's shot and then push the follow-up round the post for a corner. Sleet and snow made the conditions difficult, but Watford missed enough chances to win the game.

The next two games resulted in a 1-1 draw with Southend at Vicarage Road and a 3-1 win over Southport at Haig Avenue.

Watford travelled to Scunthorpe on Saturday, 5th February, where the game ended in a goalless draw. The headline for the match report was *"It's the Andy Rankin Show with full supporting cast."* The report went on, *"Last season, Rankin made a mockery of the most one-sided game the Hornets have been in for years, when he denied United a point after the visitors had been gifted a goal. On Saturday it was not nearly so one-sided and Rankin was not alone in the hero-stakes. But despite a full-supporting cast, the 32 year old Liverpudlian stole the show with some supreme saves."* After the game, Ron Ashman, Scunthorpe United's manager, commented, *"Rankin played his part in keeping the game goalless but this was no drab affair. It could have been 4-4."* (4)

At Vicarage Road the next Saturday, Watford *"out-fought, out-thought and finally outscored"* Cambridge, the Division Four leaders, who had suffered only one defeat in their previous 18 outings. Ross Jenkins, who had requested a transfer a few weeks earlier, as he wanted first team football, scored Watford's first three minutes after coming on as substitute for Coffill in the 72nd minute. Mercer got the second with a header in the last minute. Watford's team was:

Rankin; Geidmintis, Pritchett, Garner, Horsfield, Joslyn, Bond, Coffill, Mercer, Mayes, Downes.

Watford's four-game unbeaten run ended on Saturday, 19th February. Colchester scored the only goal of the game from the penalty spot in the 14th minute when, according to the match report in the Watford Observer on the following Friday, *"no foul was committed, no one touched the player".*

Watford defeated Rochdale at Vicarage Road the next Saturday by three goals to one. Mercer scored within a minute of the kick-off and, five minutes later, Watford were awarded a penalty. Goalkeeper Poole saved Bond's first spot kick, but the referee ordered the kick to be re-taken because of encroachment by Rochdale players. Bond made no mistake with his second effort. Watford went three up minutes into the second half with a second goal from Mercer. Rochdale scored a consolation goal just before the finish. Mick Buxton, Watford's former coach, was at the ground scouting for Southend. When asked who was Man of the Match, he answered, *"Rankin and Mercer. They produced the something extra."* (5)

Watford drew their next three games, which were all away from home – 2-2 with Exeter, a game in which Watford twice pulled back from a goal down; 1-1 with Barnsley, whose equalising goal came from a wind-assisted free-kick, the flight of which deceived Andy, who could only push the ball into the net; and finally 1-1 with Halifax.

Thier next game was at home to Crewe on Saturday, 19th March. On a heavy, slippery pitch, they played some of their best football of the season to win 3-1. Crewe's goal came right at the end of the game when Watford were already 3-0 up.

Prior to the Exeter game, Watford's defence had only conceded six goals in 13 League games, but they had since given away five goals in four games. The trend continued with a 3-0 defeat at Brentford on Wednesday, 23rd March, with all the goals being scored in the first 15 minutes. This was followed by a 2-1 loss at Bournemouth three days later when Geidmintis was sent off for two bookable offences.

Watford thrashed Doncaster Rovers 5-1 at Vicarage Road on Tuesday, 29th March for their biggest win of the season. The size of the win was perhaps surprising as Doncaster were unbeaten for a run of ten games, which included eight wins. Watford's next match, on 2nd April, was also at home and this time they beat Workington 2-0. They were now 7th in the League with only eight points separating the top seven teams. Promotion seemed a possibility.

Watford's unbeaten run at home had lasted for 25 games, but it came to an unexpected end on Saturday, 9th April, when Brentford beat them 1-0. An uncharacteristic mistake by Andy led to the goal when he came out for a cross, hesitated and allowed a Brentford player to beat him to the ball. Despite Andy's error, Watford should have won. Three minutes after Brentford's goal, Bond missed a penalty, only for Mayes to miss a second penalty with seven minutes of the match remaining when he side-footed the ball straight at the goalkeeper.

Watford were twice ahead at Stockport the following Monday but allowed the home team to equalise both times. Andy was at fault for Stockport's second goal when he stooped to collect a low shot and allowed the ball to bounce off his shoulder to a Stockport player who easily netted. Andy pulled a muscle in that game. The injury meant that he missed the last eight games of the season; Steve Sherwood took his place. Even without the injury, Andy might have been dropped as his form had slumped in the previous two games.

Watford were unsuccessful in their push for promotion, finishing seventh. Cambridge United, Exeter City, Colchester United and Bradford City were promoted. Wimbledon were elected to the Football League for the first time at the expense of Workington Town.

Andy had played in 37 of the League games, four League Cup and three FA Cup ties. He missed the fourth and the last eight League matches through injury.

Mike Keen left the Club just before the end of the season after four years as manager.

1977-78 Season

Mike Keen's replacement as manager was 32 year old Graham Taylor, a former Grimsby Town and Lincoln City defender. In the 1975/76 season, Taylor had guided Lincoln to promotion from Division Four and had been described by the then England manager, Don Revie, as the *"brightest young coach in the country".* (6)

Watford FC 1977/78: From left to right, back row: Brian Pollard, Keith Mercer, Ross Jenkins, Sam Ellis, Albert McClenaghan, Dennis Booth.
Middle row: Pat Molloy (Physio), Dave Butler (Physio), Ian Bolton, ?, Andy Rankin, Luther Blissett, Steve Sherwood, Trevor How, Alan Garner, Tom Walley (1st team Coach).
Front Row Dennis Bond, ? , Roger Joslyn, Bertie Mee (General manager), Graham Taylor (team manager), Bobby Downes, Keith Pritchett, Alan Mayes. Courtesy of Alan Cozzi/Watford FC

Taylor signed two defenders before the start of the season – Sam Ellis from Lincoln for £6000 and Ian Bolton for £12,000 from Notts County.

Steve Sherwood started off as the first choice goalkeeper, playing in the first ten League games and four League Cup ties. Watford had lost only three of those games, the first leg of a league cup-tie with Reading and league games against York City and Barnsley.

However, Taylor decided on two changes for the away game against Brentford on Monday, 3rd October. These were to include Ross Jenkins at centre-forward and to replace Sherwood with Andy. The team was:

Rankin; How, Ellis, Garner, Pritchett, Joslyn, Bolton, Downes, Jenkins, Mercer, Mayes.

The 14,500 spectators were looking forward to an entertaining and high scoring game, as Watford were the highest scorers in the Football League and Brentford had the most wins. The travelling Watford fans were certainly not disappointed. Their side was 2-0 up within 22 minutes and the recalled Jenkins sealed victory with a goal ten minutes from time. Andy did not have a great deal to do on his return. Following the win, Watford moved to the top of the table.

Watford's 2-1 home win over Swansea, with the same eleven that had faced Brentford five days earlier, meant that they had recorded more wins than any other team in the Football League. Downes gave them the lead in the eighth minute. They then went on to miss a number of chances before Swansea equalised just before the interval. Minutes later, *"Rankin was forced to make his first real save of his comeback, diving high to brilliantly catch a magnificent shot from Evans."*(7) Five minutes from full-time, Mercer secured both points for his side with a glancing header well out of the keeper's reach. The match was watched by a crowd of more than 10,000 spectators, a far cry from the gates of four and five thousand of the previous season.

Despite dominating most of the game away to Aldershot on Saturday, 15th October, Watford were beaten 1-0 when Sam Ellis deflected the ball into his own net with Andy appearing to have the ball covered. Three days later, Sherwood kept goal in the 1-0 defeat in the League Cup by West Bromwich Albion at The Hawthorns.

Andy was back in goal for the home league win over Newport County the following Saturday. Mercer scored the opening goal in the 17th minute, but victory was not secured until Downes headed home seven minutes from time. Although Andy kept a clean sheet, he did not have a particularly good 90 minutes, mishandling the ball on several occasions.

After only four league appearances, Andy found himself back in the reserves. However, following a run of only one win in four games at the end of November and in early December, Taylor recalled Andy for the FA Cup tie at home to Third Division side Colchester on Saturday, 17th December. The team was:

Rankin; Geidmintis, Garner, Bolton, Pritchett, Booth, Joslyn, Downes, Pollard, Jenkins, Mercer.

Almost 12,000 spectators, the highest of the season, watched Watford score a goal in each half to go through to the next round.

Watford then faced four games in eight days over the festive season for which Graham Taylor had set a target of six points from the eight available. The players reported to a local hotel on the evening of Christmas Day, ready for the home game against Northampton on Boxing Day.

There was only one change to the FA Cup team – Mayes coming in for the injured Mercer. A record-breaking crowd of just over 15,000 turned up to see Watford beat Northampton 3-0.

Immediately after the game, the players and staff travelled to Torquay where they stayed overnight. Taylor selected an unchanged team to face Torquay, who were unbeaten at home for 15 matches. Coffill, who had been transferred to Torquay a month before, played against his former club. Watford were 2-1 down at the interval. An injury to Joslyn with 20 minutes left changed the game. Luther Blissett came on as substitute and, nine minutes later, Watford were level when a Bolton shot was deflected past the Torquay keeper. Soon afterwards, Mayes headed in a Downes cross to win both points for Watford.

On Saturday, 31ˢᵗ December, Watford's next opponents were Wimbledon, newcomers to the Football League. A crowd of 16,324 at Plough Lane watched Andy make two fine saves to keep his team on level terms before Mayes scored just before half-time. Soon after the restart, Jenkins scored and two minutes later a Downes' goal effectively sealed the game for Watford. Wimbledon did get a consolation goal eleven minutes from time.

Two days later, another record crowd -16,842 – turned up at Vicarage Road to see Watford overcome defensively-minded Hartlepool 1-0 to maintain a hundred percent record for their festive programme.

It was back to the FA Cup on Saturday, 7ᵗʰ January 1978, when Watford faced West Ham at Upton Park. The teams were:

Watford: Rankin; Geidmintis, Pritchett, Garner, Bolton, Booth, Joslyn, Downes, Blissett, Jenkins, Mayes.
West Ham: Ferguson, McDowell, Lampard, Bonds, Taylor, Curbishley, Devonshire, Robson, Cross, Brooking, Hales.

Watford put up a great display against the First Division side but lost by a single goal, scored by Pop Robson with ten minutes left. *"Rankin was sound, got his angles right and his catching was clean."*(8)

There was much speculation about the likelihood of Watford signing another goalkeeper as Andy had asked for a transfer earlier in the season. When asked about the situation, manager Graham Taylor said, *"The goalkeeper problem is not in our hands. Andy Rankin wants to go back north. That situation is unchanged so we have been studying the sort of players, including a goalkeeper, who we would be interested in next season."* Taylor added, *"He's (Andy) shown in the last four or five games the sort of form everyone told me he was capable of. "*

Watford then went on an unbeaten run of eight games, which included six wins. In that time, they only conceded three goals, all in the one game – a 3-3 draw away to Swansea – and scored 17.

Against York City at Bootham Crescent on Saturday, 21ˢᵗ January, Taylor decided to replace Jenkins with Blissett because the snow-covered pitch would not suit the 6'3" forward. It was a masterstroke, because Blissett scored in 52 seconds. Mayes later scored a hat-trick to make the final score 4-0.

The following Saturday, Watford put six goals past Doncaster Rovers without reply to equal a 43 years old club record of seven successive league wins; it was also their tenth clean sheet of the season.

In February, the Watford Observer reported that Graham Taylor had tried to sign Tony Gennoe, the Halifax goalkeeper, but that Watford had withdrawn from the negotiations because of the method of payment demanded by Halifax.

Watford's unbeaten run came to an end at Huddersfield on Tuesday, 14th March with a 1-0 defeat. Andy was at fault with the goal. He went for a cross, missed his punch and, in the ensuing scramble, a Huddersfield player managed to prod the ball home. Huddersfield were managed by Watford's former coach, Mike Buxton.

That was Watford's last defeat of the season as they won six and drew seven of their remaining 13 matches. Andy featured in all of those games. His 250th appearance for Watford was the 2-0 away win over Northampton Town on 28th March. The week before, when Watford beat Torquay 1-0 at Vicarage Road, Andy had set a club record of keeping ten successive clean sheets at home. The previous record was six during the 1968-69 season.

Watford needed one point to clinch promotion to the Third Division when they travelled to Bournemouth on Tuesday, 4th April. They were not disappointed. After a goalless first half, Pollard and Downes both scored, with Bournemouth getting a consolation goal two minutes from time. The Watford team was:

Rankin; How, Bolton, Garner, Pritchett, Booth, Joslyn, Pollard, Jenkins, Mayes, Downes.

Now a veteran at 34 years of age and Watford's longest serving player, Andy said after the game, "*I've spent 17 years going the wrong way down the Football League and most of it with Watford. I came here as a Division 2 player, remember. I'm not used to all this, so there was no way I counted my chickens until tonight.*" He asked to come off the transfer list adding, "*I had wanted a move before my kid started school and before the second one was born. But nothing came through early on and frankly can you blame me for wanting to be part of all this. It's tremendous after so many downhill years."*(9)

On Saturday, 8th April, Watford clinched the Division Four championship with six games of the season left when they defeated Scunthorpe by the only goal of the game. Andy was Man of the Match with a *"first class display. Not only did he make two telling saves, but his general handling was faultless as Scunthorpe put Watford under a lot of pressure in the second half."*(10)

Having won the title, perhaps Watford took their foot of the pedal for they drew their next five games, four of them finishing 1-1, the other was goalless.

Before the home game against Southend on Saturday, 15th April, the team were presented with their medals and the Division Four trophy, watched by almost 19,000 fans, Watford's largest crowd of the season. Jenkins scored for Watford in the 24th minute, but Southend equalised from the penalty spot in the second half.

Just over 10,000 spectators turned up to watch the final match of the season against Southport at Vicarage Road on Saturday, 5th May. At least, they were able to cheer a victory. Watford were two goals ahead within the first quarter of an hour – both scored by Pritchett from the penalty spot. A third penalty was awarded eight minutes from half-time, but this time it went to the visitors, who were able to pull back to 2-1. However, Blissett restored Watford's two goal lead a minute before the break. Southport got a second after the interval but could not get the goal that would have earned them a point. Watford's team for the final game was:

Rankin; McClenaghan, Garner, Bolton, Pritchett, Booth, Bond, Downes, Pollard, Mayes, Blissett.

Watford finished eleven points ahead of second-placed Southend United, and with 15 more than the other two promoted clubs, Swansea City and Brentford.

The game against Southport was Dennis Bond's last for Watford as he had been given a free transfer. He received a tremendous reception. Bond had made his debut in August 1964, apparently playing twice that day – for the youth team in the morning and the first team in the afternoon. He was signed by Tottenham

Hotspur during Easter 1967, managing only 23 league appearances in his 3½ years there, before moving to Charlton in 1970. After 75 league games for Charlton, he returned to Watford in February 1973 and made a total of 301 appearances for the club, scoring 42 goals.

Although Steve Sherwood began the season as the No 1 goalkeeper, Andy played in 30 of the 46 League games, including the last 26, and two FA Cup ties. He was obviously thrilled to have won the Fourth Division championship and promotion for the first time in his career, so much so that he decided to stay with the club, asking to come off the transfer list.

When asked about Andy's future at the Club, Graham Taylor said, "*I think Andy completely misread the situation at the beginning of the season when he put in for a transfer. He had aggravated his old injury and I think he thought his days with me would be numbered. He came into the side in the second half of the season and proved to be the keeper everyone had told me he is. There is no reason why Andy cannot go on at this standard for two or more seasons, if he believes in himself. He is by far the best keeper in Division 4.*"(11)

Almost as soon as he arrived at the Club, Graham Taylor introduced more discipline and a greater emphasis on fitness, and coupled with his coaching abilities and tactical awareness, he transformed Watford. During the season he signed midfielder Dennis Booth for £10,000 from his former club, Lincoln City, and winger Brian Pollard from York. Both players made a significant contribution to the club's success that season.

One interesting game during the season was Watford's 5-1 home win over Barnet in the quarter-final of the Herts Senior Cup on 27th February. Watford played their first team, including Andy in goal, while Barnet fielded Jimmy Greaves; it was he who scored their goal. Watford went on to win the Cup, beating Tring Town 2-1 in the final.

1978-79 Season

Just as two seasons earlier, Watford's first two games of the 1978/79 programme were home and away to Brentford in the first round of the League Cup. A crowd of 9,292 turned out to watch the home game on Saturday, 12th August, in which

Watford were 4-0 victors. Watford also won the away game, going through to the next round 7-1 on aggregate. Brentford played much better in the second fixture, forcing Andy to make five excellent saves. He also saved a penalty, diving to his right to save from Brentford's Phillips.

Their first League match in the Third Division was away to Walsall on Saturday, 19th August. The team was:

> Rankin; Stirk, Garner, Bolton, Pritchett, Booth, Joslyn, Pollard, Jenkins, Mercer, Downes. Stirk, signed for £30,000 from Ipswich Town, was the only newcomer during the close season.

Walsall took a 2-0 lead, but Pollard scored Watford's first and then set up the equaliser. Walsall were awarded a penalty just before half-time with the score at 2-2. Andy dived to his left to save Alan Buckley's spot kick and then blocked Buckley's follow up attempt with an even better save; it was his second penalty save in successive games. Ten minutes after the interval, Watford took the lead and scored another before the end.

Watford were at home three days later and, watched by 11,812 spectators, played Blackpool off the park to win 5-1. Ross Jenkins scored his second hat-trick for the club.

Watford's run of four undefeated games came to an end the next Saturday when they faced Peterborough at Vicarage Road. The team showed only one change to the side that had faced Walsall in the opening League game, with Mayes replacing Mercer. Although Watford had much more possession and a greater number of chances than their opponents, they could not take advantage of their superiority. Peterborough were two up with 15 minutes to go when Pritchett scored Watford's consolation goal from the penalty spot.

Watford were at home to Division One side, Newcastle, in the second round of the League Cup on Tuesday evening, 29th August. The team was:

Rankin; Stirk, Bolton, Garner, Pritchett, Booth, Joslyn, Pollard, Jenkins, Mercer, Downes.

In the first minute, "*Cassidy had forced Rankin to a spectacular save to his 25-yard shot and he had the goalkeeper dropping smartly as he sent another goalwards from the resultant corner.*"(12)

Newcastle were leading 1-0 when Joslyn had to leave the field injured in the 40th minute. He was replaced by Blissett, who made himself the hero by scoring the equaliser and then notching the winner eleven minutes from time. More than 15,500 fans turned out to watch the tie.

Watford came from 2-1 behind to beat Gillingham 3-2 away from home in their next League match on Saturday, 2nd September. Despite the move up to Division Three, Watford were continuing to be prolific scorers with 22 goals in seven games and the win over Gillingham moved them up to second place in the League.

They were brought back down to earth the following Saturday, however, when, in front of a crowd of 17,438 at Vicarage Road, they were beaten 2-0 by Swansea. But, they were back to their high scoring ways in midweek, defeating Graham Taylor's former club 5-0 at Lincoln. Watford's team was:

Rankin; Stirk, Bolton, Garner, Pritchett, Booth, Joslyn, Pollard, Jenkins, Blissett, Downes.

Andy was called upon to make two superb saves early in the game. In the sixth minute, a cross was sent over and he "*somehow arched backwards and across to knock the ball on to the post and away to safety*".(13) A few minutes later, he made another fine save, this time from a "*rasping*" drive. Blissett scored twice, in the 19th and 27th minutes, and Garner got a third to give Watford a comfortable lead at half-time. Pollard notched the fourth ten minutes after the interval, while Jenkins got the fifth twelve minutes later. It was Watford's biggest away win for nine years.

A few days after the win over Lincoln, Taylor signed defender Steve Harrison for £25,000. He had made 141 appearances for Blackpool but, after becoming involved in a wages dispute with the club, went to play for North American League side Vancouver Whitecaps, managed by Tony Waiters, the former Blackpool and England goalkeeper.

Watford won their next two League games – beating Bury 2-1 at Gigg Lane on 16th September and defeating Oxford 4-2 at Vicarage Road a week later. Jenkins scored all four goals in that game, the first Watford player to do so in the League for more than ten years. Watford were now top of Division Three. Harrison made his debut against Oxford.

Watford were undefeated in 12 away games, the longest in the club's history, when they travelled to face Rotherham on Tuesday, 26th September. A 2-1 reverse knocked them off the top of the table, as well as ending their away record. Watford actually took the lead in the first half through Blissett. Ten minutes into the second half, Garner headed a shot into his own net and Rotherham scored again ten minutes later.

Watford had a convincing 4-0 win over Tranmere Rovers at Vicarage Road on the Saturday to give them confidence for their League Cup meeting with Manchester United at Old Trafford on Wednesday evening, 4th October. More than 40,000 fans saw Watford beat United 2-1 in what was, according to Oliver Phillips writing in the Watford Observer, their greatest ever result. The teams were:

Watford: Rankin; Stirk, Garner, Bolton, Harrison, Booth, Joslyn, Pollard, Blissett Jenkins, Downes.
Manchester United: Roche; Albiston, Houston, B. Greenhoff, McQueen, Buchan, Coppell, J. Greenhoff, Jordan, McIlroy, Grimes.

United went ahead five minutes before half-time when Jordan hooked the ball over his shoulder past Andy into the net. Blissett equalised a minute after the interval and notched the winner with 20 minutes of the match remaining. Oliver Phillips noted: *"It was Rankin who preserved the first half hope with timely stops and confirmed them with a string of superb saves in the second period to give the Hornets their first-ever taste of the Football League Cup's 4th Round draw."*

After the match, Graham Taylor said, *"They were all great, but a special word for Andy. Oh! What a fantastic save that was. For me, it was a goal. It was one of the most fantastic saves, the best save I have ever seen. It's ironic really that Andy at 34 has reached the pinnacle moment of his career. That late save must be the crowning moment even though I know he's played for Everton. Make no mistake, he must be really pleased with himself, deep down inside."*(14)

It was back down to earth for Watford on the Saturday when Chester beat them 2-1 at Sealand Road. However, they were soon back to their winning ways with four victories in succession, scoring seven goals in the process, whilst conceding only one. In the second of those wins, 2-1 at home to Carlisle, the match reporter wrote: *"Rankin's most energetic contribution, apart from running on to the pitch, was when he did well to claim a couple of corners."*(15) Carlisle's goal came with eight minutes from the end when Joslyn headed a corner into his own net.

The 2-0 win at Chesterfield on Saturday, 21st October, put Watford back at the top of the table, and this was followed by a 1-0 home win over Exeter City.

On Saturday, 4th November, Watford slumped to their heaviest defeat for over two seasons when Hull thrashed them 4-0. Andy did not have a good match, looking particularly vulnerable at corners.

Only eleven days after defeating Exeter at Vicarage Road by the only goal of the game, Watford travelled to face Exeter in the League Cup. Watford's team was:

Rankin; Stirk, Bolton, Garner, Pritchett, Booth, Downes, Blissett, Jenkins, Mercer, Mayes.

The night did not start well for Watford. Mercer injured himself in the 27th minute when he slipped while chasing a through ball. He was taken off the field on a stretcher and replaced by Joslyn. However, things looked up later when Pritchett scored from the penalty spot and Jenkins made the game safe with a goal just over 20 minutes from the end.

Watford completed their first double of the season when they beat Gillingham 1-0 at Vicarage Road on Saturday, 11th November, watched by almost 14,000 spectators. Jenkins scored the only goal of the game, whilst Pritchett lost his 100 percent record from the spot when his penalty kick in the 77th minute was saved by the Gillingham keeper.

An unfortunate accident that very evening meant that Andy did not feature in a first team game for four months. He slipped and broke his left collarbone while fetching the coal at his club house, which was actually scheduled to have gas-fired central heating installed by the club. Later, Andy said: "*It's a big blow. I was really enjoying it. Of course, one has to find one's feet again in Division Three, but until Hull at least, I've been no busier than in Division Four. At my time of life it's not the best of timing as we are in the middle of a great League Cup run. We have a helluva chance of getting to Wembley. It was raining heavily on Saturday night and this old guttering went. I went out the new patio door and slipped. I fell between the coal bunker and the rockery.*"(16)

In January 1979, Watford signed Steve Sims, a 21 year old centre-half, from Leicester City for £200,000, smashing the record fee of £50,000 paid to Bolton for Ray Train about two months earlier.

Watford lost only two of the 19 games Andy missed. One of those was the first leg of the semi-final of the League Cup against Nottingham Forest; the second leg was a goalless draw at Vicarage Road. So, Forest went through to the final, ending Watford's Wembley dream.

However, after a sequence of five draws in the League, Graham Taylor made three changes to the side to face Chesterfield at Vicarage Road on Saturday, 3rd March. He axed the previous season's Player of the Year, Garner; dropped the club's second most expensive signing, Ray Train; and recalled Andy in place of Steve Sherwood. Of Andy's return, Taylor said: "*Steve Sherwood fared particularly well at Brentford as the culmination of a much-improved run in the first team. But Andy Rankin, given the benefit of four warm-up matches, has an obvious advantage in experience and this could prove invaluable as Watford enter the last third of the season and the increasing pressure.*"(17) The team was:

Rankin; Stirk, Bolton, Sims, Pritchett, Booth, Joslyn, Downes, Pollard, Jenkins, Blissett.

Watford won 2-0 with goals from Bolton and Jenkins in the second half. After Blissett was hacked down in the penalty box with 20 minutes of the game left, he had to be replaced by Mercer. Pritchett missed the subsequent penalty, his shot being easily saved by the keeper. Watford were on top of the table with 42 points from 30 games, two points more than Shrewsbury Town, who had played a game less.

Exeter were Watford's next opponents, the two teams facing each other for the third time that season – Watford had won both the previous games, 1-0 at Vicarage Road in the League and 2-0 away in the quarter-final of the League Cup. It was to be a goalless draw this time, which stretched Watford's unbeaten run in the League to 15 games.

However, they were unable to extend that unbeaten run further as they lost 3-2 at Swansea on Tuesday, 20th March. Swansea were the first team to complete the double over Watford since Graham Taylor became manager. Watford were 2-0 down at the interval, but pulled level midway through the second half through goals from Jenkins and Bolton. Steve Sims was later sent off for a foul and Swansea got the winner nine minutes from time. Watford still sat at the top of the table, two points ahead of Shrewsbury, having played a game more.

After going a goal up in the ninth minute at Bloomfield Road on the Saturday, an error by Andy nine minutes later allowed Blackpool to equalise and secure a point: "*Rankin, under pressure, managed to get first to the ball but was unable to push it far. McEwan was able to move on to the ball and hook it home from 12 yards out.*" The match reporter added: "*Much has been made in the National Press of Andy Rankin's mistake but scant allowance was made on his behalf for the wind.*" (18)

Watford won their next two matches, both of which were at Vicarage Road. They defeated Walsall 3-1 on Tuesday evening, 27th March and then, watched by a crowd of more than 16,000, beat Sheffield Wednesday by the only goal of the game on the Saturday. Wednesday did not win a corner until the 78th minute and, almost immediately afterwards, Pollard scored Watford's winner. It was probably sour grapes, but Jack Charlton, Wednesday's manager, described Watford as a side that plays "*hump-up, knock it back and hump up again football*".(19)

At Roots Hall, on Monday, 2nd April, Southend deservedly beat Watford 1-0. The goal came in the 69th minute and Andy was unhappy that the goal was allowed to stand as he felt that the ball was unfairly knocked out of his hands: "*I had both hands on the ball when I was knocked from behind and the ball rolled loose again. It must have looked messy from your position but when the lad squared the ball back, I got both hands to it. I'm really sick.*"

The following Saturday, Watford beat Mansfield 3-0 at Field Mill, but then slumped to their worst home defeat since 1975, on Good Friday, 13th April, when they lost 3-0 to Colchester. A crowd of just under 18,000 watched the game. Graham Taylor described it as "*the worst display by a home side since I've been a manager. It was awful – no urgency, no commitment.*" The team was:

Rankin; Stirk, Bolton, Garner, Pritchett, Booth, Joslyn, Train, Pollard, Jenkins, Blissett.

Taylor made two changes for the Easter Saturday match against promotion contenders, Shrewsbury Town, at Gay Meadow. In came Harrison and Downes at the expense of Pritchett and Train. Watford went behind to a 27-minute goal but, three minutes later, Bolton equalised when he drove in a free-kick low beyond the reach of the Shrewsbury keeper. "*Apart from one memorable moment in the first half when Andy Rankin pulled one of his special saves out of the bag, Watford created two of the best chances of the afternoon.*"(20)

Watford completed their Easter programme on Tuesday, 17th April with a 2-0 home win over Southend before another large crowd – 15,835. It was the first time Watford had beaten Southend in nine games and avenged their 1-0 defeat by them only two weeks earlier. After the Easter games, Watford were still top of the table with 53 points from 40 games. The chasing group was Swansea with 52 points from 41 games; Gillingham 50 from 39; Shrewsbury 49 from 38; and Swindon 48 from 38.

Watford lost 2-0 at Swindon the following Saturday. They fell behind in the 15th minute when Jenkins, defending a corner, headed the ball into his own net. Three saves from Andy prevented Swindon going further ahead, but they made the game safe with a minute to go. One of Andy's saves was a marvellous reflex save from former Watford colleague Mayes, who hit a dropping ball on the volley. After the match, Mayes said, ""*That was a world class save but then that's what you expect from Andy.*"(21)

They lost again on Tuesday, 24th April, going down undeservedly at Carlisle when a curling free-kick was lifted over the wall with pace. Andy got his hand to the ball but could not keep it out.

Andy missed the last four games, more for tactical reasons than because of poor performances. Graham Taylor said, "*Andy has some grating of the knee joint which is caused by wear and tear. Ian Bolton is having to take the goalkicks on occasions because Andy is experiencing pain and difficulty in kicking the ball more than 35 yards. The problem is that after taking the goalkick, Ian invariably has to sprint 30 yards forward. At the moment, we want to push up on the opposition as far as possible but it is putting a lot of pressure on Ian. Steve Sherwood has lived in the shadow of Andy Rankin. Although I left him out I have a lot of confidence in his ability and would not hesitate in bringing him back.*"

Watford won three and drew one of the four games that Andy missed and finished runners up with 60 points, one point behind the champions Shrewsbury. Swansea, third with the same number of points as Watford but with a poorer goal difference, were also promoted to Division Two. Until the 1976-77 season, second and third place would have been decided by the goal average scheme i.e. the number of goals scored would have been divided by the number of goals conceded and the team with the highest "score" would have been placed second. However, at the start of the 1976-77 season, the simpler goal difference system was introduced whereby the difference between the goals scored and the goals conceded was the deciding factor, the team with the greater difference was better placed.

Andy played in 30 of the 46 League games and five League Cup ties. He started off as first choice goalkeeper, playing in the first 22 games, but then had an unfortunate accident at home in November 1978, breaking his collarbone. Steve Sherwood took his place for the next 19 matches, until Andy's recall in March 1979, after which he featured in 13 consecutive League games before being replaced by Sherwood for the final four fixtures.

Luther Blissett won the Watford Observer's Goal of the Season, whilst Andy received the Best Display Award for his goalkeeping against Manchester United in the League Cup in October 1978. Andy got 940 votes for his Manchester United display; second and third were Blissett for his two goals against United (501) and

Jenkins (367) for his display at home to Oxford. Speaking about Andy's award, Graham Taylor said, "*That save by Andy to Gordon McQueen was out of this world but he did more than make one save. There was two absolutely first class saves to Jordan, one which came up to him sharply but he held it well and made it look much easier than it was.*"(22)

Luther Blissett (extreme right) holds the Best Goal trophy presented by Mrs Wendy Sibthorp of J. M. Sibthorp of Sibthorp, Leavesdon, whilst Andy Rankin receives his Best Display trophy from Ron Moore, company director of Brooks and Moore Ltd , sponsors of the award.
Courtesy of the Watford Observer

In a Watford Observer Supplement of 29th May, celebrating Watford's promotion to the Second Division, Graham Taylor was asked to assess his goalkeepers: "*I think Andy would look back over the season and regret the decision to get the coal in. We had just beaten Gillingham – Manchester United and Exeter had fallen to us in the League Cup and we had gone to the top of the table.*

Andy had an outstanding night at Old Trafford and quite properly he won the Display of the Season Award. Steve came in and in my opinion his keeping has improved. He too did very well in the League Cup at Stoke and accounted for himself well in the League. But with due respect to Steve we did start to concede a few goals. I am not saying that they were his fault but, despite his size, I felt he was not exercising his authority and not giving his fellow defenders enough help.

I felt we needed the calming influence of Andy who, when recalled, performed as we expected him to. Andy is not getting any younger, however, and he has had trouble with his knee, on and off, since I first came to this club.

It is very difficult to have an injury and not let it affect other parts of your play and so Steve came back to prove that there is very little difference between the two of them.

Andy Rankin has been, and is, a first-class goalkeeper. It is just that he is regarded and appreciated in such a way by the Watford public that it makes it that extra little bit difficult for other players when they come into the side.

Both goalkeepers have had good seasons without making bad mistakes but I think they will agree that at times they could have helped the back four that little bit more."

1979-80 Season

The opening match of the new season was the first leg of a League Cup tie away to Colchester on Saturday, 11th August. In only Colchester's second attack of the first half in the 39th minute, the ball struck Booth on the arm and Hodge put Colchester ahead from the penalty spot. Five minutes later, they were two up when Gough curled a free-kick round the wall of defenders and beat Andy for pace. One of the Colchester defenders was sent off late in the second half when he tripped Blissett deliberately as he was heading for goal.

Andy had twisted his ankle during the Colchester game and missed the next four games; his replacement was Sherwood. In that time, Watford won the second-leg of their League Cup tie, but went out 3-2 on aggregate, and they lost one and drew two of their first three games in Division Two.

However, Andy was recalled for the home game against West Ham on a glorious, sunny Saturday afternoon, 1st September. A marvellous crowd of 23,329 turned up to watch, and the teams were:

Warford: Rankin; How, Sims, Bolton, Harrison, Joslyn, Booth, Train, Jenkins, Blissett, Downes.

West Ham: Parkes; Lampard, Brush, Bonds, Martin, Holland, Pike, Pearson, Cross, Brooking, Devonshire.

Watford recorded their first league victory of the season with a 2-0 win, despite being reduced to ten men for the last 19 minutes when Bolton was sent off. Watford took the lead in the 36th minute, Blissett heading home a cross from How. Blissett also scored the second, 16 minutes into the second half, when he followed up his shot, which had been saved by Parkes, to head the rebound over the keeper into the net.

Garner replaced Bolton for the away game against Bristol Rovers the following Saturday. The match was goalless at half-time. A minute after the interval, *"Blissett hit a 30 yard back pass which put Watford in all sorts of trouble but Rankin eventually saved after Barrowclough was presented with something of a gift."*(23) In the 61st minute, the Bristol goalkeeper saved a shot from Blissett but Jenkins pounced on the rebound to give Watford the lead. Eleven minutes later, How was penalised for handball when there was no immediate danger and Barrowclough equalised from the spot.

In the next league game, Watford drew 1-1 with Cardiff City at Vicarage Road and then faced Chelsea at Stamford Bridge on Saturday, 22nd September. The teams were:

Watford: Rankin; How, Garner, Bolton, Harrison, Booth, Joslyn, Train, Blissett, Jenkins, Downes.

Chelsea: Borots; Locke, Wilkins, Bumstead, Droy, Nutton, Britton, Fillery, Langley, Johnson, Walker.

Watford lost 2-0, their second defeat in the league. Andy had a good game and had no chance with the goals.

After beating Charlton 2-1 at Vicarage Road on Saturday, 29th September, Watford had a run of three successive defeats – 2-1 at home by Queens Park

Rangers, and then two 1-0 losses away from home to Swansea and Orient. Watford lost Jenkins in the first half of the Swansea game with a broken ankle.

Andy was not to blame for those defeats. Indeed, the match reports mentioned that he had made a number of excellent saves and that the defeats were the result of Watford's failure to take chances.

Five days after the defeat by Orient, Taylor completed the £100,000 signing of 25 year old goalkeeper Eric Steele from Brighton and Hove Albion and also midfielder Wilf Rostron, 23years, from Sunderland for £150,000. Rostron stayed at Watford for a decade and in that time played in 404 League and Cup games, scoring 30 goals. He subsequently played for both Sheffield clubs and Brentford.

Of Steele's signing, Taylor said, "*I can't determine the availability of a player – I have not bought a goalkeeper because of a particular display or anything like that. Andy Rankin has been doing well and will continue to do so, but the signing of Steele must strengthen my goalkeeping situation and one must always seek to strengthen the squad.*"

Andy kept his place for the home fixture against Newcastle United on Saturday, 20th October, which Watford won 2-1, watched by a crowd of almost 18,000.

Perhaps surprisingly, Andy was granted a free-transfer the following week, in recognition of his services to the club. Garner, the previous season's Player of the Year, Sherwood, Downes and Joslyn had also been transfer-listed. Graham Taylor stressed that only one of the two goalkeepers on the list would be allowed to leave. He said, "*If we receive a satisfactory offer for Sherwood then I would be quite happy to have Andy Rankin understudying for a couple of more seasons.*"(24) Andy was fairly philosophical about the situation, saying "*We will have to wait and see what turns up.*"

Andy's last first team appearance for Watford was a 3-0 defeat at Wrexham on Saturday, 27th October – hardly the ideal manner in which to step down after such a glorious career at the club. Eric Steele replaced him in the first team, whilst Andy featured in the Reserves during November.

The following month Andy joined Huddersfield Town, who were seeking promotion from Division Four, on a month's loan with a view to a permanent transfer. Huddersfield's manager was former Watford coach, Mick Buxton. Watford paid up the remaining seven months of Andy's contract in recognition of his eight years' loyal service. Andy, whose wife was expecting their fourth child on New Year's Day, was quoted in the Watford Observer as saying of his move, "*It's a chance of a game. I know Mick otherwise a loan deal wouldn't have been on at this particular time. He's agreed to let me train down here and going up on Fridays. One of their keepers is injured and the other faces a suspension but the deal is with a view to joining them permanently. I'll have to see how the month goes.*"

Despite Andy's philosophical view about his free transfer, according to his brother Terry, he always felt that he had been pushed out of the club by Graham Taylor. Regardless of that, Andy was clearly a crowd favourite. They twice voted him Player of the Season and he also won the vote of the fans for the Best Display of the Season in the 1978/79 season for his performance in the League Cup tie with Manchester United.

Moreover, in 1999, the Vicarage Road fans were asked to name their Top 100 All-Time Greatest Watford Players. From that list four judges, including Oliver Phillips of the Watford Observer and Trefor Jones, author of "Watford, Season by Season", selected "The 60". Andy was included in both lists. Indeed, he was included in almost every list submitted by the supporters and the four judges each included him in their own submissions.

In a rather humorous article "Andy Rankin: Goalkeepers Are Different", Kevin Birdseye wrote about "his all-time Hornet hero" – Andy Rankin. Birdseye described how "*Andy Rankin had sideburns which simply oozed class. He was hip and trendy in a way that the man he replaced – the no-frills, crew-cutted Mike Walker – could never hope to be. Walker's sad attempts to ape his successor's cred by growing a comedy moustache and letting his hair down an extra inch or two failed to move me (or, slightly more crucially, the Watford manager).*"(25) Despite the humour, as a young Watford supporter, Kevin Birdseye, clearly "*worshipped*" Andy.

There were moments when Andy must have wondered what he was doing at Watford, particularly as they slipped from the Second to the Fourth Division. There were occasions when luck was against him, such as the coal incident when he broke his collarbone. However, looking back on his time at Watford, he must be proud of his contribution at the club and the high regard in which he was held by the supporters.

Eric Steele remained at Watford until the end of the 1983/84 season, making only 65 appearances in his 4½ years at the club. After taking over from Andy in November 1979, he only missed the final match of that season. He then played the first 27 games of the following season, but was replaced by Steve Sherwood, and made only a further six appearances before being transferred to Derby County.

Sherwood remained at Watford until 1987 when he moved to Grimsby Town. He had made 269 appearances for the club and had had to compete with Andy, Eric Steele and then Tony Cotton for the No 1 goalkeeping position. Having joined Watford in November 1976, there were only three seasons when Sherwood could truly consider himself to be the No 1 choice – 1981/82 when they were promoted to Division One as runners-up; 1982/83 when they were runners-up to Liverpool in the First Division; and 1983/84 when they finished 11th in Division One.

Graham Taylor, of course, completed "the impossible dream". He took Watford into Division One in 1982, ending their first season there as runners-up to Liverpool, and he then led them to Wembley in May 1984 where they lost 2-0 to Everton in the FA Cup Final at Wembley.

Taylor moved on to become manager of Aston Villa in 1987, and later became the England manager.

In terms of Watford's success, mention must be made of Bertie Mee, who as manager of Arsenal from 1966 to 1976 led the club to the League and Cup double and won its first European trophy. He joined Watford in September 1977 to work with Graham Taylor as assistant manager, taking charge of scouting and youth policy. He later served as the club's general manager and, after retiring, became a director. Taylor is reputed to have said that Bertie Mee was the best signing that he ever made.

References:

1. Watford Observer, 3rd September 1976

2. Watford Observer, 10th September 1976

3. Watford Observer, 10th November 1976

4. Watford Observer, 11th February 1977

5. Watford Observer, 4th March 1977

6. Watford Centenary by Oliver Phillips; Watford Football Club

7. Watford Observer, 14th October 1977

8. Watford Observer, 20th January 1978

9. Watford Observer, 7th April 1978

10. Watford Observer, 14th April 1978

11. Watford Observer, 5th May 1978

12. Watford Observer, 1st September 1978

13. Watford Observer, 15th September 1978

14. Watford Observer, 6th October 1978

15. Watford Observer, 20th October 1978

16. Watford Observer, 17th November 1978

17. Watford Observer, 9th March 1979

18. Watford Observer, 30th March 1979

19. Watford Observer, 6th April 1979

20. Watford Observer, 20th April 1979

21. Watford Observer, 27th April 1979

22. Watford Observer, 11th May, 1979

23. Watford Observer, 14th September 1979

24. Watford Observer, 26th October 1979

25. www.bsad.org/tribute/rankin/kev.htm

10

ANDY AT HUDDERSFIELD (1979-82)

1979-80 Season

Andy joined Huddersfield Town on loan at the beginning of December. Eleven years earlier, Huddersfield pulled out of a £25,000 transfer deal with Everton following Andy's medical examination. This time, however, the Club was in desperate need of a goalkeeper. Regular keeper Alan Starling, who had been sent off the previous week after an FA Cup defeat by Darlington for foul and abusive language in the players' tunnel, was likely to be suspended, while reserve Richard Taylor was suffering from a back injury. Manager Mike Buxton said, *"I was coach at Watford when Andy joined us from Everton. He's a good goalkeeper and there have certainly never been any problems with his fitness."*(1)

Initially, the Huddersfield management had thought that Starling would miss the match on Saturday, 8th December, but later found out that off-the-field dismissals were not punished by automatic suspension. So, he was able to play in the 3-1 defeat away to Torquay United. However, Starling hurt his ribs in training the following week and was expected to be out of action for over a month.

There was no game on Saturday, 15th December, so Andy made his first team debut the following Friday evening at home against Rochdale, who were only one place off the bottom of the League and had not won away all season. It was an easy 5-1 victory for Huddersfield. Rochdale only had two shots, one of which was deflected wide of Andy for a consolation goal.

Following the game, Huddersfield signed 29 year old Steve Kindon of Burnley for £50,000. Huddersfield's team was:

Rankin, Brown, Robinson, Stanton, Sutton, Hanvey, Laverick, Hart, Fletcher, Robins, Cowling.

In his second game, a 2-1 away defeat at The Shay by Halifax Town on Boxing Day, Andy was named "Man of the Match". According to the match report, "*He was clean, positive and sure in all he did and had to be alert as Halifax tried their luck with shots from well outside the penalty area.*"(2) Huddersfield were a goal down when Kindon was brought on to replace Robins and made an immediate impact. His hard, low cross was turned into his own net by Halifax full-back Dunleavy to level the scores. Huddersfield's joy was short-lived, however, as six minutes later Halifax scored what proved to be the winner. A crowd of 10,061, the highest for a League match at The Shay for 10 years, watched the game. The defeat left Huddersfield third in the League.

Huddersfield's final game of 1979 was away to Doncaster Rovers, whose manager was Billy Bremner of Leeds United fame. Town went ahead in the sixth minute and were two up 26 minutes later when Steve Kindon scored his first goal for the Club. Doncaster reduced the arrears 20 minutes into the second half and then threw everything at the Town defence, but Andy kept them out with a series of excellent saves. After the match, Mike Buxton said of Andy, "*He's got so much experience and that counts for a lot. He is a very calm person and doesn't get ruffled. That makes a big difference.*"(3)

On New Year's Day, Huddersfield defeated Darlington at Leeds Road by two goals to one. Town were two up four minutes into the second half through goals from Hanvey and Robins before Darlington pulled a goal back ten minutes later. Cowling missed the opportunity to make the game safe for Town when he failed from the penalty spot.

The following day, Buxton announced that he was trying to sign Andy permanently. He said, "*It doesn't need me to say how well Andy has done since joining us. Anyone who has seen our holiday games will realise that. He made a good save at Doncaster late on and I mean a good one. The ball, struck by Alan Little, bounced badly in front of him as he was going for it. Then, he made another fine stop from Alan Walsh's free kick when we met Darlington. You can say I am happy to have three good goalkeepers on my staff... though unfortunately two of them are injured at the moment."*(4) Andy later signed an 18-month contract.

On Saturday, 5th January, league leaders Walsall maintained their season's unbeaten run at home with a 1-1 draw with Huddersfield before their biggest crowd of the season. However, Walsall had two opportunities to secure both points. The first was when their player-manager Alan Buckley hit the post from the penalty spot with Andy well beaten. The second followed Andy's only error in the game. Racing 20 yards from his goal line, he totally missed his clearance, leaving a Walsall player with an open goal, only for him to send the ball wide. The draw meant that Huddersfield were second in the league, one point behind Walsall and one ahead of Portsmouth, but having played a game more than each of their rivals.

The following week, Huddersfield narrowly beat Lincoln City 3-2 at Leeds Road. It was a tale of two penalties and a substitution. Town were 1-0 up when they were awarded a penalty in the 37th minute. Keith Hanvey took the spot kick and beat goalkeeper Eric McManus. However, the referee ordered the kick to be re-taken because, he later explained, a player was still walking out of the penalty area when he had told Hanvey to wait. His second attempt was saved by McManus – Huddersfield's second penalty miss in successive matches at Leeds Road. However, they were awarded a second penalty ten minutes after the interval with the scores level at 1-1. Steve Kindon took the kick this time and blasted the ball past McManus for his first goal before the home crowd. Lincoln equalised again in the 74th minute but substitute Fletcher scored the winner with two minutes to go.

Town's next three games were draws away from home – 2-2 with Newport County on Friday, 18th January; 1-1 at Hartlepool United on Saturday, 26th January; and 1-1 with Port Vale on Saturday, 9th February. These three games were memorable for Andy for different reasons. Against Newport, he gave a superb display, ensuring his team did not lose and earning praise from Newport's boss Len Ashurst. Against Hartlepool, however, it was a sad day. He was booked for the very first time in his long career for disputing the award of a penalty kick. According to the match reporter, Andy, *"the most placid of players"* threw the ball away in frustration. Hartlepool took the lead from the spot kick but Kindon equalised later with his fourth goal in six games. Against Port Vale, he gave another memorable display, rescuing his team with a number of fine saves until Vale's equaliser in the 83rd minute.

Following an easy 5-0 victory over Stockport County on Saturday, 16th February at Leeds Road, Huddersfield had a four-day break in Guernsey to prepare for their top of the table clash with Portsmouth at Fratton Park the next Saturday.

Portsmouth had won at Leeds Road in October so Town were eager for revenge. But, it was not be. Huddersfield lost by four goals to one, despite taking the lead from the penalty spot after 19 minutes. They were never in the game after that. Andy made several fine saves, making only one error when he failed to collect a corner, which bounced into the net through a mass of bodies.

Town got back to winning ways on Saturday, 8th March with a 4-0 away win against York City but the next three matches, against Peterborough United, Bradford City and Tranmere Rovers ended in stalemate 0-0 draws. The home game against Bradford was watched by 14,857 spectators, the second highest crowd of the season and it was the third goalless draw between the two teams in the last three encounters. The Tranmere match was Andy's 400th Football League appearance and Steve Kindon's 300th.

The next two games against Rochdale away and Halifax Town at home were comfortable 2-0 and 5-0 wins respectively. The shine was taken off the Halifax victory, according to manager Buxton, by a section of the home crowd who "*crucified*" Cowling, forcing the manager to replace him with Fletcher to save him from further abuse. Buxton said later that the crowd "*had killed a good professional*" and that it was the first time in management that he had had to do something like that.

The Fourth Division's "Match of the Day" on Saturday, 12th April, was the Leeds Road clash between the top two clubs Walsall and Huddersfield; Walsall were top, five points ahead of Huddersfield but had played a game more. Some 17,000 spectators watched the game, Town's largest crowd of the season. Huddersfield dominated the first half but only led 1-0 at the interval. Walsall equalised in the 61st minute so Town had tossed away the chance to reduce Walsall's lead at the top of the table.

Huddersfield's 2-1 win over Scunthorpe United at Leeds Road three days later guaranteed them promotion to Division Three. They could still win the championship as they were only three points behind Walsall with three games left, providing Walsall slipped up.

Town won their last three games convincingly – 3-1 away over Hereford United, 4-2 at home against Torquay United and 2-1 at home over Hartlepool United – whilst Walsall stumbled with two defeats and a draw in their final three games. In the end, it was Town who were crowned Fourth Division champions, scoring more than 100 goals in the process, and they were promoted along with Walsall and Newport County.

Before the start of the next season, midfielder Hart, who had played more than 200 games for Huddersfield, asked for a transfer as he was unhappy with his improved contract. He was sold to Walsall for £70,000. Days later, Town signed 19 year old Mark Kennedy as a replacement from Halifax Town for £55,000; he had been an ever-present at Halifax that season.

1980-81 Season

Town's first two games of the new season were against Second Division Blackburn Rovers in the League Cup. The first game, at Ewood Park, was a goalless draw thanks mainly to three superb saves by Andy. Afterwards, Howard Kendall, the Blackburn manager and former colleague of Andy's at Everton, said, "*The two centre-backs and the goalkeeper were tremendous. They stopped us winning.*"

Three days later, the sides draw again, 1-1 this time at Leeds Road. Blackburn took the lead a minute after the interval, only for Huddersfield to equalise with seven minutes left. Rovers went through to the next round of the Cup on away goals, but Town held their heads high after two drawn games against Second Division opposition.

Huddersfield's league campaign began at Chesterfield, joint favourites for the Third Division championship, on Saturday, 16th August with a 2-1 defeat. The Town team was:

Rankin; Brown, Robinson, Stanton, Sutton, Hanvey, Laverick, Kindon, Purdie, Robins, Cowling, sub Kennedy.

Huddersfield Town FC 1980/81 From left to right, back row: K Hanvey, MA Lillis, P Fletcher, T Austin, RH Taylor, R Picton, AG Rankin, DW Sutton, M Brown, SM Kindon, P Valentine.

Front row: P Wilson, B Stanton, DI Burke, MFM Kennedy, JJ Haselden (Coach), MJ Buxton (Manager), MG Laverick, BC Purdie, D Cowling, FJ Robinson.

Courtesy of Huddersfield Town FC

Chesterfield scored from the penalty spot after 16 minutes and their lead lasted until 20 minutes to go when Kindon put Town back on level terms with a headed goal. But, their delight lasted less than a minute, as they found themselves a goal behind again when a deflected shot eluded Andy.

After three substitute appearances, new signing Mark Kennedy started a game for the first time against Carlisle United at Leeds Road on Tuesday, 19th August. Carlisle took the lead in less than three minutes when centre-half Keith Houghton diverted the ball into his own net. Town drew level just before half-time with a goal from Robinson and then had a number of chances to win the game in the second half. Andy had little to do after the interval, but was called on to make an excellent save to deny centre-forward Bannon and prevent an undeserved win for Carlisle.

Three days later, Huddersfield drew 1-1 again at Leeds Road, this time against Alan Ball's Blackpool. They should have won after taking the lead within three minutes. However, they lost their cutting edge when Steve Kindon was carried off in the 17th minute with a depressed fracture of the cheekbone.

Stanton, who had featured in 44 consecutive games for Huddersfield, was dropped for the first time for the away game against Rotherham United on Saturday, 30th August; his replacement was 21 year old Bobby Davison. Andy was named as "Man of the Match" in the goalless draw that saw Town gain their third point of the season. "*The roar that rattled the Millmoor rafters on Saturday was reserved exclusively for Andy Rankin. In one spell-binding moment, the 36-year-old goalkeeper plunged to his left to beat away the penalty that threatened further injustice on a Town side beset by injuries and ill-fortune.*" Afterwards, manager Mick Buxton described Andy as "*one of the best penalty savers in football*".

Andy's heroics did not end with the 73rd minute penalty. Soon afterwards, centre-forward Ronnie Moore attempted to clip a shot over him, only for Andy to somehow get a hand in the way. Later, Andy said, "*I went down a shade too early, but as he tried to lift the ball over me, I was just able to do enough.*"(5) Andy also gave much of the credit for his penalty save to team-mate Fred Robinson, who told him where Forrest would place the spot kick. One of Rotherham's defenders was dismissed five minutes from time for a foul on Mark Kennedy, who had suffered some rough treatment from the Rotherham defence.

The following Saturday, Huddersfield faced Reading, the Fourth Division Champions of 1979, at Leeds Road. They secured their first win of the season by an impressive margin of 4-1, and Andy gave a safe, confident display of goalkeeping. Purdie, who tore a calf muscle in the first half, had to be replaced by Lillis, who was making his first League appearance for 19 months.

Huddersfield then lost their goal-scoring touch, only managing to score two goals in their next five games. These included two hard-fought home wins by the only goal of the game against Sheffield United and Gillingham; a goalless draw away to Gillingham; and two away defeats by the only goal of the game by Barnsley and Swindon Town, the bottom club in the league.

Against Sheffield United, Town took the lead in the 24th minute through

Stanton. Kindon, who had returned to the team after a month's absence with a fractured cheekbone, almost cost Huddersfield the game in the second half. His error allowed Stewart Houston, the former Manchester United full-back, to crash a 25 yard shot which was goalbound until Andy pulled off a great save, diving at the foot of his post to knock the ball away. He made another important save in the final minute to ensure that Huddersfield got both points.

A disputed goal was at the centre of the 1-0 defeat at Swindon on Saturday, 27th September. Eight minutes after the interval Andy had made a spectacular save to keep the score goalless but, 15 minutes later, his ecstasy turned to agony. As far as he was concerned, he got both hands to a header from Swindon's centre-forward Rowland to deny him a goal, only for the referee to rule that the ball had crossed the line. Despite the protests from the Huddersfield players, the goal stood.

Three days later, Huddersfield recorded their third victory of the season with a 1-0 home win over Gillingham, despite playing with ten men for almost two-thirds of the game after Lillis was sent off. Andy was hardly tested, being more or less a spectator for most of the 90 minutes.

Town followed this up with two further wins, beating Colchester 2-0 at Leeds Road and overcoming Oxford United away by a similar score. Three successive wins in eight days pushed Huddersfield into sixth place, four points behind leaders Plymouth.

Andy was named "Man of the Match" at Oxford following three fabulous saves. The first was in the 21st minute when a 25 yard drive was heading for the top corner of the net until Andy tipped the ball over the bar at full-stretch. Seconds before the interval, he blocked a close range shot with his body and, with just over 20 minutes to the end, he produced a *"third miracle"* to keep a header out.

On Saturday, 11th October, Huddersfield recorded their second away win of the season, beating Exeter 4-1 at St James' Park. The odds were stacked against them, however, for Exeter were unbeaten at home since February and had beaten Huddersfield in their previous four meetings. This time, it was Steve Kindon who was "Man of the Match", scoring only the second hat-trick of his career. His first was ten years earlier for Burnley against Nottingham Forest.

During the following week, 29 year old goalkeeper Alan Starling left the club by mutual agreement. He had not played for the first team since his injury and suspension following Andy's arrival. Starling had made 112 Football League appearances for Huddersfield, having joined them from Northampton during the 1976-77 season.

On Saturday, 18th October, Huddersfield beat Plymouth 2-0 at Leeds Road to leapfrog over them into second place on goal difference. A second championship in successive seasons was beginning to look a possibility.

Three days later, Andy was named "Man of the Match" in the goalless draw at home to Burnley. The match report headline read "*Superb Rankin reflexes won a point for Toon*" and it went on:

"*For once it was a goalkeeper and not goals that captivated a huge Leeds Road crowd last night. All 15,741 fans – the highest of this Third Division season by far – marvelled at the gravity-defying heroics of Town's Andy Rankin. As Mike Buxton's men have swept from one victory to another in the last three weeks Rankin has, for much of the time, been no more than a penalty area observer. Last night Burnley changed all that…. and how. Twice in the second half the Lancashire invaders looked to have shattered the all-consuming deadlock only for the 36-year-old veteran to respond in the most spectacular style. First, in the 55th minute, Rankin stretched elastically to claw a header from inside his right-hand post, then twelve minutes later twisted in the opposite direction to keep out another. Burnley's boss, Brian Miller, was only stating the obvious when he said, "The goalkeeper had an excellent game."* "

Andy's own manager said light-heartedly, "*It's about time he had something to do,*" adding, "*Andy is a good goalkeeper and a great lad. He really earned his corn tonight.*"(6)

On Saturday, 25th October, Huddersfield were beaten for the first time in seven games at Newport County by three goals to two. Newport were two goals up within the first eight minutes, but Steve Kindon scored from the penalty spot in the first half and then again 13 minutes after the interval to draw his side level. Just when it seemed that Huddersfield would get a draw, Newport scored again. Andy was not at fault for any of the goals.

Huddersfield defeated Chester 2-0 in midweek at Sealand Road, but then lost at home the following Saturday for the first time in eleven months - Charlton scoring the only goal of the game with 18 minutes to go. Andy, who was the hero against Burnley a week earlier, was at fault for the goal. He was caught in two minds when a cross came into the penalty area and he allowed Walker to steal in and prod the ball into the net. He had little to do beforehand and Huddersfield had created enough chances to at least have gained a point. The win moved Charlton to the top of the table.

Three days later, Huddersfield were back on the winning trail with a 2-0 victory over Oxford United, recording their first double of the season but, then, suffered a 2-1 defeat away to Millwall the following Saturday. Millwall took the lead with a header which struck Mick Kennedy and was deflected wide of Andy's despairing reach. Huddersfield equalised with about ten minutes left, only for Millwall to get the winner when Andy blocked a close range shot, only to see the loose ball fall to an opponent, who promptly smashed it into the net.

On Tuesday, 11th November, Huddersfield managed a 1-1 draw away to Carlisle, in which Andy was by far the busier of the two keepers. The following Saturday, they then beat Chesterfield 2-0 at Leeds Road. Chesterfield mustered only two attempts at goal, which Andy dealt with splendidly. After 31 minutes, he sprawled acrobatically to his right to hold a low drive from Bonnyman, and then, on the stroke of half-time, he denied full-back Colin Tartt, whose 25 yard drive seemed destined for the back of the net. Steve Kindon scored his 100th Football League goal to put Huddersfield ahead after only four minutes.

Huddersfield faced Northwich Victoria from the Alliance Premier League in the first round of the FA Cup on Saturday, 22nd November. They were just four minutes away from the second round for the first time in five years when a Northwich player, lying in the muddy goalmouth, somehow managed to divert a cross past Andy.

In the replay at Leeds Road, the Northwich part-timers were no match for Huddersfield, losing 6-0 after being 4-0 down in the first half-hour. Andy was virtually a spectator, his one and only save coming in the 72nd minute.

Despite having the best away record in the Third Division, Brentford slumped to their heaviest defeat on their travels when the lost 3-0 at Leeds Road the following Saturday. Again, Andy had little to do and did not even have to make a save after the interval. The win put Huddersfield in fourth place, five points behind leaders Charlton.

A week later, with eight minutes to go against Fulham at Craven Cottage, Huddersfield looked to be cruising comfortably to their fourth away win. Instead, Gordon Davies, the Welsh international, won an unexpected point for Fulham with a goal for which *"the defence has to take a lot of the blame"*, according to manager, Mike Buxton.

It was back to the FA Cup on Saturday, 13th December, when Huddersfield faced Tranmere Rovers at Prenton Park. Huddersfield were leading 1-0 with 25 minutes of the game left when Tranmere's player-manager, Bryan Hamilton, formerly of Ipswich and Everton, struck a 20 yard shot towards Andy's goal. *"The shot was struck with such velocity that it should have screamed into the roof of the net. The save – surely scorching the fingertips of Andy Rankin's left hand – was equally spell-binding. They came together in a 64th minute flashpoint that ultimately settled Saturday's FA Cup tie at Prenton Park....".* (7) Huddersfield then went on to score two further goals, both by Robins, to secure a home tie against Second Division Shrewsbury Town.

Later that week, Mansfield striker, Terry Austin, signed for Huddersfield for £120,000, a club record. The previous record - Ian Greaves paid Manchester United £66,666 for Alan Gowling in June 1972 – had stood for more than eight years.

Following the Cup victory, Huddersfield then had a run of three games undefeated. The first was a goalless draw with Portsmouth at Leeds Road, a match they should have won easily, but the forwards failed to convert their chances. They were then held to another draw on Boxing Day, 2-2 this time away to Walsall. Terry Austin scored both Huddersfield's goals on his debut and looked to have given his new team a victory but his former club equalised with virtually the last kick of the match. Huddersfield were a goal down at the interval and could have been in trouble seconds after the restart. *"They were saved by Andy Rankin's eternal athleticism and the escape inspired them to their finest football of the afternoon."*(8) The following day, they signed off the old year in tremendous style against bottom club Hull at home, scoring five goals without reply.

Huddersfield's first game of the New Year was against Shrewsbury in the third round of the FA Cup. It certainly was not a "Happy New Year" for Andy – his team lost 3-0, each of the goals against a different goalkeeper. Andy was carried off injured in the 38th minute, when his side were already a goal down. Andy and Shrewsbury's Chic Bates collided as they went for a cross and he was carried to the dressing room, clearly concussed with his left eye closed and swollen. Kindon took over in goal. Shrewsbury scored their second two minutes after the interval, whilst manager Mike Buxton was still with Andy in the dressing room. He re-appeared on the touchline after Andy had been taken to hospital and signalled yet another change of goalkeeper with Lillis replacing Kindon. Shrewsbury completed the scoring 12 minutes from time.

Andy suffered a fractured skull and was expected to be out for three weeks, a surprisingly short time for such an injury. However, according to the Daily Examiner on Tuesday, 6th January, the crack was "*a clean one with no displacement or movement of bone and Rankin hasn't had to undergo an operation.*"

Andy had had a run of 51 league matches before his injury, including all 27 Third Division games that season in which he had kept a clean sheet on no fewer than 14 occasions. In view of his injury and Starling's departure, Huddersfield signed 25-year-old goalkeeper Nick Freeman on a month's loan from Birmingham City. Mike Buxton had coached Freeman at Southend, from where he had joined Birmingham in the summer of 1978 for £85,000. Freeman made 29 appearances for Birmingham in the First Division in the 1978-79 season when they were relegated, but played only three times for them the following season. He had also spent some time at Walsall on loan.

Andy played his first game a month after his injury when he helped beat Preston North End's Reserves 4-0, a match in which he was not called upon to perform any heroics.

Freeman's loan was extended to three months whilst Andy continued to play in the Reserves. On Saturday, 14th February, he produced three excellent saves in the first 10 minutes to enable Huddersfield Reserves to hang on for a goalless draw against Liverpool Reserves at Leeds Road. Later, manager Mike Buxton said, "*I was pleased to hear that Andy played so well. It must have been a great boost for* him…*it certainly was for me. He was playing against players of First Division stan-dard – Fairclough, Heighway, Kennedy, Cohen and the rest, some of whom are inter-nationals. As far as his head injury is concerned, he's feeling better every day."*(9)

At the end of his loan period, Freeman was told by Jim Smith, the Birming-ham manager, to report to St Andrews on Monday, 30th March. His final match before returning was a goalless draw with Chester at Leeds Road. He had played in 11 league games for Town, conceding only nine goals.

Buxton was sorry to lose Freeman, telling the local press, *"I have a lot of confi-dence in Andy. He's done a great job for this club and will continue to do so. But, I'm the type of fellow who likes to keep things stable,* " before adding, *"The pleasing thing about it is that when Andy played last week against Bolton for the reserves he did well and he himself felt happy for the first time with his performance. He's convinced in his own mind that at last he's back on song and he's right. That's what counts."*(10)

Andy returned to the first team after three months absence for the top-of-the-table clash with Charlton Athletic at the Valley on Saturday, 4th April. Charl-ton broke the deadlock in the 18th minute when their defender Lawrie Madden headed in a corner kick for his first goal of the season. Fifteen minutes after the interval, however, Huddersfield drew level when Kennedy touched a free-kick 30 yards from goal into the path of Brown, who smashed the ball into the net. Three minutes later, Kennedy hurled a long throw into Charlton's penalty area. Sutton flicked the ball on to Kindon, who volleyed the ball home, giving the goalkeeper no chance. Two fine saves by Andy in the final 15 minutes helped Town to hold on for a welcome 2-1 victory.

After the match, manager Mick Buxton said, *"What Andy proved today is that he's a very good goalkeeper and will be playing top level football for a long time."* In his match report for the Daily Examiner, Paul Clark wrote: *"Rankin…returned to the pressure and demands of a Third Division promotion campaign as though he'd never been away. …could not have come back into more of a pressure cooker occa-sion than this one but his vital saves at the finish were match winners."*(11)

However, on Monday, 6th April, Freeman returned to Leeds Road on loan from Birmingham for the remainder of the season. Although Andy had clearly demonstrated against Charlton that he was back to the form he had shown before his injury, manager Buxton selected Freeman for the home game with Exeter City the following evening, which Town won easily by five goals to nil. They were in fourth position in the league, three points behind Charlton, the team immediately above them in a guaranteed promotion spot.

Huddersfield then lost their next three games, including one against bottom club Hull City, and drew the fourth. Promotion was still a possibility as Charlton had had an identical run of poor results, still leaving them just three points above Huddersfield.

In the end, Charlton did not slip up and Huddersfield finished fourth just three points behind Charlton and Barnsley and five behind champions Rotherham. They were left to rue that sequence of three defeats and a draw in the final run in to the end of the season.

At the end of the season, Huddersfield released six players. Topping, 30, was the only one to have featured in Town's promotion challenge, making seven league and one FA Cup appearances. Freeman returned to Birmingham City. Buxton said that he would not be signing him, as *there were too many problems (in negotiations with Birmingham)*.

1981-82 Season

There were two new signings during the close season – youngsters David Burke and Phil Wilson, both from Bolton Wanderers. Between them, they had made 120 appearances in the First and Second Divisions.

In the three pre-season friendlies, Andy and Richard Taylor shared the goalkeeping duties, both appearing for 45 minutes in each game.

The first league fixture was at home against Exeter City on Saturday, 29th August. Andy was preferred in goal to Taylor and the team was:

Rankin; Brown, Burke, Stanton, Sutton, Hanvey, Lillis, Kennedy, Fletcher, Kindon, Cowling.

Town had achieved the double over Exeter the previous season with 5-0 and 4-1 victories. If the team had been expecting another easy win, they were soon shocked when Exeter went ahead in the first half. Two minutes after the interval, Kindon equalised with a penalty, but Town were unable to break the deadlock and had to be satisfied with a 1-1 draw.

The following Tuesday evening, Huddersfield faced Rochdale from the Fourth Division at Leeds Road in the first leg of the opening round of the League Cup. Town were 3-0 up at half-time but allowed Rochdale to pull a goal back after the interval. Manager Buxton was very unhappy with his team's display in the second half, particularly with the performance of his two central defenders.

Huddersfield lost their first away league game at Oxford United on Saturday, 5th September by a goal to nil. Andy's penalty save in the second half was not enough to win a point for his side.

Their next league meeting was at home to Third Division newcomers Wimbledon the following Saturday. Huddersfield found themselves behind in the 56th minute, but replied with a goal of their own nine minutes later. They then had a number of opportunities to win the game, but three fine saves by Beasant and two goal-line clearances denied them a victory.

On Tuesday, 9th September, Town were at Rochdale for the second leg of their League Cup tie. After ten minutes, Rochdale reduced Town's aggregate score to 3-2 but Fletcher soon restored the two-goal lead. Town then scored three further goals after the interval, but a goal from Rochdale ten minutes from time gave the scoreline a greater degree of respectability. Andy did not have a great deal to do, but was called on to make two superb saves in the second half. After their 7-3 aggregate win, Town were drawn out of the hat with First Division Brighton for the next round.

Huddersfield were at Turf Moor on the Saturday for a league fixture against Burnley. Andy produced several excellent saves to keep a clean sheet and gain another point for his side. According to Paul Clark of the Daily Examiner, *"Rankin's eternal athleticism kept Town alive with critical saves in 14th minute and again in the 64th. First he plunged smartly to his right to parry a fierce shot from Hamilton, which was the first of many problems the big striker created, then he managed to turn a low shot from Tommy Cassidy on to his left hand post."*(12)

Having drawn three and lost one of their first four games, Town had three points from a possible 12 – the system of three points for a win and one for a draw had been introduced that very season – and were lying fourth from bottom, seven points adrift of leaders Swindon Town. Huddersfield had been expected to be competing at the top of the table after just missing out on promotion the season before. Although they had suffered injuries to several key players, they were just not playing well enough.

Their next match, away to Preston North End on Tuesday, 22nd September, was yet another draw. Preston took the lead after 10 minutes with a 20 yard drive by centre-forward Bruce but Huddersfield were back on equal terms on the half-hour mark with a goal from Kennedy. Preston were on top for almost the whole of the second half, peppering Andy's goal with shots from every angle. However, he *"showed how unflappable he is and his handling and instincts were reassuringly safe in keeping Preston at bay."*(13)

Finally, the following Saturday, Town achieved that all important first league win at home to Southend United. Their first goal came on the half-hour when Kindon scored with a penalty kick. Robins made it 2-0 on the stroke of half-time, only for Swindon to pull a goal back seconds later. Twenty minutes from the end, Huddersfield found themselves pegged back to level terms when Andy was beaten by a shot that deflected off Keith Hanvey. With nine minutes to go, Town were awarded a second penalty. This time Kennedy stepped up to beat goalkeeper Causton.

Three days later, Town were deservedly beaten 2-1 at home by Chester, who had only managed to score one goal in their previous six games. Chester forced five corners in the first ten minutes, but it was Town who unexpectedly took the lead in the 22nd minute when Robins scored his 100th league goal. Andy was the busier of the two keepers and an equaliser seemed inevitable. It came in the 33rd minute. Robins hit the post for Huddersfield in the second half, but it was Chester who scored the decisive goal with quarter of an hour to go. Manager Buxton said that it was one of the worst performances he had witnessed in almost three years at the club.

Reading, joint leaders of the Division were expected to defeat Town at Elm Park on Saturday, 3rd October. However, the joint leaders found themselves 2-0 down at the interval – first, Kindon scored with a penalty kick and, soon afterwards, a Reading defender headed a Brown cross beyond his own keeper. Reading did manage to pull a goal back in the 62nd minute when Andy was beaten from ten yards, but it was not enough to prevent Town from recording their first away win of the season.

On Tuesday evening of the following week, almost 10,000 supporters, the biggest crowd of the season at Leeds Road, witnessed one of Huddersfield's greatest nights in the League Cup when they overcame First Division Brighton by a goal to nil. Austin scored the decisive goal, his first of the season, with just over 15 minutes to go to the final whistle. Brighton never looked capable of mounting a comeback and Town could easily have won by five or six clear goals. Andy was a spectator for much of the game and only had one save to make the entire evening.

On the Saturday, Town notched their second successive league victory with a win by the only goal of the game over Fulham at Leeds Road. It was a dour game, with all the excitement in the first five minutes of each half. Robins scored Town's goal after only four minutes and, then, three minutes after the interval Kindon hit the bar with his penalty kick. There was little else of note for the other 80 minutes; Huddersfield just could not match Tuesday's performance against Brighton.

Huddersfield were unable to maintain their winning run the next Saturday when they lost 3-2 to Gillingham at Priestfield. All Gillingham's goals were scored in the first 20 minutes, leaving Town with an almost impossible task to secure at least one point. In the 70 minutes following Gillingham's third goal, they managed only one shot at Andy. It was all Huddersfield. An own goal in the 29th minute reduced the leeway to 3-1; a second with just over 20 minutes to go to the final whistle gave them hope. But Town just could not get the ball into the net again.

Three days later, Huddersfield managed their third win of the season, defeating Carlisle United 2-1 at Leeds Road. They went ahead in the 17th minute when Burke scored his first goal since his move from Bolton. A minute later, Carlisle were almost on level terms. Peter Beardsley's well-struck, swerving shot was superbly touched over for a corner by Andy. But Carlisle were not to be denied. Soon afterwards, "Pop" Robson was in the right place to place a low header beyond Andy's reach. Cowling put Town ahead again just before the half-time whistle and, after the interval, Andy produced another superb save from Beardsley to deny Carlisle a second equaliser.

As Huddersfield had just missed out on promotion the previous season, they were expected to be fighting for a place at the top of the table. However, after eleven games, they were only 12th in the league. One of the reasons they had failed to make an impact was their long injury list. Only five players, including Andy, were ever-present after 11 games.

Town faced Bristol Rovers at Eastville on Saturday, 24th October, hopeful of a win as Rovers had sacked their popular manager, Terry Cooper, only four days earlier, replacing him with Bobby Gould. There were demonstrations by the Bristol fans in support of Cooper before, during and after the game. Rovers were one up at half-time having scored as early as the sixth minute when Bernard Purdie's pass back to Andy was short, allowing Rover's Paul Randall to nip in and slip the ball past Andy into the net. Twelve minutes later, Andy produced an excellent diving save to prevent Rovers from going further ahead. However, they were two up three minutes after the break. Andy managed to beat away a tremendous drive from substitute Barratt, who had been allowed to run 40 yards with the ball. Two defenders failed to clear allowing Stephens to smack the ball into the back of the net. In the 66th minute, Huddersfield scored to put themselves back in the game but then conceded a third goal twelve minutes later. Kennedy made the score more respectable in injury time, when he followed up his penalty kick, which had been saved by the Bristol keeper, to ram the rebound into the net.

Town's next match was the much-awaited return leg with Brighton on Tuesday, 27th October. Huddersfield outplayed Brighton for the second time in three weeks and, with their 1-0 advantage from the first leg, it looked as if they would advance to the third round with the score at 0-0 with five minutes to go. But, the tie was turned on its head in those last five minutes. Brighton scored when Andy was beaten inside his left- hand post. Then, in injury time, centre-forward Mike Robinson chased a long ball from Jimmy Case. Andy managed to block his fierce shot, but the rebound fell for Tony Grealish, who scored his first goal for Brighton. It was an undeserved Brighton victory for Town should have gone in at half-time four or five goals in front. Brighton were knocked out in the next round by Barnsley.

Huddersfield played their eighth fixture of the month the following Saturday, facing Millwall at Leeds Road. Despite going ahead on the hour, they found themselves on level terms a minute later and then Milwall snatched the winner six minutes from the end.

Later that week, it was announced that Steve Kindon, who had been injured since the Gillingham game, needed a cartilage operation and would be out of action for the remainder of the year.

Andy was replaced for the game away to Chesterfield on Tuesday, 3rd November by 24 year-old Richard Taylor. Chesterfield won 1-0 with a penalty kick. Taylor kept his place for the next three months until he received an injury in training.

Andy was recalled to face Preston North End at Leeds Road on Tuesday, 9th February 1982. Town had suffered three successive defeats and only 6,674 spectators – the lowest crowd of the season – turned up to watch the game. Andy found himself picking the ball out of the net inside two minutes. He could not hold on to a free-kick from outside the area and Preston's Elliott stabbed the ball into the net. Within fifteen minutes, the crowd was jumping with joy as two goals from Fletcher saw Town take the lead. However, Preston scored twice in the second half to take the three points. Any faint chance of promotion was now well and truly gone.

There was an even smaller crowd – just over 6,000 - for the home fixture with Reading on the Saturday. The supporters went home much happier this time having seen Town score six goals with only one in reply. Reading almost scored after Town's first goal: "*Pat Earles almost equalised and would have done but for a marvellous reflex save from veteran Andy Rankin.*"(14)

Andy played in the 1-1 draw away to Walsall on Tuesday, 16th February, but was replaced by a fit again Taylor for the game against Chester at Sealand Road the following Saturday.

Two weeks later, Taylor was again injured during training. Andy stepped in to replace him for the home game against Gillingham on Saturday, 6th March. Huddersfield won 2-0, with Andy a virtual spectator – he was only called into action three times and one of those was to deal with a strongly hit pass back.

Carlisle needed a win against Town the following Tuesday evening to move to the top of the league. However, the match ended 2-2. Andy was called on to make a fine save in the first minute, diving to hold the ball at the foot of the upright. Town went ahead through Robins in the 27th minute. Ten minutes later, Staniforth equalised and then scored a second on the hour to give Carlisle the lead. Lillis equalised just before the final whistle.

Andy made his final appearance for the first team in the 2-0 defeat away to Bristol Rovers on Saturday, 13th March. Andy was the only fit keeper available as Richard Taylor and Robert Picton were both injured; Picton had broken his leg ten months earlier. Clearly, the club would face a real crisis if anything happened to Andy. Buxton had failed in his attempt to sign Sunderland keeper Barry Siddall on loan, but he did manage to bring in 20 year old Brian Cox from Sheffield Wednesday in a loan deal following the Bristol defeat.

Cox went straight into the first team on the Saturday and played in the final 14 games of the season. He signed on a permanent basis in the close season and went on to make more than 200 league appearances for the club, before moving to Mansfield Town and then Hartlepool United, finishing his career with Buxton.

Andy appeared for the reserves until the end of the season and was released on a free transfer by the club along with goalkeeper Robert Picton, Fred Robinson, Bernard Purdie and Ian Thompson. Ian Robins and goalkeeper Richard Taylor retired, while Steve Kindon also retired but remained with the club in a public relations role.

Manager Buxton said, "*It's sad losing players like Andy and Bernard, both tremendous professionals, but they are getting on a bit.*"(15)

Life after Football

Following his playing career, Andy did try his hand at coaching at Huddersfield for a while but, in an interview some years later, he said, "*…coaching is an art and I simply don't have it – I was just no good at it unfortunately so I knocked it on the head.*" When he finished playing, he was earning £125 a week - not big money but certainly a living wage, according to him in that same interview. So, like many players of that era, Andy found it necessary to find employment outside football. He eventually joined a local printing company, initially as a packer and later as a fork-lift driver in the warehouse, and remained there for 18 years, finally retiring in 2003.

During his football career, he made a total of 513 League, Cup and European appearances for his three clubs. As Howard Kendall, a former Everton colleague and Everton's most successful manager, said of Andy, *"No goalkeeper plays as many games in their career as he did without being a good keeper."*

References:

1. Huddersfield Daily Examiner, 3rd December 1979

2. Huddersfield Daily Examiner, 27th December 1979

3. Huddersfield Daily Examiner, 31st December 1979

4. Huddersfield Daily Examiner, 3rd January 1980

5. Huddersfield Daily Examiner, 1st September 1980

6. Huddersfield Daily Examiner, 22nd October 1980

7. Huddersfield Daily Examiner, 15th December 1980

8. Huddersfield Daily Examiner, 27th December 1980

9. Huddersfield Daily Examiner, 16th February 1981

10. Huddersfield Daily Examiner, 30th March 1981

11. Huddersfield Daily Examiner, 6th April 1981

12. Huddersfield Daily Examiner, 21st September 1981

13. Huddersfield Daily Examiner, 23rd September 1981

14. Huddersfield Daily Examiner, 15th February 1982

15. Huddersfield Daily Examiner, 18th May 1982

11

Gavin Fraser (1979-00)

Introduction

Gavin Fraser was born in Liverpool on 23rd February 1972, the third of four children. His mother, Maureen, was Bruce Rankin's granddaughter. Gavin moved to Formby in October 1978 with his family and attended Woodlands Primary School. From 11 years of age, he was educated at Merchant Taylor's School for Boys in Crosby and then completed his education at the University of Humberside in Hull and Liverpool John Moores University.

Primary School years (1979-83)

Gavin first played organised sport in 1979, when he joined the Formby Junior Sports League, affectionately known locally as Rourke's League. A local man, Jim Rourke, had set up the league some 25 years earlier, and each season it gave hundreds of local boys the opportunity to play football, regardless of their level of skill and ability. Each boy was allocated to a team in his age group, but if that team proved to be too good for all of the others, then Jim would "transfer" boys from the successful teams to provide more evenly matched games. The fathers of some of the boys participating would act as referees. Jim was awarded an MBE for his work with the local youth and his son, Frank, has now taken over his father's role.

At first, Gavin played in goal, having been encouraged to play there by his father, who had been a goalkeeper in school, church and works teams. Gavin proved to be an excellent keeper, having a safe pair of hands and quickly coming off his line and fearlessly going down at opponents' feet. But, he also enjoyed being an outfield player when the occasion arose, and was a strong runner with the ball at his feet.

Gavin was an all-round sportsman as a youngster. He represented Woodlands Primary School at football, athletics, cricket and rugby. He played in goal for the football team. It had its most successful year ever in 1982-83, Gavin's final year at the school, winning the Formby Schools League, Cup and 5-a-side competitions and the Merseyside Schools' 5-a-side Cup and reaching the quarter-finals of Merseyside Schools' Echo Cup and the Merseyside Schools' 7-a-side competition.

Gavin was selected to play in midfield for the Formby Primary Schools representative team for the 1982-83 season. The team played in a league with teams from other local Primary School Associations including Bootle, Maghull, Crosby, Kirkby, Southport, South Wirral, St Helens and Warrington. According to the Formby Times, the team's record in 1982-83 *"surpassed any other since Formby joined the competition".*

Formby Primary Schools football squad (December 1982): Left to right, back row: Jonathon Owen, Jamie Robinson, Gavin Fraser, Julian Culshaw, Neil Delaney, Tommy Nickson, David Barrowclough, Robert Shalliker. Front row: Alex Russell, Martin Palmer, Richard Mortimer, Richard Scanlon, Chris Kirkham, Simon Richards, Jason Given. Courtesy of Trinity Mirror

Gavin represented Woodlands in the school's annual rugby game against Holm-wood, a local public school. Despite his footballing successes, Gavin's teacher, Mr Morris, told Gavin's father that Gavin *"would be a much better rugby player than a footballer"*.

Senior School years (1983-90)

1983-84 Season

In September 1983, Gavin moved to Merchant Taylors' Boys School in Crosby. As football was not played at the school, he now had to take up rugby, but continued to show all-round sporting ability, representing the school at cricket and athletics as well as rugby.

It took Gavin a little time to break into the 1st Year rugby team as the boys who had played for Merchant's Preparatory School team were selected in the first instance. However, once Gavin broke into the team he was selected regularly, play-ing mainly on the wing or at full-back and occasionally at fly-half and centre.

Gavin continued to play football at weekends whenever his rugby commit-ments permitted. By now, he had joined Redgate Rovers, another Formby team, and was captain of the Under-12 team, playing in midfield. He featured in 21 of the 22 League games and in the five Cup games. His team won the Ball and Per-cival Craven Minor League, losing only the last game of the season, when the League title had already been secured. Redgate also reached the final of the Swan Athletic Cup at Haig Avenue, Southport FC's ground, losing in a tightly contested game to Town Green by two goals to one.

1984-85 Season

Merchant Taylor's Under-13 rugby team played 11 games and Gavin featured in every one, playing on the wing and at centre. He was the leading try scorer among the backs with 11 tries. Merchant's lost only one game. Gavin was also a member of the 7-a-side team, which won the Birkenhead tournament.

Gavin was again captain of the Redgate Under-13 football team, but had to play in goal as the previous season's goalkeeper, Julian Culshaw, had moved up an age group to the Under 14s. That year, the team was playing in the Bootle and Litherland League, which was much tougher than the Craven Minor League. The team finished mid-table in the League but, as the Formby Times reported, the side *"wrote a new page in the club's history on Sunday lifting silverware from the Bootle and Litherland League for the first time. The under-13s won a nerve racking KO Cup Final against Spooner on penalties."*

The game had finished two goals apiece after normal time. It had been end-to-end football with Gavin making some excellent saves. One save in the last minute was brilliant, when he threw himself to divert a shot heading for the top corner over the bar to thwart Spooner. As extra time failed to separate the teams, *"a penalty shoot out came into operation with Jamie Robinson, Richard Scanlon, Steven Younger and James Clark all successful for Redgate. Gavin Fraser then saved a penalty and watched another balloon over the crossbar to give the trophy to the Formby side."*

The Redgate Rovers first team played in the Bootle and Litherland League on Sunday mornings, whilst the second team played in the Craven Minor League on Saturdays. When his school rugby commitments permitted, Gavin also played for the second team. Indeed, he managed to take part in 15 league and cup games, playing on the left side of midfield. The team finished in mid-table in the League and reached the final of the Catherine Oldfield Cup, which was played at Southport FC's ground, Haig Avenue. Although Redgate were heavily beaten by Dynamo Burscough, the League Champions, it was still an enjoyable day for the players.

Gavin was selected to play left midfield for the Craven Minor League representative side in the Lancashire FA Inter League Cup and was appointed captain. Unfortunately, the team lost 4-2 to Rainhill in the first round, despite leading twice.

1985-86 Season

Gavin played 12 times for the Under-14 school rugby side, missing two games through injury. He scored five tries, the best of which was in the first game against Rossall away when he stooped down low to take an awkward pass then ran some 30 yards to score.

That season, Gavin started to play for Waterloo RUFC at Under-14 level. The highlight of his first season was beating Littleborough 32-0 in the Lancashire Under-14 Cup Final. He played at fly-half, scoring a try. A number of people at the game, including the team manager, said that Gavin was "*man of the match*".

Gavin was captain of the Redgate Rovers Under-14 football team in the Craven Minor League. Unfortunately, the previous season's successful team broke up, which meant that the team struggled, finishing 6th in the League and being beaten in the first round and in the semi-final of the two Cup competitions.

However, Gavin achieved individual success when he was selected to play for the Craven Minor League representative team in the Liverpool FA and Lancashire FA Cup competitions and was again appointed captain. The team was knocked out in the first round of the Liverpool competition by Skelmersdale, but gained their revenge when they beat them 4-2 in the Lancashire Cup. The Craven Minor team went on to reach the final at Haig Avenue, only to be beaten 2-1 by Blackpool. Nevertheless, it was a great achievement for Gavin to play in Lancashire Cup Finals at rugby and football in the same season.

1986-87 Season

Gavin only played five of the 14 games for the school rugby team, receiving two injuries that kept him out for a total of 10 weeks. In October, he was knocked unconscious in a Sevens tournament at Liverpool St Helens ground and was detained overnight in hospital for observation. The rules at that time meant that he could not play for eight weeks. No sooner had he returned to the team when he damaged shoulder ligaments and missed another two weeks. He still scored six tries in those five games.

He was selected to play at full-back for North Merseyside Schools against Manchester Schools, but missed the game because of injury.

His injuries also restricted Gavin to eight appearances for Waterloo Under 15s, but he managed to score seven tries. Two of his games were in the semi-final and final of the Lancashire Under-15 Cup when he gave two excellent performances. In the semi-final, he scored two tries and two conversions in the defeat of Preston Grasshoppers by 26pts to 4 and, in the 28-0 defeat of Orrell in the Final, he scored a glorious drop goal from a considerable distance, three conversions and a penalty.

He had obviously made an impression with his tackling, strong running and try scoring as he was selected to play for Lancashire Clubs, but again injury prevented him from making an appearance.

The Redgate Rovers football team folded up that season. Having played 119 League and Cup games for Redgate, a number of them as goalkeeper, and scoring 43 goals, Gavin joined the Formby Junior Sports Club. He played 19 games, 13 in the Craven Minor Under-15 League and Cups on Saturday mornings and six in the Maghull and District League and Cups on Sunday mornings. About half of his appearances were in goal, the remainder in midfield. He still managed to score six goals.

Ball & Percival Craven Minor League Under-14
Representative Squad 1985/86
Back row (left to right): Andrew Holmes, Richard Mortimer, David McGuire,
Philip Nimmo, Matthew Chorley, Gareth Farrington, Jason Bridge,
James Clark, Drew Collard
Front row (left to right): Gary Hughes, Justin Hunter, Stephen Brady, Gavin Fraser
(Captain) Martin Palmer, Christopher Kirkham, Steven Younger.

The season proved to be far more successful than Gavin could have imagined. The team won the Maghull and District League and a Cup competition and was runners-up in the Craven Minor League and two Cups. In the programme for one of the Cup-Finals, Gavin's pen picture described him as *"Centre midfield. Strong in the air and on the ground. Has a long throw-in."*

1987-88 Season

This season saw Gavin's first real recognition for his undoubted ability at rugby when he was selected to play at full-back for the Lancashire Schools Under-16 side. In all of the County games, the ground was heavy, which prevented Gavin from demonstrating his strong running, but he nevertheless gave a competent display throughout the series of seven games, including two friendlies. In the North of England series of games, Lancashire were undefeated, beating Cumbria, Northumberland, Cheshire and Durham and drawing with Yorkshire.

Gavin managed nine games for the school's Under-16 side, two for the Second XV, and he was a reserve for the first team on one occasion. Because of his versatility, he played in three different positions - wing, fly-half and full-back, and he scored eleven tries.

At Club level, Gavin played eight times for the Waterloo Under-16 team and three games for the Colts, scoring five tries. Again, he played in three different positions - full-back, fly-half and centre.

He played in the Lancashire Under-16 Cup Final in which Waterloo beat Littleborough by 7 points to 6, with Gavin giving an excellent display at full-back. He was also a member of the Waterloo Sevens team that won two competitions, at Mold and Newton-le-Willows.

Another highlight of Gavin's season was his selection for Lancashire Clubs. However, he only managed to play in two games because of his selection for Lancashire Schools, which took precedence. His first game was against Northumberland Schools at Vale of Lune on 15th November 1987, when he scored a try in the dying seconds to tie the game at 18 points each. He also played in the Lancashire Clubs' final game of the season on 29th April 1988 against North Midlands under floodlights. Lancashire won and Gavin scored a brilliant try, running the full length of the pitch from his own 22. Both his games were at full-back.

Being chosen as Waterloo's "Player of the Year" brought a wonderful end to a great season for Gavin.

With Gavin's increasing commitment to rugby, he no longer had the time to continue with football.

Gavin in his Lancashire Schools Under-16 strip. Courtesy of Trinity Mirror

1988-89 Season

Mike Slemen, former England and British Lions winger, and Gavin's rugby coach at Merchant Taylor's, wrote Gavin a glowing reference for a trial for the Scottish Under-18 squad. He attended Murrayfield for the first trial, only to find that it had been cancelled because of a heavy snowfall; the school would not release him for the second trial, which was midweek. As a consolation, however, he was invited to attend a three-day training session with the Scotland Under-19 and Under-21 squads in the summer of 1989. The coaches included some well-known former Scotland players such as Roy Laidlaw, John Rutherford and Colin Deans.

Merchant Taylors' School First XV 1988-89
Left to right, back row: Nick Scott, Peter Maguire, Paul Coats, Tony Dickson,
Philip Jones, Philip Banks, Stephen McGee, Mark Webster. Middle row: Gavin
Fraser, James Heather, Tim Ryan, David Clift (capt), Gareth Glynne-Jones, Stephen
Trollope, Mike Hanlon. Front row: Graham Stubbs and Richard Harris.

Gavin was a regular for the School 1st XV. The team had one of its best seasons ever, losing only three of the 21 games and winning the Hymers Sevens competition. Gavin missed four of the 21 games through injury, but still managed to score 20 tries, 23 conversions and nine penalties. He shared the kicking duties with Gareth

Glynne-Jones and the captain David Clift. The team's coach Mike Slemen wrote in the school magazine, The Crosbeian, *"Fraser had an exceptional season scoring 20 of the team's 78 tries"*, and, in awarding Gavin his colours, he added, *"He had pace, elusiveness and the willingness to look for work"*.

Because Gavin was in the 1st XV at Merchant Taylors', he did not play for Waterloo, as Mike Slemen did not want his players to turn out on a Sunday after playing for the school team.

1989-90 Season

For Gavin's final year of school rugby, the 1st XV had lost all of its backs with the exception of Gareth Glynne-Jones, the fly-half, and Gavin and the entire pack apart from Paul Coates, the hooker. On a personal level, it proved to be a rather disastrous year for Gavin. He suffered from an ankle injury in the first game of the season, missing almost half of the games and, despite being selected for the Lancashire Schools Under-18 representative team, he was unable to make a single appearance. In March 1990, he eventually had to have an operation on his Achilles tendon to cure tendonitis.

Hull and East Riding RUFC (1990-91)

1990-91 Season

Gavin went to Humberside University in October 1990 to study European Business Studies. Mike Slemen, his rugby coach at school, advised him to go to the Hull and East Riding Rugby Club. However, it turned out that it was no longer the top team in the area and only played in the North Division 7.

Nevertheless, it was quite a good move for him. He was selected at full-back for the first team immediately and the team included two Zimbabwean internationalists, Billy Schultz and David Walters, who had come over to England to acclimatise themselves for the Rugby World Cup in 1991.

Gavin quickly made a good impression at full-back. In the team's first league game against Rowntrees of York on 13th October 1990, which Hull won 32-3, he *"beat two men to score a fine try near the posts"*.(1)

On 10th November, Hull and East Riding played Wilmslow from North West Division 2, some seven leagues above them, in a friendly game away from home. Surprisingly, Hull were leading 12 pts to 4 at the interval and managed to keep their opponents from scoring in the second half. Gavin scored one of Hull's three tries and the match report stated: *"Gavin Fraser was cool under pressure, bravely taking several high balls and markedly improves each game."*(2)

On 24th November, Hull beat the league leaders Hornsea away from home by 11 points to 9. According to the match report, *"Gavin Fraser and Mal Cressey were the pick of the backs."*(3)

The team was top of the league in February of 1991, when Gavin left Hull to study for six months in Bordeaux in France, and was eventually promoted to Division 6 as runners-up.

In France, Gavin played a number of games for the Begles Bordeaux Under-21 team on the wing and at full-back.

Although Gavin was away in France, the Hull and East Riding team selected him for the squad to tour Zimbabwe during Easter 1991. He played in the four games, one of which was against Karoi (Billy Shultz's and David Walter's team). Hull won three games and lost one. Gavin came off injured in two of the games. Some years later, Gavin described his experiences on the tour: *"I was staying with a family on a farm just outside Karoi. I remember them having a swimming pool and, immediately on arrival, I jumped into the pool. The weather was very warm and I ended up staying in the sun too long and spent the next 24 hours in bed with sunstroke. I also got shingles on my shoulder, which meant it was very painful to put a rugby shirt on.*

We were really well looked after and were taken to see Victoria Falls and Lake Kariba. The rugby highlight of the tour was the game against a Zimbabwe Select XV. The pitch was on a plateau on the top of a hill, with a steep drop all around it. As a result, we agreed there was to be no kicking, as we would lose the balls. The game was like a sevens match, with the ball thrown around and was end-to-end. It was boiling hot and we were all exhausted within minutes of the start."

Waterloo RUFC (1991-95)

1991-92 Season

Gavin was back at Humberside University when the rugby season started, but he decided that he would travel home most weekends to play for Waterloo rather than Hull and East Riding. He was captain of the under- 21s, but also played several games for the 2nd and 3rd XVs.

1992-93 Season

Gavin broke into the first XV on 24th October 1992 against Wakefield and kept his place for the remainder of the season. The Liverpool Echo reported: *"Promotion chasing Waterloo take another of their talented youngsters off the assembly line for their Courage League Division Two clash with Wakefield at Blundellsands tomorrow. Man of the moment is the strongly built 20-year-old ex-Merchant Taylors' schoolboy Gavin Fraser, who makes his debut on the wing where his weight and speed is expected to cause problems for the opposition."* (4)

Waterloo beat Wakefield by 22 points to 11, but if Wakefield's place kicker, Rob Lilley their fly-half, had kicked a reasonable percentage of the penalties awarded against Waterloo, then Wakefield might have been out of sight at half-time. That was not to be and Waterloo consolidated their third position in the League. Gavin had a good game on his debut: *"New boy Gavin Fraser, on the left wing, kept his opposite number Jon Sleighthome, subdued and showed he can kick well for advantage, but had little opportunity for anything else."* (5)

Gavin certainly made a name for himself in the next game, against Richmond in London. Waterloo won 16-12, despite having hooker, Paul Hackett, sent off early in the second half, and *"Winger Gavin Fraser, a member of Scotland Under 21 squad, who made his senior debut last week, was the hero of the hour. He lifted Waterloo to 11-9 with his first try and, after Richmond had re-taken the lead with a drop goal, Fraser kicked through in injury-time to score the winning points."* (6)

Early in January, Waterloo found themselves at the top of Division Two when they trounced Bedford 28-8. *"Gavin Fraser raced over for the second try"* and almost scored a second in the closing minutes of the game when he and *"Handley*

raced the Bedford fullback for a kick ahead. Both beat him, Handley claiming the
final try, Grayson converting."(7)

Gavin in action for Waterloo against Sale in November 1993.
Courtesy of Trinity Mirror

Waterloo, however, were unable to hold on to the top spot. Going into the final
League game of the season, they had to win at home against Blackheath by a land-
slide and hope that Newcastle Gosforth would lose at Moseley. Newcastle did lose,
but only by three points, while Waterloo could not overcome the 69 points deficit,
which separated them and Newcastle. Waterloo beat Blackheath by 27-6, con-
signing them to relegation, and *"the second half belonged to Waterloo, with winger*
Gavin Fraser always in the picture. He made the running for Peter Buckton to plunge
over and then finished late on with two great match-clinching tries."(8)

Waterloo sign off with dazzling demolition of Blackheath

Two seconds to touchdown . . . winger Gavin Fraser is tackled by Blackheath players before flicking the ball to Peter Buckton (right) to score.   *PICTURE BY MIKE GRIFFITHS*

Courtesy of Trinity Mirror

The disappointment of failing to win promotion was somewhat tempered by a tremendous run in the Pilkington Cup, with victories over Lichfield, Bath and Orrell, before losing controversially to Harlequins at home in the quarter-finals.

Gavin played in all of the games, scoring a try against Lichfield in the first round. In the second round, Waterloo faced Bath, England's champion club side, at Blundellsands on 28th November. When local reporter, George Withy, suggested that it was an awesome task, Gavin replied,

"I'm looking forward to it. It's going to be such an experience. And in any case I think we can win it. Our crowd gets behind us now. I think the biggest obstacle we have to overcome is the actual psychological thing."(9)

Bath, who had won the Cup seven times in the past, had a team full of internationals, including Jonathon Webb, Tony Swift, Jeremy Guscott, Phil de Glanville,

Richard Hill, Gareth Chilcott, Graham Dawe, Jon Hall and Andy Robinson, who later became the England head coach. Despite the Cup game, Bath released Stuart Barnes and Ben Clarke, both current England internationals at that time, to play for the Barbarians that Saturday. Over-confidence, perhaps! The Waterloo team was:

Steve Swindells; Austin Healey, Murray Craig, Nigel Hill, Gavin Fraser; Paul Grayson, Christian Saverimutto; Mark Becket, Paul Hacket, Steve Peters; Nick Allott (captain), Paul White; Jonathon Ashcroft, Stuart Beeley, Peter Buckton.

Mark Reason, Sunday Times reporter, described Waterloo's 9-8 victory before a crowd of 4000: *"Upsets do not come much bigger than this. The Cup-holders, Bath, came to Waterloo with firm resolve and confidence, to them just another step on the well-worn golden path to 1993 glory. Three Grayson penalty goals later, they were unceremoniously dumped out of the Cup by the determined minnows. England's champions were rattled to their back teeth by a magnificent display of tackling from the Second Division side."*(10)

In the next round, on 23rd January 1993, Waterloo faced their local rivals, Orrell, who, like Bath, were a Division One side. Waterloo showed only one change from the Bath game with Nigel Wilkinson replacing Paul White in the second row. Orrell's team was:

N. Heslop; P. Hamer, G. Ainscough, S. Langford, P. Halsall; B. Wellens, D. Morris; M. Hynes, N. Hitchen, D. Southern (capt); R. Kimmins, G. Cusani; D. Clearly, S. Gallagher, N. Ashurst.

Playing with the strong wind behind them in the first half, Waterloo were 5-0 up after 24 minutes, when Austin Healey went over in the right-hand corner from short range. Orrell reduced the arrears to two points with a penalty ten minutes later, before Paul Grayson's penalty in the 35th minute restored Waterloo's five-point lead. There were no further scores in the remaining 45 minutes, with Waterloo emerging 8-3 winners.

Gavin with the Lancashire Cup, which was won by Waterloo when they defeated Preston Grasshoppers by 48 points to nil. Other players from left to right are Christian Saverimutto,
Mike Hayton, Jason Ashcroft and Steve Swindells

Stephen Jones, the Sunday Times' rugby correspondent wrote: "*Waterloo arrived at the quarter-final stage of the Cup by knocking off yet another giant and in one sense, this startling victory was even more of an achievement than their win over Bath in the previous round. They existed on starvation rations throughout the game because Orrell dominated possession completely and … Waterloo must have been in Orrell territory, playing against the driving wind in the second half for all of five seconds.*" Waterloo's defence stood solid for the entire second half despite relentless pressure: "*their back three of Swindells, Healey and Fraser lay deep for the long, downwind Orrell kicks and all three defended magnificently.*"(11)

Next, it was Harlequins in the quarter-final on 27th February, again at Blundellsands. Victory would put Waterloo into the semi-finals for the first time since 1977.

For Waterloo, there were two changes to the team that defeated Orrell – Ian Aitchison came in at fly-half for the injured Paul Grayson, whilst Tony Ireland replaced Ashcroft in the back row. Harlequins fielded a strong side, full of internationals, including the England captain, Will Carling. Their team was:

N. Bray; M. Wedderburn, W. Carling, G. Thompson, E. Davis, P. Challinor, J. Le Roux; J. Leonard, B. Moore, A. Mullins; A. Snow, R. Langhorn; M. Russell, P. Winterbottom (capt), C. Sheasby.

Despite taking an early lead through a Saverimutto try, Waterloo were beaten 21-14 in a game full of controversy and which, according to John Reason writing in the Mail on Sunday, *"almost degenerated into another Battle of Waterloo".*

Waterloo club officials and players accused Harlequins of using illegal studs and foul play, with England hooker, Brian Moore, named as the chief culprit. After the match, Derek Murphy, the Waterloo chairman said, *"Our-full-back, Steve Swindells, is in the neurological ward of Walton Hospital after being elbowed in the face"*; the Waterloo team manager, Jed Poynton, alleged that *"Steve Peters needed nine stitches after being kicked in the nose and Austin Healey's back has been ripped to pieces by the illegal studs"*; while the Waterloo hooker, Paul Hackett, added, *"I asked the referee three times to deal with the problem of Harlequins' illegal studs each time one of the players was hurt. He told me that he would do so and some of their players did change their footwear. But people like Moore, Mullins and Leonard are in the England squad and I want to know if the England hierarchy are condoning England players wearing illegal studs."*(12)

The only success for Waterloo that year was winning the Lancashire Cup. Gavin played in all of the Cup games, including the final.

The highlight of Gavin's season was probably being selected to play on the left wing for Scotland Under-21s against Wales at Myreside in Edinburgh on 19th February 1993. He was in the original squad of 40 players, but had missed the squad training sessions because of injury. As Scotland had lost their first three games, the selectors decided to make sweeping changes and Gavin was called up unexpectedly to play on the left wing in the final game of the home countries series against Wales. The Scotland team was:

Gavin with his younger brother Neil (right) and cousin Robbie Angus after the
Scotland v Wales Under 21 international on 19th February 1993

M. Thomson; K. Milligan (both Stewart's Melville), R. Brown (Melrose),
M. Tonkin (Currie), G. Fraser (Waterloo); D. Lee (Watsonians), G. Burns;

R. McNulty (Stewart's Melville), D. McGavin (Bedford, captain), G. Rigby (Stewart's Melville); G. Paxton (Gala), M. Rudkin (Watsonians); M. Ballantyne (Gala), G. Burns (Boroughmuir), N. Penny (Stewart's Melville).

Scotland were trailing 8-3 at the interval, but equalised early in the second half with a try. However, Scott Quinnell, who was later to be a formidable presence in the senior Welsh forward line, scored a try when he ran through a number of the Scottish defenders, including Gavin. Wales later scored a penalty to end the match with a 16-8 victory. Because of the dominance of the Welsh forwards, Gavin was restricted mainly to a defensive role.

Earlier in the season, Gavin had played four games for the Scottish Exiles Under-21 side in the District Championship. The Exiles finished next to bottom in the league, with only one win - 36 points to 12 against the North and Midlands, with Gavin scoring a try - and a draw against the South of Scotland.

This had been a tremendous season for Gavin, probably best summed up by Gavin himself in an interview with the Liverpool Echo titled *"A Glorious Year I Will Never Forget"*. He said: *"So much has happened in such a short time, that I am still a bit confused to be honest. I only made the first team in October, when we played Wakefield, and there I was last Friday playing for Scotland Under-21 against Wales. I have never felt so emotionally drained in my life as I did then, after we lost. The atmosphere was terrific, as it must be when you play for your country, and a lot of my family came to watch, though of course I wasn't aware of them until afterwards....Whatever happens now, this has been a fantastic season. There are not too many people who can say they have played in the company I have been keeping, and clashes with teams like Bath and Harlequins are the stuff of stories you tell your grandchildren."*(13)

Although Gavin was still a student at Humberside University, it was his placement year and he was working as a marketing assistant for the Liverpool Echo.

1993-94 Season

Gavin only managed to play ten League games for Waterloo this season, mostly on the left wing, as he was injured in the home game against Sale at the end of January

1994. Waterloo lost 28-10 and Gavin had to leave the field with an ankle injury. He also appeared in one Pilkington Cup game and two Lancashire Cup ties.

Gavin shone in the home game against Moseley in the League on 20th November. Waterloo won by 12 points to 5 and *"Scottish exile Fraser (ran) riot to cause countless problems for Moseley on the left wing".*

The highlight of Gavin's season was his selection on the left wing for two games for the full Scottish Exiles team. The first was against Leinster In October to mark the opening of the floodlights at Landsdowne Road in Dublin.

The second game was against Auckland, New Zealand's provincial champions, in November in London. In their first game of their seven match tour, Auckland fielded what was effectively a second-string fifteen, but were still far too strong for the Scottish Exiles, weakened by the withdrawals of Damian Cronin, Kent Bray and Fraser Harrold. The Exiles were in the game for the first 40 minutes but, with the wind at their backs, the New Zealanders came into their own scoring six second half tries and running out winners by 33 points to 12. The Exiles team was:

Nick Grecian (London Scottish); Ian Bruce (Orrell), Murray Craig (Waterloo), Rob MacNaughton (Northampton), Gavin Fraser (Waterloo); Murray Walker and Kevin Troup (both London Scottish); Alan Sharp (Bristol), Brian Gilchrist and Paul Burnell (both London Scottish); Neil Edwards (Northampton), Chris Gray (Nottingham); Peter Walton (Northampton), Ian Smith (Gloucester), David Leckie (London Scottish). The best known opposition player was the New Zealand international forward, Pat Lam.

After a very successful season the previous year, this season proved to be a great disappointment for Gavin, with a lack of tries and an ankle injury in January, which effectively brought his season to an early finish. The one bright spot for him was playing for the full Scottish Exiles team, which gave him encouragement to aim for higher international honours.

Fitting in the Waterloo training sessions around his work and his University commitments was somewhat problematic for Gavin throughout the year. Upon the completion of his placement in the summer of 1993, the Liverpool Echo management offered him full-time employment as a marketing assistant, on the condition that he completed his marketing degree on a part-time basis at John Moores University. He eagerly accepted the offer, but this necessitated attending John Moores University two nights each week for a further two years to complete his degree.

Season 1994-95

Because of an ankle injury, Gavin was unable to play for Waterloo until 12th November when he took his place on the wing against the leading Scottish side, Boroughmuir, in a friendly at rain-soaked Blundellsands. Waterloo won convincingly by 29 points to 16, and Gavin looked really sharp, scoring one try. According to the Liverpool Daily Post reporter, Gavin *"scored the try of the match late on. Thompson (the Waterloo full-back) side stepped the defence to set up Fraser on the right. After a lost year on the sidelines through injury, the Scottish Exiles player showed tremendous pace in the corner."*(14)

Gavin did not play for Waterloo again until after the New Year because he was selected to represent the Scottish Exiles in the McEwan's Inter-District championship, playing in the four games at full-back.

The first game was against the South of Scotland on Saturday afternoon, 3rd December, in an eerily empty Murrayfield stadium in Edinburgh. It was a fairly dour game and Graham Law, the rugby correspondent for the Scotsman, reported that *"the only play worth describing was a superb fifth-minute try from Gavin Fraser which emanated from Reed's lineout provision, a break by the strong-running Ronnie Eriksson, augmented by Murray Craig and sustained by Derek Patterson before Laing sent in the fullback on the overlap."* (15)

Although the Exiles went on to win easily by 25 points to 9, that was the only try of the game. Domination of the lineout by the Exiles' forwards was a key contribution to the victory. The teams were:

South of Scotland: Dods (Gala); Joiner (Melrose), Nichol (Selkirk), Swan (Gala), Suddon (Hawick); Sheil (Melrose, captain), Farquharson (Gala); McIlroy (Jed-Forest), Hay (Hawick), Lunn; Brown, Weir; Aitken (all Melrose), Renwick (Hawick), Kirkpatrick (Jed-Forest).

Scottish Exiles: Fraser (Waterloo); Kemp (Saracens), Craig (Waterloo), Eriksson (London Scottish), Appleson (Sale); Laing (Istonians), Patterson (West Hartlepool); Hilton (Bristol), Mair and Burnell (both London Scottish); Cronin (Bourges), Reed (Bath, captain); Blyth (Waterloo), Holmes (London Scottish), Peters (Bath).

Scottish Exiles v South of Scotland at Murrayfield on 3ʳᵈ December: The Exiles Gavin Fraser (right) dives over the line to score the only try of the game despite the efforts of the South's Grant Farquharson. Courtesy of The Scotsman Publications Ltd

The following Saturday, again at Murrayfield, the Exiles faced Glasgow. There were two changes to the Exiles side, both in the forwards – Gilchrist replaced his London Scottish clubmate Logan Mair at hooker and Ian Morrison also of London Scottish took Simon Holmes' place in the back row. The Exiles outshone their opponents to win rather easily by 34 points to 13. However, the points difference might have been even greater had the referee not judged Gavin to have interfered with Kenny Logan in a kick and chase effort and awarded Glasgow a penalty try, a decision that infuriated Gavin.

The Exiles' third game in the series, on the following Friday evening, nearly did not start, as the main Murrayfield pitch was frostbound. Luckily, it was possible to hastily arrange the match on one of the back pitches. This did not seem to bother the Exiles, who overwhelmed the North and Midlands 41-13. Murray Craig of Waterloo scored three of the Exiles tries, with Mark Appleson of Sale adding the other two.

This meant that the winners of the Championship would be decided in the final game between the Exiles and Edinburgh on Wednesday evening, 23rd December. The result of the game was in doubt until the last kick of the game when Gavin Hastings, the Edinburgh and Scotland full-back, had a chance to equalise with a penalty from 46 metres, but it fell short to leave the score at 19-16 in favour of the Exiles. The Exiles managed only one try, in the fourth minute, when Gavin ignited a move that led to a try by Appleson when he chipped ahead and touched down. That try effectively killed off any hope Edinburgh may have had of winning the title. They then needed to outscore the Exiles by nine tries to edge the title.

Victory gave the Exiles the Inter District championship trophy for the very first time. They did it in style, with a clean sweep of victories over the other four District sides. Surprisingly, very few of the Exiles team were selected for the Scotland A team against Italy in January, creating something of an outcry in the Scottish press. Gavin had played well throughout the championship and he was disappointed when he did not attract the eye of the selectors for the Scotland A summer tour of Zimbabwe.

The Scottish Exiles team that won the Inter District Rugby Championship for the first time in December 1994. Left to right, standing: Ronnie Ericksson (London Scottish), Mark Appleson (Sale), Dave Millard, Logan Mair (both London Scottish), Stuart Laing (Istonians), Ian Smith (Gloucester), Rob Scott, David McGavin , Simon Holmes, Paul Burnell (all London Scottish), Murray Craig (Waterloo), Ian Morrison (London Scottish), Eric Peters (Bath), Roger Whittaker (Assistant Coach).
Kneeling: Malcolm Kemp (Saracans), Kevin Troup (London Scottish), Dave Hilton, Andy Reed (both Bath) captain, Damian Cronin (Bourges), Dave Blyth, Gavin Fraser (both Waterloo) Courtesy of Herald & Times Group

After a successful comeback as a member of the Scottish Exiles team, Gavin was recalled to the Waterloo first XV on the wing for the first League game of 1995 against Newcastle Gosforth at Newcastle. Waterloo's hopes of maintaining their Second Division promotion challenge were dashed with a defeat, but Gavin *"celebrated his recall with an individual effort to spark off a late revival."*(16)

Waterloo's biggest game of the season was against Wasps from the First Division at Blundellsands in the Pilkington Cup. In an interview with John Sanderson of the Liverpool Daily Post, Gavin outlined the routine that would be followed before the game: *"(it) begins with a meeting at the nearby Blundellsands Tennis Club about three hours before kick-off. We have a light meal, sandwiches, pasta, coffee that sort of thing, followed by a team talk lasting about an hour, during which our coach Dick Greenwood runs through the game in a kind of question and answer session. Mostly, he is shouting out questions to make you think what you will do in any given situation. By the time he finishes, you shouldn't be in any doubt. We drive back to the rugby club in our own cars, change and then either run out on to the pitch to limber up or wander around chatting to people according to your own inclination…After I've changed I clean my boots, immediately before the final team talk from our skipper Peter Buckton."*

Waterloo took a 6-0 lead after 30 minutes over their more illustrious opponents, but were made to pay heavily for their audacity. Wasps, raising the tempo of the game by tapping every penalty, ran in eight tries in the remaining 50 minutes to one by Waterloo, triumphing 54-13. The game was marred, however, by two dismissals in separate incidents. Matt Greenwood of Wasps was sent off after 55 minutes for stamping, while Waterloo's Nick Allott followed him six minutes later for punching. The teams were:

Waterloo: Steve Swindells; Gavin Fraser, Chris Bibby, Murray Craig, Gary Meredith; Neil Ryan, Simon Wright; Mark Beckett, Stuart Turner, Steve Peters; Sean Fletcher, Nick Allott; Peter Buckton (captain), Stuart Beeley, Tony Ireland.

Wasps: Ufton; Greenstock, D. Hopley, Childs, P. Hopley; Rob Andrew, Bates; Popplewell, Delaney, Dunston; Greenwood, Hadley; Dallaglio, Ryan (captain), Wilkins.

Gavin's last game for Waterloo was a Lancashire Cup tie at home against Manchester, from the Division below. Surprisingly, Waterloo were deservedly beaten in a poor game. Gavin was dropped for the next League match and did not play again as he was injured and had signed to play the following season for London Scottish, also a Division Two team.

Gavin had been approached by London Scottish and felt that a move to them would assist his chances of playing for Scotland. Moreover, Waterloo had already lost their best young players over the previous two years with Paul Grayson moving to Northampton, Austin Healey to Orrell, Will Greenwood to Harlequins, Chris Saverimutto to Sale and Andy Northey turning professional with the St Helens Rugby League Club. The loss of these players ripped the heart out of their backs and midfield. The first four of those players later became full internationals. It was a good time for Gavin to further his rugby career elsewhere.

Gavin summed up his time at Waterloo: "*Whilst I had a very successful time at Waterloo, it was in the amateur era and, as a result, the best memories were probably the social side of the game. That said, I was one of the youngest ever first team players at the club and so was initially in awe of the rest of the team as these were players I had only previously seen playing on the pitch. From a rugby perspective, the thing that sticks in my mind most about my time there was the Pilkington Cup run where we beat Bath and Orrell and lost in the quarter finals to Harlequins. Having beaten Bath, there were massive celebrations and I remember picking out Dad from the hoards of fans running onto the pitch at full-time and we literally jumped into each other's arms! What was disappointing was I wasn't able to celebrate the victory as I had to leave straight after the game to get on a train to London for a Scottish Exiles training session the following day. I made some fantastic friends both on and off the pitch at Waterloo and have some amazing rugby memories.*"

Whilst at Waterloo, Gavin had played alongside four members of the original England World Cup winning squad of 2003 - Paul Grayson, Kyran Bracken, Will Greenwood and Austin Healey. Healey did not make the final cut. Waterloo also provided a fifth member of the squad, Ben Kay, who was several years younger than Gavin, so they did not play together. Stuart Turner, another Waterloo colleague, also played for England, making his debut when he had turned 30.

In his three seasons with Waterloo, Gavin had played 40 first XV games scoring 11 tries – 20 Courage League games (six tries), six Pilkington Cup ties (one try), six Lancashire Cup ties (three tries) and three friendlies (one try).

During his last season there, Gavin had continued to fit in his training sessions around his work and university commitments. However, he graduated in the summer with a BA Honours Degree in Marketing.

London Scottish (1995-96)

Gavin moved to Guildford during the pre-season and worked for CLI Connect, based in Guildford, as a Business Development Manager. He travelled to Richmond in London, a car journey of 30 miles, to train with London Scottish two evenings a week.

He had a tremendous first half to the season at full-back for London Scottish. His performances were such that a report in Rugby World of February 1996 said, *"Gavin Fraser has had a fine season at full-back and will be putting pressure on Melrose's Rowen Shepherd, who won his first cap for Scotland against Western Samoa."*

By the end of January, London Scottish were second in the Second Division, having lost only once, to Northampton, the league leaders, at Franklin Gardens on 4th November. The teams were:

Northampton: M. Dods; N. Beal, G. Townsend, M. Allen, H. Thorneycroft; P. Grayson, M. Dawson; M. Volland, T. Beddow, M. Hynes; J. Phillips, M. Bayfield; T. Rodber (captain), B. Pountney, G. Seely.

London Scottish: G. Fraser; T. Watson, F. Harrold, R. Eriksson, M. Sly; C. Russell, T. Withers-Green; D. Signorini, L. Mair, P. Burnell; A. Nesbitt, D. Orr-Ewing; M. Duthie, S. Holmes (captain), I. Morrison.

Before a crowd of 7,500 spectators, Scottish held Northampton to a 12-8 lead at the interval, but the home team ran in six tries in the second half, including a hat-trick by Gregor Townsend, the Scotland international, to win eventually by 54 points to 11. This meant that Northampton had scored 474 points, beating Sale's League Two record with half the season still to go.

Despite the heavy defeat, Gavin played well. Ian Malin of the Guardian wrote, *"Their back row was outstanding and the full-back Gavin Fraser a lively attacker.* (17)

After the match, Northampton's coach Ian McGeechan said, *"I know it sounds condescending but London Scottish made it difficult for us. It was a very competitive first half, our hardest game of the season and the best refereed."*

In an earlier game, against Bedford on 4th October, Gavin made a name for himself for all the wrong reasons. *"A frenzied outburst of fisticuffs from Fraser who might have been sent off but was not even shown the yellow card"*(18) was the only blemish on an impressive 50-10 victory for Scottish. Fortunately, Gavin also made his mark on the game in the true rugby sense when he went over for *"a tapped penalty overlap try"* in the first half.

Gavin was again selected in the Scottish Exiles squad for the Inter-District Championship. The Exiles began their defence of the title against Edinburgh at Richmond on 6th December in an evening game in appalling conditions. It was bitterly cold and there was a light dusting of snow on the pitch. Not surprisingly, it was rather a dull game, with the Exiles winning narrowly by 17 points to 6. Gavin played at full-back, but had little chance to make a name for himself.

Victory for the Exiles in the second game three days later over Glasgow at Burnbrae was by the narrowest of margins, 28 points to 27. Gavin featured in one of the Exiles' tries, early in the second half: *"...then Laing probed the blind and linked with Gavin Thompson, who broke in-field, the switch in direction ending with Murray Craig scoring from the admirable Gavin Fraser's searching little chip."*(19)

Despite seven tries and a closely fought game, it was hardly an entertaining game and the Exiles' coach Alastair McHarg was not impressed: *"We played like horse manure out there – and we were dead lucky to win... It's hard to fathom how top class players can perform so far below the standard they are capable of."*(20)

The following Saturday, the Exiles beat North and Midlands 21-9, and then secured their second successive Scottish Districts' title when they easily beat South of Scotland by 34 points to 9. Gavin played in the first three games, but missed the final game against the South because of another ankle injury he suffered in a League game for London Scottish.

This was to be the last season that rugby would be a totally amateur sport. During the District Championship, the Scottish Rugby Union announced its plans for professionalism and European Rugby. There were to be only three Scottish-based super-district sides, Edinburgh, Glasgow and the Borders, excluding the Scottish Exiles. After watching the Exiles win their second District Championship title in a row, their coach Alastair McHarg raged, *"It's a disgraceful plan, and the SRU are only cutting off their noses to spite their faces. To say that there is no role for us in Europe is impossible to understand. Don't they realise most of their top forwards over the past five years have been discovered and coached south of the border..."*

Just before the New Year, London Scottish suffered their second defeat in the League, which effectively ended their promotion chances. The morale of the Scots suffered so much that they lost several more games, leaving Northampton and London Irish to be promoted from Division Two.

That second defeat came on 28th December 1995, when Scottish lost away to London Irish by a single point – 21 points to 20. Defeat was all the more galling as London Scottish played running rugby, scoring three tries to none by the Irish. Gavin's replacement at full-back, Nick Robinson, scored two tries. The difference in the end, was the kicking of the Irish left winger, Michael Corcoran, who put over seven of the eight penalties awarded against the Scots, giving the Irish that decisive point lead five minutes from the end of the game.

Gavin played only one more game for London Scottish, a friendly against Bristol. However, his ankle injury flared up again and he had to leave the field in the second half. He had played 11 League games, scoring two tries, and one game in the Pilkington Cup in a defeat away to Nottingham, when he scored a try.

Luckily, Gavin's season did not end in December. He was selected at full-back for the Scottish Development XV, which had two games in February 1996. In an effort to play in those games, he went for treatment to Margot Wells, wife of the Olympic gold medalist, Allan Wells. Somehow, she managed to get him fit and, on 1st February, he played in the 84 points to 3 victory over Durham County at Pennypit, Prestonpans. The Development XV scored 12 tries, all of them converted by stand-off Mark McKenzie. Gavin scored two tries and could have had a hat-trick, but he passed unselfishly for the left-wing, Neil Renton, to score when he could have strolled over the line himself.

After the game, the Development XV captain, scrum-half Andy Nicol, who was returning to representative rugby after recovering from a serious knee injury, said, *"In a way, it was like a training run but we had a number of repertoire moves to practice. In the circumstances, we could have played a very loose game, but we tried to keep some shape to it even although the tries were being scored easily. The big challenge will be a week on Sunday when we play New South Wales."*(21)

Murrayfield was the scene for the game against New South Wales on 11th February. The teams were:

Scotland Development XV: G. Fraser (London Scottish); A. Stanger (Hawick), I. Wynn (Orrell), A. James (Wasps), K. Logan; M. McKenzie (both Stirling County), A. Nicol (Bath); R. McNulty (Stewart's Melville), S. Scott (Melrose), M. Stewart (Blackheath); M. McVie (Edinburgh Academicals), K. Stewart (Cardiff); B. Ward (Currie), G. Mackay (Stirling County), S. Holmes (London Scottish).
New South Wales: M. Burke; A. Murdoch, R. Tombs, M. Dixon, M. Mostyn; S. Bowen, A. Ekert; M. Harthill, M. Bell, A. Blades; W. Waugh, J. Welborn; S. Talbot, F. Finau, D. Manu.

One of the world's top teams, New South Wales had eight internationals on parade, whilst there were only three in the Development XV side, which had a host of players on the fringe of representative recognition. Their only big names were the captain Andy Nicol and the wingers Tony Stanger and Kenny Logan. Unfortunately, Stanger, who, like Nicol, was returning from serious injury, had to leave the field after 12 minutes with a groin injury. His replacement was Matt McGrandles of Stirling County.

New South Wales, winners by 48 points to 11, were simply too good for the Development team. Scotland struggled to take the ball over the game line against the strong and powerful Australians, whose superior physical presence caused problems for the Scots in the area of ball-retention.

Gavin was not disgraced and made several strong tackles. One in particular, was at full-length when he brought down one of the wingers near the corner when a try looked a certainty.

In his own time and at his own cost, Gavin had been attending training sessions under the guidance of Margot Wells in order to improve his fitness. More than ten years later, she described how she came out of retirement to begin coaching again, "...*but the phone kept ringing. London Scottish: 'We've a great full-back here Margot, but he's not quick enough'. Surrey University: We've had Dan Luger and Dominic Chapman in and they want to do some sprint work.*"(22) Gavin was the full-back she referred to at London Scottish.

London Irish (1996-97)

This was the first season of open or professional rugby. Paul Burnell's father (23), who seemed a very influential figure at London Scottish, had told Gavin and his parents that he would definitely get a professional contract at the Club. Indeed, on the basis of that "promise", Gavin turned down the offer of a position as Promotions Co-ordinator for Rugby Union, Rugby League and Track and Field for Mizuno. The job involved extensive travel for all the major sporting events for these sports, such as to the Olympics, the Rugby World Cup and so on.

Before the start of the season, Tony Tiarks, who bought London Scottish, brought in Gavin Hastings, the former Scotland full-back and captain, who had just retired from playing rugby, as a sort of broker in negotiating contracts with the current playing staff and recruiting new players. After weeks of uncertainty during the close season, neither Gavin nor Nick Robinson, the other full-back at the Club, were offered a professional contract. Derek Lee was brought in from Scottish rugby on a professional contract to fill the full-back position.

Understandably, Gavin was unhappy with the situation, particularly as he had given up the opportunity of a very attractive job. He talked to several clubs, including Saracens and Moseley, without anything concrete being offered. Meanwhile, Alistair McHarg, his coach at Scottish Exiles, recommended him to Clive Woodward, who was the coach at London Irish. Gavin subsequently joined the Club three or four weeks after the beginning of the season on a non-contractual basis, but being paid for first team appearances.

Clive Woodward had taken London Irish into the First Division of the Courage League the previous season, when London Scottish narrowly missed out on promotion. So, at the AGM in July 1996, he had been expecting "*a little bit of a hero's welcome... But the reception I received was just the opposite.*"(24)

A special agenda item was introduced for discussion at the AGM – an amendment to the club's constitution that only people of Irish descent could be involved in the management of the club, with exceptions at the discretion of the committee. Woodward was assured by the chairman that this would never apply to him, as the committee would have a discretionary veto to waive the rule in his case.

When Woodward argued that this was "*totally utterly wrong*", a member of the old faction at the club jumped up, pointed his finger at Woodward and shouted, "*We know what you're trying to do. You're trying to turn this into a whole team full of English players! You're trying to make this club an English club.*"

Woodward left the meeting, after telling members that he did not wish to be part of a club that sanctioned discrimination. He left the club formally in October 1996 when he was stopped by a committee member from going into a team meeting and told that his services were no longer required.

So, Gavin had no sooner joined London Irish than the person who had signed him left the club. His replacement as coach was Willie Anderson, a former Ireland captain.

Gavin played mainly for the Second XV at London Irish, although he did play a number of first team games. He was a replacement in a Courage League Division One game against Gloucester at Kingsholm, coming off the bench with 20 minutes to go. London Irish were beaten, however. He also played in a number of home games in the Anglo-Welsh League and in at least one game in the European Conference cup competition.

However, Gavin does remember Anderson speaking positively about his performances, particularly because he put big tackles in on large forwards and always gave 100%.

The highlight of Gavin's season was his selection for Scottish Districts against Australia, at McDiarmid Park, Perth, on 5th November. He was originally chosen to play on the wing but, because of the withdrawal of Michael Dods, he was moved to full-back. The coaching staff at London Irish congratulated him on his selection as they intimated that honours such as these also reflected on the club.

The game against Australia was played in torrential rain and, although the Scots were ahead by six points after 25 minutes with two penalties from Gary

Parker, they were down 8-6 at half-time. After an Australian try in the second half, Gavin decided to trap a long kick forward with his foot in his own 22, rather than risk handling the slippery ball, but he only succeeded in knocking it into the path of Joe Roff who aquaplaned over the line to score. David Campese came on as substitute in the second- half, which pleased Gavin, as Campese was one of his rugby heroes. The final score was a comfortable 25 points to 9 for Australia, but the incessant, heavy rain and waterlogged conditions reduced the game to a scrappy affair for the crowd of only 2,307. The teams were:

Scottish Districts: G. Fraser (London Irish); D. Officer (Currie), P. Rouse (Dundee HSFP), I. Wynn (Wakefield), G. Parker (Melrose); J. Steele (London Scottish), D. Patterson (Heriots FP); W. Anderson (Kirkcaldy), M. Scott (Orrell), M. Stewart (Northampton); D. Burns (Boroughmuir), I. Elliott (Hawick); D. McIvor (Glenrothes, captain), M. Waite (Edinburgh Academicals), B. Pountney (Northampton).

Australia: S. Larkham; B. Tune, A. Magro, R. Tombs (captain), J. Roff; T. Wallace, G. Gregan; C. Blades, M. Caputo, A. Heath; J. Welborn, T. Gavin; D. Williams, O. Finegan, T. Kafu.

Later in November, Gavin went with the Scottish Exiles to the Barrington's training camp in the Algarve, Portugal, for a week. The Exiles played the Spain and Portugal national teams, winning both games and beating Spain by 56 points to 12 in Seville. Gavin played at full-back in both matches. However, it is a non-rugby incident that sticks in Gavin's mind about the trip: *"The one thing I remember is going to a karaoke bar one night with all the players and some of us left to go on to another bar. We had just got to the end of the road and we heard police sirens and looked around to see a police van screech up outside the bar. The next minute, policemen jumped out of the van with guns and went and dragged out the remaining Exiles from the bar and took them to the local police station. Apparently, one of the lads had knocked over a glass in the bar and the manager had immediately called the police. The Exiles management team had to go to the police station to get the lads released."* A lucky escape for Gavin!

Unfortunately, the Scottish Rugby Union resolved to eject the Exiles from the District Championship, as they had already decided that they would not be permitted to represent Scotland in the European Cup.

At the London Irish's AGM in July 1997, some supporters of the club expressed the view that all club players should be of Irish origin, otherwise the club would lose its integrity. The players did not support this point of view. Gavin had already been told that he was likely to receive a professional contract at the end of the season but, following the AGM, he was informed that the club felt that they would have put the decision on hold until the start of the 1997-98 season. He decided to leave.

Gavin enjoyed his time at London Irish. He said, *"The players and most of the officials were very welcoming and friendly. It goes without saying that, being Irish, there were a lot of good times. I felt I was also very fortunate to play and train with individuals like David Humphries, Conor O'Shea, Victor Costello, Kieran Dawson and Rob Henderson, who all represented Ireland and, in some cases, the British Lions."*

All in all, not a very happy season for Gavin, although a high spot was the game against Australia.

Glasgow District and Kilmarnock RUFC (1997-98)

Gavin signed for Edinburgh Accies as an amateur before the beginning of the season and played for them in a Sevens tournament at Preston Lodge, near Edinburgh. However, due to an ankle injury he received in one of the early games, he was unable to complete the tournament.

Before the season started properly, however, he was offered a professional contract with Kilmarnock Rugby Club, with the possibility of a full professional contract with Glasgow District. Alastair McHarg, who had been his coach for the Scottish Exiles, had recommended to the SRU that he receive a professional contract with Glasgow. Kevin Greene, the Glasgow coach, subsequently telephoned Gavin and invited him to Glasgow. He was unable to play in any "trial" for Glasgow for some weeks because of his ankle injury, but was eventually offered and accepted a professional contract with the District side.

Gavin's contract at Glasgow was £15,000 per season plus match fees. Kilmarnock offered to pay him £3000 for the season, but he asked for and received a leased Ford Explorer in lieu of the £3000 cash.

Gavin only managed to play seven games for Kilmarnock – four in the SRU Trophy against Biggar, Jedforest, Watsonians and Dundee HSFP, all of which were won by Kilmarnock, with Gavin scoring a try in the game against Dundee; two League games against Musselburgh and Biggar, losing the latter game by 25 points to 22, with Gavin again scoring a try; and one game in the Cup against Biggar, which Kilmarnock won 11-0.

Gavin had an incident-filled debut for Kilmarnock in their 38-18 victory over Biggar in the SRU Trophy. According to the local reporter *"Fraser looked very much the part at full-back, setting up a try for Kenny Sinclair with a delightful 60-metre break, but he found himself sin-binned – a trifle harshly – around the hour mark."*

He played five games for Glasgow. In the European Cup, he came off the bench against Swansea and Leicester, but Glasgow lost both games. Against Swansea, he came on as a replacement with ten minutes of the game left, so was unable to make any real impression. He played 55 minutes of the game against Leicester, coming on as a replacement for the injured Derek Stark; Glasgow lost this game by a record margin for the European Cup competition, 90 points to 11, despite taking the lead with a try early in the game.

Gavin played in two of the Inter-District Championship games, both of which Glasgow won. He came on as a replacement at full-back against Edinburgh with 15 minutes left and made some excellent catches from high balls and made a tremendous head-on, try-saving tackle on a big forward in a one-on-one situation. His second game was against the South of Scotland, when he came on for an injured player after 15 minutes and played well.

He also played on the right wing in a friendly against the Australian side, ACT, in early December on a miserable, wet and windy evening. Gavin had to come off for a short period to get three stitches in a head wound. Glasgow lost 22-6.

Gavin's last game that season was for Kilmarnock against Biggar in the Cup in December. He had to come off at half-time, suffering from a back problem. It proved to be a prolapsed disc, which was not healing itself. Eventually, he was admitted to Ross Hall Hospital, a BUPA Hospital in Glasgow, where he underwent a discectomy, in which 90% of the bulging disc was removed; the operation was paid for by the Scottish RFU. Gavin was unable to play for the rest of the season and did not get his contract renewed by Glasgow.

Gavin before the Glasgow v Edinburgh game in October 1997

Watsonians (1998-00)

1998-99 Season

Gavin continued to live in Portobello in Edinburgh and took up the position of marketing manager with the Scottish Mirror. He started playing rugby again when he signed for Watsonians of Edinburgh in February 1999, at a time when the Club was one of the favourites for relegation. By the end of the season, however, they were safe in Division 1. Gavin made his debut against Glasgow Hawks and played every game afterwards. At the end of the season, he *was "congratulated by many of the Club members for my contribution in helping the Club avoid relegation".*

1999-00 Season

Gavin remained with Watsonians for the following season, but he did not play many first team games. Although he lived in Portobello, he continued to work in Glasgow, and was, therefore, unable to make the twice-weekly training sessions. As a result, he was dropped to the Second XV and gave up playing seriously at the end of the season because of the travel problems. He did play in the pre-season Edinburgh Cup, when Watsonians reached the final, only to lose to Boroughmuir by 24 points to 5.

Edinburgh Cup Final Watsonians v Boroughmuir: Gavin Fraser is unable to stop Graeme Kiddie of Boroughmuir scoring a try.

Gavin's stay in Scotland in terms of rugby did not live up to expectations. He summed up his feelings: *"I regretted moving, as the set up in Scotland was so unprofessional - they were light years behind rugby in England. Having trained with Margot Wells, I was aware how fit and good I could feel, but the training methods in Scotland were archaic. The mentality was to run everyone into the ground during the week and expect them to feel fresh for the game at the weekend. This culminated in us being forced to do 10 x two minute runs three days before the European Cup quarter final play-off against Leicester. We were due to travel to Leicester the following day by coach, so we should never have done anything like two minute runs three days before what was the biggest game of our season. I made my feelings known, as did several other players, but it was to no avail. Suffice to say we experienced our heaviest loss of the season with many players citing tiredness as the main factor. There was also a massive drinking culture in Scottish rugby. After every game, we would immediately hit the clubhouse bar and then go out drinking all night, coming home in the early hours of the following morning. I have always said I drank more as a professional rugby player in Scotland than I ever did as an amateur player in England. I think, prior to my injury, my rugby had regressed as a result of moving to Scotland."*

Post-rugby

Gavin eventually moved to live in Glasgow as he continued to work in the city, by this time as Marketing Manager for the Scottish Daily Mail. In May 2005, he was appointed as Head of Newspaper Sales and Marketing for Northamptonshire Newspaper, part of Johnston Press, moving to live in Mawsley just outside Kettering.

He continued to keep active through cycling. He played the occasional game for Scottish Legends, a team of former Scottish Rugby internationals and, in 2006, began to play football in the same Sunday League football team as his brother, Neil. Neil had joined Johnston Press' Advertising Department in Northampton in the summer of 2006, following his graduation from Manchester Metropolitan University, and he moved in with Gavin.

Continuing his cycling, Gavin completed several Sportifs, including La

Marmotte, which incorporates several difficult climbs culminating in the infamous Alpe d'Huez. In June 2009, he cycled from Land's End to John o' Groats with two friends, completing the 900 miles in five days at an average of 17.5 miles per hour. He has now moved on to triathlons.

He left Johnston Press in December 2007 to become Regional Press Controller for Smith's News. In August 2009, Gavin married Amanda Hamilton and they live in Mawsley with their two daughters.

References:

1.   Hull Daily Mail, 15th October 1990

2.   Hull Sports Mail, 10th November 1990

3.   Hull Sports Mail, 24th November 1990

4.   Liverpool Echo, 23rd October 1992

5.   Liverpool Daily Post, 26th October 1992

6.   Liverpool Daily Post, 2nd November 1992

7.   Liverpool Daily Post, 11th January 1993

8.   Liverpool Echo, 26th April 1993

9.   Liverpool Daily Post, 27th November 1992

10.   Sunday Times, 29th November 1992

11.   Sunday Times, 24th January 1993

12.   Sunday Telegraph, 28th February 1993

13.   Liverpool Echo, 24th February 1993

14.   Liverpool Daily Post, 14th November 1994

15.   The Scotsman, 5th December 1994

16.   Liverpool Echo, 9th January 1995

17.   The Guardian, 6th November 1995

18.   Daily Telegraph, 6th October 1995

19.   The Scotsman, 11th December 1995

20.   Daily Mail, 11 December 1995

21. Dundee Courier, 1st February 1996

22. The Sunday Times, 20th April 2008

23. Paul Burnell was capped many times by Scotland at prop forward and was a team-mate of Gavin's at London Scottish

24. Winning! by Clive Woodward; Hodder & Stoughton 2004; P 124

Bibliography

Everton FC

Football on Merseyside by Percy M. Young; Stanley Paul & Co. Ltd (1963)

Goodison Glory, The Official History by Ken Rogers; The Breedon Publishing Company Limited (1998)

Gladwys Street's Hall of Fame; By D H France; Skript Publishing (1999)

Everton - a complete record 1778-1988 by Ian Ross & Gordon Smailes; The Breedon Books Publishing Co. Ltd (1988)

Everton Football Club 1878 – 1946 By John K Rowlands; Tempus Publishing Ltd (2001)

Still Talking Blue by Becky Tallentire; Mainstream Publishing (2001)

Who's Who of Everton by Tony Matthews (2004)

Dr Everton's Magnificent Obsession: The David France Collection by David France and David Prentice, Trinity Mirror Sport Media (2008)

Across the Park by Peter Lupson; Trinity Mirror Sport Media (2009)

When Football was Football: Everton – A Nostalgic Look at a Century of the Club by Michael Heatley; Haynes Publishing (2011)

Huddersfield Town FC

Huddersfield Town: 75 Years On by George S. Binns; Huddersfield Town AFC Ltd (1984)

The Light at the End of the Tunnel: An a-z History of Huddersfield Town Football Club by Tony Matthews; 90 Minutes Publications (2004)

99 Years & Counting: Stats and Scores 1908-2008; Huddersfield Town AFC

Luton FC

The Luton Story 1885-1985 by Timothy Collings (1985)

Marine FC

The Mighty Mariners by David Wotherspoon (1997)

Southport FC

The Sandgrounders: The Complete History of Southport FC by Geoff Wilde and Michael Braham; Palatine Books (1995)

Tranmere Rovers FC

Tranmere Rovers: The Complete Record by Gilbert Upton, Steve Wilson and Peter Bishop; The Breedon Books Publishing Co Ltd (2009)

Watford FC

The Watford Football Club Illustrated Who's Who by Trefor Jones (1996)

The Golden Boys: A Study of Watford's Cult Heroes by Oliver Phillips; Alpine Press Ltd

History of Watford FC 1881-1991 by Oliver Phillips; Watford Football Club

West Bromwich Albion FC

West Bromwich Albion: Soccer in the Black Country 1879 – 1965 by Peter Morris; Heinemann (1965)

Albion Memories, Express and Star (1998)

100 Years at the Hawthorns by Tony Matthews, The Breedon Books Publishing Company Limited (1999)

The Essential History of West Bromich Albion by Gavin McOwan, Headline Book Publishing for WH Smith (2002)

The Who's Who of West Bromwich Albion by Tony Matthews; Breedon Books (2005)

The Official Encyclopedia of West Bromwich Albion compiled by Tony Matthews, Britespot publication (2002)

Wrexham FC

Wrexham: A Complete Record 1872-1992 by Peter Jones, published by The Breedon Books Publishing Company Limited (1992)

Wrexham Football Club 1872-1950 compiled by Gareth M Davies and Peter Jones, published by Tempus Publishing Ltd (2000)

Football - General

The Encyclopaedia of Association Football; Compiled by Maurice Golesworthy; Robert Hale Ltd (1956)

Association Football and English Society 1863-1915 by Tony Mason; The Harvester Press Ltd (1980)

Football League Players' Records 1946 – 1988, compiled and edited by Barry J Hagman; The Arena Press (1988)

Pay up and Play the Game: Professional Sport in Britain, 1875-1914 by Wray Vamplew; Cambridge University Press (1988)

Football League Players' Records 1888-1939 by Michael Joyce; SoccerData (2002)

Living to Play by John Harding, Robson Books (2002)

Boots, balls and haircuts: An illustrated history from then to now by Hunter Davies; Cassell Illustrated (2003)

My Father and other Working-Class Football Heroes by Gary Imlach; Yellow Jersey Press (2005)

Aristocrats v Artisans by Ian Maxwell in Ancestors Magazine; The National Archives, Kew, Richmond (July 2006)

When Football was Football: A Nostalgic Look at a Century of Football by Richard Havers; Haynes Publishing (2008)

Football and the English: A Social History of Association Football in England 1863-1995 by Dave Russell; Carnegie Publishing (1997)

The Association Game: A History of British Football by Matthew Taylor; Pearson Education Ltd (2008)

Thank God for Football! The Illustrated Companion by Peter Lupson; Society for Promoting Christian Knowledge (2010)

Baseball

British Baseball by Andrew Welch (2008)

Rugby Union

Winning! By Clive Woodward; Hodder & Stoughton (2004)

Sport - General

Sporting Ancestors: Tracing Your Family's Athletic Past by Keith Gregson; History Press

Sport in Britain: A Social History Edited by Tony Mason; Cambridge University Press (1989)